Resurrection in Retrospect

Cover picture: Resurrection of Christ and Women at the Tomb
Florence: San Marco Convent Museum fresco
Fra Angelico
Born: 1395, Vicchio, Italy; Died: 18 February 1455, Rome, Italy

Resurrection in Retrospect

A Critical Examination of the Theology of N. T. Wright

Peter Carnley

 CASCADE *Books* · Eugene, Oregon

RESURRECTION IN RETROSPECT
A Critical Examination of the Theology of N. T. Wright

Cascade Books
An Imprint of Wipf and Stock Publishers
199 W. 8th Ave., Suite 3
Eugene, OR 97401

www.wipfandstock.com

PAPERBACK ISBN: 978-1-5326-6751-0
HARDCOVER ISBN: 978-1-5326-6752-7
EBOOK ISBN: 978-1-5326-6753-4

Cataloguing-in-Publication data:

Names: Carnley, Peter, author.

Title: Resurrection in retrospect : a critical examination of the theology of N. T. Wright / Peter Carnley.

Description: Eugene, OR: Cascade Books, 2019. | Includes bibliographical references and indexes.

Identifiers: ISBN 978-1-5326-6751-0 (paperback). | ISBN 978-1-5326-6752-7 (hardcover). | ISBN 978-1-5326-6753-4 (ebook).

Subjects: LCSH: Jesus Christ—Resurrection. | Wright, N. T. (Nicholas Thomas)—Criticism, interpretation, etc.

Classification: BT482 C37 2019 (print). | BT482 (ebook).

Manufactured in the U.S.A.   04/29/19

For the students of the Systematic Theology classes
of the
General Theological Seminary of The Episcopal Church,
New York,
2010–2013
Halcyon days.

Peter Carnley's other publications:

The Structure of Resurrection Belief, 1987
The Yellow Wallpaper and Other Sermons, 2000
Reflections in Glass, 2004
A Kind of Retirement, 2016
The Reconstruction of Resurrection Belief, 2019

Contents

Preface

This book, along with its companion volume *The Reconstruction of Resurrection Belief*, is the fortuitous product of retirement. The windfall of an unforeseen teaching opportunity, and a precious gift of time, free of pastoral and administrative responsibilities of the kind that dominated life in full-time Christian ministry, enabled me in 2010 to return to some sustained theological work once again. This was a huge privilege, which has come with all the surprising sweetness of something entirely unplanned.

I am grateful to the Acting President of the General Theological Seminary of The Episcopal Church in New York, Lang Lowry, and to the Interim Dean of the time, Bishop Peter Lee, for inviting me to come out of retirement to fill a temporary teaching gap during a difficult period of the Seminary's institutional history. Initially this was to be for only one year, but when for various reasons this morphed into a longer commitment than was at first envisaged, it was with no sense of calamity; indeed, it became natural to think instead in terms of life's providential ordering. Believe it or not, my wife Ann and I submitted to the twenty-four hours of flying time from Perth in Western Australia to New York and return, following different routes and on a variety of airlines, on at least twelve occasions between 2010 and 2013—so many times, in fact, that I have actually lost the exact count.

Amongst other things, this provided the opportunity to revisit the theology of the Resurrection of Christ, which I first tackled in *The Structure of Resurrection Belief*, as long ago as 1987. By 2010 it was well overdue for a critical review and revamp. I am particularly grateful to the students of the Systematic Theology classes of the Seminary during the years from 2010 to 2013 for wrestling with the New Testament resurrection traditions, and for squarely facing the challenge of producing a theology of the Resurrection of Christ for today, in the language of today, and hopefully with some traction in the context of contemporary ways of viewing the cosmos and the human experience of life within it.

This seminary course on the Resurrection of Christ was repeated a number of times over these years, with N. T. Wright's magisterial 2003 book *The Resurrection of the Son of God* as the set text. I hope its author appreciates my contribution to his increased sales during this period. Members of these classes worked carefully through

Wright's book, and at the end of the term were asked to write a critical review as the primary item of their course assessment. I am indebted to them for wrestling with the complex issues it raises, and for persisting with its detailed prose. I am also grateful to them for providing a sounding board as I endeavored to unpack Wright's arguments, and to highlight what appeared to me to be the book's most concerning problems. The key issues canvassed with them in lectures are now presented in what follows in this book, which I dedicate to them.

Then, as this teaching assignment was ending, my name was suggested to the very lively Episcopal Parish of St. Peter, Morristown, New Jersey, where there was a temporary position in ministry with a focus on Adult Education. The parish teaching sessions between the two major community Eucharists at 10am of a Sunday morning, that were attended by upwards of about fifty keen-to-learn adults, allowed for the further airing of the theology of the Resurrection of Christ—though not just the Resurrection, but also other equally demanding topics: the Persons-in-Communion of the Trinity, St. Mark's Redaction of the Gospel, and Issues in Christian Moral Theology. I am very grateful to the Rector of the Parish, the Reverend Janet Broderick, for making all this possible, and to Mikael and Beth Salovaara, for attending to the logistics of our time and accommodation at St. Peter's. Ann and I remember appreciatively the contribution of Constance Silverman to the decorative flair and enthusiasm that Beth brought to this enterprise, and we salute the lively and welcoming group of "informed laity" who were adventurously prepared to tackle the challenges of thinking theologically. Hildegard Bucking is to be thanked for her role in stretching our minds in a different direction by organizing us into a parish group to learn and to play Bridge. It was a huge amount of fun.

These New York/New Jersey assignments have undoubtedly helped me clarify my own thinking about what is without doubt the most abidingly important subject in the specifically Christian theological tradition. Indeed, there is no substitute for having to work through the issues of philosophical and systematic theology with as much intellectual honesty as can be brought to the task and with the aim of producing a reasonably coherent statement of a position, than to have to communicate it to others, and then defend it in the cut-and-thrust of critical discussion and questioning.

On the other hand, mere thinking *about* the Resurrection does not get us very far without a concrete experience of the fundamental reality that we identify in faith as "the presence of the Raised Christ." The prayerful and humanly enriching worship, and the vibrantly caring community life of both Seminary and Parish, provided ample avenues, not just for engaging in some systematic thinking, but for the experience of engagement with the concrete reality to which St. Paul referred as "the Spirit of life in Christ Jesus" (Rom 8:2), and which in faith we still claim to have to do today. After all, there are "two stems" of knowledge, as Immanuel Kant once explained them: with one stem things are thought; with the other, experienced reality is encountered, identified, and named. Without the thoughts we are "blind" to what there is to be perceived and known; without the concrete experience that "fills" them such thoughts are empty.

For the last three years since 2015, now back to a more normal form-of-life, re-united with our children and delightful grandchildren, and comfortably settled in our East Fremantle townhouse with an undemanding pocket-sized garden to care for, it has at last been possible to massage the verbal precipitate of these years of teaching and talking since 2010 into what I hope is a coherent and helpful publishable form.

I am indebted to my very good Perth friends for their continuing care and support through all this: amongst them especially, the Warden of Wollaston Theological College, Gregory Seach, not least for providing a home for my library; David Wood, for being prepared to read a very early draft of what started life as a single book that then become two; and Susan Maushart who is always on hand to provide computer and publishing advice. I especially want to thank Luke Hoare whose keen critical eye, and the technical expertise he brought to the pressured work of checking references and copy editing, has been an invaluable help to me—in fact, life-saving.

Needless to say, I am grateful also to Dr. K. C. Hanson, the editor-in-chief of Wipf and Stock Publishing, and the team of dedicated staff who work behind the scenes in this splendid publishing house. They have been unfailingly prompt, generously courteous, and very impressively professional. The company's Author Guide, especially for those having to learn the intricacies of *The Chicago Manual of Style*, is remarkable for its attention to detail and helpful clarity.

I also thank Bishop Tom Wright for generously receiving the first news that his big 2003 book on the Resurrection was to be subjected to critical public scrutiny. I know he is accepting of the fact that the *The Resurrection of the Son of God* was unlikely to remain unassailed in perpetuity. On the other hand, he is to be thanked for producing *The Resurrection of the Son of God* in the first place. It remains the "reigning paradigm" of the approach to the Resurrection understood as an event of past historical time, that must necessarily therefore be approached employing the methods and techniques of critical historical research. I happen to come at it from quite another angle, but I fully appreciate the sustained and detailed argument that has been mounted for handling the Resurrection as a "historical event."

Finally, I wish to thank my loving wife, Ann, who is a very gifted teacher, and a writer in her own right, but who has tended to shelve many of her own interests in her steadfast commitment to managing our joint well-being and the stable organization of our lives during these busy years. As well as caring for our two children and their spouses, and four grandchildren, especially through those times when we were separated by the "tyranny of distance," Ann has ensured that I have not been distracted from the task in hand and has kept me focused on the goal of completion. Certainly, I feel much loved and supported. Words are inadequate to express how appreciative I am of her care right through what has been an eight-year-long project that has gobbled up much more of our time and mental energy than I ever imagined it would—and probably much more than I should have permitted. Hopefully, we may now both look forward to some time of relative tranquility together, and to the pleasures of "growing old in the company of friends."

Despite the fact that there is always more to be said about what is essentially a "mystery" and thus "beyond words," I think these books are probably just about as good as I can do on the topic of the Resurrection of Christ. Now that this project is finished, at least roughly to my own satisfaction, it will be up to others in a new generation to continue the discussion in whatever way they will.

+Peter Carnley
East Fremantle, Western Australia
10 September 2018

Abbreviations

Ancient

1QH	*Hodayot* from Qumran Cave 1
4Q385, 386, 388	Pseudo-Ezekiel from Qumran Cave 4
4Q521	Messianic Apocalypse from Qumran Cave 4
Ag. Ap.	Josephus, *Against Apion*
Ant.	Josephus, *Antiquities*
b.	Babylonian Talmud
B. Qam.	*Baba Qamma*
Deus	Philo, *Quod Deus sit immutabilis*
ʿEd.	*ʿEduyyot*
J. W.	Josephus, *Jewish War*
Jub.	*Jubilees*
Ketub.	*Ketuboth*
m.	Mishnah
Opif.	Philo, *De opificio mundi*
Roš Haš.	*Roš Haššannah*
Sacr.	Philo, *De Sacrificiis Abelis et Caini*
Sanh.	*Sanhedrin*
Šebu.	*Šebuoth*
Yebam.	*Yebamoth*

Modern

LCL	Loeb Classical Library
RSG	N. T. Wright, *The Resurrection of the Son of God*
WUNT	Wissenschaftliche Untersuchungen zum Neuen Testament

I

Introduction
Matters of Method

In 2003 the eminent British New Testament scholar N. T. Wright[1] published the third volume of a series on Christian Origins and the Question of God. This particular volume was titled *The Resurrection of the Son of God*.[2] It is an impressively detailed and weighty tome, which, including indices and bibliography, runs to a whole 817 pages. Given its sheer length and the detailed nature of its prose, I am sure I cannot have been the only reader to have wilted in the course of the first attempt to read it. Indeed, if I am honest, I think I must own that on more than one occasion I skipped through some sections in order to get to the conclusions.[3]

Quite apart from the daunting task of working through Wright's detailed discussion, it must be said that this lack of enthusiasm at the time of the first reading of *The Resurrection of the Son of God* also surfaced because it almost immediately became apparent to me that I held some very serious reservations about the fundamental thrust of the book's basic argument. While it could be contended that the judgment "that Jesus Christ was raised from the dead" is a judgment of faith, given that it is usually understood by Christians to be a transcendental "act of God" with profound cosmic implications, not least for the salvation of humanity, Wright's contention is that Christ's Resurrection is to be handled straightforwardly, at least in the first instance, as an event of the past history of this world. Before the Resurrection is spoken of in theological terms as a "mighty act of God" for the salvation and transformation of humanity, and as something therefore that must necessarily be appropriated by faith,

1. Who had been Canon Theologian of Westminster Abbey since 2000, and was appointed to the See of Durham in 2003.

2. Wright, *The Resurrection of the Son of God* (hereafter *RSG*).

3. Markus Bockmuehl confesses to tending to "reach swiftly for the smelling salts" when faced with such a daunting prospect as tackling Wright's "high octane" and encyclopedic work. "Compleat [*sic*] History of the Resurrection," 489.

Wright's contention is that it is to be handled quite simply as an event of historical time. It is of a piece with any other historical event that might be located in a particular geographical place and at a datable time in the past, such as Caesar's crossing of the Rubicon in 49 BC,[4] or the death of Augustus in AD 14, or the fall of Jerusalem in AD 70.[5] That it actually happened can therefore be established using historical reasoning alone, employing the secular techniques of critical historical research. Thus, Wright sets out on a quest for "historical knowledge about the resurrection, of a sort that can be discussed without presupposing Christian faith."[6]

In this way, Wright's fundamental methodological contention is that the exercise of the historical reason may be relied upon to provide what is imagined to be a sure foundation for consequent interpretive judgments, including judgments of faith. These might include belief in God as the ultimate author of the event, or the belief that Jesus' Resurrection was an event with transcendental implications for the restoration and renewal of humanity. Alternatively, appeal may be made to it to ground the more general belief in life beyond death for all human believers. Once the actuality of its occurrence is proved by historical research it can be interpreted in faith as the promise of an ultimate fulfillment relating to the eternal destiny of all people. In this case, judgments of faith of this variety become a kind of optional extra that may be entertained by religiously minded people. However, the affirmation of the actual occurrence of the Resurrection itself is said by Wright not to be a judgment of faith of this kind, but a conclusion of critical historical research. This may be reached by anybody, whether religiously inclined or not, using the historical reason. Wright therefore claims that there is "no reason in principle why the question, what precisely happened at Easter, cannot be raised by any historian of any persuasion."[7] What he means, more specifically, is that any historian of any persuasion may not only "raise the question" as to whether the Resurrection occurred, but may actually come to the conclusion that it did in fact occur, simply by employing the secular methods of critical historical research. Indeed, Wright claims that he, working purely as a historian, can actually prove the occurrence of the Resurrection to any right-thinking person of any or no religious persuasion at all. This is what he sets out to do in *The Resurrection of the Son of God*.

4. *RSG*, 685. See also Wright, *The New Testament and the People of God*, 95, where Wright uses Caesar's crossing of the Rubicon to distinguish carefully between the factuality of an event and the multiplicity of interpretative meanings that may be assigned to it.

5. *RSG*, 710, where the Resurrection of Jesus is said to be as historically secured as the death of Augustus or the fall of Jerusalem, though as we shall see in chapter 7, at this point some questions are begged by Wright about the status of historical judgments generally. Even the death of Augustus in AD 14 and the fall of Jerusalem in AD 70 are said to be established only with "historical probability" but "historical probability so high as to be virtually certain."

6. *RSG*, 22.

7. *RSG*, 21. See also Wright, *The New Testament and the People of God*, 15: "The great advantage of this task is that it can be seen quite clearly as a public operation. It is open to all and sundry; its methods are those of any historian reconstructing any society and its belief-systems."

Introduction

My immediate misgivings about the validity of these contentions are explained by the fact that when I myself wrote on the theology of the Resurrection in *The Structure of Resurrection Belief*, which was published in 1987, I argued an entirely contrary thesis: that the primary category of "divine mystery," if we are prepared to allow it to be brought to the discussion of the Resurrection (as St. Paul surely invites us to do[8]), entails that assent to the occurrence of the Easter Event is itself a judgment of faith, and not just a conclusion of the historical reason. It involves the interpretation of the reported experiences of the first Christians from the perspective of faith in God and even from the point of view of a pre-existing belief expressing the eschatological hope for resurrection beyond death. This already presupposes a set of dogmatic assumptions, which allowed the first Christians to interpret their Easter experiences in faith using the category of "resurrection." Indeed, even before we begin to try to come to a conclusion about whether the Resurrection of Jesus happened or not, we have to edge towards an understanding of what it is we are setting out to prove, for questions of meaning are logically prior to questions of truth. If it is rightly approached as essentially a transcendental mystery of God we have to anticipate that we may find ourselves humbly confronted by the fundamental limitations of human reason—something quite the opposite of an over-confident conviction that Christ's Resurrection was the kind of event that can be proved to have occurred by the exercise of the critical historical reason alone. We may anticipate therefore that the category of "mystery," by contrast with something that is clearly and distinctly manifest to all who care to attend to it, will therefore dictate the need to utilize a multiplicity of different avenues of approach as we seek to handle its surpassing transcendental qualities.

The kind of multi-faceted approach to the theology of the Resurrection of Christ, which was therefore pursued in *The Structure of Resurrection Belief*, is anathema to N. T. Wright, who contends that the category of "historical event" is to be employed exclusively, as the only really legitimate means of dealing with it. Indeed, as he sets out to convince his readers that he can actually prove the occurrence of the Resurrection of Christ as a historical event, Wright contends that the evidence constituted by the story of the empty tomb together with the accounts of the first Easter appearances or "meetings" with Jesus, as he calls them, provides both the necessary and sufficient conditions to warrant the judgment that Jesus *was* raised from the dead and restored to life in this world, leaving the tomb in which his dead body had been laid empty.[9]

---

8. 1 Cor 15:51: "Behold, I show you a mystery . . ."; perhaps following *1 Enoch* 103:2–4: "I know this mystery; for I have read the heavenly tablet . . . goodness and joy and honor are prepared and written down for the souls of those who have died pious. And their spirits will rejoice and not perish." See also 14:8 and 39:3 for Enoch's vision and translation into heaven. *First Enoch* accepts the idea of resurrection of the dead but does not develop it in any detail (51:1; 62:15; 91:10). In Ephesians Paul is said to speak of "the mystery of the gospel" that had been given to him to make known (Eph 6:19).

9. *RSG*, 706–10.

This, he says, is the *only* really plausible conclusion that can be drawn from the available evidence.

It can readily be conceded that Wright's approach to an understanding of what is meant by the term "resurrection," together with an examination of the evidence relating specifically to Jesus' purported Resurrection, using the historical reason, may indeed be *one* way of attempting to handle the Easter Event. However, if it is not the kind of event "that can be discussed without presupposing Christian faith"[10] that Wright assumes it to be, and if by definition the Resurrection is a mystery of God which "surpasses all understanding," the use of the historical reason alone is bound in the long run to be found wanting. In order to reduce the transcending mystery of it, even to reasonably manageable proportions, not just one but various hermeneutical models may have to be employed, none of which may be entirely satisfactory in and of itself. This means that no single avenue of approach is likely to be without some difficulties, not least and quite specifically, the approach to it simply as a historical event. Indeed, in *The Structure of Resurrection Belief* I argued that even the most impressive past attempts to handle the Resurrection exclusively as a historical event (notably, for example, the earnest and high-quality attempts of B. F. Westcott in the nineteenth century and of Wolfhart Pannenberg in the twentieth century) turn out, at the end of the day, to be ultimately unsatisfactory. I have come to the same conclusion in relation to N. T. Wright's own attempt in *The Resurrection of the Son of God*.

Wright himself does not suffer fools gladly. Indeed, those in the past who have pursued a quite different line of approach from his own in wrestling with the theology of the Resurrection of Christ tend to be summarily dismissed, and even abruptly put down in a thoroughly unceremonious way.[11] Despite the fact that Wright claims to have been "in implicit dialogue" with the corpus of publications on the Resurrection over the last generation,[12] there is little apparent attempt in *The Resurrection of the Son of God* to try to understand or accommodate alternative points of view, or to see them as complementary to his own. Indeed, one reviewer, noting Wright's overall "apologetic tone" and "calculating rhetorical defensiveness," has questioned the ethics of interpreting the biblical texts while failing to accept responsibility for representing "substantial interpretations different from the author's." Wright, he says, "never seriously presents the positions of the primary scholars of our day" or "engages any of

10. *RSG*, 22.

11. Among those who receive Wright's finger-wagging reprimands, Alan Segal, for example, is numbered among commentators on Wisdom of Solomon who agree "with the wicked in making an alliance with death," *RSG*, 168; the views of Gerd Lüdemann, in *The Resurrection of Jesus* are simply written off as "almost entirely worthless," *RSG*, 319 n.17.

12. *RSG*, 4 n.3.

the critical perspectives of modern and post-modern biblical scholarship."[13] Another reviewer charged Wright with playing narrowly to a conservatively minded audience, particularly those contemptuous both of liberal theology and of contemporary historical-critical exegesis, "with remarks about the mental deficiencies of those of us who disagree with his gospel of salvation history and attachment to narrative realism as historical evidence."[14]

In fairness, it has to be said that the discussion of whether a particular piece of theological writing stands aloof from the conclusions of others who have written on the same subject in recent times, or fails to take sufficient account of them, or of whether it falls within one specific kind of theological style rather than one that meets a reviewer's preference, is of less importance than the public examination and discussion of the author's own actual work in order to pass critical judgment on his or her own specific arguments. It is now well over fifteen years since the publication of *The Resurrection of the Son of God,* and it continues to stand as the reigning paradigm of the approach to handling Christ's Resurrection as an event of the historical past, using the techniques of critical historical research. We are now challenged to move beyond concerns about whether it passes muster when judged against a canon of theological preference or style of theologizing. We may take issue with a piece of theological writing by categorizing it as "liberal," "conservative," "defensive," or lacking in respect for "modern and post-modern" historical-critical exegesis, however, this kind of judgment is to some degree a matter of subjective preference. Irrespective of judgments of this kind, few will disagree that Wright has performed an important service by pursuing his own particular approach to the understanding of the Resurrection of Christ with a sustained and single-minded determination. This throws down the gauntlet of challenge to those who prefer to approach the theology of the Resurrection of Christ from other perspectives. I hope this book will be found to be just as single-minded and focused as it pursues a thorough analysis and assessment of the viability of his arguments.

Apart from Wright's commitment to the use of critical historical research as the preferred, indeed the *only*, really legitimate method of approach to an understanding of the Resurrection of Christ, there is another basic element of Wright's thought that needs at the outset to be brought to the foreground of the discussion of his views. Wright is anxious to persuade us to think in what he imagines to be exclusively "Jewish" or "biblical" categories of thought, almost as though it is possible to come to the biblical texts without having to take account of any extraneous considerations. We

13. Taussig, "Review," 244–45.
14. Perkins, "Review," 412.

are encouraged to read and understand them from *within* as it were,[15] in a pristine or unadulterated "biblical" or "Jewish" way. In the specific case of the Resurrection of Jesus, we must think in the manner of a mind-set inherited from Second Temple Judaism, which Wright alleges was received without significant developmental tampering either by the Pharisees of Jesus' day or subsequently by, also allegedly, the first generation of Christian believers. He is therefore anxious to urge that in order to understand the Resurrection of Christ one must be free of the contamination of modes of thought derived from external sources; instead, we are to think exclusively in the same categories of thought that were allegedly bequeathed to the first Christians, whose Easter experience is said to have conformed to this inherited Second Temple preunderstanding. Indeed, their Easter experience is said to have confirmed this specific inherited understanding of things.

Already it may seem that Wright's contention that critical historical research using the historical reason alone can establish the occurrence of the Resurrection as a historical event, which can then be used as a basis for judgments of faith and theological interpretations of its significance, actually presupposes some pre-existing faith commitments and dogmatic assumptions after all! However, to be fair to Wright, in the case of the Resurrection, the pre-existing understanding does not involve mention of any transcendental reality, such as "God" or "heaven," for he narrows down the specific preunderstanding inherited from Second Temple Judaism relating to the Resurrection simply to the empirical dimensions of the restoration of a dead person to life in this world of historical time. This is not a faith commitment, but simply how Second Temple Judaism thought of "resurrection," he says, and how the Pharisees and first-century Christians thought of it, and how we must think of it too. God, of course, is understood to be the author of this event, but is located at one stage remove in the background of it. Belief in a divine behind-the-scenes role might be a matter of faith, but as a historical event it is to be handled as something contained within space and time that can be literally described, and proved to have occurred, using the techniques of critical historical research.

Wright's methodological commitment to the handling of the Resurrection as a historical event that is in principle of a piece with any other event of human history, therefore holds at bay any suggestion that the Resurrection is to be understood as "a going of Jesus to God," whatever the precise sense in which these words might be used. In other words, the Resurrection is not to be understood in any sense as Jesus' entry to a heavenly destiny or as a sharing in the immortality of the God; it is simply to be understood as a happening of this world of space and time, albeit if ultimately at the hands of God. Indeed, it might even be thinkable that it could be handled without any explicit reference to God at all, for the word "resurrection" is said to refer simply to the return of a dead person to life in this world of historical time after a period

---

15. See his declaration of the need Christian theology has of "biblical studies" in *The New Testament and the People of God,* 138.

of having been dead, regardless of how this extraordinary happening was actually brought about. Explanation by appeal to its divine cause would be a kind of second order religious judgment based upon a purely rational historical conclusion as to its occurrence.

The received dictionary definition of the meaning of the word "resurrection," allegedly derived from its Second Temple Jewish source, therefore becomes prescriptive for Wright. The mind-set of Second Temple Judaism, he says, requires us to think not in faith-charged theological terms of a going of Jesus to heaven, or of his being vindicated by being raised and exalted to be with God, but simply in terms of his historical return from the dead to *this* world. This then allows for the accommodation of very matter-of-fact historical "meetings" with him by the first witnesses of the Resurrection in the days immediately following Jesus' crucifixion and burial. These "meetings" are spoken of as though they were in principle not unlike the historical meeting of David Livingstone and H. M. Stanley in Africa on 10 November 1871. As in the case of Livingstone and Stanley, the reports of the occurrence may be historically examined and a judgment made as to their veracity. Paul's "kerygmatic summary" of the Easter appearances in 1 Cor 15:3–8, and the narrative records of the discovery of the empty tomb and the various accounts of the Easter appearances in the Gospels, likewise constitute the primary evidential material upon which this purely historical judgment may be made.

Wright therefore contends that it is impossible to think of the Resurrection in any other way than as a historical event in which Jesus was restored to life in this world, for this is the way in which Second Temple Judaism thought of "resurrection" generally, and the first Christians can have thought of it in no other way. Their Easter experience simply fulfilled this aspect of their pre-existing apocalyptically colored expectations as these had been generated within this inheritance from Second Temple Judaism. To suggest that the Resurrection of Jesus may be understood, somewhat more mysteriously and in transcendental terms, as a divinely crafted and disclosed event that involved a "going to God," in some way located in a heaven beyond this world, is entirely anathema. Furthermore, to suggest that the Easter Jesus may have "appeared" in a revelatory way *from* the heaven to which he had gone, and was therefore mysteriously perceived by witnesses in this world in a judgment of *faith* is not to be countenanced.

Indeed, in contending that the Resurrection is to be understood in only one way, which he alleges is *the* biblical or Second Temple way, Wright bids us surrender any suggestion that the first Easter experiences might actually have led the first Christians to modify, at least in any substantial way, these inherited preunderstandings.[16] As we shall see, he acknowledges that they did in fact add to the inherited Second Temple understanding by attaching the rider that Jesus' raised physical body had become "incorruptible." But this simply "firms up" the nature of Jesus' raised body and in no way diminishes the purely observable and historical nature of it. The original Easter experiences therefore continue to be interpreted in the light of categories of thought that are said to have been acquired from the mindset of Second Temple Judaism, and we are discouraged even from entertaining the thought that these received understandings may have been in any really significant way changed, perhaps even transformed, in the light of those very experiences themselves. Instead we are obliged to think only of a rigid conformity to a "strictly limited"[17] and fixed, single understanding of what "resurrection from the dead" allegedly literally meant as this form of words was inherited by the first Christians from Second Temple Judaism.

In a way that is entirely consistent with this, Wright also attempts to draw a kind of *cordon sanitaire* around "Second Temple Judaism" itself and its understanding of the term "resurrection," as though this is something generated entirely from within itself, and free of any possible influence from ideas derived from outside sources in the ancient world. It is abundantly clear that at this point it is Greek thought that he has in his sights. For, while his concern is to exclude all possible alien influences from what he imagines to be a set of purely Jewish ideas, it is clear that Wright's methodological commitment to an alleged Jewish mode of thought is understood to be in radical contrast particularly to Greek philosophical categories. Most notable among these identifiably Greek notions is the idea of the "immortality of the soul." It will not be a surprise that, by pursuing this strategy of excluding what he believes are the entirely alien philosophical modes of thought of the ancient Greek world, Wright reveals that he has a particular aversion to Plato. After all, Plato is, if not the author, then the most definitive promoter, of the Socratic idea of the "immortality of the soul"[18] in the tradition of ancient Greek philosophy.

But Plato's fault is not confined narrowly to the idea of the soul's immortality. The idea of a timeless eternity outside space and time, which is the immortal soul's ultimate destination, is equally offensive to Wright. Indeed, Plato may be said to be guilty of

16. Luke Hoare has drawn my attention to the fact that it may be acknowledged that Wright does state that "there are substantial mutations from within the 'resurrection' stream of Judaism." *RSG*, 210. E.g., there is no "socio-political" metaphorical sense any more. But there is nothing in terms of a significant ontological difference apart from the alleged early Christian belief in "incorruptibility" as below.

17. *RSG*, 204.

18. As found in his account of the death of, and eulogy to, his teacher Socrates in *Phaedo*.

leading us into a fundamentally mistaken mode of thinking of a much broader kind, given that Plato initiated thought of a dualistic epistemology and its pre-supposed ontology by quite famously drawing a sharp distinction between changeless, eternal Forms or Ideas and their shadowy representations in the passing things of this material world, or between the eternal perfection of ideal changelessness by contrast with the change and decay of this passing imperfect world of matter. This kind of epistemology and its cosmological implications concerning the nature of reality are of no interest to Wright; it is altogether incompatible with the primary thrust of a genuinely Biblical eschatological understanding of things.

This dichotomy between Greek and Hebrew views of reality and especially of the afterlife is reflected in the fact that Wright tends to draw a thorough-going methodological distinction between an alleged "biblical" interest in the historical events of this world, and a more characteristically theological or philosophical focus on transcendental realities, such as, most notably, the timeless eternity of God, above and beyond history. Any theologian of the Resurrection who is inclined to focus on it from the perspective of Jesus' vindication "at the right hand of the Father" in a transcendental life with God beyond space and time, so as to speak in turn of the Easter appearances as revelations "from heaven," is mistaken. This alternative to an interest in the discovery of the empty tomb and the "meetings" with the Raised Jesus as evidence relating to an event of historical time in *this* world, is therefore condemned and written off as "platonic" and *ipso facto* as fundamentally mistaken as Plato himself.[19] The same may be said of interpretations of Paul's references to a heavenly "spiritual body" as though this is to be contrasted with "physical bodies" in 1 Corinthians 15. This too is said to be "platonizing."

The background to this methodological stance, which lines up a Jewish mode of thought antithetically to Greek categories of thought, lies in the so-called "Biblical Theology Movement," which flourished internationally across the world of New Testament studies in the generation immediately following the Second World War. Even though Wright says that he draws also on other more recent methodological approaches to New Testament studies in an eclectic kind of way, it is clear enough that the Biblical Theology Movement accounts for this fundamental orientation of his thinking. Among the more notable proponents of this post-war fashion in New Testament studies were scholars such as G. B. Caird, with whom Wright actually worked at Oxford as a research student, and Oscar Cullmann and Krister Stendahl, both of whom worked explicitly on the theology of the Resurrection and vigorously promoted

19. In this work, where possible, a lower case "p" is used to indicate a very general or generic kind of "platonism" as an orientation of thought beyond time to the timeless eternity of God. An upper case "P" will be used of "Platonism" in the more technical sense to indicate ideas that more closely originated specifically with Plato himself.

conclusions with which those of Wright resonate. At the very least, we may think of them as kindred spirits, if not as Wright's intellectual mentors as far as his theology of the Resurrection is concerned.[20]

The basic presupposition of this movement was the belief that there was a distinctively "biblical" or "New Testament" view of things, which could be isolated and expounded in a kind of "dictionary definition theology." Indeed, in this period the "dictionary of the Bible" or "theological word book" of the Bible became a very popular genre of theological writing. The numerous contributors to Gerhard Kittel's celebrated *Theological Dictionary of the New Testament* in Germany, for example, and to *The Interpreter's Dictionary of the Bible*[21] in the USA, exemplified this quest to unpack what was claimed to be a distinctively "biblical" way of thinking.[22] In England and the extended British theological world, Alan Richardson's *Theological Word Book* was a standard and much-used primer for that generation of theological students.[23]

The assumption was that *the* meaning of key Biblical terms such as "God," "Spirit," "time," "eschatology," or whatever, could be synthetically understood and presented as *the* Biblical or New Testament view of things. Unfortunately, this imposed a false harmony of viewpoint across the documents of the New Testament, which overlooked the theological diversity to be found among the various New Testament authors, not to mention nuances of meaning thrown up by the specific socio-historical contexts within which individual writers worked. In the next generation of New Testament scholarship, this homogenizing tendency was therefore enthusiastically challenged and corrected. From the mid-1960s, Redaction Criticism[24] began to focus on the rich variety of theological emphases that are disclosed once close comparative attention is paid to the specific editorial changes, additions, and omissions made to the Gospel traditions by successive individual New Testament authors, each of them working from their own distinctive theological perspective.

Another important methodological commitment of the Biblical Theology Movement, which also came to be challenged at the same time, and which is of particular relevance to our present concern, was that this movement very often achieved its goal by contrasting an alleged distinctively "biblical" or "New Testament" understanding of the key terms in which it took specific interest, with alternative, nonbiblical understandings of many of their semantic counterparts in differing linguistic and

---

20. For an outline of the agenda of the "Biblical Theology Movement," which Wright locates in the 1950s and 1960s (*The New Testament and the People of God*, 21), see Stendahl, "Biblical Theology," and Wright, *God Who Acts*.

21. See also, as representative of a more conservative approach, Morris, "Resurrection" in *New Bible Dictionary*, 1010–12.

22. For a more thorough-going critique of the methodology of this movement see Barr, *The Semantics of Biblical Language*, especially chapter 8 on the analysis of Kittel's *Theological Word Book of the New Testament*; also *The Concept of Biblical Theology*.

23. Richardson, *Theological Word Book of the Bible*.

24. A term coined by Willi Marxsen (*Redaktionsgeschichte*).

religio-cultural traditions. In particular, it drew a radical dichotomy between "biblical" or Hebrew/Christian modes of thought and pagan or "Greek" ways of thinking. Oscar Cullmann, in stressing "the fundamental differences between the two points of view,"[25] went so far as to say that "we must recognize loyally that precisely those things which distinguish the Christian teaching from the Greek belief are at the heart of primitive Christianity."[26] The coloring of this style of Biblical theology flows on into the work of N. T. Wright.

The following generation of New Testament scholarship pointed up the fallacy of this over-drawn opposition between so-called Greek and Hebrew/Christian modes of thought. Since the seminal work of James Barr on the semantics of biblical language,[27] and also of Martin Hengel on Judaism and Hellenism,[28] we have become much more conscious of the pervasive influence of Hellenistic culture around the ancient Mediterranean world, including Palestine, and even reaching as far east as modern Iraq and Iran. At least from the conquests of Alexander the Great in the fourth century BC onwards, the Greek language gradually became the *lingua franca* of the ancient world, and this naturally included Palestine. By the second century BC, the Pseudo-Aristeas saw it as no unusual thing that it was possible to recruit six scholars proficient in the Greek language from each of the Tribes of Israel to undertake the translation of the Hebrew Scriptures into Greek at Alexandria, which resulted in the production of the Septuagint (LXX). A further consequence of the Hellenization of the ancient world is that the New Testament itself was, of course, also written in Greek.

However, it was not just the Greek language as such but Greek modes of thought, that were necessarily crafted and expressed in the words and concepts of the Greek language, which permeated the cultures of the ancient world as well. The conquests of Alexander the Great thus transformed the ancient world, making trade and cultural exchange possible across great distances, but also facilitating a very fertile exchange of ideas. Indeed, if there was one thing that Hellenism excelled at it was the export of education. Hellenistic civilization thus created a meeting place of Greek and oriental ideas of such a kind that a good deal of shared outcome was inevitable. The great intellectual tradition of Greek philosophy that we associate with Plato and Aristotle naturally began to permeate neighboring cultures, including that of Palestine.

The fall of Athens at the hands of Mithridates, King of Pontus, in 88/87BC signaled an abrupt end of the orthodox philosophy of the traditional Greek philosophical schools of Athens. When the Roman general, Sulla, besieged and flattened the city

---

25. Cullmann, *Immortality*, 16.

26. Cullmann, *Immortality*, 8.

27. See Barr, *The Semantics of Biblical Language*; and Barr, *The Garden of Eden*.

28. Hengel, *Judaism and Hellenism*.

in the following year, the enforced closure of the philosophical schools if anything facilitated the dispersal of Greek learning; as scholars scattered they founded new centers of learning at such places as Rome,[29] Rhodes, Pergamon, Ascalon in southern Palestine, and of course, the enormously important neighboring center of Alexandria. In this way the demise of Athens actually assisted the wider energizing of philosophical endeavors across the Hellenistic world. The resulting dispersal of intellectual talent also meant that no single philosophical teacher could dominate the scene in the way Plato and Aristotle had done in ancient Athens. The result was a rather more complex and "mixed" intellectual atmosphere.

From the second century BC, Stoicism had already established itself widely across what was to become the Roman Empire, but from 86 BC onwards down to AD 200, an amalgam of Platonic, Aristotelian, and Epicurean ideas struggled for air within the prevailing environment of popular Stoic thought. As a direct consequence of the disaster of 86 BC, a new edition of Aristotle was produced in Rome by Andronicus of Rhodes in the middle of the first century BC, which stimulated a renewed interest in Aristotle, often if only to critique his views. But it was Plato's thought that, with the help of a transcendentalist thrust of a resurgent Neopythagoreanism,[30] gradually came to dominance. For this reason the period from 200 BC, when Stoicism enjoyed an ascendency, to AD 200, when Plato had once again assumed pride of place, is justifiably spoken of as a "Transitional Period" in Greek philosophy.

Already around 50 BC Cicero had identified three schools of philosophy: Stoicism, Epicureanism and the New Academy, which developed the nondogmatic side of Plato. This transitional phase of the revival and development of the fundamental notions of Plato is therefore generally referred to as "Middle Platonism."[31] With some input also from the Peripatetic school derived from Aristotle, the philosophy of Plato gradually began to get the upper hand over Stoicism. Certainly, it was Platonism that was destined to rise to the ascendant. The very influential Antiochus of Ascalon (130–69 BC)[32] who, after fleeing Athens was the teacher of Cicero in Rome around 79 BC, and who is often identified as the founder of Middle Platonism[33], quite intentionally sought to integrate elements of Plato's thought with the prevailing Stoicism, and at the same time rejected inherited skeptical theories in relation to the capacity both

29. Which also benefitted from Sulla's seizure of a library in which the works of Aristotle featured prominently.

30. The fascination with the abstractions of numerical truth, and the conviction that truth could be acquired by reason alone, in independence of countable material objects, is clearly in tension with the more empirical approach to truth through the deliverances of sense of epistemologies including the Stoic that were developed in the wake of Epicurus.

31. See the excellent survey of this period in Dillon, *The Middle Platonists*.

32. Antiochus had been teaching at Alexandria around the time of the closure of the school at Athens in 86 BC.

33. Probably incorrectly; this accolade goes to Eudorus who re-established a more transcendental orientation of thought than is found in Antiochus.

of the senses and the intellect to discover truth. In the wake of these advances, Eudorus of Alexandria, who flourished around 25 BC, is credited with turning the very Stoicized Platonism of Antiochus in an even more transcendental direction under the influence of Neopythagoreanism, and it was this that eventually led to the eclipse of Stoicism and the triumph of Platonism in the early Christian era.[34] One important sign of the success of this growing Platonism was the production of a new edition of Plato's writings by Emperor Tiberius' court astrologer, Tiberius Claudius Thrasyllus (who originally came from Alexandria), around AD 25.

This is not to say that there were not significant differences of religious and cultural outlook between Jews and Greeks. At times of tension and crisis, which naturally precipitated a heightened sense of Jewish self-identity, it was obviously felt necessary for Jews to define themselves over against the Greeks. Generally speaking these times of acute crisis were relatively short-lived, however, and focused on foreign interference particularly in relation to the observance of the law. The Maccabean revolt is the paradigm example of this. However, Jewish resistance to interference with its own political and cultic organization, and its more general negative reaction to foreign rule, does not countermand the contention that in the world of ideas and in literary production, extensive Hellenization is undeniable. Some of the later books of the Hebrew Bible itself exhibit the Greek influence very noticeably.[35]

Indeed, in relation to the mind-set of Second Temple Judaism itself, we have to acknowledge that we are dealing essentially with an amalgam of thought forms made up of Hebraic and Greek elements. For all the self-conscious exclusiveness of Jewish self-identity of the kind which surfaced particularly in times of tension and crisis, we need to appreciate that in less fraught times Judaism found a natural ally, not only in an ethical monotheism of the kind that could be historically connected back to Plato's philosophical speculation, but also in his fundamental focus on the reality of what is transcendentally "other" than this passing world of space and time.

While it is true that, following the publication of Martin Hengel's major work *Judaism and Hellenism*, there have been a few who have raised questions about some of his isolated conclusions, in general terms his thesis about the cross-fertilization of Jewish and Greek thought-forms across the Hellenistic world still stands. Sometimes it is imagined that Hellenistic influences on Judaism were somehow confined to the Jewish communities of the Diaspora, such as were found in Alexandria, or Antioch, or Rome, while back in Galilee and Jerusalem a more authentic and purified form of Jewish thought prevailed. However, Hengel has convincingly demonstrated that

34. Such as we see in Clement of Alexandria, Origen, and Philo of Alexandria.

35. For example, Koheleth (Ecclesiastes, possibly around 300 BC), Ben Sira (Ecclesiasticus, second century BC), and The Wisdom of Solomon, usually dated between 50 BC and AD 50.

Hellenizing pressures were so all-pervasive that it is no longer possible to draw a distinction between Palestinian Judaism and the Hellenized Judaism of the Diaspora in this kind of way. Hengel's follow-up book, specifically on the Greek influence on the culture of Jewish Palestine in the first century, which is supported by a plethora of recent archaeological finds, including even bilingual inscriptions (for example on ossuaries and in epitaphs), seems even more decisive than his earlier analysis of the influence of Hellenism upon Judaism. As Hengel himself says:

> It is not so simple to distinguish between the 'Jewish-Hellenistic' literature of the Diaspora and the 'genuine Jewish' literature of Palestine. Almost all accounts of intertestamental Jewish literature suffer from their desire to make too simple a distinction here. There were connections in all directions, and a constant and lively interchange.[36]

This process of Hellenization thus included the religious and cultural center of Jerusalem itself, and there is clear evidence that Galilee was likewise not exempt. To Hengel's mind, the processes of Hellenization were so extensive and all-pervading that it is even at least a thinkable proposition that Jesus was himself perhaps bilingual; witness his conversation with the Syro-phoenician woman recorded in Mark 7. In this episode the woman is specifically identified as a Greek. Also, some of Jesus' inner circle of disciples had Greek names (Andrew and Philip), and Peter (Andrew's brother) by tradition later prosecuted the Christian mission among the Jewish Diaspora of the West, which spoke only Greek.[37] We might also question whether it is even possible for Jesus to name Peter as "the rock" in Aramaic; at this point the use of the Greek *Petros*/rock may also indicate that in the mind of the Gospel writers it was not out of place to suggest Jesus' own acquaintance with the Greek language. However speculative these particular suggestions may be, they do alert us to the need to take Hellenization seriously in first-century Palestine.

The Jews were certainly conscious of their historical ancestry and of the historical roots of their religious identity as the covenant people of the God of Abraham, Isaac, and Jacob. Very notably, their eschatological hope orientated them towards a future vindication and release from foreign oppression. However, insofar as the fundamental thrust of thought inherited ultimately from Plato helped to point Hellenistic culture towards another world, in broad terms defined as "heavenly," and to think of an ideal reality above and beyond this passing world of time, then this was not only compatible with Jewish theological sympathies but could be a positive support to them.

Conversely, in a world of decaying polytheism both Plato and Aristotle propagated the idea that the perfect order of the heavenly bodies proves the existence of a Supreme Being who governs the universe. Despite the idolatry of much popular Greek culture of the time, for the more philosophically sophisticated "It was a windfall to

---

36. Hengel, *The 'Hellenization' of Judaea*, 26.

37. Hengel, *Judaism and Hellenism*, 105.

discover a people who rejected false gods and adored the God of Heaven alone."[38] Even in times of crisis when Jewish and Greek identity was most polarized, and it was necessary for Jews to stand apart from Greeks, and particularly from visual tokens of Greek culture (most notably its idolatry), it is nevertheless much less likely that people became consciously aware of a "Jewish way of thinking" over against a "Greek way of thinking," particularly about the existence of a transcendent God. On the contrary, in the eclectic world of Jewish philosophy from Aristobulus and the *Letter* of Pseudo-Aristeas in the middle of the second century BC onwards, down to Josephus in the closing decades of the first century AD, there were those who positively argued that, even if known by other names, the God of the philosophers was fundamentally also the God of Israel.[39] Indeed, at the hands of Aristobulus, Moses actually came to be identified as the teacher of Plato.[40]

It is incontrovertible that by the first century the use of the Greek language also meant that characteristically Greek ways of thinking informed the intellectual and cultural atmosphere. If Hellenistic influences penetrated religion and culture across the ancient world in a way that was all-pervasive, then the idea that purely Jewish modes of thought persisted in complete independence of the influence of more characteristically Greek ideas, in the way championed by the Biblical Theology Movement, has therefore become entirely problematic.

Moreover, in speaking of the Hellenization of Jewish thought by the first century AD we are not just speaking in very general terms. Rather than the integration of an alleged "Greek" way of thinking with a "Jewish" one, what we have to come to terms with was the incorporation into an identifiably Jewish worldview of an amalgam of philosophically diverse streams of thought that were quite specifically of Stoic and Platonic origin. While some quite justifiably refer to this as a Transitional Period leading to the fully confident emergence of Platonism of the triumphant kind we see in the Neoplatonism of Plotinus (ca. AD 204/5–270), this Stoic/Platonic amalgam that was characteristic of the philosophy of the time, with Plato clearly on the way to becoming the dominant partner, is what allows the period from 100 BC to AD 200 to be distinguished as the time of "Middle Platonism."

The specific form of the Hellenization of the intellectual atmosphere out of which the New Testament emerged might naturally therefore be thought of as a type of philosophical "eclecticism" of a Stoic/Platonic kind. It is important to note, however, that this is a matter of some debate. John Dillon has questioned the appropriateness of the use of the term "eclectic" in reference to Middle Platonism on the ground that this word usually suggests a kind of freewheeling selectivity of a fairly chaotic kind. However, what we are dealing with is really a progressive "blending" and development

---

38. Rajak, "The Location of Cultures" 18.

39. Hengel, *Judaism and Hellenism*, 266.

40. Hengel, *Judaism and Hellenism*, 163–69. This was still being affirmed in Paul's time by Philo of Alexandria.

of various carefully selected elements of thought under the influence of key influential thinkers, all broadly contributing to the growing interest in Platonism within the already popular Stoicism. As the Danish scholar Troels Engberg-Pedersen says: "One thing particularly striking about the Transitional Period is that almost all philosophers within the period to some degree adopted ideas from philosophies other than their own."[41] In the process of the overall change from Stoicism to Platonism as the dominant force, what we find is that "many philosophers who were basically Stoics, and who saw themselves as such, also drew on ideas that had a specifically Platonic pedigree."[42] Similarly, those who thought of themselves as Platonists appear to have had no hesitation in drawing upon input from Stoicism if it was deemed helpful. Sometimes language was co-opted from an opposed school of thought while at the same time taking issue with it.

It should not be a surprise to find that, even though no New Testament writer would have called himself either a Stoic or a Platonist, traces both of Stoic philosophy and Platonism may fairly easily be detected in the books of the New Testament. Paul provides the paradigm case. He certainly saw himself as a "Christian" rather than as a Stoic or a Platonist, but the cultural complexion of the communities to which he wrote his epistles necessarily required him to use words and concepts understandable to them. Paul was a Jew and he worshipped the Jewish God, but inevitably his Epistles nevertheless reflect the Stoic/Platonic amalgam of concepts and ideas that informed the intellectual world of which he was part. These days we dare not try to understand Paul as the inheritor of Second Temple Judaism as though this could be conceived in independence of this Hellenistic milieu. The principal thrust of Paul's apocalyptically-colored eschatology was undoubtedly drawn from a Jewish source. But even here the Stoic belief in a final conflagration may also have been within earshot; the Stoic view being that instead of *aether* beyond the heavens there was divine fire and that the end of the world would be marked by an all-consuming divine conflagration. Paul's references to the shining brightness of the glory of God in the face of the Raised Jesus Christ, and especially to the Day of Judgment as a day when the final purposes of God will be "revealed with fire," almost certainly echo Stoic images (1 Cor 3:13–15).

In recent years the remarkable congruence of Stoic ethical language with some of the key themes of the thought of St. Paul has triggered a succession of publications. Indeed, this has emerged as one of most fertile areas of advance in contemporary New Testament studies.[43] Troels Engberg-Pedersen, who has spearheaded this important

41. Engberg-Pedersen, "Setting the Scene," 4–5.

42. Engberg-Pedersen, "Setting the Scene," 5. On Stoic use of Plato, see Sedley, *Greek and Roman Philosophy*, 24.

43. Largely pioneered by Troels Engberg-Pedersen. See the collections of essays edited by him: *Paul in His Hellenistic Context*, *Paul and the Stoics*, and *Paul beyond the Judaism/Hellenism Divide*.

development, makes the salient point that we do not turn to the philosophical tradi-tions of Hellenistic culture so as to illuminate the "background" against which Paul is to be understood, for this suggests that he, as a Jew, in some way "stands out" from it. Rather, this is the intellectual and cultural context *in which* Paul is to be placed; he is a participant in it. Certainly, apart from his apparent reliance on a model of ethical argument conditioned by the popular Stoic moral philosophy of the culture of which he was part, not to mention his use of characteristically Stoic words and phrases, there is good reason to believe that he was open to a wider range of additional philosophical influences of an epistemological and ontological kind.[44] From time to time, therefore, Paul certainly uses language that is also characteristically Platonic; this is true particu-larly in relation, for example, to 2 Corinthians 4 and 5.[45]

We must, as a consequence, necessarily take account of the fact that from the very start, Christianity was born into a world that, for some centuries, had been thor-oughly "Hellenized." As Tessa Rajak has said, "In reality, even if contemporaries were not themselves wholly aware of the strands, Jewish and Greek cultures were deeply intertwined from the early hellenistic period."[46] Likewise, Diarmaid MacCulloch, in his history of Christianity, aptly reflects upon "what a tangle of Greek and Jewish ideas and memories underlies the construction of Christianity."[47]

In view of this cross-fertilization of Greek and Hebrew ideas, a clear consciousness of a direct and sophisticated opposition between ideas of "the resurrection of the body" and the "immortality of the soul," of the kind that inhabited the minds of those involved in the twentieth–century Biblical Theology Movement, calls for very care-ful scrutiny. Indeed, it is not unreasonable to say that an alleged consciousness of a radical dichotomy between the two was actually very unlikely, if not virtually impos-sible, in the fluid and eclectic context of ancient speculation about life beyond death. Certainly, we have therefore to be open to the specific theoretical possibility that even what was understood by the idea of "resurrection" was not immune from Hellenistic modifying influences.

The crucial issue for the theology of the Resurrection of Christ is whether the concept of "resurrection" must be understood in terms of categories of thought that are exclusively in line with the apocalyptic imagery of Second Temple Jewish eschatol-ogy, as the return of the Raised Jesus (after having been dead for three days) to *this*

44. It has been argued that he also followed a set of rhetorical strategies that can be traced back to Aristotle, the founding father of the study of rhetoric. See David Hellholm's analysis of the argument in Romans 6 in relation to Aristotelian rhetorical principles in "Enthymemic Argumentation in Paul."

45. A discussion of this facet of Paul's thought will be found in the companion volume to this: Carnley, *Reconstruction of Resurrection Belief*, chapter 11.

46. Rajak, "The Location of Cultures," 4.

47. MacCulloch, *Christianity*, 19.

world, and thus as a historical event, as N. T. Wright vehemently contends. Or, alternately, whether commerce with transcendentalist ideas of Greek origin meant that the notion of "immortality with God" in a timeless eternity beyond this world was brought to bear on the understanding of resurrection. If so, we have at least to take account of the possibility that this may well have been modified by being removed from the arena of historical time to the arena of God's eternity. In this case, it becomes an object of faith and the subject matter of theology, with only a secondary toehold in history in the form of the religious faith–claims and reported experiences of the first generation of Christian believers. The question of interest thus becomes whether the originally Greek idea of the "immortality of the soul" and the originally Hebrew idea of "the resurrection of the dead" rubbed shoulders so as to produce a kind of amalgam of these two streams of thought.

N. T. Wright is, of course, sufficiently attuned to the contemporary appreciation of the Hellenization of Palestinian culture in the first century to try to distance himself from the Biblical Theology Movement, and to avoid speaking in terms of a rigid polarity between "biblical" and "Greek" categories of thought. To his credit, for example, he is wary of drawing a clear dichotomy between the "Greek" belief in the immortality of the soul and the "Jewish" belief in resurrection, given that this is now somewhat passé in the world of New Testament studies.[48] However, after a perfunctory distancing of himself from the Biblical Theology Movement, its fundamental orientations of thought are nevertheless re-affirmed. For in practice, despite his protestations of innocence, it is abundantly clear that Wright has not been able to shake himself entirely free of the dichotomizing mind-set of the Biblical Theology Movement. *The Resurrection of the Son of God* is peppered with disparaging comments about Plato, and more generally about a theological "platonism" that is said to characterize any kind of interpretation of the Resurrection of Christ other than in terms of a return to *this* material world. Specifically in relation to the understanding of the Resurrection, he does not hesitate to draw a radical contrast between Hebrew and Greek modes of thought, and he does this repeatedly. To think of the Resurrection of Christ in terms of his going to a transcendent world so as to be eternally with God "in heaven" is branded "platonizing" and is for this reason alone declared to be anathema. This is in a sense understandable, for it is a conclusion that is methodologically driven. After all, only by locating it squarely within this world can the Resurrection of Christ be handled purely as a historical event, employing the techniques of argument of critical historical research.

48. *RSG*, 162–64: "The old assumption that Greeks believed in immortality and Jews believed in resurrection is not merely historically inaccurate; it is conceptually muddied." He will later clarify this muddiness by explaining that when Paul used the term "immortality" he really meant "resurrection," for "resurrection is a form of immortality"!

Wright's contention that there can be only one meaning of the word "resurrection" which is *the* Second Temple or Jewish view, and that it connotes a return of a dead body to life in *this* world of space and time, is therefore not just regularly contrasted with the technically Platonic view of the "immortality of the soul." It is even contrasted with a far more general contemporary theological propensity to think of the destination of the resurrected dead in essentially "other worldly" terms. Even the idea that the Resurrection of Christ involved a "going to God" as to a timeless eternity, outside of space and time, from whence he might then be said to have "appeared," and from whence he is in hope expected to return at the Eschaton, is written off as an essentially alien "Greek" or "platonic" idea.

Likewise, those who understand Paul to speak of the body of the resurrection as a radically transformed celestial or "spiritual body," as against the restoration of a purely physical and material body and its return to this world, are also written off as "platonizing." Clearly, it is not just a technical, full-blown Platonism with which Wright takes issue, but anything with what Ludwig Wittgenstein would have called a "family resemblance" to Platonism. What is to be contrasted with the alleged pure and unadulterated Second Temple view of resurrection becomes a kind of extended quasi-platonism, constituted by a platform of broadly related "other-worldly" or "heavenly" orientated ideas.

At the height of the Biblical Theology Movement, Oscar Cullmann confidently declared that "The teaching of the great philosophers Socrates and Plato can in no way be brought into consonance with that of the New Testament."[49] In a similar vein, Wright's antipathy and even hostility to Plato is the other side of the penny of his attempt to articulate an uncontaminated "Jewish" view of things. Sometimes his hostility to Plato is couched in somewhat intemperate language: Those who think of Paul's references to the "spiritual body" in 1 Corinthians 15 as something radically transformed and "heavenly" or nonphysical, for example, or as something "which you could not touch" and "could not see with ordinary eyesight" are said to fall into "Plato's ugly ditch."[50] Indeed, Plato is charged with conceiving unwelcome views of the afterlife; not only including images of eternal heavenly bliss for the souls of the righteous, but of hellish punishment for the wicked, accompanied by graphic scenes of judgment of the kind that became so characteristic of the Middle Ages. These, Wright suggests, may be written off, not just as "Platonized Christianity" but possibly as "Christianized Platonism," and thus categorized as an essentially pagan way of thinking.[51]

49. Cullmann, *Immortality,* 60.

50. *RSG,* 348.

51. *RSG,* 50. Elsewhere, in the face of this kind of possibility, Paul is said to belong "on the Jewish map rather than the pagan one," (*RSG,* 372).

It was Oscar Cullmann's view that we must "guard against any accommodation to Greek philosophy, if we wish to understand the New Testament doctrine."[52] This amply encapsulates Wright's methodological stance specifically in relation to the understanding of "resurrection."

⁓

As a consequence of all this, it is important to note that, insofar as God is spoken of at all by Wright in relation to the Resurrection, it is therefore only the background activity of God in some way "behind" events of historical time, and the future eschatological act of God of the End Time, that hold any real interest for him. What we might appropriately call "salvation history" (*Heilsgeschichte*) replaces any focus on the timeless, heavenly life of God as God is in God's self. This explains why Wright is disinclined to speak of the Resurrection of Christ as a "going to God" in a heaven above and beyond this world. Indeed, instead he also thinks of heaven itself in historical terms. The term "heaven" is really only legitimately used by Christians in the phrase "the Kingdom of Heaven." Rather than as the imagined timelessly eternal abode of God outside of this world of space and time, heaven awaits us in the future of *this* world, for the "Kingdom of Heaven" will only be realized on earth at the future Eschaton. This yet-to-be-realized future is the ultimate destination beyond the grave of Christian believers.

The fact that it "has not happened yet," because it is a reality that will only come to be at the End of all history as we know it, does not appear to be an issue for Wright. At that future time, all the righteous dead will be raised to be with Christ, and God will be all in all. Meanwhile, all the righteous dead are said somehow to be asleep, in an (intermediate) state of suspended animation,[53] awaiting their restoration to life in this world. While this will only happen in the denouement of the End Time, we are assured that they are all safely "in the hands of their maker";[54] but exactly where the Raised Christ with his materially-restored body, now made physically incorruptible, might be thought to be located in this interim period, which has now extended over two thousand years, if not with God in a heaven beyond this world, is not made altogether clear.

⁓

The idea of the Resurrection of Christ as essentially a mystery of God, an event with a transcendental face, is in this way abandoned in favor of a kind of monistic theological horizontalism. This alone is what is said to be congruent with the fundamental

---

52. Cullmann, *Immortality*, 49.

53. At this point, Wright also exhibits a close relationship with the seminal thought of Cullmann on this subject. See Cullmann, *Immortality*, 10.

54. *RSG*, 170.

emphasis of the apocalyptic hope regularly expressed in Second Temple Judaism, which is in turn said to have been taken over by the first generation of Christians. Wright's attempt to disconnect us from thinking in ahistorical transcendental terms also means that any suggestion that the Resurrection might be thought of in terms of "exultation" and "heavenly glorification" also tends to be dismissed as "purely platonic," and therefore as foreign to authentically "biblical" and historical categories of thought. This is despite Paul's propensity to speak in this way, apparently quoting an early hymn, in Phil 2:5–11 with its affirmation that God "highly exalted" the crucified Jesus without, perhaps significantly, any explicit reference to the concept of resurrection.

This then, is the Second Temple understanding of resurrection that is said to have been bequeathed to us also in the twenty-first century. We are allegedly bound to it no less than the first generation of Christians, who are said not to have departed from it. This basic orientation away from the quasi-platonic view of the timeless eternity of God above and beyond this world allows Wright to believe that the Resurrection of Christ may be thought of quite simply as a time-bound historical event in the sense of the return of the dead historical Jesus to life in *this* world of space and time.

In all this Wright is clearly not only anxious to keep our understanding of the Resurrection contained within spacio-temporal parameters, but also to make sure that it remains the *kind* of event that can be handled by the techniques of critical historical research. We can fully acknowledge the pressure on Wright in methodological terms to hold on to an understanding of "resurrection" in "strictly limited," clear, and distinct terms. In order to qualify for its handling as a historical event, it must conform in principle to any other happening of this world and must obviously be contained within space and time. What might be appropriate to an imagined heavenly world, or acknowledged to be less material and more immaterial and spiritual, or what might be thought to be located away from this world of time in the timeless eternity of God, might become the religious object of faith and the subject matter of theology, but hardly the subject matter of critical historical inquiry. While a historian may write an account of the way in which the first Christians described an experience that was in essence understood to be directed towards an "other-worldly" reality, the analysis of the nature of the experience of an alleged heavenly reality itself becomes a matter for speculative reflection rather than the subject matter of a purely historical enterprise.

This is why, by contrast with an understanding of the Easter appearances as revelatory or even visionary experiences that were appropriated by faith and perceived by some but not by others, Wright is obliged to portray the appearances as matter-of-fact historical "meetings" with the historically restored and reanimated Jesus. By the same token, for this methodological reason, an understanding of the Resurrection as a "going to God" has necessarily to be entirely ruled out of court. The same applies to any inclination to speak of the first Easter experiences as "revelatory disclosures" of the Raised and exalted Christ, appearing "from heaven" and appropriated by faith. For the methodological reasons to which Wright is committed, the word "resurrection" can *only* mean the return of Jesus to life in a visibly material body after a period of having been dead, and its restoration therefore to this world of space and time. This is what he contends happened to Jesus, and given that Jesus is "the first-born of the dead," this is what will also happen to all the righteous dead at the End of the World, when they are finally awakened from their current state of sleep: they will all be restored to life and accommodated back in this world. Only at that point of time will it be appropriate to speak of "the Kingdom of Heaven." Thus, when "heaven on earth" is finally actualized at the Eschaton, all the righteous dead who have ever lived will be bodily restored to this world in the manner of the resurrected Jesus, with reanimated bodies made no less incorruptible than his, and with him they will rule over the entire world. At that point, "God's people will actually be running the new world on God's behalf."[55]

By contrast with this aggressively anti-platonic orientation of Wright's approach to the theology of the Resurrection, it will be argued in this book that Christian thought of the kind that Wright condemns as "platonic" actually starts with the first generation of believers. This, of course, is not to suggest that the first Christians were necessarily students of Plato, or had any immediate or direct acquaintance with his writings, though this is of course not impossible. Rather, the suggestion is that their theological understanding, not least in relation to the specifics of the Resurrection of Christ, was formed within a Jewish intellectual environment already energized by the popular amalgam of Platonism and Stoicism of the day. Even for Jews, this was inescapably the world of Middle Platonism. As important as it certainly was, Second Temple Jewish apocalypticism was not the only component of their intellectual inheritance. They were certainly not uninfluenced by a basic Hellenistic orientation of thought towards a world above and beyond this one, of the very kind that Wright labels "platonic" and then urges us to avoid at all costs.

We can appreciate the difficulty for Wright of this way of thinking, for it entails that the resurrection experience upon which Easter faith is based must become essentially revelatory, "from heaven" as it were, and therefore something that must necessarily be appropriated by faith. This is clearly at odds with Wright's own fundamental methodological commitment, which entails that it must be contained within historical time so as to ensure that access to it is by the critical historical reason alone

55. Wright, "Christians Wrong about Heaven." Whether contemporary Christianity will respond warmly to this prospect is problematic. Leslie Houlden, in *Connections*, 149, may speak for many when he says "The apocalyptic 'package' can scarcely be given new currency."

2

2 *Baruch*, Josephus,
and The Wisdom of Solomon

N. T. Wright laments that so many who have written about Jesus' Resurrection over the last generation have paid "scant attention" to the "complete Jewish context" of the language used by the early Christian disciples.[1] In particular, despite the wide spectrum of belief in Second Temple Judaism regarding the fate of the dead, insufficient attention, he says, has been paid to the emerging "definition" of the term "resurrection" that was called forth by the new circumstances of post-Exilic Judaism. Wright contends that his own study of the Jewish context shows that, at least by the time of 2 Maccabees, a highly specific definition of "resurrection" was in circulation with a "strictly limited range of meaning."[2]

Wright plots the emergence of this "strictly limited" definition over time. First, the concept of "resurrection" is said to have been used metaphorically of the restoration of Israel. As in Ezekiel's prophecy of the valley of dry bones (chap. 37), the metaphor of resurrection was used to point to the political return of Israel from exile "with corpses coming to new bodily life."[3] But "By the time 2 Maccabees was written the metaphor has become literal"; being now used to connote "the concrete referent of re-embodiment—getting back hands, tongues, entire bodies—without losing the larger concrete referent of national restoration."[4] According to this received "definition," the term "resurrection" refers not to some vaguely defined continuing life after death, but only to the second phase of a two-stage process. The first phase is a *kind* of "life after death" characterized by a form of sleep for departed souls who are in an "intermediate state" while they await their resurrection. Rather than being used just to affirm a form

---

1. *RSG*, 200–201. Peter Carnley is cited as being particularly at fault in this regard!
2. *RSG*, 204.
3. *RSG*, 202.
4. *RSG*, 202.

of disembodied heavenly life after death, the term "resurrection" was then used quite specifically to affirm a new re-embodied life as an ultimate return to this world *after* "life after death" in the alleged "intermediate state."

This is the "strictly limited" definition that he believes was firmly set in place and bequeathed to the first generation of Christians, who are said very dutifully to have used it only in this way. This means that the use of the term "resurrection" in reference to Jesus cannot have to do with a going of Jesus to an eternal heavenly existence after death, from whence he was reported to have appeared, and from whence he would show himself in gloriously vindicated victory at the End of the Age. Rather, "resurrection" refers only to the return of Jesus from a temporary three-day intermediate form of "life after death" to resurrected life understood as a return to re-embodied life in this world.

I have some difficulty comprehending Wright's account of a development from a metaphorical use of the term "resurrection" to its literal use. Usually, the metaphorical use of a term starts with a literal image and applies it to an object of reference of an altogether different kind. For example, when Shakespeare wrote of "Sleep that knits up the ravell'd sleave of care,"[5] he takes the literal image of a knitter with needle and yarn, darning a hole in the frayed sleeve of a garment, and applies it metaphorically to the phenomenon of the balm of sleep in relation to a care-worn person. So, to unpack the metaphor in more prosaic and literal language, the meaning is that sleep operates to renew a care-worn person in a way similar to the way in which a knitter mends a frayed hole in a garment. Unless there is a prior understanding of a literal use of words, the metaphor does not work.

In the case of the appeal to the notion of resurrection, the literal restoration of a dead corpse to life might be used metaphorically of the renewal and restoration of a political reality, such as Israel. The metaphor depends upon a prior understanding of the "resurrection" of human bodies literally understood. But Wright's contention is the reverse of this insofar as an original metaphorical use in a political context (the restoration of Israel) is said to develop to its literal use as the restoration of individual bodies of flesh and bones, albeit in a mass phenomenon involving all the departed at the Eschaton. It is hard to see how a metaphorical understanding can lead to a literal one in the way that Wright would have us believe. Furthermore, Ezekiel envisages this metaphorical political event in terms of corpses apparently literally and very graphically coming to new bodily life.

It is already obvious that metaphors may of course themselves be unpacked in more literal and prosaic language. Thus Ezekiel's use of the metaphor of the "resurrection of Israel" may be explained in detail simply as "the return of Israel from exile and the political reconstitution of its national sovereignty." This is the political reality, which is being expressed in the image of bodily resurrection. On the other hand, when Wright explicitly speaks of Ezekiel's metaphorical reference to the return

5. *Macbeth,* Act 2, scene 2.

of Israel from Exile "with corpses coming to new bodily life," it is hard to discern whether he means that Israel's return was *accompanied by* or *figuratively expressed through* the image of "corpses coming to new bodily life." If this is to be understood as metaphorical language, then the latter must be the case. But his account of this event nevertheless then draws upon a literal understanding of individual "corpses coming to new bodily life." It is difficult to see how the metaphor can work without reliance upon this logically prior literal understanding of things.

In any event, Wright, along with most other scholars, argues that whatever its antecedents, a literal understanding of the fate of the dead, and particularly of martyrs, in terms of the reconstitution and return of their mortal bodies, began to flourish around the time of the persecution of Antiochus IV Epiphanes. In the Hebrew Bible, Daniel 12 and 2 Maccabees bear witness to the emergence of explicit resurrection belief in relation to individuals. In circumstances of foreign domination and persecution, an unwavering belief in the justice and faithfulness of God in this way found expression in the hope of vindication through the dramatic reversal of fortunes.

It is pertinent to note that, while Daniel 12:2–3 definitely appears to speak of the resurrection of individuals,[6] it is less than clear that the author of Daniel thought in terms of a return to earthly life. T. W. Manson promoted this view,[7] but Daniel's references to resurrected leaders "shining like the brightness of the firmament," and to those leading others to righteousness being "like the stars for ever and ever" prompts H. C. C. Cavallin to conclude that "the least one might say is that the resurrection statement of Dn 12:2 does not describe a mere return to physical life. On the contrary, by the addition of v.3, it is open to the idea of transformation into heavenly existence."[8] By contrast, 2 Maccabees represents a much more graphic picture of the restoration of material bodies, apparently to life in this world. In any event, Wright's contention is that appeal was increasingly made, specifically in the context of the apocalyptic belief in the vindication of all the righteous dead at the final day of the Eschaton, to the concept of "resurrection" understood in more literal terms as the physical restoration of individual martyrs and their return to this world from the dead. This is the "strictly limited definition" that is said to have gained exclusive currency at least from 2 Maccabees onwards, which N. T. Wright identifies as *the* mind-set of Second Temple Judaism.[9]

He then seeks to persuade his readers that this specific mind-set *and no other* was ultimately bequeathed to the inhabitants of first-century Palestine by this immediately preceding religious culture. This Second Temple approach to the specific question of

6. Very likely inspired by Isa 26:19.

7. See Manson, "The Bible and Personal Immortality," 12.

8. See Cavallin, *Life after Death*, 27.

9. A roughly similar account of the emergence of belief in personal survival beyond death in Judaism, with a clear emphasis on the pivotal role of Daniel at the beginning of resurrection belief, may be found in Segal, "Life after Death," 91–102.

"life beyond death" is said to have viewed the future resurrection of the dead exclusively as a post-mortem restoration to life in this world after a period of having been dead. This means for Wright that those whose thinking was formed by this mind-set, including the first Christian believers, cannot have thought otherwise of Jesus' Resurrection than as a restoration of his physical remains to life in this world of space and time, leaving the tomb in which he had been laid empty. It is thus something that may today be handled purely as a historical event of this world of space and time.

It is significant that Wright argues that this Second Temple preunderstanding of "the resurrection of the dead" was shared across a spectrum of diverse groups in the Palestine of the Greek diaspora. Given that the Sadducees denied that there would be any resurrection of the dead at all, exactly what it was that they explicitly denied was the belief that the dead might be restored to life in this world. The Pharisees, on the other hand, who received the view of Second Temple Judaism in a more positive way, accepted the very same belief, which the Sadducees denied. This also necessarily involved the hope of the restoration of physical remains to life in this world. Whether it was denied, therefore, or received and positively accepted, Wright contends that it was tacitly agreed within the culture of Second Temple Judaism that the term "resurrection" meant only one thing—the restoration of a dead person to life in this world after a period of having been dead.

Given this linguistic fact of the contemporary religio-cultural environment, Wright's thesis is that the first Christians unwaveringly shared this very same view. This means that their Easter faith involved a judgment that was based on experiences that conformed with, and thus confirmed, this received understanding of things. When they claimed that Jesus had been raised, they can *only* have meant that he had been physically restored to life in this world; they cannot have imagined an alternative understanding, such as, for example, that he had left this world in order to go to a timelessly eternal and glorified life with God of a more heavenly, exalted, transcendental kind. Somebody influenced by the basic otherworldly schema of Plato might have thought in this way, but the first Christians did not.

Furthermore, Wright's contention is that they could not have thought that in their Easter experiences Jesus appeared to them from any other place than from somewhere else within this world of space and time. Because he was necessarily understood to have been restored to this world, what we speak of as his "appearances" could not therefore have been apparitions, visions, or revelatory appearances "from heaven," but instead, and unavoidably, quite straightforward occasional "sightings" of a physically-restored person within the spacio-temporal parameters of this world. Indeed, as has already been noted, Wright prefers to speak of these appearances in unambiguously matter-of-fact terms as "meetings."

It is manifestly clear that N. T. Wright urges that the view of resurrection within the mind-set of Second Temple Judaism, particularly as it was entertained by the Pharisees, was able to keep itself untainted from outside influences of a Hellenistic kind which would have encouraged thought, less in terms of a restoration to life in this world, and more in terms of a release from it to eternal immortality. The term "resurrection" meant only one thing in the ancient world, he says, and that entailed the restoration of the dead to life in this world, after a period of having been dead. This single, "strictly limited" and firmly set meaning had been adopted by conventional agreement across many sub-cultures; whether one was a Pharisee, a Sadducee, or a Christian, it made little difference. Indeed, even a pagan in the same environment, perhaps actually believing in the immortality of the soul as against the notion of resurrection, would have agreed that the term "resurrection" meant only one thing.

The immediate question, therefore, is whether it really is the case that this single "strictly limited" way of conceiving the resurrection of the dead was the *only* current option available in the world inhabited by the first Christian believers, or whether some variety of belief may have been in circulation in relation to this matter. This obviously has a direct bearing on whether the first Christians themselves must *necessarily* be understood also to have thought of Jesus' Resurrection precisely and exclusively in these same prescribed terms.

While N.T. Wright insists that there was no variety of opinion, and that the ancient world shared a uniform understanding of resurrection as a return of a dead person to life in this world, account must be taken of the alternative contention that there was indeed some variety of belief relating to the afterlife at the time. In 1987, in *The Structure of Resurrection Belief*, I myself observed that in the first and second century AD "an array of understandings appear to have been on offer concerning exactly what was materially involved in making the formal assertion that the dead would be restored to life."[10] My contention was, and still is, that as people struggled to discern the more specific "shape" of their belief in life beyond death and the nature of "the resurrection of the body," they would necessarily have been involved in imaginative and speculative thought. By nature, this is not just a matter of factual reporting but of discerning the possible outline understanding of a yet-to-be-experienced mystery and a yet-to-be-realized object of an ultimate hope. It is reasonable to anticipate that this might naturally have led therefore to a variety of speculative outcomes and that, for this reason alone, a number of different perceptions about the fate of the dead is likely to have been current at the same time. Moreover, if the culture of the time was heavily influenced by Hellenistic modes of thought, as I have already suggested was certainly the case, then some variety of resurrection belief may also be anticipated to have

10. Carnley, *Structure of Resurrection Belief,* 53–54.

resulted from modifications introduced by syncretizing cultural pressures. Wright's handling of the evidence upon which he grounds the contention that the mentality of those who inherited the mind-set of Second Temple Judaism in the ancient world was uniformly monochrome has therefore to be examined carefully.

The argument that Jewish views about the resurrected afterlife were single, fixed, and resistant to variety of viewpoints, is based upon an extensive array of documents. Fortunately, we can avoid such an exhaustive analysis, given that we will only have to find evidence of a few contrary viewpoints in some of the most important literature to demonstrate at least the possibility that the understanding of things within the culture of Second Temple Judaism may not have been quite as univocally monochrome as Wright would have us believe.[11] Our primary concern will be to examine the strategies of argument employed by Wright in reaching his conclusions, and to come to a judgment concerning their validity.

As it turns out, indicators of the existence of some variety of resurrection belief due to the conditioning of Hellenistic coloring may be found in two of the most important evidential sources available to us, namely *2 Baruch* (also known as *The Apocalypse of Baruch)* and the writings of Josephus. To these may be added the Wisdom of Solomon, for Wright's handling of Wisdom is also helpfully instructive.

From the outset it can readily be acknowledged that belief in the literal restoration of a material body to this world was almost certainly *one* of the paradigms current at the time.[12] For example, the rabbis interpreted Ps 16:9–10 as a reference to resurrection in terms of the preservation of the physical flesh beyond death, presumably within this world. This is in keeping with the classic articulation of this viewpoint that is expressed in very graphic terms in 2 Maccabees, where the third Maccabean martyr in his last gasp, "holding forth his hands manfully, said courageously, These I had from heaven and for his laws I despise them; and from him I hope to receive them again" (2 Macc 7:11). A similar view is expressed where the wounded martyr Razis hurled his own bowels upon the assembled throng and called "upon the Lord of life and spirit to restore them to him again" (2 Macc 14:46).

However, an alternative, less graphically physical, and more "spiritual" understanding of things cannot be excluded from consideration. The possibility of thinking of the resurrection body in a radically transformed heavenly, exalted, and glorified sense has been promoted by a number of modern authors. Once again, we do not have to compile a compendium; a number of representative thinkers will serve our present purpose: in particular, Kirsopp Lake of an earlier generation of New Testament

11. Surveys of the background literature are now legion. Among the more significant are Glasson, *Greek Influence*, and the very balanced and carefully considered work of Cavallin, *Life After Death*.

12. This is noted in Carnley, *The Structure of Resurrection Belief*, 53, in the course of arguing that the mental furniture of the time appears to have been somewhat complex and various.

scholars; the more contemporary British New Testament scholars A. E. Harvey and C. F. D. Moule; and also the conclusions of Strack and Billerbeck based upon their study of the Talmud and Midrash.[13]

Kirsopp Lake, in speaking of the possibility that the first Christian believers thought in terms of the "non-material nature of the resurrection body" coined the idea of the "transubstantiation" of the body of flesh and blood into some kind of "spiritual" body, by which he means a nonmaterial and thus "heavenly" body. C. F. D. Moule speaks in broadly similar terms of the "transfiguration" of the body.[14] Wright's predecessor at Westminster Abbey, also a New Testament scholar, A. E. Harvey, on the other hand, points out that Josephus indicated that some Pharisees appear to have assimilated resurrection belief to the more clearly Greek belief in the transmigration of souls.[15] Finally, H. L. Strack and P. Billerbeck[16] contended that while some rabbis in apocalyptic Jewish circles certainly thought in terms of a very mundane return to life on earth with the same body, even with the same blemishes and the same clothing,[17] others thought in less purely material terms. In particular, Strack and Billerbeck concluded that in the *Apocalypse of Baruch* 49–51, there are explicit references that indicate an understanding "in which the body of the resurrection is spiritualized."[18] N. T. Wright understandably has little sympathy with these statements.[19]

It is clear that this diverse group of scholars are agreed that *2 Baruch*, and Josephus in particular, are of crucial significance in furnishing us with the key material for justifying the view that there was indeed some variety of viewpoint with regard to the detailed nature of thought about the possibility of resurrection within post Second Temple religious culture. We must therefore first examine the *2 Baruch* and then turn to the contributions of Josephus to this discussion.

Second Baruch is to be distinguished from the book of Baruch in the Old Testament Apocrypha.[20] The full text of the most relevant passage for our present purposes (*2 Baruch* 49–51) is attached as Appendix 1 at the end of this book. From it, the reader

---

13. See also Carnley, *The Structure of Resurrection Belief*, 231.

14. See Moule, "St Paul and Dualism."

15. Harvey, *Jesus and the Constraints of History*, 150. Segal, "Life After Death," 108, also notes that "Josephus envisioned another, different kind of body for imperishable souls. The body which we have in this life is corruptible; therefore, like Paul, he sees a new incorruptible flesh to be the reward of the good."

16. Strack and Billerbeck, *Kommentar zum Neuen Testament*, 3:475, and also 4:1166–98, esp. 1173–76.

17. See 2 Macc 7:11 and 14:46, and also the graphic image of Ezekiel 37.

18. Carnley, *The Structure of Resurrection Belief*, 231.

19. *RSG*, 161.

20. The *Apocalypse of Baruch* may be found in Charlesworth, *The Old Testament Pseudepigrapha*, chapters 49–51 of which may be found in Appendix 1 of this book.

should note at the outset that the author raises a series of very pertinent questions that are addressed to God, as in a prayer:

> In which shape will the living live in your day? Or how will remain their splendor which will be after that? Will they, perhaps, take again this present form, and will they put on the chained members which are in evil and by which evils are accomplished? Or will you perhaps change these things which have been in the world, as also the world itself?

The fact that these very questions are being asked already suggests that, at least in the mind of Baruch, the exact shape of resurrection belief was far from clearly settled. Otherwise, why ask these rhetorical questions in the first place? In effect he is posing the Pauline question: "How are the dead raised? With what kind of body will they come?" (1 Cor 15:35). Already it is clear that this was a live question; the answer to it may not have been nearly so firmly fixed by the first century, as N. T. Wright would have us believe. Indeed, we should note essentially the same question in the minds of Jesus' disciples when "They discussed among themselves what this 'rising from the dead' could mean" (Mark 9:10). In the case of *Baruch*, there is an element of indecision insofar as "different types of resurrection belief are skillfully combined" in a way that suggests that different possibilities were current—on one hand, the restoration of the body "to its pre-existing state," and on the other, "the transcendent glorification of the righteous into an angelic state."[21]

It is also important to note especially Baruch's interest in at least the theoretical possibility of some kind of bodily change through death, which leads to his further affirmation that though "the earth will give back the dead, just as it received them," they will share the "splendor of angels" and be "like angels." *Baruch's* actual words are: "They will live in the heights of that world and they will be like angels and equal to the stars." In the face of this statement alone, it is hard to sustain N. T. Wright's contention that only one "strictly limited" understanding of the term "resurrection" was in circulation in the ancient world of Second Temple Judaism and that it merely involved a material and physical restoration to life in this world. Indeed, the contention that it meant *only* that the bodies of the dead were materially restored to life in this world of space and time, and this without significant change in form, save for the fact of being "firmed up" as it were by being made incorruptible, as Wright contends, already appears somewhat problematic.

Those of us who interpret this reference to suggest that 2 *Baruch* might have thought of life beyond death in less purely mundane and material but more spiritual or nonmaterial and heavenly terms, see this conclusion as the logical implication of *Baruch's* statement that the righteous dead will be "like angels." It is fairly clear that

---

21. This is the considered view of Cavallin, *Life after Death*, 88. Unfortunately J. D. G. Dunn emphasizes only the first half of this equation in Dunn, *Jesus and the Spirit*, 118. As we shall see, N. T. Wright goes a step further in attempting positively to neutralize the second half of the equation.

in the ancient world even the angels were understood to have some kind of body. They appear not to have been understood just as disembodied spirits. But, however we might envisage the similarity that *Baruch* draws between the resurrected bodies of the righteous dead and the bodies of angels, N.T Wright is determined not to allow them to be understood to be too much alike, if alike at all. Certainly, for him the righteous dead are not like angels in the sense of being heavenly or spiritual—in other words nonmaterial. Wright's strategy of argument in handling these references from *2 Baruch* is therefore very informative.

It has already been noted that at least some element of bodily transformation is actually conceded by Wright as an integral part of Christian resurrection belief.[22] Indeed, he admits that some kind of "radical transformation is obviously envisaged."[23] Moreover, he is even prepared to concede that this particular text from *2 Baruch* is noteworthy precisely because it provides "the only clear anticipation of what we do certainly find in the New Testament: the sense that resurrection will involve some kind of life-enhancing transformation."[24] He also concedes that this passage from *2 Baruch* has indeed been appealed to in support of an "immaterial" resurrection, and hence as a possible corroboration for interpreting Paul's talk of a "spiritual" body in the sense of some kind of nonmaterial body in 1 Corinthians 15. At this point he makes explicit reference to my quoting of Kirsopp Lake in this regard in *The Structure of Resurrection Belief*.[25]

However, despite all these concessions, he then cavalierly dismisses what appears to be the unavoidable implication of *2 Baruch*'s actual simile. After all, as *Baruch* says, it is not only that the righteous dead will be "like angels" but that "they will live in the heights of the world and be equal to the stars." Surprisingly, Wright clutches somewhat desperately at *2 Baruch*'s saying that the righteous dead are *like* angels: it is not, he argues, that they are said to be *the same as* angels! He then seeks to avoid suggestions of a possible Hellenistic conditioning of *Baruch* in the direction of a future immortal life in the nearer presence of God by saying that *2 Baruch*'s "careful distinction between the righteous and the angels in 51:12 should also be noted."[26] *Second Baruch* 51:12 says that "the excellence of the righteous will be greater than that of the angels." For Wright, the excellence of the righteous dead, entirely unlike the angels, hinges upon their becoming incorruptibly material by a kind of divinely contrived biological alchemy. This is what it means to enjoy an excellence "greater than that of the angels"! In other words, Wright would apparently have us conclude that Baruch meant that the righteous dead are really entirely unlike angels!

22. *RSG*, 162.

23. *RSG*, 162.

24. *RSG*, 162.

25. *RSG*, 161 n.133; Carnley, *The Structure of Resurrection Belief*, 231.

26. *RSG*, 162.

What we clearly have in 2 *Baruch's* speculative reflection about the righteous dead being "like angels" is that, whatever this may mean, it must mean that they may *not* be just restored to *this* world in a sense somewhat akin to the matter-of-fact way in which a nearly-drowned body might simply be pulled from the water and resuscitated on a beach and restored to life in this world. Rather, the implication must surely be that they are transformed and renewed in some kind of way appropriate to a heavenly existence. At the very least, the imagined possibility of the transformation of the righteous dead to be "like angels" takes us away from the idea of a mundane restoration to life in this world and in the direction of the heavenly and spiritual. Curiously, this understanding of things appears to have been endorsed by none other than Jesus himself, who in answering the skeptical Sadducees on the basis of the teaching of the Torah,[27] purportedly characterized the state of those raised from the dead as being "like angels in heaven" for they neither marry nor are given in marriage![28] We may hesitate before being too over-confident about the historicity of Jesus' purported teaching concerning his *own* future resurrection given the operation of the evangelist's perspective of hindsight, but the suggestion of the Gospel tradition is that Jesus' understanding of resurrection generally was of a piece with the reflections of the author of *Baruch* on the subject.[29] If this is so, and N. T. Wright is correct in his reading of *Baruch*, then we would have to conclude that Jesus had it wrong. In any event, this encounter of Jesus with the Sadducees, quite apart from illustrating their denial either of immortality of the soul or resurrection of the dead, also illustrates and confirms that ancient Jewish understandings of resurrection were ill-defined and even "confused and muddled."[30] The question "What would be the nature of the resurrected body?" was a live issue.

It is also pertinent to note that right at the beginning of his reflection about the resurrection of the righteous, when 2 *Baruch* raises his initial questions about whether they will simply be reclothed with their "present form" and with "chained members which are in evil and by which evils are accomplished," the author then speculates that perhaps God will change not just the things that have been in this world, but also "the world itself" (49:3). In other words, the precise form of the world itself on the Last Day is not altogether clear to Baruch. In purely logical terms, of course, the object of an ultimate speculative hope must necessarily remain ill-defined in this kind of way.

Finally, lest we be in doubt with respect to Baruch's openness to Hellenistic influence, such as, specifically, belief in the immortality of the soul along with a general orientation of thought towards a post-mortem heavenly reality, we need to note that

27. On the institution of levirate marriage in Deut 25:5–6.

28. Mark 12:25, Matt 22:30; Luke 20:34–36. Markus Bockmuehl notes that in this Jesus appears to have operated "in good Pharisaic fashion," (citing *m. Sanh.* 10.1) and further observes "the New Testament's repeated placement of Jesus' own resurrection, ascension and parousia in the company of angels." See Bockmuehl, "Resurrection," 115.

29. Whether resurrected bodies are thought of as angel-like and thus celibate, but never-the-less physical, or whether nonphysicality is also to be assumed, is not altogether clear.

30. Klawans, *Josephus and the Theologies of Ancient Judaism*, 102.

Baruch then goes on to exhort his readers to "prepare your souls for that which is kept for you, and make ready your souls for the reward which is preserved for you" (52:7). In the absence of an exhortation to prepare the physical body, perhaps by a quest for moral purity, this concentration on the soul is language unmistakably reminiscent of the Platonic tradition. It seems that we have here *prima facie* evidence to suggest that Platonic ideas of an eternal and immortal destiny for the dead beyond this passing world of space and time has begun to condition the more physical and material approach of understanding resurrection as a restoration and return to this world. Unmistakably, the effect of Hellenistic influence is to orientate eschatological hope towards the timeless eternity of God, though this does not exclude, of course, the future eschatological *revealing* of an eternal and ultimate cosmic state of affairs at the End of all history.

In any event, as if by deft sleight of hand, Wright then directs our attention away from *2 Baruch* to his own discussion of Phil 3:20–21, 1 Cor 15:35–58, and his summary of "Resurrection in the New Testament," at the end of *The Resurrection of the Son of God*, chapter 10.[31] In other words, we are immediately invited to interpret the transformation of the body to which reference is made in *2 Baruch* by bringing it into association with what is said by Wright himself in his own discussion of resurrection in the New Testament. Clearly, there is a danger of circularity entering into Wright's argument here. For he interprets the New Testament evidence itself on the basis of the predetermined conclusion that only one fixed and limited understanding of resurrection was inherited from Second Temple Judaism. While the assertion in Phil 3:20–21, for example, is that any bodily transformation will be "from humiliation to glory," "glory" is held, somewhat predictably, to be understood only in the sense of a transformation from material corruptibility to material incorruptibility, and not from "earthly lowliness" to "heavenly glory."[32] Unfortunately, rather than reading and interpreting the New Testament in the light of *2 Baruch*, at the end of the discussion of *2 Baruch* itself, we are invited to understand *2 Baruch* by reference to Wright's own discussion of passages from Philippians and 1 Corinthians. And that, astonishingly, is the end of N. T. Wright's discussion of *2 Baruch*. At this point his discussion moves quickly on to talk about the *Psalms of Solomon*.

Wright's discussion of *2 Baruch* is hardly sufficient to convince us that there was no variety of viewpoint in the speculative thought of the ancient Jewish world about the precise form that the resurrected bodies of the righteous dead might take. I think we must conclude that, on the basis of his treatment of *2 Baruch* alone, Wright's contention that we cannot possibly think that within the religious culture of Second Temple Judaism there were various approaches to the understanding of resurrection

---

31. *RSG*, 162 n.134. Wright's discussion of Phil 3:20–21 is in *RSG*, 230–31; and 1 Cor 15:35–58 in *RSG*, 340–61; and his summary of "Resurrection in the New Testament" at the end of *RSG* chapter 10 is found at 476–79.

32. *RSG*, 231.

is, to say the least, very questionable. *Second Baruch* suggests that the transformation of the resurrected body could be envisaged as a transformation of the body that would make it more appropriate to a heavenly or celestial life, with bodies somehow akin to angelic bodies (however these might be imagined), rather than to a temporally extended life in this world, with terrestrial bodies made incorruptible and thus resistant to death and decay.

∿

But, let us do as Wright suggests and fast forward to his own discussion of Phil 3:20–21. In this passage, Paul says:

> Our citizenship is in heaven, and it is from there that we are expecting a Savior, the Lord Jesus Christ. He will transform the body of our humiliation that it may be conformed to the body of his glory, by the power that also enables him to make all things subject to himself.

In order to avoid what Wright would undoubtedly categorize as a "platonic" reading of this text, he would no doubt have us think of the "heaven" to which Paul refers, not as a heaven "above" this world, or as a platonic-style "timeless eternity," but essentially as the heaven which he believes is yet to come to this world at the future Eschaton. In other words, Wright says that what Paul means is that we are citizens of a future-orientated Kingdom of Heaven that is already dawning, rather than citizens of the heaven above and beyond this world where we imaginatively place the God whom we address, for example, as "Our Father in Heaven."[33]

However, while St. Paul undoubtedly thought in terms of a kind of over-lap of the ages, with one world passing away and another dawning within it from the future, he in fact seems to be thinking in Philippians of heaven also as the place of origin from whence the awaited returning Christ will come to this world at the final showing of the Eschaton. The fact that his kingly reign might be said to be dawning by anticipation in this world, in the sense of the arrival of the future, does not rule out the possibility that it, as in the case of the image of the new Jerusalem, "comes down from heaven" at the hands of God (Rev 21:2). Indeed, in some of the texts in which this hope is expressed, it is suggested that, because "Jesus died and rose again," at the time of his eschatological return "through Jesus, God will bring with him those who have died"; the suggestion being that they will be brought by God "from heaven" (1 Thess 4:14). It is in this way that those "who are (still) alive, who are left, will be caught up in the clouds together with them to meet the Lord in the air. And so we will be with the Lord forever" (1 Thess 4:17).

That Wright's avoidance of all things even vaguely "platonic" is conditioning his discussion of this passage of Philippians is suggested by the fact that he seeks to head

---

33. *RSG*, 229–30.

off any suggestion that Paul envisages that the bodies of the resurrected righteous will be transformed in the direction of a preparation for "heaven above," by assuring us that "the body will be *transformed*, not abandoned."[34] Here he seems to be suggesting that the only alternative to belief in the resurrection in his preferred sense of the restoration of an essentially mundane body to this world is Plato's full-blown doctrine of the immortality of the soul, which involves the abandonment of the material body. Indeed, that Wright is thinking in exactly this Platonic way is betrayed by the fact that he then says that the body is not "a prison from which to escape; what it needs is transformation."[35] But this still begs the question as to the precise impact of the alleged transformation of the body, which he admits is an integral part of early Christian resurrection belief. A body which *2 Baruch* imagines might be like the bodies of angels "who live in the heights of heaven and are equal to the stars" might naturally be conceived as a body suited to "life with God" (however we might imagine that), rather than as a material body simply restored to this world. At this point we are in no better place than *2 Baruch*. We can only speculate about what life with God might be like.

Certainly, if we think of heaven as the radically hidden place of "divine habitation" where the Raised Christ metaphorically "sits at the right hand of the Father," that seems to be the most natural reading of what St. Paul has in mind when he says in Philippians, that the resurrected and vindicated Christ is awaited "from heaven." His revelatory return as the object of Christian hope may be located at an indeterminate future date in temporal terms, but insofar as it is possible to think in a locative way of a place from whence he will "come," the most obvious option seems to be "from the place where he now is with the God who raised him from the dead"—in other words, from a heaven that is thought to be "above and beyond" this world.

This conclusion is well summed up in the words of H. C. C. Cavallin who, in his magisterial study of the Jewish background of Paul's discussion of the resurrection of the dead in 1 Corinthians 15, says categorically that *2 Baruch* has no systematized discussion of resurrection, and rather, that the particular sense of the meaning of "resurrection" as a restoration and return of the material remains to this world tends to be displaced by the clear expression of "the transcendence of the new postresurrection world beyond time and human sensation."[36]

In any event, the chief point at the moment is simply that Wright's attempt to persuade us that *2 Baruch* does not represent an alternative to a matter-of-fact restoration of the righteous dead to life in this world does not convince. In fact, *2 Baruch* indicates by his speculative reflection about the nature of the resurrection body, that there is at least the possibility that there was not just one single monochrome option to hand, but a more fluid variety of views, some of which might even be diametrically opposed to others. If some rabbis thought of the resurrection body in very concrete material or

34. *RSG*, 230.

35 *RSG*, 231.

36. Cavallin, *Life after Death*, 90. See also 1 Cor 6:1–4; 1 Pet 1:12; Heb 2:16; and 1:4–14 and 2:5–8.

physical terms of the kind we find particularly in 2 Maccabees, *2 Baruch* suggests the clear possibility that others may have entertained a much more "heavenly" and less purely mundane alternative. In this case, despite Wright's insistence that there was no cross-cultural borrowing, we must also allow for the benign outcome of a mutual conditioning, the one of the other.

At this point we might venture to ask whether what appears to be special pleading in Wright's treatment of *2 Baruch* may in fact stem from his initial methodological commitment to the handling of the Resurrection purely as a historical event. For him, any degree of bodily change or "transformation" cannot be admitted to involve a shift away from the physical and material nature of bodies of the kind that might be restored to this world for fear of removing the Easter Event out of the theatre of historical inquiry. Clearly, for him, the body of the resurrection must be of a piece with the more regular life of this spacio-temporal world because only so can the Resurrection of Christ be handled as a historical event. This is entirely undone just as soon as the Resurrection of Christ is understood to be about something beyond or away from this world—beyond space and time. As a consequence, he seems to be determined at all costs not to allow the bodies of the righteous dead to be thought of even as quasi-material "heavenly" bodies, but only as bodies that are, as he himself says, even "more incorruptibly material." They cannot be thought to be "immortal" or "heavenly'"; they must be contained within this material world of space and time, like all other human persons and material things that are involved in the events of human history.

N. T. Wright's contention that a "strictly limited" meaning of the term "resurrection" was rigidly established within the mind-set inherited from Second Temple Judaism, and could therefore mean only one thing in first-century Palestine, is further challenged by some relevant comments made by Josephus. It has already been noted that A. E. Harvey observed[37] that Josephus, when describing the beliefs specifically of the Pharisees,[38] "unmistakably suggests a doctrine of the transmigration of souls" as one of "a variety of ways of expressing the hope of survival beyond death found in Jewish writing of the Hellenistic and Roman periods."[39]

This judgment of A. E. Harvey is based upon some references of Josephus to the beliefs of the Pharisees, where he says that they maintain that "every soul is *aphtharton*," meaning immortal or imperishable, and that the souls of the good pass "into another body," while the souls of the wicked suffer eternal punishment. H. St. John Thackeray, in a note to the Loeb translation of the *Antiquities,* understood Josephus'

37. Harvey, *Jesus and the Constraints of History,* 150. This is referred to in Carnley, *Structure of Resurrection Belief,* 53, in justification of the contention that views of the resurrection in the first century were various.

38. Josephus, *J. W.* 2.154 and 163. See also *Ant.* 18.14; and *Ag. Ap.* 2.218.

39. This is also noted by Barr, *The Garden of Eden,* 107; see also 44.

reference to the good passing into "another body" to mean "reincarnation" rather than "resurrection," but in *Josephus: The Man and the Historian*, he revised this judgment to speak of "the return to bodily existence" of the souls of the righteous.[40] As Jonathan Klawans makes clear, the problem with interpreting "another body" to mean transmigration or reincarnation "is that it denies subtlety to ancient Jewish belief in bodily resurrection." It is not that Josephus says the souls of the righteous return to the *same* body but to "*another* body." This means that "While it is likely true that those who believed in resurrection imagined that their renewed bodies would be recognizably theirs (*2 Baruch* 50:1–4), it is equally true that a number of the fuller reflections on the nature of resurrected bodies also imagine that new bodies would be in many ways different from the old ones (*2 Baruch* 51:1–5)."[41] Thus, in the *Jewish War* 2.163, what Josephus has in mind regarding the belief of the Pharisees is that "the reward for immortal souls is to pass into some *immortal* body." In this case Josephus' reference to the belief of the Pharisees may not be far from Jesus' answer to the Sadducees (in Mark 12:25) to the effect that resurrected bodies would be celibate and angelic. For that matter, what Josephus had in mind may not be far from Paul's description of the essential difference between mortal and resurrected bodies and "heavenly bodies and earthly bodies" in 1 Cor 15:40–44. Klawans concludes that while 2 Maccabees 7 is often cited as the paradigm for Second Temple Jewish understanding of resurrection "it may turn out to be the case that the classic Maccabean martyrdom narrative is rather extreme and probably unique in its emphasis on the similarity between mortal and resurrected bodies."[42]

Josephus' reported views of the Essenes appear to represent, if anything, an even increased level of Hellenistic influence. He says that the Essenes believe that "bodies are corruptible . . . but souls are immortal (*athanaton*) and continue for ever." Indeed, in Josephus' view, the Essenes even believed the soul to be "imprisoned" in the body.[43] While only a few of the Dead Sea Scrolls speak of resurrection,[44] there is an unmistakable sense that the Essenes viewed the physical body and the physical world generally with disdain, and even contempt.[45] This kind of "soul-talk" in relation to the beliefs of the Essenes, especially when coupled with negative and disparaging views of the material body, immediately alerts us to the insistent influence of Plato in Jewish culture in the Hellenistic period.[46] In relation to this we should note in passing the view of

40. Thackeray, *Josephus*, note *a* to *Jewish War* 2.163; Thackery *Josephus*, 97.

41. Klawans, *Josephus and the Theologies of Ancient Judaism*, 108.

42. Klawans, *Josephus and the Theologies of Ancient Judaism*, 109–10.

43. Josephus, *J. W.* 2.154.

44. E.g., Pseudo-Ezekiel 4Q 385, 385B, 385C, 386, 388, and 391 and Messianic Apocalypse 4Q521 (the last, in the view of Geza Vermes). See Vermes, *The Complete Dead Sea Scrolls in English*, 89.

45. See for example, the Thanksgiving Hymns, 1QH 2.20–23; 4:29–37, 9:23–25, 12:30–32, 20:27–39.

46. See, e.g., Plato, *Phaedo* 81d–82c.

the body expressed by Paul in Phil 3:21: "Who shall change our vile body, that it may be fashioned like unto his glorious body . . ." The pertinent question is: Do we detect a hint of Plato here?

This is all the more remarkable because Josephus himself claimed to live "as a Pharisee," even though he may not have actually been a Pharisee. In his autobiographical piece, *Life*, which he composed late in the first century at around the same time as *Against Apion*, he says that he had lived his life as a Pharisee,[47] even though for a short time in early manhood he experimented with life as a desert ascetic with a guru called Bannus. This came at the age of nineteen immediately after three years in which he says he studied the teachings of all three Jewish schools—the Sadducees, Pharisees, and Essenes.[48] Thereafter he lived as a Pharisee. There is therefore no real reason to doubt Josephus' descriptions of Pharisaic belief and of his own resurrection belief in this context. This is especially so given that Josephus' own presentation aligns reasonably well with what we know of the Pharisees from other sources, not least from the New Testament itself.[49]

It therefore seems incontrovertible that Josephus is a "reliable guide to ancient Jewish theological disputes"[50] when he attributes both to the Pharisees and the Essenes, if in different ways, a capacity to appropriate Greek notions of the afterlife with more characteristically Jewish beliefs. Certainly, Josephus gives us clear enough indication that Jewish thought, at least as it represented by some Pharisees and by the Essenes, was not quite as diametrically opposed to Greek ways of thinking as we once were led to believe by the proponents of the Biblical Theology Movement and, in the wake of that movement, by N. T. Wright. Indeed, given the separate origins, respectively of belief in resurrection and in the immortality of souls, Alan Segal is of the view that Josephus "was the first of many to try to bring the two concepts together."[51]

While N. T. Wright is naturally obliged to take note of the affirmations of Josephus about the views of the Pharisees, he nevertheless interprets them in a way that brings them into line with his own view that resurrection was understood only to have involved a physical restoration to this world, specifically on "the day of the Lord," at the world's Eschatological End. He admits that in the account of Pharisaic belief about the fate of the dead given by Josephus that "they go to heaven," but then, Josephus

47. Josephus, *Life* 12.

48. Mason, *Life of Josephus*, 15–21. In *Life* 12, Josephus compares the Pharisees with the Stoics; significantly in *Antiquities* the Sadducees are compared with the Epicureans by virtue of their denial of life after death and divine providence (*Ant.* 10.277–280).

49. See Mason, *Flavius Josephus on the Pharisees*.

50. Jonathan Klawans's conclusion in *Josephus and the Theologies of Ancient Judaism*, 115.

51. Segal, "Life after Death," 110.

says, "Then they return to live in a new kind of body, a holy one."[52] Even though "heaven" in this context cannot be the "heaven that has not happened yet," for the future Kingdom of Heaven is reserved until the Eschaton, Wright believes it is admitted by Josephus to be a destination to which the righteous dead go at least temporarily, *until* the appointed day of their bodily return "at the revolution of the ages." By this strategy Wright contends that Josephus' reference to the belief that "they go to heaven" is to be understood as a reference to a going to a kind of intermediate state, prior to the return of the righteous to this world; it is only then that they re-appear in a "new kind of body."

Though Josephus also seems to attribute a Hellenistic belief in the immortality of souls to the Pharisees, their full belief is therefore said by Wright ultimately to involve a return to this earth in a "new kind of body"! It is far from clear, however, that when Josephus speaks of a "new kind of body" he actually means their old mortal body refurbished and made incorruptible, or any kind of rejuvenated physical body appropriate to life in *this* world. Josephus could just as conceivably have been thinking of a body of a more transcendental kind. For example, in *Against Apion* 2.218 God is said to have granted those who keep the law "renewed existence and a better life"; furthermore, in *Jewish War* 3.374 Josephus says that in his own opinion (which may not necessarily be that of the Pharisaic party) the righteous dead "are allotted the most holy place in heaven." In going beyond mere immortality of a classic Platonic kind to affirm some form of bodily renewal (as in *Jewish War* 3.734) Josephus appears nevertheless to have embraced a generally platonic "other-worldly" orientation of thought.

In any event, though the unmistakable assimilation of Hebrew belief with a more characteristically Platonic or Hellenistic mode of thought in Josephus' understanding of things is at least admitted by Wright, at this point he will not allow his readers to entertain the assumption that Josephus might be accurately reporting the situation of his time with regard to the actual beliefs of the Pharisees. The implication is that what we hear from Josephus is more the creation of Josephus himself than a reliable report of the actual belief of the Pharisees. Rather, Wright contends that Josephus himself regularly "translated" Jewish ideas into Greek ones. In support of this, he points out that Josephus also portrays the Jewish parties as being like philosophical schools among the Greeks. Josephus cannot therefore be relied upon as an accurate observer of Pharisaic belief. Other commentators, however, see nothing sinister in Josephus's categorization of the Sadducees, Pharisees, and Essenes as "schools."[53]

At this point, in relation to the reported beliefs of the Pharisees, Wright appears to be dependent upon some earlier conclusions of Krister Stendahl, who also suggested that Josephus makes "a drastically apologetic translation of their actual belief in resurrection into more Hellenistic modes of thought." In other words, Josephus

---

52. *RSG*, 176.

53. For example, Steve Mason regards "schools" rather than "sects" as the preferred translation of *airesis*. *Flavius Josephus on the Pharisees*, 125–28.

himself is charged with being guilty of assimilating resurrection belief to the idea of the immortality of the soul, and then of falsely attributing this to the Pharisees.[54] Wright also contends that we cannot accept this as an accurate account of Pharisaic belief because of the fact that elsewhere in his writings Josephus speaks more explicitly of resurrection belief among the Pharisees, but without the coloring of quasi-platonic ideas of immortality of the soul. In this way, Wright, apparently following Stendahl, feels justified in dismissing Josephus as a reliable source of evidence, either in support of the actual existence of a variety of beliefs within Hellenistic Judaism, or of the possibility of there having ever been an amalgam of Hebrew and Greek views in the minds of the Pharisees of the time.[55] These are misrepresentations that are said to be contained within the mind of Josephus alone.

Wright adopted a similar strategy of argument in relation to Josephus' account of the words of Eleazar at Masada in the first volume of his series on "Christian Origins and the Question of God": *The New Testament and the People of God* (1992). When the insurgent leader urged mass suicide as a "liberation to the soul,"[56] Wright acknowledged this to be "strikingly Hellenized."[57] However, this Hellenized account of what Eleazar had to say is judged by Wright to be "almost certainly" wrong. What Eleazar would really have said is conjectured to have been closer to the views of some unnamed Pharisees who, in a similar speech created by Josephus,[58] are also said to have urged their followers to die in a noble cause. Though they too are represented as offering the hope of the soul's immortality (whether as an innate natural property or as a reward of God is a moot point), all this is dismissed by Wright as a "smokescreen" created by Josephus, whose "apologetic stance" resulted in an account of things specifically intended for the ears of a "respectable Roman audience."[59] Wright contends that in reality these teachers to whom Josephus refers would have actually offered the hope of resurrection, rather than the immortality of the soul in their understanding of vindication of God.[60] Josephus is not therefore to be accepted as a reliable witness of Jewish views, whether of Eleazar or of these unnamed Pharisees. In his endeavor to distance these Pharisaic teachers, no less than Eleazar, from Josephus's portrayal

54. Stendahl, in the Introduction to *Immortality and Resurrection*, 7. This is a position typical of the Biblical Theology Movement's assumption of a fundamental dichotomy between Greek and Hebrew thought.

55. Even though he does refer in passing to James Barr who argues explicitly for this position. See Barr, *The Garden of Eden*, 133 n.32.

56. Wright, *The New Testament and the People of God*, 324.

57. Wright, *The New Testament and the People of God*, 326.

58. Josephus, *J. W.* 7.349.

59. On Josephus's alleged tendency to try to please Greek readers see the original insights in 1920 of Wilhelm von Schmid, *Christs Geschichte der Griechischen Literatur*, II: I, 600. More recently C. D. Elledge has spoken of Josephus's "apologetic translation" of Pharisaic and Essene beliefs into Hellenistic philosophical terms. See Elledge, *Life after Death in Early Judaism*, 3, 45 and 81–82.

60. It is once again noteworthy that the treatment of these two views as polar opposites in this kind of way is characteristic of the earlier Biblical Theology Movement.

of their views, Wright even gratuitously proffers the suggestion that in actuality "they might have been reading 2 Maccabees"[61] and that in this case they would actually have been thinking in terms of an unadulterated Jewish "orthodoxy"!

More recently, this kind of negative assessment of the veracity of Josephus as a historian has been systematically challenged by Jonathan Klawans, who insists that Josephus in fact accurately represents not only the importance of theological differences among the three schools of ancient Judaism, as well as their obviously different approaches to interpretation of the law,[62] but also that these theological differences represent broader trends in first-century Jewish society. Even allowing for "diversity within the group or change over time,"[63] as against Josephus' tendency to stereotypical description and even exaggeration and over-simplification, Josephus emerges in Klawans' view as "our best guide to a general understanding of ancient Jewish theological disputes . . ."[64] This judgment is based upon Klawans' careful reading of Josephus, which shows that "Josephus's descriptions, when measured against the extant evidence, suggests that he accurately describes positions we can find articulated among other Jewish sources . . ." Indeed, Klawans notes that "Josephus's descriptions find confirmation on these matters among rabbinic sources and the New Testament, especially with regard to the complexity of Pharisaic hopes regarding reembodiment."[65]

Surprisingly, despite his attempted discrediting of Josephus, at the end of the day even Wright himself at least acknowledges that the erring Josephus nevertheless demonstrates clearly that the doctrine of bodily resurrection "could quite easily be described, for rhetorical reasons, in language which by itself could easily be taken to refer to the immortality of the soul."[66] He is also prepared to concede that, in all this Josephus shares the mentality of the first-century AD work 4 Maccabees, which is a reworking of 2 Maccabees. In 4 Maccabees 8–17, he notes that "mention of the bodily resurrection has been toned down almost completely, in favor of a much more Hellenistic approach."[67] In this passage of 4 Maccabees, persecuted young men declare their hope that they "shall be with God" (rather than restored to earthly life *by* God).

Clearly, Josephus was therefore not alone in assimilating Hebrew belief to concepts originally deriving from Greek philosophy. Indeed, it comes as a surprise to find that Wright cites 4 Maccabees as an "excellent example" of what is also found in Josephus: it demonstrates that "a firmly physical account of the resurrection can easily,

61. Wright, *The New Testament and the People of God*, 327.

62. See his discussion of Lawrence Schiffman's placing of "halakhic issues at the centre of Jewish sectarianism in the Second Temple period," in Klawans, *Josephus and the Theologies of Ancient Judaism*, 15–16, and 5. Also, Heger, *Cult as the Catalyst for Division*, 4.

63. Klawans, *Josephus and the Theologies of Ancient Judaism*, 12.

64. Klawans, *Josephus and the Theologies of Ancient Judaism*, 43; and his summing up of Josephus' general reliability: Klawans, *Josephus and the Theologies of Ancient Judaism*, 134–36.

65. Klawans, *Josephus and the Theologies of Ancient Judaism*, 134–35.

66. Wright, *The New Testament and the People of God*, 327.

67. Wright, *The New Testament and the People of God*, 324.

under the right rhetorical constraints, be 'translated' into a Hellenistic doctrine of the immortal memory of the virtuous dead."[68] Indeed, despite attributing all this to "rhetorical constraints," Wright is prepared to concede that in Josephus we have a single writer, who demonstrates the same transition that we see in the development of ideas from 2 Maccabees to 4 Maccabees. Clearly, between 2 Maccabees and 4 Maccabees we do after all have evidence, not of a single monochrome viewpoint in relation to the afterlife, nor of something peculiar to the mind only of the errant Josephus, but of a development and combination of ideas in an apparently rich and complex religious culture within which there was a somewhat fluid spectrum of belief concerning the nature of life beyond death.

It can readily be admitted that the views of 4 Maccabees can be contrasted with the more fleshly doctrine of the Pharisees such as is expressed in the fourth Sibylline where, immediately after the destruction of Jerusalem, God is envisaged forming "men from dust and bones" and making them "the mortals they were formerly."[69] This is essentially the same view that was also clearly expressed in time of persecution in 2 Maccabees, and in what is said by Wright to be the more "explicit passage" of Josephus concerning the Pharisaic belief in restoration of the physical body to this world. However, by focusing on these references in Josephus rather than others, Wright clearly aims to deflect our attention away from 4 Maccabees, and the more Hellenistic sounding comments of Josephus about the beliefs of the Pharisees.

It seems abundantly clear that Josephus's account of the resurrection beliefs of the Pharisees is less than systematically clear and distinct. But this, of course, is the point: Josephus simply reflects what was undoubtedly the case in wider Jewish society in more general terms. We have to accept that speculative views about the exact nature of the afterlife, and particularly the exact nature of the resurrected bodies, in the minds of those who believed in resurrection in the world of Hellenistic Judaism of the first century were ill-defined and various. There was no clear and distinct, rigidly fixed "dictionary definition" of what was entailed in the afterlife. As Jonathan Klawans aptly puts the point: "There can be little doubt that Josephus's descriptions of the Pharisees are cryptic; but one possible explanation for this ambiguity is, in fact, accuracy; it appears that the precise nature of resurrected bodies was something of a conundrum among ancient Jewish believers in bodily resurrection."[70]

At this point it should be noted that, in any event, Wright has undercut his argument: if Josephus the quasi-Pharisee was himself capable of assimilating inherited Jewish resurrection beliefs with Hellenistic modes of thought, particularly those relating to

68. Wright, *The New Testament and the People of God,* 324.
69. *Sibylline* 4.180.
70. Klawans, *Josephus and the Theologies of Ancient Judaism,* 110.

immortality and the timeless eternity of heaven, and if he was capable of understanding Pharisaic belief from this point of view, then others could have done exactly the same thing. Whether Josephus was motivated by a rhetorical desire to try to please his Greek readers or not is immaterial at this point.[71] For, who can say that there were not other Pharisees who themselves were also capable of this fusion of ideas, perhaps while holding also to the hope that the Eschaton would involve a return of the righteous dead from the place of their heavenly reward in an ultimate apocalyptic revelation (in time or at the end of time) of a gloriously triumphant eternal immortality with God?[72] This possibility also includes the early Christians, including specifically St. Paul, in relation to the understanding of the Resurrection of Jesus, particularly if the quality of their own resurrection experiences led them in that direction. In other words, if Josephus (and perhaps many others) could conceive Pharisaic belief in this way, it is at least logically possible that St. Paul could have conceived resurrection belief in a similar kind of way, quite specifically in relation to his understanding of the Resurrection of Jesus. Understandably, the Jewish scholar Alan Segal sees Josephus "as the first of many" who try to bring the two concepts, of the immortality of the soul and the resurrection of the body, together. Segal notes that "Paul is apparently engaging in the same kind of hermeneutical enterprise when he answers the question of the nature of the resurrection in I Corinthians 15:35–45."[73]

The real possibility of the existence of an amalgam of Jewish and Greek ideas in the Jewish world of the Greek diaspora specifically in relation to views of the afterlife, has received additional support from the considered conclusions of Martin Hengel. In his early work of 1969/74, on the basis of his exhaustive studies in Judaism and Hellenism, Hengel came to the view that "Spiritualized and realistic conceptions" of resurrection "stand side by side with relatively little connection."[74] He illustrated the increasing impact of Hellenism particularly in relation to the beliefs of the Essenes: "This lack of unity is also shown in the fact that in the Essene wing of the Hasidim the idea of physical resurrection retreated so far into the background that we must ask whether

71. It must also be noted that, even though Josephus wrote in Rome for Greco-Roman Gentiles who may have been comparatively ignorant of Judea and the schools of Judaism, it should not be assumed that he did not expect his work to be read as well by literate Jews who were well-acquainted with the three "schools." See Mason, *Josephus, Judea, and Christian Origins,* 47; and Feldman, *Josephus's Interpretation of the Bible,* 49–50 and 132–62.

72. Cavallin, *Life after Death,* 145–46, acknowledging that the avoidance of usual resurrection terminology by Josephus may be due to his desire "not to confront his readers with the most difficult parts of Jewish thinking," together with "his own assimilation of popular Greek philosophy." Yet Cavallin notes that "we cannot be sure this was not the common way of expressing the belief in after life in wider Jewish circles."

73. Segal, "Life after Death," 110.

74. Hengel, *Judaism and Hellenism,* 1, 198. Also, Glasson, *Greek Influence,* 29.

this concept is still appropriate in their case, and whether for them eschatological salvation did not rather consist in the heavenly communion of the exalted spirits with the angels."[75] As might be expected, given the essentially speculative nature of such things, a lack of unity is an unavoidable result; internal logical consequences may not have been thought through with any clarity.

Certainly, while the Qumran writings contain only a couple of possible references to resurrection, Hengel noted that the Essenes might nevertheless have entertained the possibility of a physical resurrection. In this case there seemed to him to have been a degree of variety and flexibility even within the Essene community itself. Hence, a more restrained and generalized tendency to talk of "eternal life," or "eternal joy," or "eternal salvation" without elaboration seems very often to have sufficed. At the end of the day, for Hengel it is an open question whether the Essenes did not know the concept of resurrection and had already opted for a more vague belief in immortality of the kind expressed in Wisdom 2–5, or whether they entertained a variant of resurrection belief. Even so, he nevertheless confessed that he was inclined to accept K. Schubert's rejection of the possibility that the Essenes thought in terms of a "resurrection of the flesh" of individuals after death, and so endorsed Schubert's conclusion that they thought of "a new spiritual and corporeal life," or of a resurrection of the soul endowed with corporeal functions. Furthermore, he declared that he believed this was "significant for the Pauline conception of the resurrection" as we find this expressed in 1 Cor 15:44 and 50, and in Phil 3:21.[76]

Essentially the same conclusions were re-affirmed by Hengel, explicitly in relation to beliefs current in first-century Palestine, in his 1989 book *The 'Hellenization' of Judaea in the First Century after Christ*. Indeed, building on his magisterial work on *Judaism and Hellenism* of 1969/1974, he also observed that while Josephus may certainly have been right in attributing to the Essenes a doctrine of the immortality of the soul, the major Qumran fragment 4Q181 1 II, 3–6, long withheld from publication at that time, nevertheless reportedly showed that the Essenes taught the physical resurrection.[77] This then led him to conclude with regard to the Essenes: "Perhaps as in earliest Christianity and Pharisaism both conceptions existed side by side."[78]

Very importantly, apart from the possibility that ideas of resurrection and of the immortality of the soul may have existed concurrently, Hengel entertained the further possibility that as the result of the cross-fertilization of ideas, the one may have had a modifying impact upon the other. He came to the view that a less material, more Hellenized or "spiritualized" approach to an understanding of the resurrection may

---

75. Hengel, *Judaism and Hellenism*, 198. See also Hengel, *Judaism and Hellenism*, 223–24.

76. Schubert, "Die Entwicklung der Auferstehungslehre," 204; and Schubert, "Das Problem der Auferstehungshoffnung," 158.

77. Hengel, *'Hellenization' of Judaea*, 90 n.235. This fragment is discussed by Cavallin, *Life After Death*, 65.

78. Hengel, *'Hellenization' of Judaea*, 46.

actually find echo in the writings of St. Paul, for it is at least thinkable that Paul's talk of a "spiritual" body in 1 Corinthians *15* may well also fall into this category. Hengel therefore came to the view that "in the earliest testimonies the resurrection does not have the massively realistic form which it takes on in the later Pharisaic haggada, but still has a spiritualizing character similar to Paul's statement in I Cor. 15.42–50."[79] He concluded that "The contrast in principle which scholars are so fond of making between a Hellenistic-Jewish eschatology of the rise of the soul to the heavenly world after death, orientated on the Greek conception of immortality, and an apocalyptic Palestinian hope of resurrection at the dawn of the kingdom imagined as taking place on earth, just does not exist in such an abrupt form."[80]

While I think Hengel was a little too inclined to assimilate the more clearly Hellenized belief in the immortality of the soul of the Essenes with the beliefs also of the Pharisees, it is clear enough that, given an admitted lack of clarity, the evidence of clear variants among the beliefs of the Pharisees represented by Josephus, means that Wright's thesis that resurrection can be understood in *only* one way in Second Temple Judaism has become very problematic. The contention that Hebrew and Greek notions were kept entirely apart so as to preserve their individual integrity also seems implausible, particularly given that in logical terms it is not difficult to marry a vertical thrust towards personal heavenly immortality with a more horizontal apocalyptic hope of the eventual revealing to the world of this eternal reality at the Eschaton. Even if Josephus spoke of "the revolution of the ages" as the time of the revealing of the righteous dead in "another body" this does not exclude the possibility of a heavenly life in transformed and renewed bodies in the timeless eternity of God "prior" to their revealing in time at "the revolution of the ages." This kind of synthesis may be well illustrated also when St. Paul himself says that at the day of the Lord, "God will bring with him" the righteous dead (1 Thess 4:14) so as to catch up those still living with them, and that "so shall we ever be with the Lord" (1 Thess 4:17). The emphasis is on the re-gathering of the living and the righteous departed to be with God in Christ at the Eschaton, rather than just the somewhat mechanical return of the righteous dead to be with the living in material and physical form in the continuing history of *this* world. As Jonathan Klawans says "the evidence of the New Testament (as well as later rabbinic literature) suggests that Josephus was not alone in his understanding that believers in resurrection understood resurrected bodies to be distinct from those that humans possess in the present world."[81]

79. Hengel, *'Hellenization' of Judaea*, 90 n.234. Hengel supports this statement by appeal to *2 Baruch* 30:1–5 and 49:1—52:7, and the conclusions of Strack and Billerbeck, *Kommentar zum Neuen Testament*, 4:1166–98, esp. 1175.

80. Hengel, *'Hellenization' of Judaea*, 46.

81. Klawans, *Josephus and the Theologies of Ancient Judaism*, 115.

The same kind of heavenly destination appears to have been envisaged in relation to the sons of Job in the *Testament of Job* (perhaps 100 BC—AD 100) where Job intervenes when his first wife, Sitis, seeks the bodies of her children and asks for a decent burial for them. Job says: "My children will not be found, they have been taken up into heaven."[82] Christian belief in Jesus' entry into heaven to "sit at God's right hand" (Ps 110:1) involves a great deal more than these references, given that it was understood to be an indication that God had vindicated Jesus and confirmed his messianic status. It was also understood in his case that, as Messiah, he would return from heavenly glory as judge at the Eschaton. However, the *Testament of Job* does at least indicate that a straightforward general restoration to this world appears not have been the only way of understanding what was involved in resurrection from the dead. There were clearly other options in the air so far as the fate of the righteous dead was concerned.

It is pertinent to note that the reach of Hellenistic ideas about the destiny of the righteous dead in a heaven beyond this world, rather than being realized only in the historical future of the world at its Eschatological End, is also indicated explicitly in Rev 11:11–12, where the two martyred prophets, as innocent sufferers, are envisaged being transported to the heavenly dwellings of the righteous:

> After three and a half days the breath of life from God entered them and they stood on their feet . . . Then they heard a voice from heaven saying to them, "Come up here!" And they went up to heaven in a cloud.

It is something of a surprise to find that the apparent variety of belief to which the inheritors of Second Temple Judaism were heirs was also illustrated by Wright himself, if unwittingly, in this earlier work (*The New Testament and the People of God*) in his consideration of the *Psalms of Solomon*.[83] There, he apparently assumed the actual existence of a spectrum of belief between bodily resurrection and the immortality of the soul, in asking "Where on this scale should we put the Psalms of Solomon?"[84] One relevant passage from *Pss. Sol.* 3:11–16 reads:

> The destruction of the sinner is forever,
> > And God will not remember him when he visits the righteous.
> This is the portion of sinners forever;
> > But they that fear the Lord will rise to the life eternal,
> And their life shall be in the light of the Lord,
> > and shall come to an end no more.

Even though it is hardly expressed in terms that are explicitly clear, it is difficult to see how notions of immortality can be entirely milked out of this passage. The reference

---

82. See *The Testament of Job* 39:8—40:4.

83. The *Psalms of Solomon* are usually said to have been composed around 50 BC, and probably in a Palestinian cultural (though not necessarily geographic) environment.

84. Wright, *The New Testament and the People of God*, 327.

to a rising to "life eternal" may reflect Dan 12:2; however, the allusion to that life being in "the light of the Lord" seems more likely to be a symbol of "theophanic glory."[85] In this case it is an allusion to an eternal life of heavenly transcendence with God rather than a pointer to a restored earthly life.

To be fair to Wright, he does acknowledge that his namesake, R. B. Wright, in a commentary on this passage, says "that it is unclear whether it refers to the resurrection of the body (rising from the grave) or the immortality of the spirit (rising to god), or if indeed the author necessarily distinguishes between the two."[86] In response to this, N. T. Wright himself observes that "It is, however, perhaps asking too much to expect doctrinal precision from this sort of poetry" and that "by themselves they cannot be forced to yield a clear statement."[87] Though unwitting, this is probably Wright's most profound observation in relation to the discussion of these issues. We need to note, however, that it is not only poetry, but even more prosaic discourse as well, when it has to do with the question of the nature of the afterlife, that must by nature be speculative and less than systematically precise. Given that nobody has actually experienced life beyond death at first-hand, it is understandable that the verbal expression of what is necessarily imaginative must resort to metaphors and images. This is unavoidable. These metaphors and images are intended to point to something less than clearly defined, as the only way of expressing an ultimate hope in something that by nature is resistant to translation into more clear and distinct specification.

Even so, Wright endeavors to persuade us to maximize our commitment to the idea of the first-century currency of more characteristically and unadulterated Jewish ideas of resurrection and to minimize the possibility that Hellenistic "other-worldly" concepts may have had a modifying influence of any significance on them. He even tries to coax his readers into believing that language that is apparently suggestive of immortality or of "being raised to God" rather than of "being restored to this world" was used only referringly and not descriptively. At this point his contention is that references to "immortality" were used to *denote* or point to the more clearly Jewish belief in resurrection as a restoration to life in this physical world, but not to *connote* something more transcendent or heavenly, even though they at first appear to us to do so.[88] In other words, Wright admits that Hellenistic-sounding language was used, but not in such a way as to *mean* what it says, but simply to *refer* or point to something else![89] The question is: How does Wright know this? These risibly improbable mental gymnastics appear to be designed to avoid a more descriptive, if speculative,

85. See Nickelsburg, "Resurrection, Immortality and Eternal Life," 132.

86. Wright, *The New Testament and the People of God*, 328, quoting R. B. Wright in Charlesworth, *The Old Testament Pseudepigrapha*, 2. 655.

87. Wright, *The New Testament and the People of God*, 328.

88. See *RSG*, 164, where Wright says that "Resurrection, in fact, is one *form* or type of immortality . . ." In this case it is possible to speak of immortality but really mean "resurrection" with the specific meaning Wright assigns to it!

89. Wright, *The New Testament and the People of God*, 330–31.

understanding of language simply because (somewhat dangerously to Wright's way of thinking) such language would suggest an understanding of resurrection that involves a movement away from this world towards the transcendental and heavenly. And if this is so, this of course means a movement away from the possibility of handling it in a very matter-of-fact way purely as a historical event, employing the methods and techniques of critical historical research.

Finally, we come to a consideration of the Wisdom of Solomon, an originally Alexandrian Jewish tract of the late second or early first century BC,[90] which is important to this discussion given that it appears to have been immediately influential in the thinking of St. Paul. Already in the third century BC, in the book of Ecclesiastes (Koheleth), even if a direct dependence on Greek philosophy and literature cannot so easily be demonstrated, the "spirit of Hellenism" appears to be at work. Interestingly enough, this seems particularly the case in relation to issues relating to the fate of the dead: "The dust returns to the earth as it was, and the spirit returns to God who gave it" (Eccl 12:7). The influence of Greek ideas of immortality that can be detected here can also be seen in *Jub.* 23:30–31 which speaks of those who will "rise up and see great peace"; while "their bones shall rest in the earth," "their spirits shall have much joy." *First Enoch* 103–104 also speaks in very similar terms of a future restoration not of the body, but of the life of the souls of those who have died pious, whose "spirits will rejoice and not perish."

By the time we get to the Wisdom of Solomon, we have a work that is indisputably redolent of Greek influence. Indeed, Wisdom is perhaps the most Hellenized book among the Hebrew Scriptures. At the same time, much of its content appears to draw upon both Stoicism and Platonism in a way that is typical of this transitional period of philosophical thought that is usually referred to as Middle Platonism.

Wisdom provides clear evidence that Jewish ideas about the afterlife and the fate of the dead were certainly not immune from Hellenistic coloring. In fact we have to reckon with the possibility that the mentality of Second Temple Judaism, specifically relating to the resurrection of the dead, may itself have been open to much more commerce with originally Greek modes of thought than N. T. Wright was prepared to concede when he wrote *The Resurrection of the Son of God*, for Wisdom actually provides evidence of belief in immortality with no explicit reference to resurrection of the body at all.

It is regularly observed that the Wisdom of Solomon incorporates characteristically Greek notions into a Jewish frame of reference. First, it unquestionably affirms a belief in immortality, not necessarily as a gift of God to the righteous, but as an

---

90. Following Schütz, *Les idées eschatologiques*, and many others through to Reese, *Hellenistic Influence on the Book of Wisdom*. A dissenting voice is Zimmerman, "The Book of Wisdom, Its Language and Character," 1–27 and 101–38.

immediate consequence of righteousness itself: "The righteous live for ever, and their reward is with the Lord" (Wis 5:15). Secondly, a Hellenistic contrast between body and soul is uncompromisingly accepted: "for a perishable body weighs down the soul, and this earthly tent burdens the thoughtful mind" (Wis 9:14).[91] Third, a belief in immortality for righteous souls is affirmed, apparently without teaching the resurrection of the body as a physical return to this world, or indeed without teaching any variant kind of bodily resurrection whatsoever. Instead, Wisdom articulates the hope of restoration to life beyond death in unambiguous talk of a blessed continuing existence *with God*, rather than a physical restoration to a future life in this world:

> But the souls of the righteous are in the hand of God,
>
>> And no torment will ever touch them.
>
> In the eyes of the foolish they seemed to have died,
>
>> And their departure was thought to be a disaster,
>
> And their going from us to be their destruction;
>
>> But they are at peace.
>
> For though in the sight of others they were punished,
>
>> Their hope is full of immortality. (Wis 3:1-4; see also 4:7)

In this passage it is not only said that the righteous gain immortality; it is also affirmed that "they only *seem* to have died" (Wis 3:2). This might appear to be an allusion to the characteristically Platonic idea of the innate nature of the soul's immortality, which was understood naturally to survive death, leaving the body of flesh and bones to perish. In Wis 2:23, this is already suggested when the idea of the "image of God" in humanity is interpreted to imply that humans share in God's eternity or timeless immortality: "God created us for incorruption, and made us in the image of his own eternity." Wisdom also seems to assume a natural immortality, which was lost by Adam's disobedience, insofar as Wisdom is of the view that death enters the world as the punishment for Adam's sin.[92] However, it has to be said that Wisdom elsewhere suggests the more clearly Jewish belief that immortality is received by the righteous as a reward from God, rather than an inherent quality of the soul itself.

Though the Wisdom of Solomon goes on explicitly to speak of the "assurance of immortality" which "brings one close to God," it also retains an orientation towards the ultimate future vindication of the righteous that is common to Jewish apocalyptic eschatology. This was apparently thought to happen at the end of the world, though the time line is never clear in Wisdom. This ultimate vindication of the righteous is expressed in terms of an ultimate visitation (*episkopēs*) by God at a time of judgment

---

91. There appears to be an echo of Plato here, *Phaedo* 81c:"my friend, we must believe that the corporeal is burdensome and heavy and earthly and visible. And such a soul is weighed down by this and is dragged back into the visible world, through fear of the invisible and of the other world."

92. Wis 2:24: "through the devil's envy death entered the world."

marked by the punishment of the wicked and the distribution of glory to the righteous. The nature of this visitation of God is expressed by employing images of the enlivened righteous being kindled into flame and running about "like sparks that sweep though stubble" (Wis 3:7). This specific eschatological image is perhaps more Greek than Jewish and may well derive ultimately from Stoicism's fascination with the idea of divine fire, which significantly features in Stoic apocalyptic notions of a fiery end of the world. In any event, this surely suggests that Wisdom has been able to achieve a kind of symbiosis of the two concepts, immortality of the soul of Greek origin and a more Jewish emphasis on the future eschatological visitation of God.[93]

Now, it is instructive to note Wright's strategies of argument in his treatment of the Wisdom of Solomon. He acknowledges the presence of both Greek and Hebrew ways of thinking about the afterlife, with obviously different pedigrees, but he argues that, though different, they are nevertheless not entirely antithetical.[94] In fact, a kind of harmony of these two views becomes possible: even if Wisdom assumes the idea of the soul's immortality, it does not necessarily mean, says Wright, that "it cannot simultaneously teach the resurrection of the body."[95] Indeed, in the face of Wisdom's apparent references to the immortality of the soul, Wright even says at one point that the "old assumption" that the Greeks believed in the immortality of the soul and the Hebrews believed in the resurrection of the body is inaccurate.[96] He thus distances himself from this tendency of the Biblical Theology Movement out of which he originally came. However, while he seeks to avoid the tendency of this school of thought to assume that the Hebrews got everything right and the Greeks got everything wrong, it is clear enough that he himself is constantly at pains to avoid any suggestion that the Jewish mode of thought about bodily resurrection was in any substantial way modified by rubbing shoulders with the alternative (originally Greek) approaches to the question of the afterlife. His proposed "harmony" of Greek and Hebrew ideas is not to be thought of as an amalgam or symbiosis. Rather, Wright contends that the two views are conceptually held rigidly and systematically distinct, while at the same time an attempt is made to line them up and couple them together in serial order.

The use of the word "soul" is (perhaps reluctantly) retained, but any suggestion of the release of the immortal soul *from* the body and its ascent to the timeless eternity of God as its ultimate destiny is strenuously avoided. Instead, Wright opts for softer talk of the continuing post-mortem existence of the "soul" after death in an "intermediate

93. Cavallin also observes that "The manner in which Platonic anthropology is . . . combined with the theology of the main stream of Jewish tradition is remarkable" (*Life after Death,* 131–32).

94. *RSG,* 184: "we should not be beguiled into the old antithesis of 'immortality' versus 'resurrection.'"

95. *RSG,* 163.

96. *RSG,* 162.

state" characterized simply by "sleep." The "sleeping souls" of the dead are said to be "in the hands of God" (Wis 3:1–4). Whatever the cash value of this metaphor may be, their "sleep" is decidedly not to be understood metaphorically as an entry into eternal immortality or heaven. Much of the distinctive Platonic baggage of the characteristically Greek view of "the immortality of the soul" has therefore to be jettisoned. Instead of the soul's "immortality" with a focus on its ultimate eternal destiny in heaven, Wright talks of the "souls" of those who after death are said to be in *a temporary kind* of "immortality" while they are asleep. This interim state of "sleeping souls" is then used by Wright as the bridge to the eventual resurrection of the body, which, he says, though not explicitly referred to, may be assumed to be implied when Wisdom talks of God's "visitation"! In this way the "old antithesis" between Greek and Hebrew views is said to be overcome and, even if somewhat awkwardly, harmonized. Wright is adamant, however, that there was no blending of these identifiably discrete ideas, no cross-cultural borrowing or hybridization. At least with respect to the integrity of the concept of the resurrection of the body there was no alien modifying influence. Rather, the resurrected life in bodily form comes *after* a temporary kind of "life after death" in the form of a preparatory post-mortem existence of sleeping souls. Wright in this way contends that the continuing existence of the soul is treated in Wisdom only in reference to a temporary condition of the departed in an "intermediate state" immediately following death, and prior to its future return to this world in a resurrected bodily form "on the day of visitation." The separated integrity both of the Greek view of the soul (though not exactly its eternal immortality) and of the alleged Hebrew view of resurrection is in this way sustained; it is just that one follows *after* the other, in a kind of temporal succession, not that one *conditions* the other so as to produce any kind of conceptual synthesis.

In this way, though Wright happily (or perhaps not so happily) acknowledges that notions of the soul's immortality were in the air, and that it may actually have been taught by Wisdom, the more authentically Hebrew view of the resurrection of the body, particularly in the specific form of the future return of physically restored bodies to *this* world, is retained and clearly distinguished from it. The post-mortem existence of souls and the idea of the resurrection of the body are only coupled together one after the other, in temporal sequence. In this way the original difference between Greek views of immortality and the Hebrew view of resurrection is said somehow to have been transcended.

Wright thus downplays any suggestion that Wisdom's clearly Hellenistic emphasis on the belief in immortality might either displace or modify Jewish ideas of resurrection of the body. Instead, even in the face of Wisdom's weighty expression of belief in the reward of immortality with God, a valiant attempt is made by Wright to rescue the idea of the resurrection from Hellenistic taint by re-affirming an alleged commitment to it in the explicit form of an ultimate material restoration and return to this world.

RESURRECTION IN RETROSPECT

It is important to note that in *The Resurrection of the Son of God*, Wright admits that, when Wisdom talks of the achievement of immortality with God (expressed in Wis 3:1–6), the accompanying alleged references to resurrection are only *veiled references*. In other words, when the author of Wisdom speaks of the enlivened righteous "shining forth" at the time of the future visitation of God (in Wis 3:7) and "running about like sparks through stubble," this is actually a way of talking about resurrection in the form of the restoration of their material bodies to this world!

Wisdom's focus upon a future eschatological event in which the good purposes of God and the vindication of the righteous is made abundantly clear in, or at the end of, history, is not, of course, disputed. But the use of the image of kindling the righteous into flame and having them "running about like sparks through stubble" could in fact be understood as a way of expressing something of the mystery of the enlivening of life by God that, precisely because it is yet to happen, is otherwise beyond words. Wright, however, is unlikely to accept this imagery as irreducible theological metaphor. That it might also reflect Stoic conceptions of immortality of the soul in terms of a return to "divine fire," is not considered at all. Rather, for Wright, this imagery must be unpacked as a way of speaking of bodily restoration in material form and its return to *this* world. In this way the evidence of Wisdom is massaged into conformity with Dan 7:18 and 27, in which the ultimate destiny of the righteous is to "rule over all the kingdoms under heaven with power and greatness." Wright thus seeks to insist that the achievement of immortality refers only to a temporary resting place in an intermediate state prior to a resurrection back to life in this world and not really to an eternal reward of immortality at all.

Unfortunately, however, there are no explicit references in Wisdom to an intermediate state between the death of the righteous and their achievement of immortality with God, and no explicit references to resurrection either. All this has to be imported into the imagery of "sparks running through stubble," and loaded into Wisdom's talk of a future "visitation" of God. Clearly, it is a big ask to equate what appears to be a metaphor of enlivened life with a clear indication of resurrection to re-embodied material life in this world. These images of "sparks," which have a likely Stoic resonance, can be pressed into the service of resurrection belief as a way of speaking of the materially restored life of physical bodies in the continuing history of this world only by an entirely arbitrary interpretative decision.

Wisdom does contain suggestions that the ultimate visitation of God will mean that the righteous will be seen to be participating in the justice of God and in some sense to be "ruling with him" over the vanquished wicked. However, given the heavy emphasis of Wisdom as a whole on immortality and 'being with God' as the reward of the righteous, one can legitimately question whether the ultimate triumphant showing of God's justice must necessarily take the form of a physical return of the resurrected righteous to this world so as *to rule it on behalf of God*. Indeed, it is really very doubtful that this can really be the only obvious meaning of these references. The writer of Wisdom may have actually been rather more subtle than that. In fact, his obvious Hellenistic sensibilities may have led him to use these images of the enlivenment of souls as "sparks running through stubble" precisely to save his readers from an over-materialistic and physical bodily understanding of things. In other words, given the Wisdom of Solomon's overall emphasis on the reward of immortality with God, these particular images may have been designed to avoid what the author may have actually seen as a crudely materialist alternative.

This means that, instead of referring to a future life in *this* world, these images of the visitation of God and the reversal of fortunes especially of the righteous may have been intended to express a historicized revealing of an eternal, divine state of affairs in which, in the justice of God, the wicked who seem to prosper in this world are punished and the persecuted righteous are rewarded. Rather than an alleged implied "further event" inaugurating a new phase of the history of this world, the use of these poetic images of visitation, could well have been intended to point to the ultimate and eternal vindication of the righteous by God, without being unpacked precisely in the earthly and historical kind of way envisaged by Wright. Indeed, we might today be prepared to acknowledge that this kind of eschatological imagery is actually irreducible to any more literal and prosaic specification. Nobody really knows what the final revealing of the good purposes of God at the end of the world is going to be like, and the author of Wisdom was in no better place than the rest of us. Given the use of poetic images, it might be more appropriate to assume a cautious *apophatic* reserve before insisting on any one specific interpretation of them.

Certainly, Wright's interpretation of the meaning of running around "like sparks through stubble" is entirely speculative; and speculative imagery has a habit of not being amenable to verification. The fact is that the Wisdom of Solomon contains no explicit references to resurrection either in terms of a restoration of a physical or materialistic kind to this world or any other kind of resurrection. Wright's insistence that Wisdom's image of the vindicated righteous running about like "sparks through stubble" at the time of the "visitation of God" is to be interpreted *only* in that "strictly limited" way is a gratuitously unwarranted conjecture.

Curiously, in an earlier treatment of the Wisdom of Solomon in *The New Testament and the People of God*, where essentially the same two-stage argument about the interpretation of Wisdom is run, Wright once again undercuts his own argument. Given his own insistence that Wisdom teaches that after the death of the righteous a temporary state of immortality will be followed by a further event of bodily restoration to the material world, he admits that, "No doubt some Hellenistic readers of the Wisdom of Solomon might have missed the point in a casual reading."[97] Nevertheless, he insists that "against the full Jewish background" his own preferred alternative should prevail: Wisdom may have been read in this way by some, but the book actually represents "the majority" Jewish position "rather than a Hellenization."[98] Once again, we must ask exactly how Wright knows of these statistically established outcomes?

In any event, whether we are speaking of a majority position or a minority position, the point is that we cannot avoid the conclusion that there was some diversity of viewpoint in circulation in first-century Palestine in relation to these matters. Though in the interests of handling the resurrection purely as a historical event in *The Resurrection of the Son of God*, Wright insisted that there was only one "strictly limited" understanding of resurrection in circulation in first-century Palestine, in the earlier work, *The New Testament and the People of God*, he was more inclined to admit some diversity of viewpoint. He says: "No doubt a substantial and perhaps growing minority of Jews, including those who have quite clearly drunk deeply from the Platonic and general Hellenistic well could write of the immortality of the soul. But the majority speak of the bodily resurrection of the dead . . ."[99] Indeed, he even admits that "These two groups would, of course, be likely to overlap quite heavily, i.e. political and philosophical assimilation would go together, both causing the assimilators to tone down the mainline Jewish expectation."[100] That resurrection might be conceived in terms of an ultimate heavenly and eternal destination with God, akin to the otherworldly orientation of Hellenistic belief in the immortality of souls cannot be dismissed as, at least, a conceptual possibility.[101]

In Wisdom we have concrete evidence of an attempt to combine talk of the more characteristic Jewish belief in some kind of eschatological vindication of the righteous by God with more Hellenistic talk of the immortality of the soul and the entry by the righteous into the eternity of God. It seems that while some undoubtedly entertained the hope of a victorious restoration to life in this world of historical time, others appear to have held an alternative position—that the ultimate destination of those who are restored to life beyond death is "with God," though without necessarily denying the hope of a future visitation of God to demonstrate the victory of the righteous and the punishment of the wicked. In this latter case, instead of a return to the historical future of *this* world, "nearness to God" admits of a share in God's own immortality and eternity. In this case the final apocalyptic revealing of the good purposes of God

97. Wright, *The New Testament and the People of God*, 330.

98. Wright, *The New Testament and the People of God*, 330.

99. Wright, *The New Testament and the People of God*, 331. Talk of minorities and majorities does not help the cause of arguing that there was only one "strictly limited" way of conceiving of the nature of the afterlife open to the primitive Christians.

100. Wright, *The New Testament and the People of God*, 329 n.155.

101. Indeed, Wright concedes the influence of Hellenism at leat on Philo insofar as he apparently believed that when Abraham left this mortal life he "became equal to the angels" (Philo, *Sacr.* 5; compare Luke 20:36). The resonance with *2 Baruch* 51 does not escape us.

and the vindication of the righteous at the Eschaton may be understood as a "show-ing" in time, or revelation (*apokalypsis*), of a timelessly eternal state of affairs in which the just reward of the righteous by the gift of immortality will be made manifest.

The pressing question is, of course, whether the same Hellenistic traditions as there are found influencing the Wisdom of Solomon, Josephus, and *2 Baruch* were also influences in the thought of St. Paul. Do his accounts of the early Christian experience and primitive faith claims also reveal a kind of blending of Hellenistic views of belief in an afterlife having an other-worldly and eternal orientation akin to ideas of eternal "immortality" with God with the more characteristic Jewish eschatological belief in a final visitation of God to establish his sovereign reign in this world? Or does Paul restrict an understanding of "immortality" of Hellenistic origin only to a temporary condition of "sleep" prior to an eschatological event involving the resurrection of all the dead and their restoration to this world, in the way Wright would have us believe?

In pursuing answers to these questions it will obviously be necessary to spend some time examining the "kerygmatic summaries" of Paul and the many passing ref-erences to resurrection faith and its behavioral implications in his Epistles, along with the New Testament narrative traditions of the appearances of the Raised Jesus and the tradition of the Empty Tomb. But first, some attention needs to be paid to the impact of experience generally upon language, for it may well be that the uniqueness of the Easter experience *itself* might well have dictated a need to revise *any* definition of the term "resurrection" that is alleged to have been bequeathed to the first Christians from the mind-set of Second Temple Judaism. In this case, whether a "strictly lim-ited" understanding of resurrection as a material and physical restoration, or a more diverse range of more "spiritual" options, was in the air at the time, it would not have been a matter of experience conforming to received expectations, so much as received expectations being radically redefined by experience.

3

Language and Experience

The discussion of the previous chapter was fundamentally historical in character. Doubts were raised as to whether there could really have been only one "strictly limited" way of conceiving the meaning of the term "resurrection," and the understanding of the afterlife said to be initiated by it, in the consciousness of those who in the first century inherited the religio-linguistic culture of Second Temple Judaism. These doubts were based primarily upon historical evidence furnished by *2 Baruch*, Josephus' account of the beliefs of the Pharisees, and the Wisdom of Solomon, all of which suggest that, in that world, notions of the afterlife were not just confined to views of resurrection as a material restoration of the righteous dead to life in *this* world, but also encompassed a more clearly Hellenistic focus upon a "going to the eternity of God" so as to receive the other-worldly reward of immortality.

Furthermore, this same historical evidence also suggests that these various views were not kept strictly apart in hermetically sealed mental compartments. Rather, it points to the likelihood of a cross-fertilization of ideas, a partial or rough-and-ready symbiosis, within the diversely rich nature of Hellenistic religious culture. Certainly, the diffused impact of Hellenistic modes of thought on the Jewish mentality appears unlikely to have been so systematically analyzed and developed as to allow the one to be aligned against the other in a way that would permit us to say that the first Christians could have thought in only one way that was entirely to the exclusion of the influence of the other. Likewise, it seems equally unlikely that the originally Greek notion of the "immortality of the soul" and the traditional Jewish notion of the "resurrection of the body" could simply be coupled together in sequential order without one coloring the understanding of the other.

In addition, it is also possible by historical argument to establish a direct connection between Hellenistic modes of thought concerning death and the afterlife and St. Paul himself, given the remarkable similarity of aspects of his thought with a theological tradition which earlier found expression in the Wisdom of Solomon, and which he appears to have used as a theological guide.[1] Whether the primitive Christian understanding of the Resurrection did assimilate Hellenistic notions of a "going to the eternity and immortality of God" rather than simply the return of Christ to this world in a restored material body now made physically incorruptible can only be determined by reviewing the actual available evidence relating to the Easter appearances and the tradition of the empty tomb.

Before we proceed to that, however, let us for the moment further consider the validity of N. T. Wright's proposition that only one "strictly limited" meaning can be assigned to the term "resurrection" and that the first Christians could have thought in no other way. For there are some other important factors that are of relevance to this issue. These are factors of a nonhistorical kind that have to do with the general nature of the development of the linguistic apparatus which we all inherit as members of linguistic communities, and the impact upon it of actual experience in the course of life. This discussion will therefore take us, at least initially, away from historical argument and into a constitutive or methodological argument about the operation and modification of the meaning of terms in languages generally. For while it is certainly helpful to probe the possibilities of thought that may have engaged the minds of the first generation of Christian believers, including St. Paul, we cannot assume that their actual Easter experiences simply conformed to *any* of their inherited preunderstandings and belief-generated expectations. This is for the simple reason that the interaction of language and experience does not always operate in that kind of way.

In fact, there is a sense in which the historical quest to isolate an exact understanding of the meaning of the inherited term "resurrection" and even a precise preunderstanding of how "the resurrection of the body" was conceived in the Hellenistic world of first-century Judaism, may not be as entirely crucial to our estimate of what it was that the first Christians experienced at Easter as N. T. Wright would have us believe. Whatever understanding of these things had been bequeathed to the first Christian believers, including whatever precise meanings may have been implicitly attached to the term "resurrection" in particular in its day-to-day use within the cultural context of first-century Palestinian Judaism, we need to be prepared to acknowledge that dictionary definitions do not rigidly define reality, nor do they necessarily dictate the exact shape of our human experiences.

It is obviously true that we employ the concepts of an inherited language in the interpretation of experience; but conversely, our concrete experiences often in turn call for the modification of those received concepts. In other words, the development of language in relation to experience is a reciprocal enterprise. While it can readily be acknowledged that the concepts expressed in the words of a language are regularly

---

1. This connection will be explored in more detail in chapter 10, below. See 243–45.

brought to the interpretation of experience, it has then to be acknowledged that experiences just as regularly dictate the need to refine and modify those very linguistically formulated concepts themselves. This obviously becomes necessary when experienced reality does not exactly conform to the received expectations generated by the language we have become accustomed to use.

Insofar as the inherited words and conceptual meanings of a learned language are used to interpret experience, they are therefore a necessary element in our claims to identify and know things. However, the words and concepts of a linguistic community, and rules for their correct use, are constantly being modified. This is not so much the case in relation to a scientifically established definition, such as, for example, that relating to the term "oxygen," which has become conventionally agreed upon and formally set within the scientific community. Speaking more generally, however, the development of words and their meanings are open to other rather more dynamic possibilities.

For example, we are able to claim to know that the object we are looking at is an "apple" only if we possess the concept expressed in the word "apple," and rules for its correct use. In the first instance we may have learned its meaning by ostensive definition: in other words, we come to an understanding of the term "apple" by being shown an actual apple by our parents and having it identified for us as "an apple" as they point to it and say "apple." This learning experience might at first lead us to think that all apples are red, or at least that all apples are red when they are ripe and sweet enough to eat. We might even be warned off eating apples when they are green. But then, when we become acquainted in experience with our first Granny Smith apple, we learn that some apples are in fact green and remain green even when they are ripe and sweet and ready to eat. In this circumstance the originally learned concept of an apple has therefore to be modified to include apples that can be either red or green when they are ripe. In this way the concept of an apple gets modified in the light of our actual expanding experience of apples. Clearly, actual experiences often call for a modification or redefinition of the inherited meaning of words and the refinement of the concepts they signify. Experience obviously does not always rigidly conform to received definitions. If we rely on linguistically formulated concepts to interpret experience, it is also true that sometimes concepts have to be modified and redefined in the light of experience.

Another example may be helpful to drive home this point. When the first European explorers came across the Indian Ocean to the western coast of Australia late in the seventeenth century, they came with the inherited concept of a "swan." This was received from the European linguistic community from which they originated. For them, the word "swan" denoted an elegant white bird, somewhat like a large duck or goose with webbed feet, but with a distinctively graceful long neck and a red bill. All swans were understood to be white. However, when Willem de Vlamingh in 1696 sailed into the mouth of what he came to call the Swan River[2] at what is now Perth in Western Australia, he and his colleagues found that their working concept of "a swan" had to be revised. They identified what they saw with the interpretative concept of "a swan," and could therefore claim to know that they were observing swans, but surprisingly, their actual experience now dictated that some swans were black and therefore somewhat different from what they might originally have expected concerning swans. The point is that the experiential encounter with black swans called for the revision and modification of the inherited European understanding of what a swan was.

It follows that the precise meaning attaching to the concepts that are brought to the interpretation of experience is subject to modification and change from time to time, precisely as those same concepts are used in the light of nuances thrown up by those very experiences themselves.

The inherited concepts that people have at their disposal are sometimes found wanting, at least in some respects, and fail adequately to describe the actual experiences to which they are applied. They may still be obliged to use them, for they may be the only concepts available in the limited array of linguistic tools at their disposal. Nevertheless, in the course of their actual use, particularly when they are used identifyingly, as objects of concrete experience are interpreted and claims are made to know them, their exact meaning may come to be modified. They thus come to be understood to mean something a little different from the inherited meaning that was originally assigned to them. So the basic principle is: actual experience dictates that inherited linguistic concepts sometimes have to be adapted to serve specific interpretative purposes.

Now, in the case of the first Christians, it is thinkable that any inherited notions of "resurrection" that they received from the mind-set of Second Temple Judaism, along with an understanding of what might therefore have been anticipated to be involved in an experience of a human person being or having been raised from the dead, would also have in principle been open to modification and revision in the light of their actual Easter experiences. In this case, the inherited meaning of the term "resurrection" that they received from Second Temple Judaism may automatically have been modified. Apart from N. T. Wright's problematic contention that there was only one rigidly fixed and "strictly limited" working definition of the term "resurrection" current at the time, we therefore also have to question his reasoning when he then goes on to contend that the first Easter experiences simply conformed to this alleged inherited idea, and thereby confirmed their received Second Temple expectations. It is very important to acknowledge that, at least in principle, instead of their experience having to conform to their inherited belief in every respect, the actual newfound Easter

2. Vlamingh actually called it *Zwaanenrivier*.

experiences which led the first Christian believers to make the explicit claim that Jesus had been raised from the dead simultaneously dictated some changes in their understanding of the term "resurrection" and its implications.

The contention that the first Christian believers inherited a "strictly limited" definition of the term "resurrection" from the linguistic tradition of Second Temple Judaism and that they could not have thought of the resurrection of Jesus otherwise than as the return of his physical body to life in this world, fails to take account of the fact that conformity to received expectations is not secured as an absolute necessity simply by the bare use of a word. We therefore need to be wary of falling victim to the unquestioning assumption that when they used the term "resurrection" it was being used strictly in accordance with a received conventionally agreed upon meaning. On the contrary, the dramatic uniqueness of their Easter experience may have dictated the need to modify the inherited meanings of the language they used to describe it.

We will grapple with the discernment of the more precise and nuanced meaning that appears to have been intended when claims were made by the first Christian believers concerning the Resurrection of the crucified Jesus from the dead in future chapters of this book. For the present it is sufficient simply to note that it does not necessarily follow that the first Easter experiences *had* to conform to the received expectations generated by an alleged "strictly limited" meaning content of the term "resurrection" as it was received from Second Temple Judaism. It is at least thinkable that the quality of their Easter experience was nuanced and that, at least in some important respects, what was experienced was entirely unexpected. The unexpected nature of the event may well have dictated the need to make modifications in their understanding of what a "resurrection from the dead" actually was understood to involve. Whether this logical or thinkable possibility is an actual possibility can only be judged by examining what they in fact claimed to have experienced. Before jumping to conclusions that might well turn out to be wrong, we need to look carefully at the New Testament Easter traditions themselves, particularly the earliest stratum of them, with a view to measuring what they actually had to say against any alleged "strictly limited" inherited definition.

Wright's contention that the meaning of "resurrection from the dead" was "constant throughout the ancient world, until we come to a new coinage in the second century,"[3] and that the first believers could not have thought otherwise than strictly in accordance with a single, clear, and distinct understanding of the term "resurrection" that was bequeathed to them by the preceding religious culture, raises another important issue: his insistence that the first Easter experiences conformed to and confirmed their

3. *RSG*, 31. The reference is to the appearance of the *Gospel of Thomas* in the mid-second century AD.

inherited expectation may in practical and missiological terms be vicious with respect to the Christian cause, given that it leads right into the possibility that the first Easter experience was nothing more than the mere wish-fulfillment of received expectations. If what happened to Jesus was exactly what the first Christians hoped and believed would happen to all the righteous dead (even if this was not expected to happen before the end of the world), then, in the arena of Christian apologetics, this becomes a quite serious difficulty. If what happened is said to be exactly what they thought would happen, or if the specific nature of the resurrection experience was exactly what they had been led to expect, then how are we to answer the charge that Easter was simply a matter of wish-fulfillment?

Fortunately, we do not have to back ourselves into that corner. There are good reasons for being open to the possibility, regardless of the tradition of their religious and linguistic tutoring, that their actual Easter experience was, in some important ways, in fact unexpectedly unique. In other words, the indications are that it did *not* conform to a preconceived stereotype. While the first believers naturally interpreted their experience using the received concepts of their Second Temple religio-cultural tradition, for these are all they had at their disposal, it is at least thinkable that those very concepts had to be adapted and modified as a result of their encounter with something that was in some respects incongruous with their received expectations.

The element of surprise, even disbelief, is too deeply rooted in the New Testament Easter traditions for this not to be a thinkable possibility. After all, the first recorded reactions were reactions of awe and consternation and even doubt and disbelief.[4] The words "Isn't that exactly what we expected?" do not seem to have come to their lips. Rather, the truth is that the first believers had to trawl through the Hebrew Scriptures in search of clues which might help them interpret and explain the surprisingly puzzling quality of their newfound Easter experience. As Geza Vermes rightly says, the disciples of Jesus "did not expect him to rise from the dead any more than their contemporaries expected the Messiah to do so."[5] If there was no explicit expectation among their contemporaries that the Messiah would rise from the dead, but only a generalized belief in a final eschatological restoration of all the righteous departed, how can we be sure that there was a clear perception about the detailed nature of what "rising from the dead" might mean which was simply confirmed by the claimed experience of the Resurrection of the Christ/Messiah?

That what happened was not exactly what they might have expected is also indicated by the fact that we know that they came to the belief that Jesus had been raised from the dead in a way that, in some important respects, was not just unexpected but actually contrary at least to some aspects of their inherited beliefs. For example, we

4. For example, the reactions of the women at the tomb did not lead to the judgment that this was exactly what they should have expected. In many of the appearance narratives, surprise and doubt are a regular theme, as in Matt 28:17 and Luke 24:11–12.

5. Vermes, *Jesus the Jew*, 20.

have already noted that resurrection was only anticipated on the day of the general resurrection of all the dead at the End of the world. However, the evidence clearly indicates that in reality this received understanding of things had to be reviewed in response to their reported experiences. Resurrection was no longer just a collective experience, whether of the righteous only, or of the righteous and the unrighteous together, nor was it to be temporally located in accordance with their inherited expectation at the apocalyptic End of the world. The unexpected occurrence of Jesus' Resurrection as an event, which involved a single human individual *before* the time of the general resurrection of all the dead at the Eschaton obviously dictated the revision of the expected eschatological time-line.

Of course, Wright himself readily admits this. He confidently affirms that "nobody imagined that any individuals had been raised, or would be raised in advance of the great last day."[6] Whatever the inherited meaning of the term "resurrection" when used to articulate this Second Temple apocalyptic belief in the general resurrection at the end of the world, it was now used in relation specifically to Jesus to describe the surprising and entirely unique experience of encounter with an individual three days after his death. In this way at least, the first believers were obliged to revise their understanding of what they had meant hitherto by "the resurrection of the dead."[7] Given then that, contrary to expectations, "resurrection" is what the first Christians actually claimed had happened in the case of Jesus, it is implicitly conceded that they departed from the normative apocalyptic belief that they had inherited in this very significant respect. Instead of employing it to speak of the resurrection collectively of all the righteous dead at the end of the world, it was now used to apply to a single human individual ahead of time, as it were. The concept of "resurrection" implicit in their inherited eschatological belief had necessarily to be modified in this respect.

Despite these concessions, on the basis of the assumption that the first Easter experiences must have conformed to a single and fixed inherited understanding of things, Wright argues that the first believers not only declared that Jesus had triumphed over death, but that, in accordance with an alleged inherited belief, his being raised from the dead *must* have involved the understanding that he was returned to this material world in a straightforward physical way. This implicitly entails, therefore, an *a priori* conclusion that the tomb in which his body had been laid *must* have been found empty. This inherited view of the Resurrection then in turn allowed the first generation of believers to assert that Jesus "would never die again" and, with the help of Ps 16:10, that his restored material body had become "incorruptible." All this could be said to be in accordance with the straightforward and "strictly limited" nature of their inherited understanding of things. Indeed, Wright furthermore insists that the conformity of their experiences with their inherited belief therefore positively excludes the possibility that they may have thought in terms of a "platonic" going to

6. *RSG*, 205.

7. *RSG*, 205.

"heavenly immortality" or a sharing in the eternal life of God in the interim prior to the ultimate revelation of his victorious messianic status and power at the future Eschaton.

However, if belief in the Resurrection of Jesus, as a happening involving an individual human person prior to the general resurrection at the End of the world, was at least in these respects *not* exactly what they expected, then we have to ask if it is unreasonable to imagine that the *quality* of their experience might also have dictated a modified understanding of how precisely the "resurrection body" was to be envisaged as well. They may well have come to the conclusion that their inherited belief was in need of somewhat more modification than just its timing, or the individualization of what was formerly understood to be a collective event.

Very significantly, the New Testament post-Easter traditions indicate that from a very early time the worship of Jesus was an integral element of the primitive response to him in the days following his crucifixion. Indeed, in the earliest narrative account of an appearance of the Raised Christ that we have (in Matthew 28), those who were assembled on a mountain in Galilee and who came to faith, are said immediately to have worshipped him (28:17).[8] As we shall see in chapter 8, the subsequent expressions of faith were the occasion for recourse to a rich variety of Christological titles, and images associated with them, which indicate that the primitive Easter experiences had to do with one who was understood to have been gloriously exalted to "the right hand of the Father."[9] From this exalted and heavenly place he was understood to be not only the Messiah/Christ but also one who exercised sovereignty over their lives as their "Lord." As witness to this, appeal was regularly made, to Psalm 110 to explain this newfound aspect of their experience, as something that went well beyond any preconceived notions of messiahship that they had received from Second Temple Judaism.[10]

In other words, the Easter experience was of such a kind that the question of the ultimate destination of the Raised Jesus, where he had gone, also presented itself as an additional associated item of speculative inquiry. Did this conform exactly to their anticipated resurrection beliefs? And if these inherited beliefs were various, which one most appropriately matched their experience? Was Jesus restored to *this* world, or is it thinkable on the basis of their actual Easter experience that they understood

8. Larry W. Hurtado has expounded the significance of worship in the early response of faith in a sustained series of publications: See Hurtado, *One God, One Lord*; Hurtado, *Lord Jesus Christ*; and Hurtado, *How on Earth Did Jesus Become a God?*

9. Apart from Paul's appeal to the motif of exaltation in the Christ-hymn of Phil 2:5–11 and his use of Psalm 110 in Rom 8:34, the Deutero-Pauline epistles indicate something of the significance of Psalm 110 in early Christian thinking. See, for example, Eph 1:20–23 and Col 3:1. It also features in Heb 1:3–13; 8:1; 10:12; 12:2; 1 Pet 3:22; and Acts 2:34.

10. The classic treatment of this aspect of early Christian reflection on the Easter experience is found in Lindars, *New Testament Apologetic*.

that he had been "glorified" and exalted to the eternal immortality of God? Rowan Williams has pertinently observed that the New Testament Easter traditions reveal that a "gradual convergence of experience and pre-existing language" occurred in the thinking of the first Christians, but in a way "that inexorably changes the register of the language."[11] We dare not underestimate the impact on their thinking of the fact "that Jesus was, within a generation of his death, regarded as *present* to and in the believing community, the object of personal devotion, the recipient of personal address."[12] Whatever it was that the first Christians understood was entailed by the use of the inherited term "resurrection," when it was used in relation to what was believed to have had happened to Jesus, it was charged with a new set of mind-expanding and transcendent meaning.

Certainly, the clarification and re-definition of an inherited Jewish belief in life after death as a return in physical form to *this* world, would have become absolutely necessary if the Easter experience of the first Christians itself insistently pointed them in an alternative "other-worldly" direction of a general "platonic" kind. Indeed, if the first Christians were not already thinking of the fate of the dead in more "other-worldly" terms (given that this was a real possibility in the mix of beliefs relating to the afterlife in Hellenistic Judaism at the time), then we have to reckon also with the possibility that the Easter experience itself may have been an invitation to do so. Indeed, the first Christian believers may have been perplexed to find that in this specific respect, what they perceived to have happened did not quite fit with any of their received expectations. I think therefore that we must conclude that whatever the precise preunderstanding of the first believers was, it was necessarily subject to revision in the light of their actual Easter experiences. If they were using an alleged "strictly limited definition" of the term "resurrection," and thus could only have thought in terms of the physical restoration of a material body to *this* world, then this likewise may necessarily have been subject to revision in the light of their actual Easter experiences.

Furthermore, if we are prepared at least to countenance the possibility of some variety of expectation and lack of clear definition as to the fate of the righteous dead, given the range of speculative views in circulation within the religious culture of Hellenistic Judaism, then this may be expected to have precipitated some initial confusion in relation to the interpretation of the Easter experience. In this circumstance, it is understandable that what happened among the first witnesses triggered faith for some but confused doubt for others.[13] Accordingly, in the face of reports of the Resurrection of Jesus, some may have been at a loss to know exactly what to think. Certainly, we

---

11. Williams, "Between the Cherubim," 91.

12. Williams, "A History of Faith in Jesus," 220.

13. Already in the first appearance narrative we have (in Matt 28:17), while some came to faith in the Raised Christ and worshipped him, others were clearly of a different mind for "some doubted" or "hesitated."

cannot discount the possibility that what happened also led some to a revised under-standing of their inherited beliefs and expectations.

Despite Wright's insistence on the conformity of the first Easter experience with a "strictly limited" inherited understanding of "resurrection," specifically in respect to the material nature of the resurrected body and its return to this world, he is pre-pared to admit that the first Easter experiences at least dictated the need to modify the received view with regard both to the time-line and also to the important inherited belief that resurrection was essentially a collective experience. However, it seems ar-bitrary to argue that the term "resurrection" *was* subject to revision in the light of the Easter experience insofar as it was now used to apply to a specific individual before the time of the general resurrection of all the righteous dead on the Last Day, but then to deny even the theoretical possibility that the term could also be used in the light of that same experience to refer not just to Jesus' restoration to life in this world, but to his glorification and heavenly transformation now as the one designated to be Lord and Christ "at the right hand of the Father." To characterize such an understanding of things as "platonic," and therefore to rule it out of court on that ground simply that it does not conform to a predetermined definition, hardly constitutes a convincing argument.

On the other hand, within the Hellenized culture of post-exilic Judaism, modifica-tions to linguistic usage expressive of religious belief appear to have occurred along a two-way street. If we have to take account of the possibility that the definition of the term "resurrection" may have been open to some modification in the light of the actual Easter experience of the first Christians, a similar kind of modification can already be demonstrated with respect to the concept of "immortality" as it made its way from classical Greek culture into the Hellenistic world of first-century Judaism. In this case we can actually track something of its modification. For example, in the course of its use in the context of the Greek diaspora of post-exilic Judaism, there is clear evidence that the original fully blown Platonic notion of the "immortality of the soul" underwent considerable processes of modification and conceptual change, spe-cifically as a consequence of its commerce with Jewish monotheism. Plato's original doctrine entailed that souls, being immortal before being born into earthly human existence, enjoyed a pre-existing life in which the contemplation of "Ideal Forms" occurred. The soul's alleged possession of the resulting residual "memory" of these Forms, now as "innate ideas" explained how it was possible in the course of historical earthly existence to identify and know material things; they were understood to be the shadowy counterparts which "matched up" to their remembered eternal Ideal Forms. This was the benefit in epistemological terms of the fundamental belief in the soul's immortality. Conversely, for Plato, the soul's possession of the remembered Forms or

"Ideas" that were apparently acquired prior to its temporary "imprisonment" in the earthly body (from which it in turn "escaped" at death) functioned also as a support for belief in the soul's innate immortality. The "memory" of the Forms itself indicated that the soul could therefore be understood to possess the character of immortality as a kind of natural possession or endowment.

However, this full-blown Platonic belief was clearly modified in the context of its reception in Palestinian Judaism. Insofar as Intertestamental Jewish literature began to speak in terms of the "immortality of the soul," this belief tended to be nuanced, so that it is spoken of in this literature, not as a pre-existing natural possession, but as the "gift of God." Through commerce with the fundamental concepts of Jewish theism "immortality" thus came to be regarded as a new endowment bestowed upon the soul by God, especially as a reward for a specific martyr's faithfulness unto death.[14]

In the speculative imaginings of 2 Baruch, for example, God is addressed as the author of the new life that might await the righteous dead beyond the grave; there is no suggestion that the "soul" is itself entirely in charge of its own eternal destiny. The same may be said of the Wisdom of Solomon where, generally speaking, immortality is a reward of a righteous life rather than an inherent quality of the soul, though at the same time there are some suggestions of the remnant survival of Plato's original notion of innate immortality as well.

It is a measure of the degree to which Plato's influence had gained ground in the world of Middle Platonism, that Philo of Alexandria (who was born around 15 BC),[15] actually espoused a clearly expressed belief in the soul's inherent immortality. I am not aware of any resistance to the views of Philo in the Jewish community of Alexandria, so it may have been that Jews could accommodate this more originally Platonic doctrine without too much difficulty. It is clear enough, however, that generally in a Jewish environment a pre-existing belief in God entailed that any notion of the "immortality of the soul," though ultimately inherited from Plato, underwent a process of adaption, so as to accommodate a set of more clearly monotheistic and characteristically Jewish presuppositions.

We have therefore to accept that the mere use of the term "immortality" does not entail that it must be understood in the "strictly limited" sense of its original meaning as it is found full-blown in the writings of Plato himself. In the context of the Jewish culture of first-century Palestine, this modification, and as a result the emergence of some variety in the understanding of immortality, prompts us to ask if there may have been similar permutations of belief in relation to characteristically Jewish ideas of

14. See the account of this development in Cavallin, *Life after Death*, 126.

15. This is the generally assumed date of Philo's birth. It is known that he led an embassy from Alexandria to Caligula in AD 39 (Josephus, *Ant.* 17.257–260). Interestingly, the fact that his nephew, Tiberius Julius Alexander, became Procurator of Judaea in AD 46, speaks of the real connection between the Jewish community of Alexandria and nearby Palestinian Judaism.

resurrection, under the influence of Hellenistic sensibilities about the transcendently timeless eternity of heaven.

N. T. Wright seems to have no problem at all in accepting this modification of the idea of the originally Greek idea of immortality in the context of the culture of Jewish theism. While the concept of "resurrection" is said to have been sustained with its alleged "strictly limited" univocal meaning, which is said to have remained "constant throughout the ancient world, until we come to a new coinage in the second century,"[16] he is prepared to admit that the original Greek notion of the soul's possession of an innate immortality naturally became subject to modification and change in a Jewish context. Indeed, for Wright, in this specific context notions of "immortality" were modified even to the point of being transformed into a temporary condition in an alleged "intermediate state" pending the arrival of the Eschaton. In effect, this means that we are asked to accept that a cross-fertilization of ideas impacted upon the Greek view of the immortality of the soul so as to require its modification in the context of Hellenized Palestinian Judaism, but at the same time we are urged to deny even the possibility of the modification of the notion of resurrection by commerce with the same other-worldly and eternal orientation that was potentially available as an inheritance from Hellenism. At the very least, it seems awkward to admit one possibility and deny the other.

In any event, all this alerts us to the basic truth that language itself is simply not rigidly static. Furthermore, while we employ inherited understandings, expressed in the linguistic apparatus of words and their conceptual meanings, to interpret experienced reality so as to be in the position to make knowledge claims about it, the reverse does not apply. Experienced reality cannot itself be made to conform to the received dictionary definitions of a language. The fact that the inherited concepts of a linguistic community are brought to the interpretation of experience in the making of knowledge claims does not mean that those concepts are not open to modification in the process. Contrary to Wright's contention that the first Christians cannot have come to their Easter experience other than with a "strictly limited" and fixed inherited understanding of what the term "resurrection" meant, and that their Easter experience simply conformed to it, it may well therefore be that their inherited understanding had necessarily to be revised in response to their understanding of the precise nature of what they actually did encounter.

An appreciation of the importance of actual experience as a stimulus to the possible need to modify the deliverances of all received linguistic traditions certainly invites us to revise our estimate of the actual importance of those received definitions and preunderstandings which are said to have filled the minds of the first generation

16. *RSG*, 31.

of Christians. Whatever it was in precise terms that they received from the tradition of Second Temple Judaism may not be quite as important as we may think.

Now, if it is not necessarily the case that experienced reality must conform to received definitions and understandings of things, and if sometimes the words and concepts of the interpretative grid that we apply to experience in making knowledge claims is itself subject to modification in the process, then it follows that we cannot simply assume the validity even of the most obvious of the claimed entailments of a received definition. For example, when the concept of "resurrection" is understood as a return of a dead person to this world, it might reasonably be assumed that this involved the physical restoration of a material body, perhaps also that this body had become incorruptible (as distinct from "immortal" as would be the case if resurrection is understood as a going to the timeless eternity of God). Such a belief would entail also that the tomb in which the dead person had been placed was therefore left entirely empty. However, in considering the precise meaning of the term "resurrection" when it was used with respect to the Resurrection of Jesus in the first century, and what was entailed by it, we are dealing not with logically necessary but with contingent matters. While we can be quite certain that, if a man is described as a bachelor, then it is necessarily entailed that he is unmarried, it does not necessarily follow that if a person is said to have been raised from the dead, then he *must* have been restored to this world with the same material body as he formerly possessed. This is not a necessary truth but a purely contingent one. Furthermore, it cannot simply be assumed that, if a person is said to have been raised from the dead, that his body was thereby made incorruptible. Nor is it necessarily entailed that the tomb in which he had been laid was left empty. This too is a contingent matter. Clearly, any tendency to adopt an *a priori* way of arguing on the basis of the alleged necessary entailments of a received definition undercuts the outcomes of *a posteriori* consideration of the actual evidence relating to these matters.

The inherent dangers of this procedure should give us cause to pause and proceed with caution. Even if we were inclined to concede Wright's contention that there really was only one fixed possible meaning attaching to the concept of "resurrection" in the culture of Second Temple Judaism which the first believing Christians inherited, it does not follow that their actual experiences conformed equally strictly to that received definitional understanding in terms of its possible entailments. What is entailed by the claim that a person has been raised from the dead is not itself a straightforward *a priori* judgment. The specific entailments about the nature of Jesus' resurrection body have to be demonstrated to have been of such and such a kind by an examination of the evidence relevant to the making of such a judgment. It is in this way that what specifically pertains to the understanding of "resurrection" is established. It has to be proved from the actual evidence that Jesus did appear to the bereft disciples in physical and material form, for example. This cannot simply be assumed as a logically necessary entailment of the assertion that Jesus had been raised from the dead. Furthermore, the story of the empty tomb has to be validated. Clearly, these are not *a priori* truths that *necessarily* follow from an alleged "strictly limited" and fixed received definition. They are all contingent matters. It cannot therefore simply be assumed that in using the term "resurrection" the first Christians cannot have thought otherwise than in terms of physical and material "meetings" with him. Likewise, it cannot simply be assumed that because they spoke of Jesus' "resurrection from the dead," then they *must* also have thought in terms of an empty tomb.

Clearly, it is a mistake to seek to contain the resurrection experience wholly within the realm of this mundane order, as an event like any other historical event within space and time, simply because this is how *some* Pharisees understood the word "resurrection" in the context of the apocalyptic beliefs they inherited from Second Temple Judaism. On the contrary, even if we could be confident about there having been only one single and univocal "strictly limited" definition of the term "resurrection" in circulation at the time, it may well have been the case that the original Easter experiences were of such a kind as to suggest that Jesus' body had been radically transformed in a more heavenly, glorified and exalted form, such as would have led to an alternative set of entailments—that Jesus had entered into the eternal "immortality" of God in a radically transformed and glorified body, for example. To think in terms of a sharing of the life of the eternal God who is alone "immortal, invisible" (1 Tim 1:17) therefore becomes a viable theological option, as opposed to a restoration to *this* world with a body of a physical and material kind made "incorruptible." Once again, however, this kind of conclusion can only be arrived at by considering the evidence concerning what the first witnesses concluded and reported in response to their Easter experiences, and what they said about what they thought had happened in the wake of those experiences. If it is clearly perilous to base the theological enterprise upon a received dictionary definition, and then to argue that experienced reality must conform to it, it is just as perilous simply to assume the validity of all the *a priori* entailments of a received definition. All these are contingent matters that stand or fall according to an assessment of the evidence provided by the first witnesses.

To argue, as N. T. Wright does, that Paul and other first generation Christians cannot have thought otherwise than in terms of an inherited "strictly limited" meaning of the term "resurrection," is to fail to take account of the real possibility that the Easter experience was capable itself of dictating a nuanced revision of the idea they received. It is also to fail to take account of the fact that what they came to think was entailed by it may have been entirely without precedent. What is understood to have been entailed by Jesus' Resurrection from the dead can only be determined by considering what was actually said in faith claims in response to that experience—the actual evidence relevant to establishing what the first Christians understood took place. Undoubtedly, St. Paul was using concepts inherited from the religio-linguistic community from which he came; after all he could not have done otherwise. But we cannot rule out the possibility that he was in fact stretched beyond those inherited words to express something of his own uniquely felt experience when he himself came to talk about it.

On the other hand, if the meaning of the term "resurrection" and the conceptually speculative nature of the afterlife associated with it were not nearly so rigidly set in the culture of Second Temple Judaism as N. T. Wright would have us believe, and if there was actually a spectrum of diverse belief relating to the nature of the afterlife in the received culture of the time, including the imagined nature of the body of the resurrection, then the actual Easter experience of the first Christians was destined to have functioned in a clarifying way.

We therefore have to be open to the possibility that whatever received understandings of the afterlife may have been inherited from the religio-linguistic culture of Second Temple Judaism, those very understandings were necessarily open to modification, and even radical revision, in the light of what actually happened. Whatever had been previously envisaged conceptually, what actually grounded the claim that Jesus had been raised from the dead, was the first Easter experience itself, and not simply something already predetermined by an alleged fixed definition received from Second Temple Judaism. The nature of the actual concrete religious experience of Easter that grounded the conviction and the faith claim that Jesus had been raised from the dead, cannot be made quite simply to conform to received theological perceptions and eschatological hopes, to the exclusion of its uniqueness.

The possibility that the first Christians did actually revise their inherited conceptual beliefs concerning the afterlife and the nature of the resurrection body, and also its ultimate location in the light of their concrete experience of the Resurrection of Jesus (whether back in this world or in another more heavenly place), is heightened when we observe their active modification and development in the wake of their Easter experience of other insights that they had received from their inherited religious tradition. For example, primitive Christianity also received, as part of its linguistic and cultural inheritance from Second Temple Judaism, an understanding of the role of the Messiah as a hoped-for deliverer anointed by God, long expected of the line of David. Indeed, it appears that one stereotypical (perhaps even "strictly limited"?) understanding of the nature of the messiahship he would come to exercise was widely entertained: to put it briefly, the awaited Messiah was envisaged primarily as a political figure, who was expected to deliver Israel from foreign domination and persecution by the exertion of military power. This is, of course, the inherited view that appears particularly to have motivated insurgent groups such as the Zealots. But the Gospel traditions suggest that the primitive Christians clearly understood the importance of their vocation to redefine the nature of messiahship in the light of the actual experience of encounter not only with the Raised Christ but already with the historical Jesus of the days prior to his crucifixion. While this process may even have been initiated by Jesus himself,[17] it certainly appears to have commenced in Jesus' own lifetime in response to Jesus' historical life and teaching, and the manner of his death. The evidence for the initial redefinition of messiahship exercised by Jesus in response to his historical words and works is now found in the work of the second generation of believers in the Gospels, most notably in the first of them—the Gospel of St. Mark. Certainly, the process of redefinition was complete by the time Mark finished his Gospel.

The Gospel of St. Mark shows that the experience of the earthly ministry of Jesus was understood to have dictated that the inherited Second Temple understanding of messiahship had not only to be modified, but actually turned on its head. If Jesus was the long awaited Messiah, he was not anything like the kind of Messiah that most Jews of the time appear to have expected. Thus, in the context of the Christ-Event the inherited dictionary definition of "messiahship" was perceived to be only of limited usefulness, for clearly, as Messiah, Jesus did not conform to expectation as this had been expressed in their religious and political traditions. In the light of what was experienced of him, the concept of the Messiah of Israel therefore had necessarily to be modified and redefined.

The fact that historical Christianity has received written Gospels is in large part due to the ingenuity of St. Mark who apparently perceived the need to address this issue. Mark, as far as we know, was the inventor of the literary form of the Gospel. One of his chief purposes in writing his Gospel was to undertaking a systematic redefinition of the inherited meaning of the term the "Messiah of Israel." Richard Burridge has pointed to the importance of recovering the biographical genre in relation to our understanding of the nature of the Gospels.[18] He concedes that they may not be biographies in the modern sense, but they do have a great deal in common with the biographies of the ancient world. However, whether this is a correct assessment of the Gospel genre or not,[19] it is clear that the Gospels were not biographies for biography's sake, nor were they intended just for the purpose of preserving the historical memory of the way in which Jesus had lived and the manner in which he had died, as in a mere chronicle. In Mark's case, the motivation for writing was driven by a quest not just to

17. The messianic self-consciousness of Jesus himself may be difficult to prove, given the coloring of hind-sight in the evangelists' presentation of the traditional material. James D. G. Dunn, while generally pessimistic about the security of historical judgments, adventurously enters this speculative field in Dunn, *Jesus Remembered*.

18. Burridge, *What Are the Gospels?*; and Burridge, *Four Gospels, One Jesus?*

19. Charles H. Talbert, who argued against the antihistorical views of Bultmann, contended that the Gospels come out of a Hellenistic milieu and are a form of ancient biography in *What Is a Gospel?*. This was criticized in Aune, "The Problem of the Genre of the Gospels." See also Richard Burridge's discussion of Talbert in Burridge, *What Are the Gospels?*, 80–83.

record and report, but quite intentionally to redefine a received understanding of the nature of messiahship. Without doubt, Mark wrote with the intention of producing a tract in which the true identity of the Messiah of God was demonstrated for the purpose in turn of defining the true nature of discipleship for those who would follow him. For Mark, this project of re-definition was demanded principally by the actual experience of encounter with Jesus during his historical life and by the manner of his dying.

Mark presents the true nature of Jesus' messianic identity through his arrangement and presentation of the Gospel traditions. In the first half of his Gospel, comprising the first eight chapters, Mark gathered miracle stories and accounts of Jesus' teaching in parables. By and large, with only one or two exceptions, this kind of material is absent from the second half of the Gospel.[20] Furthermore, Mark intentionally and systematically arranged this material in three sequences; in each case, after a period of Jesus' healing and teaching activity, the sequence ends with an instance of blindness or failure of apprehension. First, Scribes and Pharisees misunderstand the true nature of his identity and mission (Mark 3:6), then Jesus' family and countrymen similarly misunderstand (Mark 6:1–5a), and then this is followed even by the misunderstanding his own disciples (Mark 7:18; 8:18). In the course of this healing and teaching activity, while many are presented as failing to comprehend Jesus' message, and thus remain blind to the true nature of his messianic identity and mission, those who did come close to discerning who Jesus was are regularly bidden to remain silent. This is the celebrated theme of the messianic secret in Mark. In the first eight chapters of Mark's Gospel, Mark even portrays Jesus as one who apparently tried to keep his identity secret, and this apparently for a specific reason. For, while some might perceive something about Jesus' identity and mission and even call him "Messiah," employing the concept inherited from the socio-linguistic and religious background, their perception would still have been wrong. In other words, while in some sense it would have been right, in another sense it would have been mistaken. For they first had to learn precisely what *kind* of Messiah Jesus actually was before they could rightly and truly identify him as "Messiah." Even if some came to some insight into his identity (like the demons who declared that they knew who Jesus was), they were therefore bidden to be silent. If they were healed, they are similarly instructed to return home without telling anybody. In this way Jesus is presented by Mark as one who discouraged those who witnessed his ministry from calling him "Messiah" prematurely. In other words, from Mark's point of view, the concept of the Messiah could only rightly be used of Jesus if its inherited meaning was first modified so as to be correctly understood.

---

20. Notably the healing of Blind Bartimaeus in Mark 10, and the story of the King who sent his Son to order his vineyard in Mark 12. We will find, however, that even these turn out not to be exceptions.

In the second half of the Gospel, comprising the second eight chapters, Mark presents Jesus' "plain" or "open" teaching (Mark 8:31–32).[21] This is that Jesus was a Messiah of a particular kind: one who came as the lowly servant of others, rather than one who wielded coercive power, and indeed as one who would himself fall victim to that very kind of worldly power, and suffer and die. Those who call him "Messiah" without understanding this, like Peter at Caesarea Philippi who called him Messiah but then insisted that a destiny of suffering and death could not be envisaged for him, are said to "think as men think, not as God thinks" (Mark 8:33).

In counterpoise to the three sequences ending in the blindness of failing to comprehend Jesus' true identity and the nature of his mission in the first half of the Gospel, Mark therefore rehearses Jesus' "plain" or "open" teaching about the true nature of his mission, and his coming suffering and death three times (Mark 8:32; 9:32; and 10:32–34). On each occasion, Jesus then calls his followers to see this clearly and then to take up their cross and to follow in the same way as "true disciples." If it is argued that the Gospel fits into the genre of ancient biography, its theme of the importance of seeing clearly the true nature of Jesus' messiahship and its accompanying exhortation to take up the cross as true disciples and follow in the same way, means that this is much more than just of biographical interest.

Once again this is followed by three misunderstandings—of Peter (Mark 8:32b–33), of the disciples as a group arguing about who is to be greatest in the Kingdom (Mark 9:33–34), and by James and John whose failure to comprehend is disclosed in the faux pas of asking for exalted places on the right and left in the coming Kingdom (Mark 10:35–37). It is only once Jesus' true messianic identity and the nature of the discipleship to which he calls his followers is seen clearly that the "true disciple" can "take up the cross" and follow in the same way.

It is at that point in the Gospel that Mark, apparently quite deliberately, places the story of Bartimaeus, who receives the miracle of sight, sees clearly, and then "followed Jesus *in the way*" (10:52). This healing miracle is an exception to the general rule that miracle stories do not feature in the second half of the Gospel. But then, this is much more than just a miracle story, for Bartimaeus is the paradigm of the "true disciple." He sees clearly and is able to follow "in the way." Following in "the way" is, of course, not just a matter of walking down a road, but following as a true disciple in the way of the Cross; the passion narrative, the story of the self-effacing, self-sacrificial, and lowly surrender to death, then follows immediately (Mark 11–15).

Significantly, it is then that a Roman soldier at the foot of the Cross, who is able to stand loose to received Jewish conceptions of messiahship, after having actually witnessed Jesus' self-giving and lowly death, is therefore permitted to say "Truly this was the Son of God." In this way the soldier expresses and confirms the truth of Jesus'

21. In the second half of the Gospel Jesus' teaching is direct, "open" or "plain" by contrast with the parables and riddles of the first half of the Gospel.

true identity to which readers of the Gospel have already been alerted by anticipation by Mark at the very beginning of his Gospel (1:1).

In all this Mark, over and above any supposed biographical interest, is at pains to ensure that from a Christian perspective the inherited concept of "the Messiah of Israel" had necessarily to be modified in the light of the experience of encounter with the Jesus of history. His words and works, including specifically the manner of his death, disclose his true identity, and *this* specific identity was what was affirmed and confirmed by his resurrection from the dead. In other words, the net result of Mark's redactional handling of traditional material, particularly in his highly skilled literary arrangement of the material, is to produce not just a biography for biography's sake, but in fact a systematic theology in which the inherited meaning of the title "Messiah" is radically revised and redefined in response to what the first witnesses of Jesus ministry actually experienced. Inherited notions of the long-awaited Messiah were thus significantly modified in the light of the quality of the life of lowly servant-hood, which the human Jesus is said to have both taught and in actuality to have lived out in lowly obedience, even unto death. The Cross, as the definitive sign of the distinctively unique messiahship that was revealed in Jesus' crucifixion and death, thus became the center and symbol of the Christian faith. Though already in Paul we find the first insights of the very same theology of the Cross that Mark discerned in the life and death of Jesus,[22] as the church's first known systematic theologian, Mark is to be credited with the literary and theological achievement of producing the first Gospel.

As an accompanying theological theme, Mark also universalized the significance of the mission of the Jewish Messiah. In his Gospel, it is a foreign woman who first comes to faith;[23] and the Temple is explicitly said to be intended to be a house of prayer "for all nations" (11:17). Furthermore, it is a foreign soldier at the foot of the Cross who declares Jesus' identity as "Son of God" (15:39). Matthew, by contrast, presents Jesus' mission as being focused on the Jews; it is only universalized with the post-Easter Great Commission to preach the Gospel to all nations. Also, by contrast with Mark, St. Matthew's Gospel may be read as an attempt to establish Jesus' Jewish credentials as the hoped-for Messiah, *despite* any suggestion that by living and dying he did not conform to expectation. Hence, for example, the whole emphasis on Jesus' Davidic credentials in the first chapter of his Gospel, and his containment of Jesus' mission to Jews in his historical lifetime, with its universalization coming only with the Great Commission at Easter (Matt 28:19–20).

Without doubt, all this redefinitional activity was triggered by the injection of new confidence among Jesus' dejected disciples by the experience of his Resurrection from the dead, which cannot but have confirmed and clarified the flickering perception of his messianic identity. However, if the Resurrection was the stimulus for this

---

22. Notably as in Gal 6:14: "God forbid that I should glory in anything save the cross of our Lord Jesus Christ"; and Phil 2:5–8.

23. The Syro-phoenician woman of Mark 7:24–30.

kind of re-assessment of the significance of Jesus' historical life, the initial raw material for an entirely new understanding of Jesus' messianic identity of the kind that is presented first in Mark's Gospel, was certainly found in the string of episodes of his historical life and death.

Clearly, Jesus was not understood just to have actualized and confirmed the inherited conceptions of messiahship received from Second Temple Judaism. Here we have an unmistakable example of the way in which the lived experience of encounter with Jesus dictated the revision of received Second Temple conceptual expectations. We have, however, to ask whether the Resurrection was just the trigger for the revision of received conceptualizations, or whether the continuing experience initiated by the Resurrection itself, the perception of the continuing presence of Jesus through the medium of his "life-giving Spirit" also dictated the need to pursue this same end.

If the inherited Second Temple understanding of the meaning of the title "Messiah" came to be revised in the light of the experience of the words and works of the historical Jesus, in the way that was eventually expressed in systematic written form in the Gospel of Mark, this was certainly not the first or only revisionary process that it underwent. The primary Epistles of St. Paul provide evidence for the further modification of the received meaning of the title Messiah/Christ in response to the concrete experience of encounter in faith with the Raised Christ. Indeed, while clearly entertaining some kind of memory of the historical Jesus of a dispositional kind, and of the general tenor of what he said and did (with the obvious exception of his Crucifixion) Paul was apparently less interested in the incidents and episodes of Jesus historical life. His letters indicate that it was rather the experience of the Easter Jesus that was of more interest to him. This same interest among the first Christian believers in turn dictated their need to revise their use of the title Messiah/Christ so that it came to be nuanced and no longer just "received" as a rigidly set definition with its inherited meaning.

It has been forcefully argued by many scholars, for example, that, as the Christian mission spread beyond Jewish circles into the purely Greek-speaking Mediterranean world where specific notions of "messiahship" were no longer culturally current, the title (now as the Greek "Christ") tended to be used no longer as a title at all, but as little more than a kind of surname to refer to or *denote* Jesus. In other words, the contention is that its inherited meaning-content was quickly lost. St. Paul's letters indicate, for example, that it appears not to have been long before the title of "*the* Messiah/Christ" ceased to be used simply as a title. Once the article dropped away the former title came to be used in reference to Jesus more-or-less as a proper name. Thus, "Jesus *the* Christ," became simply "Jesus Christ." In this case, it no longer really "meant" anything of a specifically Jewish kind about the nature and role of the awaited "Messiah of Israel." Rather, it came to be used in a denotative way, but no longer connoted any particularly Jewish meaning content. "Jesus Christ" functioned as though this was a complete proper name.[24]

It has to be admitted at the outset that this argument is somewhat over-simplified. For example, Paul's own actual retention of the use of the definite article, at least on a couple of occasions where he refers to "the Christ," significantly in what is perhaps his last epistle (in Rom 9:3 and 5), indicates that "Christ" had *not* simply become a proper name. Furthermore, the representation of the primitive Christian mission as moving from a Jewish context, into an alleged non-Jewish environment also over-simplifies what was actually the case. Though it has been popular to think of the Epistle to the Romans as a final summing up of the main theological themes which had exercised Paul's mind through his life and ministry as a kind of "last will and testament," rather than a letter designed to address a specific set of problems in the church of a specific city (as in the case of all his other epistles), Romans has in more recent times been conceived as a missiological tract explicitly directed at solving a problem in Rome, precisely relating to the plight of the Jewish community. The known presence in Rome of a significantly large Jewish community immediately calls into question any talk of a simple movement from a Jewish context to a Gentile one. Karl Donfried has argued[25] that the immediate occasion for the writing of the Epistle to the Romans was the expulsion of the Jewish community from the city by the Emperor Claudius in AD 49, following disturbances that Suetonius says were caused by disputes over someone called "Chrestus" (Christus?). This edict would have encompassed those Jews who by this time were sympathetic to the Christian cause, and this would thus have left the synagogues in the hands of Godfearers and Gentile Christians. Even when the expelled Jewish community, including those Jews who by this time had become Christians, were allowed (apparently for economic reasons) to return to the city at around the time Paul wrote (ca. AD 55) they were given no public right of assembly. Donfried's thesis is that the immediate social issue that Paul was addressing in Romans therefore had prompted the question of "how it was that the promises made to Abraham were not being fulfilled among Jews, but among Gentiles?" Paul's answer is that the original promises were made to Abraham, not on the basis of the fulfillment of the Jewish law, but on the basis of his faith. Hence, Paul's fundamental thesis that justification is by grace through faith, not works of the law. Whatever we make of Donfried's thesis (and I happen to find it very compelling), the historical context of the writing of Romans to which he alerts us indicates that Jewish connections had certainly not been lost at this point in the Gentile mission. Whether or not we agree with Donfried's thesis concerning the occasion for Paul's writing to the Romans, it is incontrovertible that there

24. See for this: Dahl, "Die Messianität Jesu bei Paulus"; Kramer, *Christ, Lord, Son of God*; Hengel, "'Χριστός' in Paul"; Chester, "Messianism, Mediators and Pauline Christology"; also, Zetterholm, "Paul and the Missing Messiah."

25. Donfried, *The Romans Debate*.

was in fact a significant community of Jews living in Rome in the middle of the first century. In this case it would still have made perfectly good sense for the title Messiah/Christ to have been used by Paul in its original Jewish conative sense.[26]

This loans credibility to N. T. Wright's insistence that an alleged semantic change in the meaning content of the notion of "messiahship" did *not* occur at all. From the time of his Oxford D.Phil. thesis,[27] Wright has consistently argued that the inherited Jewish concept of "the Messiah" remained as unchanged as the alleged fixed and unchanging Second Temple concept of "resurrection." Indeed, he contends that Paul ensured that the "messianic" content of meaning inherited from its Jewish origin was in fact sustained into the Mediterranean mission; it therefore lost none of its received conventional meaning when it was taken into Gentile Christianity. In this case, early Christian experience had no significant impact upon its usage.

Wright's contention is therefore that the term "Messiah/Christ" continued to mean what it had meant prior to the Crucifixion. The resurrection experience had no significant conditioning impact upon it; rather, Jesus' resurrection simply acted reassuringly as an authenticating stamp that affirmed Jesus' identity as "the Messiah of Israel." While Paul fully appreciated that Jesus' messiahship took the unexpected form of one who had been crucified, and that for his obedience unto death on the Cross God had highly exalted him, thus confirming his messianic identity, the specific fixed meaning content of the title is nevertheless said by Wright to communicate the inherited "royal meaning" of the Messiah/Christ. Like the kings of Israel, he was one in whom the destiny and ultimate well-being of the entire people of Israel was bound up. The very concept of messiahship when applied to Jesus therefore involved the belief that Jesus was the one in whom the people of God are summed up. This alleged Pauline belief is said to have "played a massively important role in his entire theological understanding."[28]

Not least, this received Second Temple understanding of "incorporative Messiahship" is said to explain the distinctive Pauline phrase "in Christ." This "tells heavily of a messianic reference";[29] in other words, it is mistakenly interpreted simply as a proper name. Rather, references to being "in Christ" indicate that Jesus as the Messiah summed up Israel "*in*" himself." This is the import of the continuing *meaning* of the title Messiah/Christ when it is used in reference to him.

When it comes to pinning down the verbal origins of the phrase "in Christ" Wright therefore points to the royal idea that the corporate fortune of Israel resided

---

26. See Larry Hurtado's measured discussion in *Lord Jesus Christ*, 98–101. This is a point of convergence between N. T. Wright and Hurtado.

27. Wright, "*The Messiah and the People of God*."

28. Wright, *Paul and the Faithfulness of God*, 824.

29. Wright, *Paul and the Faithfulness of God*, 16.

"*in* the King" or "*in* David," "*in* the anointed one," or "*in* the son of Jesse."[30] Thus the destiny of Christians as the new Israel of God is found "*in* Christ" (in *the* Messiah).

In response to this view of things, A. J. M. Wedderburn has proposed an alternative source of Paul's incorporative language in God's promise to Abraham in Gen 18:18, which Paul actually quotes in Gal 3:8: "All the Gentiles will be blessed *in* you." Thus the redemption won by Christ was "in order that in Christ Jesus the blessing of Abraham might come to the Gentiles" (Gal 3:14). Thus, in Wedderburn's opinion, "Abraham and Christ are viewed as representative figures through whom God acts toward the human race."[31] Aquila H. J. Lee, in reviewing this material concerning the verbal origin of Paul's "incorporative" language, finds Wedderburn's suggestion "more persuasive than Wright's."[32] Clearly this speculative quest to find Old Testament precedents for Paul's incorporative phraseology invites a good deal of guesswork.

Wright himself notes that his explanation of Paul's use of the title "Christ" with its traditional inherited meaning has been challenged by Matthew V. Novenson,[33] who argues that the most appropriate category for understanding Paul's distinctive use of *Christos* is "honorific." In this case, it is used both as if it were simply a personal name but without losing something of its continuing messianic meaning. What Wright does not note, however, is Novenson's observation that many of the instances of the use of *Christos* in Paul do not *necessarily* have to be translated as "messiah" in its conative sense as an "incorporative" title; they could well still function denotatively as a kind of proper name. It is also significant that, despite the "royal" precedents cited by Wright, in the LXX "*Christos*/Messiah" is never used with the preposition "in."[34] The connection of Paul's alleged consistently used incorporative understanding of "messiahship" with alleged incorporative royal phrases found in Samuel–Kings therefore becomes difficult to sustain.

As it transpires, more recently Wright has forsaken his original account of the purely *verbal* origin of the phrase "in Christ" based on Samuel–Kings, preferring instead to point to the fact that the Second Temple hope of the corporate or general resurrection of all the righteous was anticipated "in Christ"—in other words, in the person of the single individual, as the Raised Messiah/Christ the corporate destiny of the people of God is fulfilled by a kind of experience-in-anticipation.[35] Thus, it is now for this reason that the "royal" or "incorporative" meaning of *Christos* does not disappear in Paul's writings."[36] In this way Wright is able to reaffirm his conviction

---

30. Citing precedents in Samuel–Kings. See for example, 2 Sam 19:43; 20:1; 1 Kgs 12:16.

31. Wedderburn, "Paul's Use of the Phrase 'In Christ,'" 91.

32. Lee, "Messianism and Messiah in Paul," 383.

33. Novenson, *Christ among the Messiahs*.

34. Novenson, *Christ among the Messiahs*, 124.

35. Wright, *Paul and the Faithfulness of God*, 830.

36. Wright, *Paul and the Faithfulness of God*, 824.

that the title did not lose its conventional meaning even when taken over by Gentile Christianity to the point of being used just as a denotative proper name.

Even so, despite the persistence of significantly large Jewish communities of the kind that we know existed in Rome in the middle of the first century AD, and Wright's defense of the notion that Paul sustained an inherited "incorporative" understanding of the title "Messiah/Christ," it remains true that in some contexts a denotative use of the former title, now as a proper name prevails. Especially when it is used identifyingly, its inherited traditional use as a title with an associated inherited set of meanings is put into eclipse. In other words, the actual experience of the Raised Christ insofar as it involved claims to identify his presence in faith in the form of the "Spirit of Christ" necessarily impacts upon this question of the early Christian use of the title-cum-proper name—as we shall see.

There is also another set of issues to be considered in assessing Wright's argument about the alleged sustained use of the title "Messiah/Christ" with its inherited Jewish incorporative meaning. It is important to note that Wright's interests come to focus on Paul's *theology*; that is to say, he is concerned to expound the way in which Paul *thought* of "the Messiah/Christ." Hence his focus is naturally on the *verbal* origin of Paul's thinking. It is the "incorporative *thought and language*"[37] that he says is so pervasive in Paul, and that he sets out to explain in terms of the belief that Jesus was the "incorporative Messiah." Thus he says: "The full range of Paul's 'incorporative' language can be thoroughly and satisfactorily explained on this hypothesis: that he regarded the people of God and the Messiah of God as so bound up together that what was true of one was true of the other."[38] In his concern to account for the *verbal* source of Paul's use of the phrase "in Christ" he thus unavoidably highlights the conative use of the title "Christ" at the expense of its denotative use as a kind of proper name.

However, an earlier generation of New Testament reflection on the witness of Paul proceeded on the basis that before "Paul the theologian" came "Paul the man of faith"; indeed, "Paul the man of faith" is logically prior to "Paul the theologian." Attempts to explain Paul's thinking are to be matched by Paul's more fundamental concern to commend his faith, and therefore to talk about it by describing it. Inevitably, this meant that he spoke on the basis of his experience. And this was not just his remembered experience on the Damascus Road, but his continuing experience of the presence of the Raised Christ encountered through the medium of the gift of Christ's "life-giving Spirit." He also reminded those to whom he wrote of their faith, and of the work of the same Spirit among them, and its behavioral obligations. Thus, in what is now a classic study of "The Corporate Christ," C. F. D. Moule set out to examine the

---

37. Wright, *Paul and the Faithfulness of God*, 825.

38. Wright, *Paul and the Faithfulness of God*, 826.

phenomenon which "for lack of a better term" he called "an understanding *and experience* of Christ as corporate."[39] Likewise, a few years before Moule wrote, James D. G. Dunn took great pains to emphasize the importance of Paul's *experience* in the development of his thought: "so far as Paul is concerned, his religious experience as a whole is characterized by a dependency on Jesus as Lord: it is not merely the experience of sonship, but the experience of Jesus' sonship, made possible by the Spirit of the Son; it is not merely the experience of grace, it is the experience of the grace of Christ; it is not merely the experience of the Spirit, of life and death, it is the experience of the Spirit of Christ . . ."[40] It is in the context of talking about the *experience* of faith that Dunn claims that Paul tends to use the title Christ less as a title and more as a kind of proper name. This emphasis on Paul's experience in the formulation of his faith and theology also means that we are mistaken to think of the Resurrection simply as an event of Paul's past which operated as the trigger for a theoretical development of theological ideas. It is certainly not as though Paul were the passive recipient of preformed fixed ideas for the most part received from Second Temple Judaism. Rather, his continuing religious experience of dependence on the Raised Christ continued to inform his thinking as well.

While Wright's concern is with the verbal source of Paul's "in Christ" language, which he develops as the basis of Paul's theology of "the Messiah," we therefore also have to reckon with the possibility that when Paul used the "in Christ" phrase he was also describing something which he claimed to know in faith through concrete experience. In this case, irrespective of any continuing conative meaning attaching to the term "Christ/Messiah," whether used as an honorific or otherwise, it was also used by Paul in a denotative sense *to identify and talk about* the experience of the distinctive nature of the continuing encounter with the presence of the Easter Jesus, both in his own experience and in the lives of the first believers. They were "in Christ" not just in a theoretical incorporative sense which they could appropriate in their abstract understanding, but in an ontic sense which they could thus claim to know in concrete experience. Their experience was interpreted by appeal to the identifying use of the proper name "Christ," as for example when they claimed to have to do with the "Spirit of Christ" and thus confessed to be "in Christ." In this way, that experience fed into their denotative use of "Christ" as a proper name, both referringly and, in the context of their Easter faith claims, also identifyingly. Once again, while Wright tends to pursue the *verbal* source of Paul's theology by unpacking the alleged inherited "incorporative" sense that is said to have attached to the Second Temple use of the title "Messiah/Christ," this is unfortunately at the expense of considering how the continuing Easter experience of the presence of the Raised Christ might itself have impacted on his use of the title, so as now, at least sometimes, it came to be used as a proper name.

39. Moule, *The Origin of Christology*, 46 (italics added).

40. Dunn, *Jesus and the Spirit*, 342.

Larry Hurtado, has put his finger on this very problem in Wright's account of things. In questioning how Paul was able to speak of the Spirit of Jesus as also the Holy Spirit/Spirit of God in Rom 8:9–11, Hurtado notes that Wright at one point attributes this to the way in which the post-Easter Jesus was "personally and powerfully present," and to "vivid experiences" of the presence and power of Jesus.[41] Hurtado observes, howewever, that "Wright seems curiously reticent"[42] to elaborate what he means by this, and opts instead then to explain how Paul arrived at both Jesus' "divine identity" and a matching pneumatological "divine identity" by appeal, not to the quality of the post-Easter experiences themselves, but once again to an inherited Old Testament theme—the inherited theological theme of the return of YHWH to Zion.[43] Hurtado notes therefore that "Wright focuses on the conceptual content of 'pneumatology,' leaving the specifics of the phenomena in question somewhat vague."[44] However, in the absence of a reference to some kind of distinctive experiential trigger, Hurtado concludes "we are left without an adequate answer to the question of *how* Jesus supposedly came to be seen as the personal and embodied return of YHWH."[45] Once again, this deficit is almost certainly because Wright has difficulty in according sufficient importance to the actual post-Easter experience which led to the faith claims of the first Christians.

While Hurtado finds Wright's reticence to focus on the phenomena of the post-Easter experience somewhat "curious," it is in fact of a piece with Wright's methodological commitment to establishing the Resurrection as a remembered historical event of the past, the occurrence of which he seeks to prove using the historical reason and the techniques of critical historical research. In this way, Wright's appeal is to the evidence of the appearances and the tradition of the empty tomb as the sufficient trigger of subsequent faith claims and theology. Wright is nothing if not consistent. The experience of the activity of the Spirit is therefore excluded as a datum of Easter faith. Even the strong sense of Jesus presence during worship and prayer is said to be important but essentially secondary. As a consequence, a Pauline "theology of the divine Spirit" is worked out, along with a theology of Jesus' "divine identity" with the help of the inherited Old Testament theme of the return of YHWH to Zion, employing deductively-driven processes of the kind that John Henry Newman spoke of as "paper logic." The inevitable outcome is to produce a somewhat airborne and abstract Pauline theology, even of the "divine Spirit," that does not really touch down in the continuing

41. Wright, *Paul and the Faithfulness of God,* 654–55 and 690.

42. Hurtado, "YHWH's Return to Zion," 423.

43. Wright, *Paul and the Faithfulness of God,* 727.

44. Hurtado, "YHWH's Return to Zion," 424.

45. Hurtado, "YHWH's Return to Zion," 424.

experience of faith, let alone admit of any conceptual coloring of the interpretative language called forth by that experience.

This means that, while Paul's Damascus Road experience is said by Wright to be the trigger for the Pauline theological development of the concept of the "incorporative Christ," we should not simply assume that the continuing experience of the presence of Christ through the medium of his Spirit played little or no part in conditioning his use of language, not least his use of the phrase "in Christ." Furthermore, we cannot simply reduce Paul's faith to a kind of propositional belief *that* Jesus' Resurrection *had* occurred—which then triggered a lively process of theological reflection on its meaning. In relation to the understanding of the "incorporative" meaning content of the title "Messiah/Christ," it is not just that *the events of Jesus' death and resurrection compelled Paul in this direction, and caused him to read old texts in new ways.*[46] On the contrary, what compelled Paul to speak of being "in Christ" was in fact the concrete corporate experience of the life of faith, and the perception of the continuing presence of the Raised Jesus through the medium of his Spirit among the community of the baptized. Inevitably, they claimed to know the Spirit of Christ (using "Christ" as a proper name) and thus to be "in Christ," once again thereby apparently describing a concrete experience by appeal to a proper name. A theoretical understanding of the alleged *meaning* of Paul's incorporative language, either by recourse simply to Old Testament precedents, or by recourse to the inherited belief that the general resurrection had been actualized in the person of Jesus the Christ, can hardly be lifted out of the experiential context of the faith and life of the first believers. In this context, the name "Christ" came into use to identify and describe the way in which their continuing relationship with him was actualized. In a sense it was inevitable that, in the context of identifying Christ's presence in faith and spelling out its implications for normative Christian behavior, the inherited title necessarily came to be used in a denotative way as a proper name.

Thus, in Rom 16:7, when Paul observed that Andronicus and Junia were "in Christ" before him, he was not necessarily just reminding them in a theoretical sense of the way in which "the Messiah incorporated all the people of God in himself." Almost certainly, in the first instance he was simply speaking referentially as he reminded them of the historical event that initiated their continuing Christian experience—their initial entry into the life of the community of the baptized and, at the same time, their concrete incorporation through the gift of the Spirit into the transcendental life of the Raised Christ. Something was thus being described, and the title "Christ" was necessarily now being used in fact less as a title and more denotatively as a proper name. We have to reckon with the possibility that when reminded of this, Andronicus and Junia may have thought, not in a *theoretical* way of the *meaning* of the term "Christ" in relation to its royal connotations on the basis of precedents in Samuel–Kings, so much as in relation to their concrete experience of belonging to the Christian community

---

46. Wright, *Paul and the Faithfulness of God*, 827 (italics original).

and at the same time to their sharing in the continuing life of Christ himself whom they might well have imagined to be "at the right hand of the Father" from whence he sent the gift of his Spirit. Paul's references to life "in Christ," in other words, do not just carry a burden of theoretical meaning derived from Samuel–Kings, or even from belief in Jesus' Resurrection as the anticipation of future general resurrection of all the righteous. They also have to do with the nature of the more concretely descriptive *experience* of the life of faith among the baptized.

In this case, Jesus' Resurrection may not have just *confirmed* Jesus' messianic identity in somewhat abstract and deductive terms; rather, the nature of the continuing resurrection experience of the presence of Christ may itself account more directly for their use of the term "in Christ." In this case, we definitely have a denotative use of the name "Christ" which may not bring with it any immediate overtones deriving from its Old Testament use. We have to take account of the possibility that, instead of the Resurrection providing a kind of authenticating stamp to a received *view* of the theoretical meaning of the role of the awaited Messiah/Christ, it actually infused a new content of associated meaning relating to the name "Christ" as a consequence of its use in describing and identifying their concrete post-Easter experience.

All the while, it is not just that experience is interpreted using inherited concepts, titles, and names. Rather, experience itself also dictates the modification of the language that is deemed appropriate to it. To put this in another way: faith is normative for theology; it is not that, vice versa, inherited theology is normative for faith, still less that faith must conform to inherited theology.

In all this, it is therefore important to note that language is the handmaid of experience. Despite the interpretative challenges of Paul's "in Christ" phrase, one thing seems abundantly clear: insofar as Paul speaks of being "in Christ," he is not talking speculatively or abstractly and theoretically using an inherited language, but is actually describing an important facet of the newfound concrete experience of the on-going reality of Christ in his post-Easter life. Whatever we are able to make of it, it is unmistakable that this distinctive language, insofar as it was suggestive of a kind of incorporation into the transcendent life of Christ, flowed out of and was uniquely grounded in the Easter experience.

Certainly, resurrection belief understood as Wright bids us think of it, as the restoration and return of a person who had previously been dead to *this* world in physical and material form, would hardly have been possible without an alleged "strictly limited," clear and distinct, received definition of "resurrection" in these specific terms. But this begs the question as to whether another form of resurrection experience, involving the perception in faith of the heavenly glorified and exalted Christ, who was understood to be at the "right hand of the Father," and whose earthly presence was concretely known through the medium of the gift of his Spirit, may have called for the revision of this allegedly received definition of "resurrection," and indeed, any other inherited conceptualization of resurrection belief. We shall therefore progress this discussion only by looking carefully at what the first generation of believers actually had to say about the nature of their Easter experiences.

4

The Appearances Tradition

There is rarely these days any dispute about the most appropriate point of insertion into the New Testament for commencing a discussion of Christ's Resurrection. The earliest piece of documentary evidence we have is the list of appearances now found in 1 Cor 15:3–8, in which Paul reminds the Corinthians of the content of his original proclamation to them when he first visited their city around AD 49. This "kerygmatic summary" lists those to whom the Raised Christ is said to have appeared, apparently in chronological order, starting *first* with Peter and the Twelve, *then* to over five hundred at once, *then* to James and the Apostles, and *finally* ending with the appearance to Paul himself.

Paul's mention of his own seeing of the Raised Christ at the end of this list is apparently the episode with which we are also acquainted from Luke's three accounts of it in Acts, where it is said to have occurred on the Road to Damascus.[1] Its inclusion here is important as the one first-hand report of an Easter experience from an eyewitness that we have. All the rest are second-hand accounts of the experiences of others, reported at some remove from the time of their occurrence. However, it is noteworthy that Paul says that the kernel of the tradition he had earlier passed on, and which he rehearses again in 1 Cor 15:3–8, is something that had in turn been received by him, even earlier than AD 49. In 1926 Gerhard Kittel pointed out that, in using the words "I handed on . . . what I received," Paul was using an established technical formula for the handing on of a received tradition.[2] That this really is a piece of early tradition that Paul had received from others is confirmed by the inclusion within it of language that is not characteristically Pauline.[3] It is therefore authenticated in linguistic terms

1. In Acts 9:3–9; 22:6–11; and 26:12–18.

2. Kittel, *Die Probleme des palästinenischen Spätjudentums*, 63. The words "I received/I deivered" (*parelabon/paredōka*) are the Greek equivalents of the rabbinic terms *qibbel min* and *masar lᵉ*. See also Davies, *Paul and Rabbinic Judaism*, 248–49, and McDonald, *Kerygma and Didache*, 112–16.

3. E.g., "sins" in the genitive plural rather than "sin" as a single all-pervading gone-wrongness of the

as something that originated from the hand of somebody else before him and which he had indeed received.

We are therefore able to say with a good deal of confidence that this is a very early piece of normative tradition, even though Paul himself obviously felt free to add to it. As the tradition he had received it obviously did not include his own experience of the appearance of the Raised Christ, or his passing comment in v. 6 that most of the five hundred were still alive; the observation that some of the five hundred "were still alive" can only have been added by Paul himself at the time he wrote to the Corinthians. It is even more significant that Paul added his own Easter experience to the list of appearances he had received, for this was apparently in the belief that his experience was essentially the same as that of the other apostolic witnesses. Indeed, it is important for Paul that this should be so because, even though he had not been directly acquainted with the historical Jesus, his own claim to apostleship, with a status equal to theirs, is grounded in an experience of the Easter Jesus that therefore needs also to be essentially the same as theirs. His own Easter experience was what grounded and authenticated his claim to an apostolic status no different from theirs: "Am I not an Apostle, did I not see the Raised Christ?" (1 Cor 9:1).

The question of particular interest to us right now for the development of a systematic theology of resurrection faith is: what can we discern about the nature of these Easter experiences listed by Paul, and particularly about the nature of the Object of perception that is said to have been religiously encountered in these experiences? Then there is the closely related epistemological question concerning the more precise manner of the human perception of them.

When N. T. Wright comes to the discussion of this early Pauline account of the Easter appearances, he acknowledges that the Greek word ōphthē, which we usually translate "he appeared" or "he allowed himself to be seen," is of particular significance. Ōphthē is repeated four times in the passage in relation to each of the individuals and groups to whom Jesus is said to have shown himself to have been alive, including the appearance to Paul himself. The use of the same word elsewhere, and cognates of it, especially in the Septuagint translation of the Hebrew Scriptures into Greek (LXX), suggests that it could be used of the appearance of natural material objects, such as the tops of mountains which, having been hidden, "appear" as the water levels recede in the story of the Flood (Gen 8:5). Alternatively, the word is used of the unsurprising appearance of a person before somebody else or in a particular place, in much the same way as someone might today be said to "show up" in some place, or "appear" before a magistrate in a law court. It is also used in much the same way, but in specifically religious contexts. For example, three times per year "all the males" of Israel are commanded "to appear" before the Lord their God "at the place that he will choose" (Deut 16:16). Likewise, in Acts 7:26 Moses is said to have "appeared" in an entirely

---

world; "the twelve"; "according to the scriptures" (rather than "as it is written"); the verb *egegetai*— "was raised." These are all uncharacteristic of Paul. See Jeremias, *The Eucharistic Words of Jesus,* 101–2.

natural way in a historical incident at a place where two Israelites were fighting, and is said to have tried to reconcile them. Clearly, in these cases the word simply refers to the appearance of human persons at a particular place, in a way that implies a straightforward visual seeing, or the appearance of some other material reality that offers itself to be straightforwardly seen and perceptually known. In other words, it is a word that is used in the context of narrating descriptive accounts of historical events.

However, the same word is used more often in Scripture of the appearance of the divine, a revelatory appearance, or disclosure of the formerly hidden reality of God. Of eighty-five instances of the use of this word in the Septuagint, over half of them have to do with the appearance of Yahweh, sometimes as Yahweh's glory, and sometimes as Yahweh's angel, which, upon reflection, is understood to have been an encounter with Yahweh himself. For example, in Gen 12:7, the Lord is said "to appear" to Abram. Sometimes the same word is used of theologically pregnant "dream appearances" such as the appearance of the ladder and angels in Jacob's dream in Gen 31:13. Another example is the appearance of Yahweh to Solomon in a dream in which Solomon is said to ask for the gift of wisdom (1 Kgs 3:5). In other words, apart from the ordinary and more literal or mundane sense of its use in the context of narrating historical events involving human participants, the word is used analogically in relation to a theophany.

One might be forgiven for associating the appearance of the raised and exalted Christ after having been dead for three days with this latter kind of religious phenomenon. In this case we might speak of the appearance of the Raised Christ as a Christophany to signal its family resemblance with the clearly religious Old Testament counterpart of a theophany. Many scholars are of this view. One very recent example is that of Daniel Smith, who, in relation to the use of *ōphthē* in the Septuagint, says: "When I Corinthians 15:5–8 uses the same language, it seems appropriate to infer from the way theophanies are described in the Septuagint that the risen Jesus was thought of as belonging to that realm from which theophanies and angelophanies originate."[4]

Given this possibility, N. T. Wright's treatment of the use of this term in Paul's early Easter tradition is surprising, though in another sense entirely predictable. After citing both the "mundane" and the "heavenly" possibilities with regard to the meaning of *ōphthē*, Wright opts for the former: the seeing of the Raised Jesus is said to have been more akin to the visual seeing of a natural object, rather than to the perception of a revelatory reality "from heaven."[5] While he does at least acknowledge the theoretical possibility that *ōphthē* could be used in relation to what I have been calling a Christophany, he does not enter into any argument to rule out the possibility that the word is

---

4. Smith, *Revisiting the Empty Tomb*, 15. Among others, see Collins, *First Corinthians*, 528 and 535; Thiselton, *The First Epistle to the Corinthians*, 1198; Schrage, *Der erste Brief an die Korinther*, 47–48; and Fitzmyer, *First Corinthians*, 549.

5. *RSG*, 323.

being used in this way in 1 Cor 15:3–8. That it might be intended by Paul to refer to a visionary appearance of the otherworldly raised and exalted Christ "from heaven" is therefore not seriously considered.

But Wright's own preference for assimilating the meaning of *ōphthē* in 1 Cor 15:3–8 to the seeing of a natural object of this world is not really defended in any way either; he simply acknowledges the more "heavenly" or visionary alternative as a possibility, and then very conveniently forgets about it. Indeed, after signaling that *ōphthē* may be translated *either* as "he appeared" (the deponent meaning), with Jesus himself as the active agent, or as "he was seen" (the aorist passive, the person doing the seeing being in the dative), in which case Jesus becomes the passive object of a purely human seeing (e.g., by Peter or whoever), he nevertheless quickly moves on to indicate a preferential option for the view that Jesus "was seen." Given these two possibilities: "The fact that [*ōphthē*] is followed in each case by a dative indicates that 'appeared to' may be marginally preferable. However, the verb is passive, and its normal meaning would be 'was seen by.'"[6]

Then, at the end of his discussion of the possible meaning of *ōphthē*, he declares that the meaning for Paul and for the tradition he quotes "must be judged on wider criteria than linguistic usage alone."[7] However, at this point, even though he says that this matter cannot be judged on linguistic grounds alone, on the whole topic of "seeing" the risen Jesus he commends an "important essay" by Stephen Davis.[8] This is apparently without questioning the fact that Davis argues his case on the basis of the linguistic usage of the verbs "see," "perceive," and "know" in the New Testament appearance traditions.[9] It is not a surprise that in this article Davis argues for a straightforward visual seeing by the first witnesses of the resurrected Jesus in the form of a matter-of-fact material body.

If this is a matter that cannot be settled on linguistic grounds alone, we may appropriately look for "wider criteria" concerning what Paul may have understood *ōphthē* to indicate. As it transpires a third meaning of *ōphthē* is possible. In the Old Testament tradition, the passive form may also be understood "as a paraphrase of the name of God."[10] In this case the meaning becomes "God . . . let himself be seen." In the case of the Resurrection of Christ, the meaning would be "Christ let himself be seen," or perhaps better, "God let Christ be seen." Elsewhere, the divine initiative is clear; for example, in Acts 1:3, where it is said that "Jesus presented himself alive" to the apostles "appearing to them." More importantly, Paul elsewhere speaks of his Damascus Road

6. *RSG*, 323.

7. *RSG*, 323. Marxsen is of a similar view: "It is hardly possible to establish the precise meaning with ultimate certainty from the form itself" ("The Resurrection of Jesus," 27).

8. *RSG*, 323 n.32.

9. Davis, "'Seeing' the Risen Jesus," 126–47. As we shall see below, this article by Davis includes a similarly ambivalent disucussion of the meaning of *ōphthē*, but with a clearly stated preference for interpreting it in terms of a purely occular seeing of an entirely ordinary kind.

10. Marxsen, "The Resurrection of Jesus," 27.

experience in terms of the fact that "God revealed" his Son to (or in) him (Gal 1:16). Clearly, there are other indications, which suggest the importance of the divine initiative, not just in raising Jesus from the dead, which is very securely rooted in the tradition, but also in the disclosure of his resurrection to the first witnesses.[11] As a consequence, in some of the literature on this subject, it is contended that in 1 Cor 15:3–8 *ōphthē* is to be understood as a "divine passive" conveying the meaning that "God has let Christ become visible." In this case, the divine revelatory initiative is with God rather than with Christ himself, and this resonates with those elements of the tradition that underline the divine initiative in actually raising Jesus from the dead.[12]

However, for Wright the concluding position is the contrary—that Jesus does not reveal himself from the radical hiddenness of heaven, as it were; rather, after his resurrection he is more passively "there," as any ordinary object of this world might be, to be straightforwardly and visually observed and scrutinized. In this, Wright's position is at odds with a substantial international consensus of contemporary New Testament scholarship which holds that *ōphthē* in 1 Cor 15:3–8 should be translated "he appeared" or "allowed himself to be seen" (with the initiative lying with the Raised Jesus himself or with God) rather than simply "he was seen" or passively observed by human observers (with the epistemic initiative lying with them). In other words, the consensus is that the epistemic initiative resides with the Raised Christ himself who *reveals* his presence; it is not just that "he showed up" and others saw him. Clearly, to think of the appearances as revelatory, and the perception of them as essentially religious in nature, is inimical to Wright's insistence that the Resurrection is to be handled as a historical event that is essentially similar to any other event of human history.

Also, it is not insignificant that Wright also passes over any mention of the fact that *ōphthē* is also used in the New Testament of the mountain-top appearance of Moses and Elijah with Jesus in the story of the Transfiguration (Mark 9:4). One does not necessarily have to subscribe to the view that the Transfiguration story could possibly be a misplaced resurrection appearance story to accept the suggestion that its editorial placing by Mark, in the context of the lead up to the passion narrative, suggests that it can be understood heuristically at least as a prefiguring of the good news of the resurrection and exaltation that awaits Jesus beyond his trial and crucifixion. In any event, in the Transfiguration story Jesus appears in shining light and within the enveloping Shekinah, symbolizing the nearer presence of God, accompanied by Moses and Elijah. These heroes of the Jewish tradition are almost certainly placed there not just to flank Jesus as symbolic tokens of "the law and the prophets" as is often said; rather, they are

---

11. See O'Collins, *Believing in the Resurrection*, 62: "All the contemporary translations that I have checked (in English, French, German, and Italian) render the verb as 'appeared' (or its equivalent in other languages)." See also O'Collins' very thorough review of this issue in "The Appearances of the Risen Christ."

12. This is argued for example by Wolfgang Schrage in *Der erste Brief an die Korinther*, 47–48.

able to *appear* there precisely because in the received Jewish tradition they *could* both be placed there, given that both were believed to enjoy an immortal status in heaven.[13] The Transfiguration story in this way thus prefigures by anticipation the eternal destiny with God that also awaits Jesus himself beyond the grave. Curiously, apart from passing over the significance of this for understanding the meaning of *ōphthē* as it is used in relation to Jesus' appearances, Wright has very little at all to say about the Transfiguration in *The Resurrection of the Son of God*.

The fact that Wright somewhat idiosyncratically opts for the translation "he was seen" rather than "he appeared" might be taken to be an entirely arbitrary statement of preference, save for the fact that it is almost certainly dictated by the need for the appearances to conform to his *a priori* methodological commitment to the handling of the Resurrection purely as a historical event of this world of space and time. The Easter appearances have to conform to, or be congruent with, the category of historical event. If the Resurrection must be understood to mean that Jesus' physical body was restored to this world, then there is little alternative than to think of the human perception of it in terms of the seeing of an object that is of a piece with the seeing of any other material object in space and time. Once again, Wright's "default setting," to which his account of things regularly and almost automatically returns, seems to be operating determinatively to secure this specific outcome.

This position is arrived at despite the fact that there are elements of the appearances tradition in the New Testament that clearly point us in the direction of the alternative possibility of a Christophany. Mark has no story of an appearance; the women are simply directed by the angel to tell the disciples to "go into Galilee" where they will see him (Mark 16:7).[14] However, in Matthew 28, which provides us with the earliest written narrative account we have of an appearance to the disciples, the Raised Christ appears to the assembled disciples on a mountain in Galilee, where he is said to claim to possess "all authority *in heaven* and on earth." Given the apparent ambiguity of this appearance, which allowed some to doubt (Matt 28:17), James D. G. Dunn is of the view that this story does not permit its categorization either as a Christophany (a revelatory appearance from heaven) or as a Christepiphany (a more earthly and

---

13. Elijah was assumed into heaven in the story of 2 Kings 2 and the story of Moses' assent into heaven is found in the *Assumption of Moses*. Interestingly, Moses is said to "stand and serve on high" in the Tannaitic midrash *Sifre to Deuteronomy* 357, 428; and either the *Assumption of Moses* or a legend based upon it is quoted in the New Testament in Jude 9. Wright's insistence that the Hebrew tradition had no place for an interest in immortality with God is far from correct. There is no reference that ever says that Moses, Abraham, Isaac, or David died and went to Sheol. This fate tended to be reserved for more sinister characters. See Barr, *The Garden of Eden*, 29.

14. The important issue of the theological significance of this omission will be discussed in the following chapter.

visual appearance).[15] However, the apparent ambiguity of the appearance narrated by Matthew did not trigger a debate about the precise nature of the appearance so much as about whether there was in fact an appearance at all. For, as Matthew indicates, the apparent ambiguity of the experience triggered a response of faith in some but in others doubt (Matt 28:17). This suggests that we should think of it in terms of a revelatory Christophany rather than the more matter-of-fact kind of visual seeing associated with a Christepiphany. As Reginald H. Fuller says: This means "Matthew's appearance to the eleven is a Christophany of the resurrected and ascended One."[16] In fact, in this tableau appearance, the only indication Jesus that may have been walking around on the ground as somebody restored to life in this world, and thus as an epistemically passive object of visual sight, is the phrase "he drew near and said" (Matt 28:18). But this may well be an editorial phrase of Matthew's composition. Without it the appearance to the assembled disciples on the mountain seems to be much more exalted, "from heaven" as it were. Matthew, unlike Luke, has no consecutive scheme of resurrection appearances followed then by ascension to heaven. Indeed, the oldest Easter traditions barely draw a distinction between Easter and Ascension in the way Luke does. For example, Paul in Phil 2:8–11 passes from Jesus' obedience unto death and Crucifixion to his exaltation by God. This use of elision is also sustained in Hebrews, where "having made purification for sins," Jesus is said to go straight to sit down "at the right hand of the Majesty on high" (Heb 1:3).[17] In John, likewise, the accent is on exaltation to the Father as the meaning of resurrection.[18] Indeed, the divine Spirit is given to the assembled disciples in the upper room when the Raised Christ first appears to them (John 20:22).[19] Certainly, in Matthew the Raised Christ appears as One to whom *all* authority in heaven and on earth has been given. We note the universalist coloring of the repetition of "all" in this passage, as in "*all* power" and the command to go to teach "*all* nations," to observe "*all* things" (Matt 28:18–20).[20] Understandably, when the disciples saw him, the immediate response was that "they worshipped him" (Matt 28:17). Moreover, an element of perceptual freedom seems to have been part of an experience in which sufficient was revealed to allow some to respond in faith and thus to worship him, but insufficient to compel the assent of everyone present. Whatever occurred is rendered somewhat mysteriously ambiguous

15. Dunn, *Jesus and the Spirit*, 124: "it is one resurrection narrative in the gospels which cannot be firmly assigned to one category or the other." The useful distinction between a Christophany and Christepiphany was originally made in Lindblom, *Gesichte und Offenbarungen*, 104–11.

16. Fuller, *Resurrection Narratives*, 82.

17. See also Heb 8:1: "we have such a high priest, who sat down on the right hand of the throne of the Majesty in the heavens."

18. Note may be taken of the significance of the use of *anabainein* (ascend) in John 3:13 and 6:62.

19. Significantly, with the gift of the Spirit being associated with Jesus' breath. For John, by contrast with Luke, the gift of the Spirit does not have to be delayed until Pentecost but is already bestowed by the Raised Christ in the first Upper Room appearance.

20. See Evans, *Resurrection and the New Testament*, 88.

by being described as something that precipitated *faith* for some of those present but not for others, for "some doubted" or "hesitated" to make the judgment of faith.[21] We should note that this element in Matthew's account of the appearance of Jesus upon a mountain in Galilee does not on the face of it appear to suggest a straightforward visual seeing which would have been available to anybody who was there with eyes to see. If we are to categorize it, we are obliged to think less in terms of a clear and distinct earthly "manifestation" of Jesus' presence (a Christepiphany) and more in terms of the category of a revelatory "mystery" (a Christophany). However, Wright ignores this theologically significant item entirely by speaking of all the appearances in terms of mundane "meetings" with Jesus, of which this is but one. This hardly does justice to the more mysterious elements of the story.

In any event, Wright's tendency to flatten out the appearance stories, and to milk them of any suggestion of their mysterious and revelatory character, becomes transparently clear in his handling of the appearance narratives in Luke and John. Since the rise of redaction criticism in the mid-twentieth century, the usual conclusion of many New Testament scholars has been that these later Gospels tend to make the appearances less visionary and ethereal and more concrete and material.[22] For example, when the first believers are initially said by Luke to have thought they were seeing a "spirit" (*pneuma*), in order to allay their "fear and doubt," Luke has Jesus invite them to look at his hands and feet, and to "touch and see . . . for a spirit does not have flesh and bones as you see that I have" (Luke 24:39).[23] The Raised Jesus then asks for something to eat and actually eats broiled fish and honeycomb.[24] The message is clear that the Resurrection involves the restoration of the crucified Jesus *himself*, and not just a more ethereal duplicate. This understanding of a "spirit" seems congruent with Luke's account of Peter's appearance after his release from chains in *Acts* 12. When Rhoda reported that Peter had emerged from prison and was standing before the gate at the house of Mary, the mother of John, those assembled and at prayer at first thought she was mad, and then declared "it is his angel,"[25] for they assumed that the real Peter was still in prison.

21. C. H. Dodd observed that "the appearance of the Lord does not bring full or immediate conviction to the beholders . . . the recognition of the Lord by his disciples almost always comes with the implication that such recognition was neither immediate nor inevitable." "The Appearances of the Risen Christ," 10 and 33.

22. This is the view, for example, of Evans, *Resurrection and the New Testament*; Fuller, *Resurrection Narratives*; Perrin, *The Resurrection Narratives*; and Morgan, "Flesh is Precious."

23. Luke 24:39.

24. Luke 24:42–43.

25. Acts 12:15.

For Luke, the Crucified Jesus emerged from the tomb, not as a nonbodily presence, but in a manner as concretely material as Peter's reported release from prison.[26]

It seems clear that the materializing features of Luke's story are clearly designed to allay fear and doubt, for this is explicitly declared in the text itself when Jesus said to them: "Why are you frightened, and why do doubts arise in your hearts?" (24:38). And prior to the eating of fish and honeycomb it is observed that he spoke to them: "While in their joy they were disbelieving and still wondering" (24:41). To suggest that these materializing elements accrued to the tradition in the course of the apologetic attempt to shore up wavering faith in the face of doubt is not without textual warrant.

In John, which may be more important for Luke than most scholars are prepared to admit,[27] the Raised Jesus can also in principle be touched and, as in Luke, he likewise actually offers his wounds to be physically examined, this time by an initially doubting Thomas (John 20:27).

While this materializing tendency in both Luke and John may be interpreted as a redactional development of the original tradition, designed precisely for the apologetic purpose either of commending resurrection belief in the face of fear and doubt among early believers, or of meeting the need to defend resurrection belief to answer disbelieving taunts about ghostly apparitions, Wright tries to argue in the opposite direction.[28] It is these narratives of the Easter appearances in the later Gospels of Luke and John, in which the Easter events are represented in concrete mundane terms, that are said to preserve the original and more authentic tradition. Despite the apparent lateness of their location in the narrative traditions of the New Testament, they thus provide Wright with the template for understanding all the appearances.

However, despite these materializing tendencies in Luke and John, other elements of the tradition of Easter appearances in fact point away from its presentation as a

26. I have deliberately avoided using the term "ghost" to translate Luke's use of *pneuma*, which is more correctly translated simply as "spirit." It is probably significant that Luke does not use the typical Greek terms *phasma, phantasma,* or *eidōlon,* or even *daimōn* for phantom, apparition or the ghostly presence of a dead person. While stressing the corporeality of the Raised Jesus by contrast with a mere *pneuma,* this term somehow does not have the negative overtones of contemporary talk of "ghosts."

27. There is the possibility that Luke, having used the basic narrative of Mark, had to turn elsewhere for a Resurrection tradition, given that Mark has no appearance narrative. It may be that if Luke wrote after John he in fact used either John 20–21, or the same source as John used for the appearance stories of his narrative. Luke quite deliberately relocates the Resurrection away from Galilee, however, and thus places essentially the same story that John has in John 21 in his own Gospel in Jesus' historical lifetime (Luke 5:2–9) as an incident involving Peter and a great catch of fish, rather than as an Easter appearance story. See the discussion of this in chapter 6 below.

28. Wright passes over the fact that Luke also tends to make angels more material as agents in historical events, by contrast with Matthew's "dream angels." Likewise in the Pentecost story, Luke ensures that the manifestations of the Pentecostal Spirit are not "like tongues of fire" but "tongues, like fire."

straightforward, matter-of-fact visual seeing or manifestation, or to use Wright's preferred term, "meeting" with Jesus. In Luke's three accounts of Paul's experience on the Damascus Road in Acts,[29] the appearance of Jesus is described using the images of a light and a voice (9:3–4); indeed, it is explicitly described as a "heavenly vision" (26:19) rather than a straightforward meeting with Jesus as a fellow traveler who is met walking in the opposite direction along the same dusty road. Once again there is some confusion within Luke's three accounts as to whether those who accompanied Paul also saw and heard, or simply saw but heard nothing, or else heard something but saw nothing. In other words, a similar kind of epistemic ambiguity or interpretative freedom, if not confusion, is a feature of Luke's presentation of these traditions as has been noted to have been also the case in Matthew's account of the appearance to the gathered group on a mountain in Galilee.

Wright, however, in his concern to accept the historicity of the more materializing accounts of the appearances to the apostolic band, neutralizes the historical significance of Luke's presentation of Paul's visionary experiences. Rather, Wright is committed to the view that Paul "had seen the risen Jesus in person, and that his understanding of who this Jesus was included the firm belief that he possessed a transformed but still physical body."[30] Luke's accounts of Paul's conversion in Acts are said to be major literary developments in the tradition purely at the hands of Luke himself who is "ever the artist."[31] They are typical Hellenistic literary constructs modeled on the calling of the prophets.[32] Even the discrepancies of detail in the three versions of Paul's Damascus Road experience are not the product of confusion accompanying a mysterious event which was by nature open to being interpreted somewhat ambiguously between Paul himself and those who were travelling with him. They are to be explained as "the Hellenistic convention of style according to which variation in narrative lends interest."[33] In other words, while the accounts of the more concrete and materializing appearances in Luke's Gospel are handled as though they alone are realistically accurate, Luke's account of Paul's experience as a "heavenly vision" is represented by Wright as being just a story; the invention of Luke himself. Thus, instead of concluding that the materializing and concretizing tendency of the Easter experiences in Luke's Gospel was a development of the tradition, the situation is reversed; it is Luke's own tendency to make Paul's experience more ethereal and visionary that is to be understood as a purely literary development. Whether the implication is that

29. These are the three accounts, with some internal discrepancies, that are found in Acts 9, 22, and 26.

30. *RSG*, 398.

31. *RSG*, 393.

32. *RSG*, 392. For example in Ezek 1:28, where Ezekiel fell on his face, or Daniel's vision in Dan 10:5–11. We might note also that the call "Saul, Saul . . ." of the heavenly voice is reminiscent of "Samuel, Samuel . . ." in the calling of Samuel. Alas, for Luke, John the Baptist is the last of the prophets; whether Paul can be so conveniently slotted into the prophetic tradition may be problematic for Luke.

33. *RSG*, 388.

Wright thinks that Paul's encounter with the Raised Christ on the Damascus Road was really equally as concrete and purely visual as Luke's accounts of the appearances to the first witnesses in his Gospel, or whether it was in fact an experience of an entirely different quality to theirs, is not altogether clear.

It is important to note at this point that, even if Wright's hypothesis about Luke's literary development of the presentation of the Damascus Road episode involving Paul could be proved to be right, this does not really help his cause. If it is the case that Luke's account of Paul's Damascus Road experience is a literary invention, then the original thesis of *The Resurrection of the Son of God*, that the Easter experience of the first Christians can be interpreted in "only one way" given the alleged unwavering mind-set of Second Temple Judaism is here entirely undermined by his own argument. Here at least we have an author, Luke, who is said by Wright himself to have been prepared to present the Easter experience of Paul as a "heavenly vision," involving a light and a voice. The possibility that the Resurrection could be thought of, and actually narrated, in what is admitted to be more "Hellenistic" and heavenly terms in the first century is thus also tacitly conceded. Clearly, it was not just Josephus whose mentality was colored by Hellenistic influences, but now on Wright's own admission, Luke as well. In this case, Wright allows the "spirit of Hellenism" to condition one of the key presentations of the experience of the Raised Christ, which was originally declared to be an impossibility. The fact is that instead of being Luke's own literary invention, his account of Paul's "heavenly vision" may preserve an important feature of all the early Easter experiences insofar as Jesus seems to have appeared in a transcendently transformed way "from heaven."

In this case, some attempt must be made to explain why Luke resorted to this alleged strategy of portraying the experience of Paul on the Damascus Road (in Acts 9:22 and 26)[34] in a way that contrasts with the more physical and materializing narratives of the appearances to the original witnesses in his Gospel (in Luke 24:36–49). Markus Bockmuehl inclines to the view that the first witnesses considered as a group were anxious to affirm the Resurrection both as a historical event and, at the same time, as something that *cannot* be presented simply as an event of historical time. As a consequence, while some appearance narratives are presented in very physical and material, even matter-of-fact ways, others contain elements that suggest degrees of difficulty or ambiguity in these experiences. Therefore, Bockmuehl contends that the diversity of the experienced encounters prompted their "interpretation and appropriation in

34. Allowing him to speak of it as a "heavenly vision" in his address to Agrippa in Acts 26:19.

profoundly theological terms."[35] As a consequence, when looked at synthetically, the "diverse and yet convergent experiences of absence and presence that followed the crucifixion"[36] of Jesus obliges us to accept the "intrinsic polyvalence of the resurrection tradition."[37] Luke's presentations of the Easter Jesus therefore contain very physical and materializing elements, but also elements suggestive of transcendent mystery. Luke's tendency to oscillate between material and physical representations of the Raised Jesus (even to the point of eating fish and honeycomb with his disciples), his more elusive and mysterious appearances (as on the Road to Emmaus where he was at first unrecognized, then recognized before mysteriously disappearing entirely), and the "visionary" nature of the appearance on the Damascus Road, simply illustrates this general rule that the appearances were neither "purely visionary nor straightforwardly material in nature."[38]

However, Luke's overall theological schema of salvation history must also be taken into account at this point. In Luke's idiosyncratic understanding of things, apart from disengaging the appearances from Galilee and relocating them in Jerusalem, Paul's apostolic status has to be considered in relation to that of the original Jerusalem apostles. When Judas had to be replaced, the original group looked to elect someone who, like themselves, had "come in and gone out" with the historical Jesus, and who had been witness to all that Jesus had said and done during his lifetime, Matthias filled that bill. By the same criterion, even despite his role in the subsequent historical unfolding of the Christian mission to the Gentiles, Paul did not measure up to this qualification for apostleship. Luke could therefore systematically deny apostolic status to Paul on the grounds that he had not been acquainted with the historical Jesus. Also, Luke's account of the Ascension brings down the curtain on the first phase of more concrete and material appearances to the inner circle of apostles in a way that excludes Paul. Given that it is "the *ascended* rather than the newly risen Jesus who is properly seen in 'visions,'"[39] it becomes necessarily the case in Luke's mind that Paul had not enjoyed an Easter experience equal to that of the original apostolic leaders.

Despite Paul's own contention that his Easter experience was of a piece with those of the other apostles (1 Cor 15:8), Luke therefore notoriously emphasizes the contrasting difference between Paul's experiences of a "light and a voice" on the Damascus Road (Acts 9:3–4) and his presentation of the more starkly concrete and material appearances to the first apostolic witnesses. In this way, Paul's status as an apostle is effectively downgraded by Luke in a way that is contrary to Paul's own estimate of his own apostolic status. At Luke's hands, Paul is excluded from the class of the original apostles. But this is achieved by a concomitant "up-grading" of the alleged experiences

35. Bockmuehl, "Resurrection," 104–11.

36. Bockmuehl, "Resurrection," 113.

37. Bockmuehl, "Resurrection," 109.

38. Bockmuehl, "Resurrection," 113.

39. See Farrow, *Ascension and Ecclesia*, 22.

of the original apostolic band. Thus, while Paul is said to have encountered the Raised Jesus in the visionary form of "a light and a voice" in Acts 9:3–4, Luke does not hesitate to say that the original witnesses actually "ate and drank with him."

The discrepancy between the concrete and material appearances to the apostolic band in Luke's Gospel narrative and his presentation of Paul's Damascus Road "heavenly vision" may therefore be said to reflect this theological agenda. In N. T. Wright's estimate, because Luke's account of Paul's experience on the Damascus Road in Acts is deliberately made less concrete and material and much more visionary in nature, it is not therefore to be taken as a template for understanding all the Easter appearances. In this way, Wright privileges the historical reliability of the more material and physical elements in Luke's appearance narratives. For him they do not represent a theological massaging of the historical tradition induced by the apologetic need to defend Easter faith in contexts of doubt and skepticism. Nor, therefore, are Luke's materializing tendencies in the presentation of the appearance of Jesus to be seen as a later development of the tradition, in the way that became fashionable among the practitioners of contemporary redaction criticism. An original "heavenly" and transcendent tradition is not subject to "unrestrained speculation and embellishment" or "extravagant legendary embellishments."[40] Even if Luke received these narratives already in this particular form and was not himself directly responsible for their concrete and materializing elements, he may be said to have been happy to acquiesce in their more graphic and concrete detail as a welcome positive help in conferring the original apostolic witnesses with a status superior to Paul.

However, the argument may be run in an entirely opposite way. It is equally possible to argue that the somewhat confused accounts of Paul's Damascus Road experience in Acts would have been recognized by Paul himself as a reasonably accurate description of what actually happened. After all, when Paul himself speaks of his Damascus Road experience in Galatians as the occasion when he received his commission to proclaim the Gospel to the Gentiles, he stresses that this Gospel was not of human origin, for the experience in which he received it was "a *revelation* of Jesus Christ" (Gal 1:12). It was an experience in which God "was pleased to reveal his Son" in him (Gal 1:16). Luke's account of this as a "heavenly vision" seems entirely congruent with Paul's own account of it.

Despite the discrepancies across Luke's three accounts of the Damascus Road event, which suggests that there was some confusion about what actually had been experienced by Paul and his fellow travelers, it may have been that Luke's theological agenda allowed him to acquiesce in the general shape of the presentation of Paul's experience found in them. For, from Luke's perspective, this in turn effectively allowed the down grading of Paul's status, while Luke deliberately upgraded the Easter experiences of those original witnesses who, on his reckoning, were alone to be called "apostles." This was achieved by making their experiences more visually material and

---

40. Bockmuehl's language in "Resurrection," 110.

concrete. Given that they, unlike Paul, had actually known Jesus in his historical life-time, it is understandable that physical identifying tokens could have played a role for them that could not have been played for Paul who had not "come in and gone out" with Jesus in his historical lifetime. They may therefore be assumed to have enjoyed a pre-Ascension experience of the Easter Jesus of a more clearly physical and materializing kind. In this event, it could be argued that Luke's more concrete and materializing account of the first appearances served his schematic purpose of elevating the position of the first witnesses as the original apostles over against Paul. Accordingly, their experiences are presented in a more concrete form than may have actually originally been the case. Thus, Luke's presentation of the experiences of the original apostolic band as more concrete and material also served his own idiosyncratic theological purpose. For this reason it may not be a very reliable pointer to the actual quality of the very first Easter experiences.

Clearly, to admit that the less concrete and physical, and more spiritualizing accounts of Paul's experience in Acts might approximate more closely not only to Paul's own actual Damascus Road experience, but also to the original experiences of all the first believers, also confirms Paul's own understanding of things insofar as he is apparently convinced that all the appearances listed in 1 Cor 15:5–8 were of a similar quality. Given that in that summary he simply adds his own experience to the list that had been handed on to him, it is as though he simply assumed there was no difference in kind between the quality of his own experience and that of the others. This conclusion is supported by Matthew's presentation of the appearance to the assembled eleven disciples in Galilee in a way that is more like a Christophany of the already exalted Christ, as if "from heaven."

We are thus confronted with a dilemma. The first possibility is that all the early experiences were generally speaking of a piece with Paul's own Damascus Road experience in terms of their quality, as he indeed himself suggests was the case, and the quality of them is to be understood more or less as it is (rightly) represented by Luke in the accounts in Acts as a "heavenly vision" or Christophany. In this case the more concrete and realistically material accounts of the appearance narratives in the later Gospels such as Luke may be understood as redactional developments of the original tradition. This may also be said of the materializing elements in the Easter narratives in John, even though these are in tension with John's emphasis elsewhere on the importance of the exaltation of the Raised Jesus to the Father as the essential significance of the Resurrection. It is also not insignificant that, after presenting the very graphic story of the appearance before the doubting Thomas, with Jesus' invitation to "touch his hand and his side," in John 20, John makes an apparent attempt to deflect attention away from the suggestion that this might be somehow normative for faith, by having

Jesus declare "honorable" (*makarios*) those who have not seen in this kind of way "and yet believe" (20:29).[41]

Alternatively, and this is Wright's viewpoint, all the first appearances were of a straightforward, clear and distinct visual kind, appropriate to the unambiguous seeing of any material object, and Luke has deliberately made Paul's experience less of a concrete and material manifestation and more ambiguous, revelatory and mysterious. In this case, Paul's own experience as represented by Luke in Acts is a misleadingly inaccurate literary construct. Likewise the same materializing tendency followed by John (perhaps even following a pattern established by Luke due to his alleged literary dependence on Luke) is also to be accorded priority as an indication of the nature of the original Easter experiences of the "meetings" with the Raised Jesus.

If the first Easter experiences were more or less as they are presented by Luke and John, then the seeing of the Raised Christ can more easily be accommodated to the ordinary observation of material and physical things. In this case, there is a *prima facie* case for the view that critical historical research might be a conceivable avenue of approach to the handling of them. However, if the reported accounts of Paul's Damascus Road experience which are preserved in Acts are anywhere near accurate, and the experiences of the others were in general terms actually on a par with his (as Paul himself would insist, and as Matthew's mountain top episode also suggests), we would have to say that the Easter experiences were all somewhat more mysterious and revelatory, and less concrete and material. In this case they would all have been, broadly speaking, Christophanies of the kind that could be appropriated by faith by those with eyes to see and ears to hear, but not necessarily unambiguous manifestations or Christepiphanies of Jesus that in principle would have been capable of commanding the assent of all. In this case, the capacity of critical historical research to handle such experiences using secular methods of argument is correspondingly reduced. They become the subject matter of theological reflection, appropriated by faith, rather than the kind of events that are normally the subject of critical historical research.

Which of these two options is the more likely? In pursuing his own understanding of the "seeing" of the Raised Jesus as an integral element of the post-mortem "meetings" with the disciples, Wright declares his agreement with Stephen T. Davis, who in 1997 resolutely argued for the assimilation of the seeing involved in the encounters with the Raised Christ to normal ocular vision.[42] In Wright's estimate, this as an "important essay"[43] which provides "a brief clear answer" to the view that the later Gospels of

---

41. Hanson has made a persuasive case for translating *makarios*, both here and in the Matthean beatitudes, as "honorable/honored" rather than the usual "blessed." See Hanson, "How Honorable! How Shameful!," especially 88, 90–93.

42. Davis, "'Seeing' the Risen Jesus."

43. *RSG,* 323 n.32.

Luke and John turn a primary "spiritual" vision of Paul "into a more solid 'eyewitness' mode."[44] It is imperative therefore that Davis's essay be taken seriously.

Davis contended that the seeing of the Raised Jesus was no different from the seeing of natural objects "like a tree, a house, or another human body."[45] After noting the alleged "massive physical detail of the appearance stories"[46] he concluded that, if Jesus was "seen," then his raised body must have been of a particular kind—it was the kind of object that *could* have been seen visually. That is to say, his resurrected body must be understood to be an unequivocally material and substantively physical body.

Davis contrasts this purely natural kind of seeing with the kind of seeing which might be said *not* to be open to everyone with physical eyes to see, but only to those who are especially "graced" by God, and thus enabled to see in faith with the illumination of the Holy Spirit. Davis believes that when it comes to talking of the "seeing" of the Raised Christ, most contemporary theologians are, in his estimate, erroneously committed to the defense of this latter God-assisted way of seeing.[47] In this case, it is not just that God or Christ might be said to take the initiative by determining to have Christ appear at a particular time and place, but that a divine decision was also made to ensure that some people were enabled to "see" what was revealed while others who were not so privileged saw nothing. This second, grace-assisted kind of privileged "seeing" is termed by Davis a "visualization."

I think this is a somewhat unfortunate choice of term, given that "visualizing" usually implies a purely subjective attempt to imagine something that is itself *not* really present or that is unavailable to human observation and scrutiny. Thus, to "visualize" something is normally to imagine something by bringing it before one's "mind's eye." This is far from what Davis intends. As he uses the term "visualization," instead of simply imagining something, it is meant to involve the perception of a given reality; indeed, he also speaks of it as an "objective vision." Though it is said to be a kind of seeing *of* something, it is visionary rather than straightforwardly visual. For Davis, the key difference between the visual seeing of a natural object, and the "visualization" or visionary seeing of an "objective vision," is therefore not so much a matter of objectivity; the reality of the object seen is not at issue. It is rather that in one case the capacity to see is purely natural, whereas in the alternative some kind of divine assistance

---

44. *RSG*, 376 n.4.

45. Davis, "'Seeing' the Risen Jesus," 126.

46. Davis, "'Seeing' the Risen Jesus," 141.

47. Curiously, one such theologian is Davis's co-editor, Gerald O'Collins, who, while insisting that some kind of exterior, visual perception was involved and not merely an interior "seeing," nevertheless disagrees with Davis by holding that "the appearances did not imply *merely* physical sight or a *purely* 'ordinary' seeing of an external object." Instead, a "graced seeing on the part of the witnesses" was involved. See O'Collins, "The Appearances of the Risen Christ," 138 and 139. For O'Collins, in this very carefully argued article, the appearances are "Christophanies." They involve "recognizing someone who now enjoys an exalted, 'heavenly' existence" (O'Collins, "The Appearances of the Risen Christ," 138).

is said to operate within the experience. Thus, the objects of natural vision may in principle be observed by anybody with eyes to see, who might happen to be present. By contrast, in the case of a "visualization" or "objective vision," only those enabled by God see what is presented to them, while others who are apparently deprived of this divine assistance see nothing. What he calls "visualizations" or "objective visions" are only said to occur among selected persons who are explicitly enabled by God to see what others cannot see. It seems to follow that, by contrast with a "visualization," the visual seeing of the body of the Raised Christ, like any other material object, such as "a tree, a house, or another human body" could in principle have been photographed.

Whether just these two possible ways of understanding the "seeing" of the Raised Jesus amount to a sufficiently careful analysis of this matter remains an open question. There are other understandings of seeing in which, for example, some see and interpret what they see in one way, while others, looking at the very same objective reality, interpret their experience differently, but without any suggestion that God is somehow the cause of this difference by privileging some to see and not others.[48] For the moment, however, it is sufficient to note that Davis sets himself the task of answering those contemporary theologians who are alleged to be wedded to the idea that the "seeing" of the Raised Christ was an experience of certain privileged witnesses who were enabled by God to see what others could not see. Davis himself attempts a vigorous defense of the contrary thesis—that the seeing of the Raised Christ was a purely natural seeing of a physically resurrected material body that was in principle open to being perceived and known by everyone. This is the thesis with which Wright declares his agreement.

In defending this thesis about the purely natural nature of the seeing of the Raised Christ, Davis argues that this conclusion is based upon the plain reading both of the narratives of the appearances, and of the bare factual statements of the "kerygmatic summaries" as they are now found in the canonical scriptures.[49] Davis works therefore with a basic presumption in favor of the historicity of the fully developed Gospel traditions; little or no interest is taken in peeling away any possible redactional layering that may have accrued to the tradition in the process of its transmission in an attempt to uncover its earliest kernel. The suggestion that the materializing tendencies of Luke and John arose from a concern to address issues of doubt among wavering believers, or to respond to the criticism of hostile critics and nonbelievers, is not countenanced. Rather, an alleged "plain sense," effectively of a pre-critical reading of the received New Testament texts, is said to indicate that the first witnesses simply "saw" the Resurrected Jesus in a very matter-of-fact visual kind of way.

48. This element of ambiguity and doubt in the philosophy of perception is discussed in the companion volume to this, Carnley, *The Reconstruction of Resurrection Belief*, chapter 7.

49. Such as most notably 1 Cor 15:3–8, and the summaries of the early sermons now found in Acts 2 and 3.

Many would question the propriety of this methodological starting point. Certainly, Wright is far from the mark in asserting that Davis provides a "brief clear answer" to the view that the later Gospels turn a primary "spiritual" vision, such as Acts attributes to Paul, "into a more solid 'eyewitness' mode."[50] In fact, Davis does not so much as argue against the contention that a materializing tendency is discernable in the later Gospels of Luke and John by contrast with the more "spiritual" (nonmaterial) approach to the understanding of the resurrection body that is often attributed to St. Paul, nor by contrast with the more elusively mysterious presentation of the Easter event of the earlier Gospel of Matthew for that matter. No account is therefore taken of the apparent progression from Mark's omission of any attempt to narrate an Easter appearance, to Mathew's account of the appearance of an apparently exalted Jesus to the assembled disciples on the mountain in Galilee (which was ambiguous enough to leave some people to hesitate in doubt), to the much more materializing accounts of appearances in the later Gospels of Luke and John. No account is taken of the possibility of the redactional development of these Gospel traditions from an earlier kernel of truth, or of the possibility that the more physical detail introduced in these stories was dictated by the need to respond to the expression of doubts within the community of faith, or to polemical attacks on the faith from without. Even the possibility of giving priority to Luke's accounts of Paul's Damascus Road experiences in Acts is positively avoided by Davis, simply on the grounds that it would lead to the "rejection (perhaps as legendary accretions) of all the physical detail of the appearance stories."[51] Davis thus affirms his preferred precritical and synthetic way of reading the received texts as his starting point. Because the Raised Jesus is said in the Gospel narratives to have been "seen," along with the fact that at least some of the narratives include "massive physical detail," it is therefore assumed that what was seen must have been a material object like "a tree, a house or another human body." This same precritical approach resonates with the general approach pursued by Wright in his presentation of the alleged series of historical "meetings" with the Raised Christ.

Whether a kind of seeing that is appropriate to material objects does justice to the literary complexity of the New Testament appearances traditions is, of course, precisely the issue that needs to be carefully considered. Davis therefore assembles some arguments in support of his contention that nothing more than natural seeing was involved in the perception of the Raised Christ in a physical and material form that, to all intents and purposes, was no different from the perception of any other physically material object of this world. Starting from his alleged "plain reading" of the canonical texts as the church has received them, Davis then addresses six regular objections to his thesis.

The first is the contention that Jesus only appeared to believers and not to unbelievers. If Jesus was physically raised in a material body, why was he only seen by

---

50. *RSG*, 376.

51. See Davis, "'Seeing' the Risen Jesus," 139.

believers? In defense of his thesis that Jesus appeared in a manner visibly available to everyone, Davis lists some who came to Easter faith who were *not* believers or followers of Jesus, Paul among them. The conclusion is that it is not true that Jesus only appeared to believers. Perhaps this is, however, something of an "Aunt Sally": it might have been more helpful to say that, though many of Jesus' chief opponents (e.g., Pilate, or Caiaphas) never made the claim to have seen him, Jesus is said to have appeared, if not to everyone, then at least to a diverse collection of people. However, the theologically interesting point is that some of them became believers while others did not. This is the suggestion, for example, in Matt 28:17 where it is reported that "some doubted." If the Raised Jesus was simply there to be seen by anybody who happened to be present, and could have been photographed, how is this reported diversity of response to be explained? If it was the case that Jesus could be seen as plainly as "a tree, a house, or another human body," Davis is faced with explaining how it was that some became believers and others did not. On the face of it, at the very least this suggests some kind of ambiguity in relation to what was there to be seen. As we shall see, Davis postpones attending to this issue until he comes explicitly to discuss the phenomenon of doubt, which is so much a theme of the appearance narratives, and which he admits raises questions about the material clarity of what was seen. We shall therefore return to this when we come to consider the fourth challenge to Davis's thesis.

The second reason Davis lists to explain why some (mistakenly to his mind) think that the seeing of the Raised Christ was not just a matter of ordinary visual seeing is that it is regularly contended that the Resurrection was "not a resuscitation." Had we been talking only of a resuscitated Jesus, visual sight could happily be accepted as the entirely appropriate mode of perception. But it is often said that a resurrection is something different from a mere resuscitation, because it necessarily involves some kind of heavenly exaltation and glorification. This might therefore be said to warrant a nuanced kind of "seeing." Davis seeks to answer this by complaining that there is more talk of resuscitation among those drawing the contrast with resurrection than actual serious proponents of a theory of resuscitation: "It is easier to find scholars declaring that Jesus was 'not resuscitated' than to find a single writer who says that he was."[52] N. T. Wright likewise sees the denial of resuscitation in entirely sinister terms: it is the thin edge of the wedge towards the denial of "resurrection."[53] What is actually meant here is that a discussion of resuscitation is used to deny a particular *understanding* of resurrection, which happens to be the very concrete historical understanding of it positively espoused by both Davis and Wright. It is for this reason that Davis believes that denial of resuscitation amounts to the denial of the resurrection. It actually amounts to a denial of resurrection *as he envisages it*.

While it may be true that those who insist that resurrection is not just a mere resuscitation may use this distinction to discredit the particular view of resurrection

52. Davis, "'Seeing' the Risen Jesus," 132–34.

53. *RSG*, 7 n.11.

portrayed in uncompromisingly material terms,[54] it is hardly fair to argue that it is used to discredit resurrection belief *per se*. Indeed, this distinction is usually designed to defend resurrection belief in the face of a popular inclination to write it off on the assumption that it was "a mere resuscitation." Nor is it true to argue that resuscitation is a position that is not actually espoused by anyone. The physical resuscitation of Jesus' is precisely the kind of rationalizing explanation of the Easter tradition that was promoted in the nineteenth century to support the conclusion that Jesus did not really die.[55] In H. E. G. Paulus and Ernest Renan we have notorious proponents of a resuscitation theory, who seem to have escaped the notice of both Davis and Wright in their concern to say that the search for proponents of resuscitation theories actually demonstrates that they are virtually nonexistent; the implication being that the distinction between resurrection and resuscitation need not therefore be taken seriously.

In fact, the discussion of the distinction between a "resuscitation" and the "resurrection" of Christ is important as a way of getting to the *right* understating of resurrection by following an *apophatic* line of reasoning—by saying what it is not. Even Wright himself is logically bound to admit that the Resurrection of Christ differs from mere physical resuscitations insofar as those who are resuscitated (for example, on a beach after a near-drowning, or in a hospital after a near-death experience) will at some point of time themselves still have to face death again. The Resurrection of Christ differs from such physical resuscitations in the sense that Christ will never die again. The distinction between resurrection and resuscitation thus seeks to communicate the view that resurrection, by virtue of the heavenly transformation, exaltation, and glorification that is understood to attach to Jesus' raised body, involves something more than a mere resuscitation. Integral to the concept of Jesus' Resurrection is the affirmation that, unlike a merely resuscitated body, Jesus' body was transformed by its becoming immortal, thereby ruling out the possibility of a future death.

It is important to emphasize that what the distinction between resurrection and resuscitation seeks to deny is not resurrection faith *per se*, but one specific portrayal of what is said to have happened to Jesus, which, as in the case of Paulus and Renan, actually tends to deny the reality of Jesus' death. By saying that the Resurrection of Jesus was not a mere resuscitation in the sense of just the revival and literal "standing up" again of a body to resume life in this world, an attempt is being made to deny the suggestion that Jesus did not really die.

---

54. For example, see Morgan, "Flesh Is Precious," 13: "Christians who do not believe in the physicality of Jesus' resurrection can adduce further considerations. The Gospels do not intend to relate a resuscitation. There is no question of Jesus dying again. A physical resurrection looks dangerously like a resuscitation, and invites the rationalist explanation that Jesus really did not die on the cross. It is better avoided."

55. E.g., Paulus, *Das Leben Jesu*; and Renan, *Vie de Jésus*. For a modern popular example of an attempt to articulate an understanding of resurrection by arguing that it is *not* the same as a resuscitation see Holloway, *Where Did Jesus Go?*, 28–30.

This is a distinction therefore of enormous theological importance. To say that a discussion of resuscitation is the thin edge of the wedge in denying the actual resurrection is entirely gratuitous. Curiously, despite Wright's castigation of those who find it useful to deny that the Resurrection is to be understood as a resuscitation on the grounds that it is "the thin edge of the wedge in denying the resurrection," at the end of the day Wright himself is obliged to make exactly this distinction. He says: the actual bodily resurrection of Jesus is "not a mere resuscitation, but a transforming revivification"![56] The importance of distinguishing bodily resurrection from a mere resuscitation is recognized after all! It is puzzling to fathom just how bodily resurrection, but not resuscitation, can be said by Wright to provide "a *sufficient* condition of the tomb being empty and the 'meetings' taking place";[57] for one might be forgiven for thinking that a resuscitation would also be *sufficient* to explain both the emptiness of the tomb and subsequent reports of "meetings" with Jesus. However, in this case it might also be argued that Jesus did not die. Unfortunately, it also follows that, if "resurrection" is distinguished from "resuscitation," then questions may legitimately be asked about whether a resurrected body could be seen in exactly the way a resuscitated body might have been seen, and this remains a serious challenge to the Davis/Wright thesis.

The third of the challenges listed by Davis to the proposition that the seeing of the Raised Christ was a matter of natural vision is posed by the New Testament use of the word *ōphthē*, "he appeared" in 1 Corinthians 15. Like Wright, Davis at least acknowledges that *ōphthē* could refer to a revelatory appearance of a transcendent divine reality as in a Christophany, rather than to the seeing of a material object. Also, like Wright after him, he nevertheless opts somewhat arbitrarily for the rendering of *ōphthē* as the natural seeing of material objects. The single instance of the use of *ōphthē* in Acts 7:26, where Moses is said to have come or "appeared" before others in an entirely natural way, is sufficient evidence for him to dismiss the alternative view that in 1 Corinthians 15 *ōphthē* might be understood to mean something other than natural sight.

Even so, Davis eventually concedes that the seeing of the Raised Christ connoted by *ōphthē* could indeed be other than natural visual seeing after all. Though he admits that we *could* think of it as a more revelatory or visionary kind of seeing, such as the "seeing" of the presence of God, we are urged not to feel *obliged* to think in this way. This is hardly a convincing argument in support of the contention that *ōphthē* in fact indicates that the Easter appearance of the Raised Jesus *was* a matter of natural seeing, like the seeing of "a tree, a house, or another human body."

The fourth of the reasons listed by Davis as evidence erroneously suggestive of a kind of seeing other than a perfectly straightforward natural seeing of a material object is posed in the New Testament Easter texts by the recurrent theme of failure

56. *RSG,* 717.
57. *RSG,* 717.

to recognize, and even instances of doubt in the tradition of narrative appearances. For example, in the case of the travelers on the Emmaus Road (Luke 24:13–35), he notes that their "eyes were kept from seeing." How is this to be accommodated to a purely natural seeing on the part of anybody present? Davis answers by arguing that though, according to his thesis, a special act of God is not needed for the perception of the appearance of the Raised Jesus as in what he terms a "visualization," a special act of God *was* involved in inhibiting the natural capacities of the perception and recognition of who Jesus actually was, at least for a time![58] There is something strangely perverse in this contention that God deliberately closed the eyes of the travelers, and then later withdrew this inhibition so that they then began to see naturally. In this case God inhibited recognition, but then lifted the inhibition so as to allow the perception of Jesus' presence in the breaking of bread, once again as a matter of natural vision. Though the travelers in this story are gently reprimanded by Jesus for their failure to understand, God is effectively said to be the cause of their fault. But this also raises the question as to whether those on the mountain top in Galilee who are said to have "doubted" in Matt 28:17 were also prevented by God from seeing what others saw. All this simply fails to convince.

We need not spend too much time on Davis' cavalier dismissal of the Pauline tradition. Davis's initial methodological commitment to a precritical reading of the Scriptures "as the Church has received them," already determines the issue of whether Paul's statements in 1 Corinthians 15, even though they are much earlier than the Gospel narratives, might be understood to have been Christophanies rather than being accommodated to the matter-of-fact observation of natural objects. This privileging of the "plain reading" of the narratives of the appearances in Luke and John, with their "massive physical detail," but despite their comparative lateness, over the Pauline tradition is entirely arbitrary.

When it comes to Paul's understanding of the appearances, including his own reported experience as Luke presents it in Acts, this is accommodated to the later more physical and material understanding of things. Not only does Davis say, for reasons that are not entirely clear, that Luke's accounts of Paul's Damascus Road experience should not be seen as a model or template for understanding what the other early appearances were really like, but also that no particular account is to be taken of Paul's own talk in 1 Corinthians 15 of an apparently glorified "spiritual" or "celestial" body either. This is not because Davis believes that Jesus' body was not glorified and exalted; rather, this is dismissed on the grounds that even a glorified body "is still a body—that is, it is still a material object that can be seen."[59] In other words, even though the resurrected body of Jesus is said to be transformed and "glorified" (and, incidentally, therefore unlike a merely resuscitated body after all), there is no suggestion that this

58. This is asserted even though there is no mention of God as the agent either of the closing or opening of the eyes of those present in Luke's account.

59. Davis, "'Seeing' the Risen Jesus," 140–41.

transformation was to prepare it for, and to receive it into, a heavenly mode of existence. In Davis's view, even a heavenly body is still a material body that can be naturally seen. This is not because the transformative impact of resurrection is said merely to result in making the material body resistant to corruption, as in the case of Wright's thinking; rather, a more ethereal and glorified kind of body is said by Davis to be made to "materialize" on occasion. For example, he points to the apparent "materialization" of the Raised Christ in the room behind closed doors reported in John 20. Davis at least takes account of the tradition insofar as it suggests the occasional or episodic nature of Jesus' appearances, by contrast with a temporarily extended earthly sojourn dispersed with "meetings" that might have been open to observation as and when opportunity arose. But surely, the alleged capacity of the body of Jesus to "materialize" in specific episodes in turn means that it was not "like a tree, a house or another human body" whose temporally extended existence could be naturally observed.[60] I frankly do not know where to start to try to unscramble all this.

One could be forgiven for thinking that these assertions beg all the crucial questions. All the while, Davis reveals himself to be already committed to defending the idea that the Easter experience involved a natural seeing, and that this kind of seeing therefore dictates that what was seen was a material object. The New Testament evidence concerning the manner of Jesus' appearing is then interpreted in such a way as to lead to this outcome. I think we have to conclude that Davis's article, upon which Wright relies for support, does not make any advance over Wright's own arbitrary tendency simply to assume the historicity of the materializing portrayals of the appearances in the later Gospels of Luke and John. Without convincing arguments to support this point of view, this presentation of things remains unsatisfactorily problematic.[61]

Perhaps Wright's position about the nature of the first appearances might be strengthened with the help of some more recent negative assessments of the conclusions of form criticism of the kind that were generated in the first half of the twentieth century about the oral development of the Gospel material generally. Richard Bauckham has challenged the form critics' contention about the transmission of traditional material by anonymous communities, often in the context of teaching and worship, which is said to account for its rhetorical development in a legendary and materializing direction. Bauckham challenges this basic tenet of form criticism by making a case for

---

60. Davis, "'Seeing' the Risen Jesus," 140.

61. In a more recent discussion of Wright's handling of the evidence of Acts, Eve-Marie Becker is bluntly critical of his contention that Acts cannot "be used naively as it stands as a historical source" and that "nothing massive will rest on Acts, but it will be interesting from time to time to see what new possibilities emerge" (Wright, *Paul and the Faithfulness of God*, 63). Eve-Marie Becker argues that Wright's "action plan" of referring to Acts "from time to time" reveals a kind of "positionalism" that leads to "the danger of interpretatuve arbitrariness." (see Becker, "Wright's Paul and the Paul of Acts," 155–56).

taking the role of "eyewitnesses" with some seriousness. He contends that eyewitness testimony is to be given its due, as against the prevailing form-critical assumption of the inevitable legendary development of the traditions relating to Jesus in the course of the week-to-week round of teaching and worship in communities that are now anonymous to us. This does not just bear upon the question of the reliability of traditions about the historical Jesus, but also about the original Easter testimony. In particular, Bauckham highlights the importance of eyewitness testimony behind the Gospel appearance narratives as a way of neutralizing the idea of the openness of the tradition to literary development in the course of the apologetic defense of faith of the kind that is said to account for the materializing tendencies. He argues, for example, that the developed appearance narratives show no indication of being more detailed elaborations of the early kerygmatic summaries such as we have in 1 Corinthians 15, Philippians 2, and Acts 2 and 3. The lack of specific correlations with the summaries indicates that the Gospel narratives enjoyed a life of their own, and were not designed to "fill-out" the original kerygmatic summaries. Rather, they were simply a different genre, which circulated independently of them. They are thus to be accorded more weight as the outcome of original eyewitness testimony rather than being written off as developments from the kerygmatic summaries in the period of oral transmission prior to the writing especially of the later Gospels of Luke and John.

Bauckham acknowledges that the reasons for the lack of correlation, especially between Paul's kerygmatic summary in 1 Corinthians 15 and the various narratives of the appearances in the Gospels, remain obscure, "but the fact should not be considered a reason for treating the Gospel narratives as late legends."[62] Given the theoretical possibility that some original eyewitnesses could certainly have still been alive at the time the Gospels were written, it is therefore said to be at least thinkable that the Gospel stories, as a different and independent genre of the tradition, go back to reliable eyewitness testimony.

However, even if the appearance narratives as we have them in Luke and John do not appear to be a filling out of the kerygmatic summaries, this does not itself necessarily mean that they were not a "filling out," with increased materializing detail, of earlier more elusive and mysteriously presented episodes. To demonstrate a lack of connection with the kerygmatic summaries does not resolve the question of whether they are late developments or not with respect to earlier strands of the tradition. Nor does an appeal to the role of original eyewitnesses entail that the original testimonies behind the Gospel narratives as we have them were not subject to literary development in response to apologetic concerns thrown up by challenges to resurrection faith. We have no way of plotting the *course* of the transmissional life of the material of this particular genre even if it was independent of the kerygmatic summaries. Even if the Gospel narratives may not be elaborations of the early summaries, the question is: are they elaborations of eyewitness testimonies that were originally of a less

62. Bauckham, *Gospel Women*, 147.

physical and material kind? Notwithstanding the apparent lack of dependence of the Gospel narratives upon the kerygmatic summaries, this materializing tendency may well still explain the appearance of additions that may not originally have been an integral part of the initial eyewitness testimony. In other words, the tendency to make the appearances more concrete and realistic may still be understood as a response to expressions of doubt and incredulity among backsliding believers, or as an apologetic attempt to secure the clear identity of the Raised Christ specifically with the crucified Jesus, as seems to be the case in the story of the eating of fish and honeycomb in Luke, and especially in the Thomas story in John. This possibility persists given that such materializing tendencies are not represented in the earlier stratum of New Testament material, either in the letters of Paul or the earlier Gospel of Matthew, not to mention the lack of any appearance story at all in Mark.

In other words, it does not follow from the admitted possibility that a role was played by eyewitnesses in the origination of the tradition that *ipso facto* there could have been no further literary development of it. It is still a thinkable proposition that a tradition of appearances originally understood as Christophanies later acquired more concrete and materialistic form. The fact that the appearances are represented as more concrete and material only in the later gospels of Luke and John continues to keep this possibility alive.

However, Bauckham suggests additionally that in theoretical terms some original eyewitnesses may have still been living well into the ninth decade of the first century when these later Gospels containing the more physical and material appearances narratives were written, and that in this case these eyewitnesses would have in principle been able to exercise a kind of quality control over the literary and legendary development of these narrative traditions. This would act as a restraint against permitting the development of over-imaginative redactional accretions of a materializing kind. However, while we can readily assume that eyewitnesses may certainly have been the original sources of the traditions which later found their way into the Gospels, we have no actual evidence of eyewitnesses scrutinizing the Gospels in the last two decades of the first century as they came off the literary production line. While this is thinkable (i.e. logically possible without self-contradiction), the question of whether it was an actual possibility still remains. This means that particular elements of the tradition still have to be assessed on their merits.

Moreover, even if Bauckham's case for the importance of the role of original eyewitnesses can be made, the theoretical possibility of the narrative tradition of appearances originating with eyewitnesses does not thereby resolve the question of the precise kind of seeing of the Raised Christ that might have been originally involved. Given that the appearing of the Raised Christ suggests that some kind of "seeing" is the regular mode of perception implied in the Gospel narratives, we still have to ask whether the eyewitnesses' experience is best understood as a visual seeing of an epistemically passive object which was simply there to be observed, like "a tree, a house, or another human body"; or are we meant to understand it to have been a more visionary experience, the perception of an other-worldly reality, that was "seen" in response to an essentially revelatory act initiated either by God or by the Raised Christ himself? Talk of eyewitness testimony, or of "seeing" in relation to the appearances, does not mean that we can assume that a straight forward visual manifestation was meant rather than a much more mysterious revelatory occurrence. Whether the first eyewitnesses were thinking in terms of Christophanies, understood on analogy with the many Theophanies found in the Hebrew Scriptures, remains an open possibility.

In this case, we still have to take seriously the view that the more concrete and materializing elements of the presentations of the appearances in the later Gospels of Luke and John may be best understood as redactional developments of the tradition. We must therefore look again at the relevant texts themselves to ascertain whether there are not some additional reasons to support the contention that these more physical and materializing elements in the presentations of Luke and John are in fact elaborations of an original Easter tradition of a more elusive and mysterious kind.

The contention that the Easter experiences were originally less than clear and distinct, and somewhat less concrete and material than the portrayals of Luke and John suggest, is supported by the fact that even the appearance narratives of these very Gospels themselves contain hints that indicate the possibility that they may have originated from experiences that were less than manifestly clear.

For example, the initial inability of witnesses to recognize the Raised Jesus suggests something unusual. We have already noted that the eyes of those walking with the Raised Jesus in Luke's story of the Road to Emmaus "were kept from recognizing him" (Luke 24:16); we may now further note that this was not just a momentary experience of failure to recognize, but something that was apparently extended over time, during the entire episode until mysteriously "their eyes were opened" in the breaking of bread (Luke 24:31).

The appeal to the four-fold eucharistic action of taking, blessing, breaking, and sharing of bread in Luke's story also raises a *prima facie* suggestion that this is the description of a proto-eucharistic event and is to be read in the light of the continuing eucharistic experience of Christians through time. Also, once the Raised Jesus' presence was glimpsed in this disclosure event, he is then said to have disappeared—there is no suggestion that he lingered to enjoy an ordinary meal. Something of the apparent revelatory nature of the experience is thus preserved in this story. Likewise, Jesus' appearance with the disciples is mysteriously sudden in Luke 24:36, where he appears with an air of exalted majesty.[63] The revelatory aspect of the event is particularly strik-

63. See Dillon, *From Eye-Witnesses to Ministers*, 185, on the Septuagint's use of *histanai* of the sudden arrival of angelic messengers.

ing in Luke's statement that the eyes of the Emmaus travelers had to be opened, if not explicitly by divine initiative, then at least in some kind of mysterious disclosure.[64] This is also the implication in the same story when recognition was only achieved when Jesus, at first an invited guest of the other travelers, actually seized the initiative as host and took the bread, blessed, broke, and shared it with the travelers. None of this sounds like the seeing of the Raised Jesus as the passive object of ordinary perception.

This conclusion is reinforced by the apparent ability of the Raised Jesus to vanish just as mysteriously in the Emmaus story. After being recognized in the breaking of bread Jesus then apparently instantaneously disappears; he is said to have "vanished from their sight" (Luke 24:31). This does not appear to suggest that he was simply seen walking out through the door. Again, while blessing the eleven and others on the road to Bethany in Luke 24:51–52, he is said to have been "separated from them and carried up into heaven . . . and they worshipped him." In relation to this, a good case may be made for understanding "he was separated from them" as "he became invisible." This does not sound like a Jesus simply restored to this world who was seen in purely straightforward material and physical form in localized "meetings."

The initial failure to perceive in this Lucan text finds a parallel John 20:14–16 in the case of Mary Magdalene, where she mistakes Jesus' identity until, significantly, he addresses her by name. It is not insignificant that the initiative is taken by Jesus in John 20:16 insofar as Mary Magdalene is enabled to recognize him only after he addresses her and she in response turns towards him. The intratextual significance of the good shepherd's calling of his own sheep by name (John 10:3) in relation to this address to Mary by name in this appearance story is often commented upon. All this speaks of divine revelatory initiative rather than something akin to the mundane human observation of purely passive natural objects.

Even when these stories are interpreted in a literal and materialistic way, they continue to suggest that Jesus' body was sufficiently transformed as to allow him to be portrayed as a stranger whose identity, at least initially, went unrecognized. Moreover, Luke maintains the same consistent emphasis insofar as he says in Acts that God raised Jesus, and allowed him to appear (*emphanē*) not to all people, but to those "chosen by God" to be witnesses (Acts 10:40–41). This is of a piece with the view that *ōphthē*, as it is used in Paul's kerygmatic summary in 1 Corinthians 15, should be translated "he appeared" rather than he "was seen" or observed.

Elsewhere, even in these very same Gospel narratives Jesus is said to have appeared mysteriously in a room, not just behind closed doors (John 20:26), but also in a room where the doors are explicitly said to be locked for reasons of security (John 20:19). Unless we are to suppose that the locked doors were unlocked to admit Jesus, we have to think of the appearances behind locked doors in more mysterious terms.

64. The suggestion of Stephen Davis that the opening of their eyes is to be understood as normal visual seeing, while the closing of their eyes (so that they did not recognize Jesus) is said to be an explicit act of God seems unlikely, not least for purely theological reasons.

Stephen Davis does not dispel this element of mystery when he argues that it was not that Jesus had the doors unlocked, nor that he somehow "passed through the walls" (a seemingly impossible thought for Davis given that he is just as intent as Wright to defend the thesis that Jesus' Raised body was a material body, which could be seen like any other human body). Surprisingly, however, Davis then contends that it was within the power of God simply to make Jesus body "materialize" within the room behind its closed and locked doors. Davis seems to be oblivious to the fact that talk of a body made to materialize and then to vaporize is entirely inimical to his argument that Jesus' body was as material as "a tree, a house, or another human body." After all, trees, houses and other human bodies do not normally materialize and then vaporize once again.

Also, the argument that "anything is possible for God" does not help the argument that the resurrection was a historical event secured by the evidence of the empty tomb and the appearances. For as soon as "the God for whom all things are possible" is introduced into the equation we are speaking the language of faith, rather than the language of the secular discipline of historiography using reason alone. This highlights the inherent confusion in the arguments of those who seek to defend the idea that the Resurrection was a historical event available to human proof by the exercise of the secular historical reason, but who then invoke the power of God to secure a conclusion while denying that the matter at hand is a matter of faith. This means that those who think that they can work with the category of "historical event" available to the historical reason alone are guilty of making a very fundamental "category mistake." Indeed, Richard Swinburne argues, even if somewhat brutally, that the attempt to prove the occurrence of the Resurrection purely by relying on the techniques of secular critical historical research is "a sign of deep irrationality."[65]

In any event, while this is not the only Achilles' heel in Davis's argument, most will find his contention that Jesus' Raised body materialized and then dematerialized or vaporized, while holding that it was seen in a matter-of-fact visual sense, something of a stretch. The fact is that the story of Jesus' appearance in the upper room behind closed doors confronts us with an irresolvable mystery. We have to be aware that this may be its primary purpose: we are dealing with a mysterious and revelatory appearance of the Raised Christ "from heaven" that was perceived by those with eyes to perceive—that is to say, by faith and not just by natural sight. Even though, faith itself may be understood as a knowing by acquaintance having an epistemological structure similar to that of natural perception, the object of religious perception is unique. In this sense it is wholly unlike the material objects of this world such as "a tree, a house, or another human body."

This is not to mention the apparent importance of the element of perplexity and awe that features in so many of the Easter stories, including those presented to us by Luke and John, and that is regularly said to lead to a response of worship. Even the

---

65. Swinburne, *The Resurrection of God Incarnate*, 3.

tendency of John, in his presentation of the doubting Thomas story to draw back from suggesting that the kind of tactile experience involved in the invitation to examine Jesus' crucifixion wounds, is significant. For clearly, this is not to be understood as normative for faith. Those who have *not* seen and touched in the manner that was apparently at least made possible in Thomas' own reported experience, but who yet believe, are said to be blessed/honored (John 20:29). In other words, the possibility of coming to faith is admitted *in the absence* of such clear and distinct sensory data as is suggested in the more graphic and concrete details of the Thomas story.

Along with the initial failure to recognize him and then the opening of eyes to see in these traditions, there is the persistent fact also that some were able to see and perceive while others were not able to do so, and thus were left to doubt. This element of doubt and wonderment among those for whom the experience failed to command assent is not confined only to John's doubting Thomas story. Even though Mark's Gospel has no narrative of an appearance, the same sense of mystery is not absent from his presentation of the discovery of the Empty Tomb, where the awe-struck women flee in fear, and tell no one (Mark 16:8). More importantly, we have already noted that in Matthew's account of the tableau appearance of Jesus on the mountain in Galilee, where some are said to have seen and believed and even to have worshipped him, others are said to have doubted. In other words, it is frankly admitted across a range of New Testament appearance stories that Jesus appeared in such a way as to be revealed to some and not to others. Despite the tendency in the later Gospels to make the appearances more concretely material, many of the details of these texts themselves still persistently suggest that the apprehension of the Raised Christ was other than just a straightforward natural seeing of a physical body that was of a piece with mundane material objects simply located within space and time.

It is understandable that, in his attempt to remove the appearances of the Raised Jesus from the arena of faith, and to place them firmly in the court of critical historical reason, N. T. Wright is obliged to ensure that the appearances cannot, for methodological reasons, be allowed to be understood as visionary Christophanies from heaven. Rather, they have to be made more matter-of-fact, and presented as though they were purely visual "meetings" in the interests of ensuring that they may still be handled as evidence relating to a historical event.

Wright minimizes these mysterious and revelatory elements in the interests of reducing the tradition to this series of mundane "meetings," loosely strung together almost so as to make one synthetic story. We can appreciate that this becomes necessary so as to sustain the project of treating the Resurrection purely as an event that is in principle like any other event of past history. Only so can its occurrence be amenable to proof using the historical reason and the techniques of critical historical research.

For him the first appearances have therefore to be understood in a more matter-of-fact way than as "heavenly visions" or Christophanies so as to ensure that they are amenable to being handled as historical occurrences of the kind that historians treat using reason and the tools of critical historical research. As a consequence, he has little alternative than to insist that the first appearances were in fact simply "meetings" with the Raised Jesus within this world of space and time.

However, a selective reading of the Easter stories of Luke and John which focusses attention on their alleged "massive physical detail" but which by-passes the persistent element of mystery and surprise, doubt, and questioning, that is so much a part of the resurrection tradition even as Luke and John themselves present it, is bound to lead to an unsatisfactory outcome. Any discussion of the manner of the "seeing" of the Raised Christ must take account of the apparent ambiguity of perception that is so much a feature of the narrative stories of the first appearances. If this element of ambiguity and mystery is not accounted for, but casually passed over or pushed aside in the interests of presenting the appearances as clear and distinct phenomena of the kind that can be appropriated naturally and visually, and thus handled as evidence relating to a straightforward historical event, then violence is done to the Easter tradition.

Very importantly, no systematic theology of the Resurrection can avoid the question of how it is possible to account for the fact that while some witnesses saw and claimed to recognize Jesus, others did not. On the contrary, it is precisely these elements of ambiguity and mystery which admit a high degree of freedom in perception, that suggest we are dealing with an event that could only be appropriated by faith by those "who have eyes to see" or those who, as Luke put it, were "chosen by God" to be by grace witnesses of the Resurrection. The epistemological element of perceptual freedom, either to see and perceive, or not to see, is far too much a part of the Easter traditions to be passed over as a theologically irrelevant datum. Indeed, the element of ambiguity and mystery in the manner of Jesus' appearing, and the fact that his presence could either be perceived or not perceived as the case may be, has not only to be explained but also put to creative theological purpose.

Contrary to the kind of portrayal of the appearances by Davis and Wright, I think we must frankly admit that the Easter traditions of appearances in the New Testament remain mysteriously opaque in many respects. However, the fact that they actually defy attempts to systematize them into one coherent narrative of a straightforward and literally understood kind may not turn out to be as troublesome as may at first appear. On the contrary, this may be a positive pointer to their essential value, for this makes them alluringly tantalizing. By their very nature they open us to the transcending mystery of Jesus' Resurrection and deliver us from the materialist reductionism presupposed by trying to prove the Resurrection simply as an event of human history.

We do well candidly to admit that there is a sense in which the Easter traditions themselves suggest that they must be assessed as attempts to bear witness to a transcendental Event that is in principle beyond the limits of understanding by reason alone. As a matter of principle, the Resurrection is a mystery that is in this sense "beyond words." In this case, the artistic impulse, found both in Eastern Orthodox iconography and in Western frescoes, which portrays the Raised Christ in a lozenge-shaped mandorla,[66] lifted from the ground and out of history, the surrounding clouds suggesting the timeless eternity of heaven, is an eminently legitimate and useful graphic attempt to convey something of the surpassing mystery that appears to have attached to the original Easter experience of appearances.

66. The ancient symbol of two circles overlapping one another to form an almond shape, from the Italian "mandorla" (almond), is a symbol of wholeness, and of earth and heaven coming together as, for example, famously depicted in Fra Angelico's *Resurrection of Christ and Women at the Tomb*, in the Convent Museum of St. Mark, Florence, and in many other similar representations.

5

Paul and The Empty Tomb

Given the historiographical difficulties that are encountered in handling the New Testament evidence relating to the appearances of the Raised Christ, it is sometimes argued that the tradition of the empty tomb both clarifies the nature of the appearances themselves and then positively assists the quest to establish the historicity of the resurrection.[1] This means that the question of the historical reliability of the story of the finding of the empty tomb itself becomes of crucial importance.

Fortunately, this tradition appears to involve a much more straightforward judgment of a matter of historical fact compared with the tradition of the appearances. Indeed, some scholars have argued that the meaning to be drawn from the mysteriously ambiguous accounts of the appearances is greatly clarified when the story of the discovery of the empty tomb is brought into association with them.[2] This is for the obvious reason that the emptiness of the tomb implies that the appearance narratives report not a revelatory Christophany from heaven, so much as what has conventionally come to be called a Christepiphany, a visual seeing of a thoroughly material Jesus, physically restored in bodily form to this world of space and time.

This means that we have to be open to the possibility that the empty tomb story might operate in such a way as to enhance the capacity of the appearances tradition to furnish us with historical evidence by making it clear that a living Jesus, restored to historical life in this world, simply vacated the tomb, leaving it empty. In this way, he could have been seen in a straightforward visual manner, and the first believers could clearly have engaged in "meetings" with him. In whatever way this is then explained, whether theologically as a miracle of God, or purely naturally as the revival of one mistakenly assumed to have been dead, as in the case of Paulus and Renan in the nineteenth-century, the implication of the story of the empty tomb is that Jesus' body

1. This is in fact N. T. Wright's position.

2. For example, Wolfhart Pannenberg in *Jesus—God and Man*, 1968; and Pannenberg, "Did Jesus Really Rise from the Dead," 134–35.

was a physical body, concretely material enough to be visually seen and identified. Such an understanding further suggests that the observation of the physically restored Jesus would have thus been sufficiently clear and distinct to become the object of verbal reports that are essentially the same as reports of any other historical event with which a historian might have to do. Clearly, much depends therefore upon the historicity of the story of the empty tomb.

Immediately, however, we face a further set of difficulties. The earliest written evidence for the empty tomb is found in the Gospel of St. Mark (c. AD 65+), after the elapse of a whole generation of Christian faith and worship, and a full ten to fifteen years after Paul wrote his first letter to the Corinthians in AD 52–55. Somewhat surprisingly, Paul's kerygmatic summary of the evidence for the resurrection in 1 Cor 15:3–8 contains no explicit mention of it. Indeed, the story of the empty tomb is missing from the entire corpus of the Pauline letters. Given that the story of its discovery surfaces at a comparatively late date in the literary record of Christian origins, many scholars have held that it is the product of a pre-existing faith, rather than the historical basis of faith. In other words, it has been explained as a story that was developed as a way of proclaiming the Resurrection, or as an apologetically motivated explanatory defense of resurrection faith. In this case it cannot therefore be regarded as evidence that might be used to prove the occurrence of the Resurrection as a historical event.

Most notably, this was the approach taken by Rudolf Bultmann[3] and others influenced by him. To use Bultmann's own phrase, the story of the empty tomb is to be understood as "an apologetic legend." This view has been tenaciously promoted by Willi Marxsen,[4] and also very notably by Gerd Lüdemann.[5] Bultmann argued that faith is precipitated by the church's proclamation of the saving event of the Cross, and that the Raised Christ is encountered "in the proclamation." In an existential moment in which his living Word is heard as a word of address, the Raised Christ is known as one who calls those who hear to faith and discipleship. Thus, "faith comes through hearing" (Rom 10:17). Hence, the defining catch cry of Bultmann's resurrection theology: "Christ was raised into the kerygma." The empty tomb along with the narratives of the appearances are then categorized as later legendary expressions of faith.

Willi Marxsen, on the other hand, who furnishes us with a well-argued paradigm of this general kind of approach, contended that the Easter Event was simply "the coming to faith" of the first disciples, in the sense of the dawning of a conviction

3. In Bultmann, *The History of the Synoptic Tradition*, 290. Also, Dibelius, *From Tradition to Gospel*, 190.

4. Marxsen, "The Resurrection of Jesus."

5. Lüdemann, *The Resurrection of Jesus*, 118 and 123.

among them *that* the historical Jesus was the long-awaited Messiah.[6] In this case, faith is not a commitment of trust (*fiducia*) based upon a cognitive judgment (*fides*) relating to an objective historical event involving the restoration of Jesus to life. Instead, faith is the noncognitive discernment of the theological meaning and significance to be accorded the historical life of Jesus; it is more like "seeing the light" by grasping the inner significance of the Christ Event. In other words, for Marxsen faith becomes the subjective awareness of the *real significance* or theological meaning and importance of the historical Jesus. It is a purely intellectual kind of "seeing," somewhat like seeing the point of a joke, though obviously with the gravitas appropriate to religious faith. In this case the empty tomb story becomes little more than a way of expressing this newfound faith among those who had been Jesus' original disciples, but plays no part in providing the evidential ground of faith.

Alternatively, some Roman Catholic scholars, particularly, have suggested that the story of the empty tomb arose in the course of the development of an early Easter liturgy, perhaps at a traditional Jerusalem tomb site or even some place else. To those of this mind, the liturgical context of the rehearsal of the original story is suggested by its temporal location at an early morning hour, the procession of the women to the tomb being reminiscent of some kind of religious procession, and the words put on the lips of the angel who, as if in a passion play, points to the place, and says "Look, see where they laid him."[7] This explanation has to contend with the difficulty that a set liturgical rehearsal of the story fails to account for the development of variants in the story that emerged in its apparent telling and re-telling, as we shall see.

Still others have argued that the empty tomb story was actually the literary creation of Mark himself. In this case, it is held that Mark's primary intention was to present an account of the disappearance of Jesus' body, and to explain its inexplicable absence from the tomb as an "assumption into heaven" similar to the Jewish tradition of the assumption of Enoch in Gen 5:24, and of Elijah in 2 Kgs 2:11, and also the extracanonical story of the *Assumption of Moses*. In this case, an assumption tradition based upon the empty tomb story is contrasted with a resurrection tradition based upon the appearances. Daniel Smith, following Adela Yarbro Collins, has contended, for example, that this kind of "assumption into heaven," rather than a resurrection, is actually what Mark had in mind in narrating the story of the discovery that the tomb was empty.

Apart from the biblical precedents for assumptions into heaven, this thesis is argued on the basis of alleged literary parallels with other assumption stories of notable figures in the Greco-Roman world, such as the assumption of the two most popular heroes of antiquity, Herakles and Achilles, and also of Romulus in the myth of the foundation of Rome.[8] In the case of Herakles, for example, Apollodorus says that

---

6. Marxsen, *The Resurrection of Jesus of Nazareth*, 159.

7 This view was proposed in Schille, "Das Leiden des Herrn."

8. Collins, "The Empty Tomb in the Gospel according to Mark," 107–40, esp. 130–31; Collins,

"While the pyre was burning, it is said that a cloud passed under Herakles and with a peal of thunder wafted him up to heaven."[9]

Then, in addition to this ancient literary tradition, there are the sporadic accounts that surface from time to time of an imperial apotheosis. This too is said to provide a model for what Mark intended to convey through his story of the empty tomb.

This thesis of Collins and Smith, attributing the empty tomb story to the literary creativity of Mark, is not without its difficulties. For a start, the idea that Mark had a "disappearance" and an assumption into heaven, rather than a resurrection followed by appearances, in mind does not square with Mark's own clear anticipations of the resurrection earlier in his Gospel,[10] nor with the words of the angel at the tomb, "He is risen . . . He goes before you into Galilee, there you will see him" (Mark 16:6–7). On the other hand, the idea of an assumption into heaven on the basis of literary parallels, but without clear indications in Mark's actual text of some kind of dependence on sources of this kind, seems unnecessarily speculative. Apart from these difficulties of the Collins/Smith thesis, it does not provide a persuasive answer to the question of the possible Marcan authorship of the story.

For the moment it is sufficient to note that all these suggestions that seek to account for the story of the empty tomb as the product of faith, rather than the evidential basis of it, arise as thinkable options primarily because it first comes to light in the written tradition of primitive Christianity only at such a relatively late date. The fact that it is not mentioned at all by St. Paul in 1 Cor 15:3–8 is particularly arresting. Its absence there is doubly troublesome given Paul's insistence that he was passing on a normative piece of early tradition that he himself had received.[11] We have to conclude from this that the absence of the empty tomb from this normative tradition pre-dates Paul. Though this is passed over by N. T. Wright, who says that the fact that the empty tomb "does not appear to be specifically mentioned in this passage, is not significant,"[12] many may beg to differ.[13] At the very least, Paul's omission of it is surprising, given that one of Paul's aims in writing to the Corinthian Christians was to remind them of the original Easter proclamation that he had himself delivered to them when he first visited them in AD 49–50, and that first established them in their

---

Mark, 791–93. Also Smith, *Revisiting the Empty Tomb,* chapter 3.

9. Apollodorus, *The Library* 2, 7, 7.

10. For example the clear predictions of Mark 8:31; 9:31; and 10:34.

11. As we have already noted, since 1926 when Kittel first made the observation, it has been well appreciated that Paul uses the technical rabbinical formula for the receiving and handing on of a tradition.

12. *RSG,* 321.

13. The priority of Paul and his silence with regard to the empty tomb along with his allegedly nonphysical understanding of resurrection is Lüdemann's basic reason for thinking of the empty tomb tradition as a crude materialistic development that post-dates Paul. See Lüdemann, *The Resurrection of Jesus,* 121.

faith. Was the story of the empty tomb then not an item of his original proclamation of the Easter message?

Given that this reminder in 1 Corinthians 15 was intended to address the problem that some Corinthian Christians were apparently doubting the Resurrection,[14] Paul was intent upon calling them back to their original Easter faith. It is very difficult to avoid the conclusion, particularly in view of the fact that Paul indicates that this "kerygmatic summary" of the Easter proclamation which he handed on, and had at an even earlier time been received by him, that he regards this as a piece of Christian tradition that is normative for faith. This makes the puzzle posed by the absence from it of any mention of the empty tomb confrontingly troublesome. If that original normative proclamation was without explicit reference to the empty tomb, it seems to be entailed that an understanding of Easter faith could possibly get by without it. We dare not simply try to side-step the potential importance of its absence by passing this off as "not significant."

Sometimes it is argued that, while Paul does not explicitly mention it, a reference to the emptiness of the tomb could be said to be *implied* in some of the phrases used by him in 1 Cor 15:3–8. For example, in v. 3 the statement "that Christ died for our sins in accordance with the scriptures, that *he was buried*, and that he was raised . . ." is sometimes said to presuppose or suggest a raising from out of the tomb in which he had been buried. However, it can be argued that this reference to the burial really underlines that fact that Jesus was actually dead; i.e. that he was "dead and buried." It does not necessarily imply that he was raised from out of the tomb in which he had been buried in such a way that the tomb was itself left entirely empty.[15] This is to read far more into Paul's words than they are capable of bearing.

Also, it has been argued that because the verb *egēgertai* ("he has been raised") is usually followed by the phrase "from the dead," it can be inferred from the use of this word that this really means "*from the grave*" and that likewise this verb therefore implies the emptiness of the tomb. However, even if the association of "he was raised" with the phrase "from the dead" were to suggest a resurrection "from the tomb," that still leaves all the key questions unanswered: does his being raised "from the grave," or "from the dead," simply mean that he was restored to *this* world in the manner of a literal "standing up of a corpse" or did the raising "from the grave" instead involve a transformation through death characterized by exaltation, and glorification of a more transcendental, heavenly kind? Jesus may certainly have been raised "from the dead,"

14. 1 Cor 15:12: "How can some of you say there is no resurrection of the dead?"

15. With regard to Paul's expression "that Christ died . . . and was buried" (1 Cor 15:3–4), Christopher Evans remarks that "this expression may simply be used to underline the reality and apparent finality of the death itself, and say nothing beyond this" (see Evans, *Resurrection and the New Testament*, 75 n.67).

but that still leaves this important question without answer: was the tomb left empty and entirely "without remainder" in this process, and was it actually discovered to be so? The answers to these historical questions still hang in the air.

The significance of the omission of any explicit reference to the tradition of the finding of the empty tomb from 1 Corinthians 15 is compounded by the fact that the empty tomb is not mentioned in the course of the whole of the Pauline corpus of letters. Clearly, it can hardly be said that Paul regarded it, if indeed he knew of it, as an important evidential ingredient of the make-up of faith. Effectively, this also means that it does not feature at all in the earliest written stratum of New Testament evidence relating to the Resurrection. Whether it enjoyed an earlier life prior to its inclusion in Mark's Gospel, or whether it was the literary creation of Mark himself, therefore unavoidably becomes an unresolved Christian hypothetical.

Paul's silence with regard to the tradition of the empty tomb, presents a clear problem for anyone seeking use the evidence of the empty tomb to prove the occurrence of the Jesus' Resurrection. The alleged historicity of the empty tomb tradition is clearly therefore of enormous importance for N. T. Wright's whole project. His insistence upon trying to prove the Resurrection as a historical event, and particularly as the kind of event in which Jesus was restored materially and physically to this world, precisely in such a way as to leave a tomb empty, brooks no alternative. Even if the lateness of the tradition and the discrepancies in the various versions of the story across the four Gospels are acknowledged, it is clearly necessary for him to come up with some kind of proof of the historicity of at least the original kernel of the tradition that is common to all versions of the story. We can sympathize with his quest, while entertaining very serious reservations about the logical safety of his conclusions.

If we set aside the set of issues relating to the variety of detail, and even actual discrepancies, among the four Gospel versions of the story, and discount their importance as indicators of the redactional development of the tradition in the course of its transmission, the chief obstacle Wright has to overcome is the apparent lateness of the first written tradition we have (i.e. its first appearance in Mark) and our inability actually to demonstrate the existence of a prior tradition, whether oral or written. On the other hand, its *absence* from the earliest stratum of the written Christian witness represented by the writings of St. Paul remains a major stumbling block. Given that Wright has no alternative than to admit its comparatively late appearance in the documentary record of Christian origins, he is obliged to argue that the story *could* possibly have been known much earlier, perhaps as part of an oral tradition or perhaps even in a document long since lost. In the explicit case of Paul, Wright contends that, despite the fact that Paul omits any mention of the empty tomb, it can seriously be contended that it was nevertheless actually known to him, and that he simply chose not to mention it explicitly, and this with good reason. Clearly, at this point Wright has to enter into the risky business of arguing to Paul's authorial intentions even from Paul's silence.

He admits that it is strange that Paul does not mention it, particularly in reminding the Corinthians of the content of his original preaching to them. Had it been a key feature of his original preaching in Corinth, it would surely have been mentioned in this reprise in 1 Corinthians 15. As we have already noted, its absence is doubly troublesome given Paul's insistence that this was something that he himself had received as a normative piece of early tradition. This is particularly so in view of the fact that he was then attempting to win the wavering Corinthians back to an authentic Easter faith. It is also admittedly strange, if Paul knew of the empty tomb tradition, that he consistently continued to omit or suppress any mention of it through the writing of the entire corpus of his letters. The question as to whether Paul regarded the story of the empty tomb as a very important element of Christian resurrection faith thus becomes very problematic.

Nevertheless, despite all these difficulties Wright believes that there is a decisive argument in favor of the historicity of at least the kernel of the empty tomb tradition, and also for Paul's alleged knowledge of it, even if he did not ever mention it. The nub of his argument is that women witnesses rather than men were said to have discovered the empty tomb.[16] The significance of the appearance of women as witnesses in the story is that the Mishnah and Talmud make it clear that at Jewish law women did not qualify as competent witnesses.[17] This is backed up by the evidence of Josephus, who also observed that women were not regarded as competent witnesses in Jewish law.[18] The fact that the testimony of women was not valued in the ancient Jewish world and that their testimony was not admissible at law,[19] Wright believes, is sufficient to account for the quite deliberate omission of the story of the empty tomb by Paul, even in his account of his first Easter proclamation to the Corinthians. There was no point in mentioning it, so the argument runs, if the women witnesses were not legally competent and were thus disqualified from providing such testimony.[20]

---

16. *RSG*, 326 and again, 607–8.

17. Though there is no explicit prohibition on women witnesses in the Torah, the view that only men could be competent witnesses was derived from Scripture by the method of *gezerah shavah*. Maimonides gives as the reason for the disqualification of women the fact that the Bible uses the masculine form when speaking of witnesses. However, Joseph Caro questioned the validity of this derivation in view of the fact that the whole Torah always uses the masculine form. Nevertheless, the place of a woman was in her home and not in court, as the honor of the king's daughter was within the house (Ps 45:14).

18. Josephus on the law of witnesses (Deut 19:15) in *Ant.* 4.219: "From women let no evidence be accepted, because of the levity and temerity of their sex."

19. See *RSG*, 607.

20. The same point is made by Gerhardsson, "Mark and the Female Witnesses," 225–26; and Witherington, *Conflict and Community in Corinth*, 300.

N. T. Wright apparently sees no contradiction in arguing that Paul deliberately omits mention of the empty tomb because it was only attested by women, while Mark (Mark 16:1–8 and synoptic parallels) and John (John 20:1–2, 11–18) apparently felt no such compunction in reporting it, presumably despite the operation of the same legal inhibitions. On the contrary, the appearance of women in the Gospel traditions is a positive for Wright. He argues that, had it been a fabricated story or had it been generated in the course of the early church's preaching and/or liturgy or, we may add, even if it were the literary creation of Mark himself, it would naturally have been furnished with male witnesses and not untrustworthy women: "If they could have invented stories of fine, upstanding, reliable male witnesses being first at the tomb, they would have done it."[21] The actual inclusion of women in the Gospel stories is therefore said to speak of the authenticity of the empty tomb tradition. As Gerald O'Collins put this same argument some years in anticipation of Wright's use of it: "Legend-makers do not normally invent positively unhelpful material."[22]

We might add to this that Paul's alleged failure to use the empty tomb tradition because women were associated with it is of a piece with the fact that elsewhere Paul, somewhat notoriously, seems to entertain subordinationist views of women anyway, and bids them, for example, to be silent in the churches, for "they are not permitted to speak" (1 Cor 14:34–35). If they are to be kept mute in church, they may likewise be entirely eliminated from the tradition by Paul, even to the point that any references to the empty tomb is sacrificed along with them.

Certainly, given the submission of women in the ancient world, Wright argues that the resurrection tradition quoted by Paul, "precisely for evangelistic and apologetic use, has carefully taken the women out of it so that it can serve that purpose in a suspicious and mocking world."[23] Indeed, it is not just that women have been eliminated from the tradition, but the entire empty tomb story has been eliminated from Paul's public discussion of the Resurrection along with them.

Against this hypothesis, if the empty tomb story was late in comparative terms, and if it was generated as an apologetic story either to support or further explicate resurrection belief, we have to note that it could hardly have been furnished with male

21. *RSG*, 608.

22. O'Collins, *Christology*, 94; also much earlier, *The Easter Jesus*, 42–43: "The role of women in the story provides a sound argument for its historical reliability." The number of scholars who have made the lack of legal qualification of the women as witnesses serve as evidence against theories of the fabulous nature of the empty tomb story is legion. See Bode, *The First Easter Morning*, 157–58, 160–61, and 173; also Perkins, *Resurrection*, 94; Coakley, "Is the Resurrection a 'Historical' Event?" 100; Hebblethwaite, "The Resurrection and the Incarnation," 158; Schweizer, "Resurrection—Fact or Fiction?" 147; Cranfield, "The Resurrection of Jesus Christ," 384. Dunn promotes the same argument in *Jesus Remembered*, 833.

23. *RSG*, 607.

witnesses, anyway. If we can rely on the Gospel tradition that the male disciples fled from Calvary and appear to have headed back to Galilee (Mark 14:27, 50), which was therefore the location of the first experiences of the appearance of the Raised Jesus to them, and that *only* women (Mary Magdalene and Mary the mother of Joses, Mark 15:47), therefore, were left behind to observe "where he was laid," it follows that only women disciples were on hand and in possession of the relevant information to go to the right tomb, and thus to discover it empty. Women may appear in the empty tomb story, despite their inadequate legal status as witnesses, precisely because there was no alternative.[24]

I am not at all persuaded that some of the male disciples may have remained in Jerusalem, even despite the obvious danger to themselves. This has been argued by A. J. M. Wedderburn on the ground that there is no convincing evidence that the disciples returned to Galilee immediately after Jesus death.[25] Richard Bauckham's observation that "They would, in any case, not have travelled on the sabbath"[26] is surely a quibble. To have fled even in the direction of Galilee so as to have traveled just a few kilometers from Jerusalem before sunset on the day of Jesus' crucifixion would have been sufficient to remove them from the burial scene. The over-whelming thrust of the evidence, however, is nevertheless that they scattered in fear (Mark 14:50), and that the first Easter experiences were in Galilee, and there is no positive evidence whatever that they were present at the burial of Jesus' body. Mark makes it clear that Mary Magdalene and Mary the Mother of Joses are clearly the primary witnesses of the whereabouts of the tomb. That Luke's mention of Peter at the site of the tomb (Luke 24:12) and of other disciples going to the tomb (Luke 24:24) qualifies as reliable historical evidence, as suggested by James Dunn,[27] seems very doubtful, given Luke's interest in relocating the original appearances to the disciples from Galilee to Jerusalem (even to the point of changing the message of the angel at the tomb from the directive to "go into Galilee," to a remembrance about the disciples once "being in Galilee," Luke 24:6). This is at variance with the Matthean tradition that the eleven all went to Galilee (Matt 28:16). The other alleged evidence cited by Dunn to shore up his contention that some disciples remained in Jerusalem, is that John 21 mentions that only seven of the eleven were present when Jesus appeared on the Galilean shore as they were fishing (John 21:2). Apart from the fact that this asks us to assume that if they were not fishing they could not have been elsewhere in Galilee, but must have remained in Jerusalem, which is a big ask,[28] Dunn has to contend with the fact that

---

24. Williams, "The Trouble with the Resurrection" 233, notes that women *had* to be represented as the ones who found the tomb empty because the males discipels had all fled.

25. Wedderburn, *Beyond Resurrection*, 58–60.

26. Bauckham, *Gospel Women*, 258 n.2.

27. Dunn, *Jesus Remembered*, 834.

28. After all, Mark seems clearly of the view that they "fled" and were "scattered" (Mark 14:27 and 50).

Peter is explicitly named as one of the seven in John 21:2. This hardly squares with Luke's concern to have him by the tomb in Jerusalem. Dunn cannot both have his cake and eat it.[29] His contention that the women were not left alone in Jerusalem when the disciples scattered into Galilee is hardly convincing.

On the other hand, despite Bauckham's (admittedly muted) support of Wedderburn's contention that there is no evidence that they fled immediately to Galilee, and that they would not have travelled on the Sabbath, he nevertheless acknowledges that Peter (assuming the historicity of Luke 24:12 and John 20:2–10) was dependent upon the women "since only they knew which tomb was Jesus."[30] Clearly, despite all this special pleading in the nervous quest for the historicity of eyewitness testimony, it is clear that the dominant presence of women in the story of the discovery of the empty tomb, despite their inadequate legal credentials as witnesses, may not really be evidence of the historicity of the tradition, but merely the inconsequential result of the fact that women and not men were the witnesses of Jesus' burial and are explicitly said to have observed the place where his body was laid. Any story of the discovery of his tomb empty therefore had no alternative than to rely on them.

I will return to this issue below. For the moment it is enough simply to say that perhaps a set tradition of the absence of the male disciples in Jerusalem immediately after the crucifixion is sufficient to explain why Mark's version of the story is furnished with women witnesses despite the drawback of their perceived unreliability and lack of legal competence.

However, the real question is: can we be quite so sure that Paul's culturally conditioned inclination towards the subordination of women was quite so thoroughgoing as to cause him, if he did know of the empty tomb, to omit mentioning it for that specific reason in the "kerygmatic summary" in 1 Cor 15:3–8? He may have directed that women should not disturb the meetings for worship of the Corinthian Christians by restraining them from asking questions at worship, and exhorting them to remain silent until they could consult their husbands quietly at home (1 Cor 14:35). But does this really mean that they had to be kept entirely mute, even when they were not in a position of ignorance but were actually in possession of such a crucial piece of evidence, given that they were the first, and perhaps only witnesses, of the empty tomb?

In seeking to defend the general credibility of the women's witness, Richard Bauckham has pointed out that, though the status of women generally in the ancient world led men to very negative views of their reliability, particularly in matters of

---

29. We may note in passing that John mentions five disciples by name, and then adds "two other of his disciples" to make a total of seven—the complete number (John 21:2).

30. Bauckham, *Gospel Women*, 279.

religious belief, this may not have been so in the Jewish cultural-religious context.[31] Bauckham is impressed, for example, by the tradition of Pseudo-Philo's *Biblical Antiquities*, which on two occasions portrays biblical women receiving and communicating the revelation of God. In one instance, Moses' sister Miriam is said to have received a prophecy in a dream, which as it happens is not believed by those for whom it was intended.[32] In the second instance, Samson's mother is told about his coming birth and she reports it to her husband Manoah.[33] In this case Manoah did not believe his wife. Bauckham points to the similarities between these stories and the account of the women at the tomb, whose report also was not at first believed. Bauckham is impressed, however, by the fact that there were Jewish precedents for the communication of revelation to men by women.

Even so, the usual argument both in favor of the historicity of the empty tomb story, and at the same time in defense of Paul's refusal to reply upon it or even to mention it, is that women were regarded as ineligible to be witnesses at Jewish law. However, in this case we have to ask if we are right in taking some abstract legal formulae about the status of Jewish women as witnesses in Jewish law as clear indications of actual practice. In other words, can we be at all sure that there was complete parity between the unreliability of women perceived by Josephus and the abstract provisions of law attested by some of the Rabbis, and the actual jurisprudential practice "on the ground" as it were? Can an alleged parity between theory and practice be proved? The existence of a law is one thing; whether human behavior patterns always conform to it is quite another. After all, people drive motor vehicles today at excessive speed, despite the existence of legal provisions designed to prohibit above-limit speeding. People do not always or necessarily adhere to the provisions of law. And can the prohibition on relying on the evidence of women be said to have operated in all cases, particularly in situations where there were only women witnesses, and in a context that was not strictly speaking a legal courtroom? To cite a few texts from the Mishnah and Talmud is one thing, but can we simply assume that people conformed to them in every conceivable circumstance?

The Mishnah and Talmud exist in large part because of the need to develop oral (and eventually written) traditions precisely about the interpretation and application of the abstract and necessarily general provisions of law. Indeed, the Talmud clearly shows that among those skilled in the interpretation of Jewish law and its application in specific circumstances, this became something of an art form.

---

31. Bauckham, *Gospel Women*, 274.

32. Pseudo-Philo, *Biblical Antiquities* 9:10. When Miriam reported her dream "Her parents did not believe her." Even so, as Bauckham points out (*Gospel Women*, 272) she is called "a prophet" in Exod 15:20.

33. Pseudo-Philo, *Biblical Antiquities*, 42:1–5.

There are three texts from Mishnah and Talmud[34] that are regularly cited by contemporary Christian theologians in support of the contention that women suffered from a fundamental incapacity to bear testimony in the ancient Jewish world. When these three texts are examined a little more closely, we find that the story is not quite as simple as those who have appealed to them suggest. For example, the first of these references, *m. Šebu.* 4:1, actually says:

> The law about "an oath of testimony" applies to men but not to women, to them that are not kinsfolk but not to them that are kinsfolk, to them that are qualified [to bear witness] but not to them that are not qualified, and it applies only to them that are fit to bear witness; and [it applies whether uttered] before a court or not before a court; but it must be uttered out of a man's own mouth. If [he was abjured] at the mouth of others, he is not liable until he has denied his knowledge before a court. So R. Meir. But the Sages say: Whether [he swore] out of his own mouth or [was abjured] at the mouth of others, a man is not liable until he has denied his knowledge before a court.

If Paul was intent upon conforming so scrupulously to the vow of testimony[35] as not to make reference to the story of the empty tomb because of its reliance on women witnesses, then what do we make of his positive inclusion of the reference to the appearance of the Raised Jesus to "James and the apostles" as witnesses (1 Cor 15:7)? Given that it was not just women to whom the vow of testimony did not apply, but "close" relatives as well, this would have excluded the testimony of James. James was the brother of the Lord. If this legal requirement were really being followed, that would surely rule out any reliance on the testimony of such a close relative. Of course, it could be argued that bearing witness to reports of the Resurrection is not the same thing as hearing evidence upon which an individual might be either convicted or acquitted of a crime in a court of law, and that this law does not apply in this case. But that simply concedes the point.

Furthermore, there is evidence to suggest that in some circumstances even in matters of legal procedure the evidence of women may have in fact been acceptable. The contention that women were never considered reliable witnesses is challenged by the fact that we read of women witnesses even in the Torah. The classic example is that of the Prophetess Deborah who, as a judge of Israel (Judg 4:4), was also qualified as a witness.[36] Also, it was two women who were interrogated by Solomon in the celebrated story about the correct ownership of the disputed baby, which became a much

---

34. *m. Šeb.* 4:1; *m. Roš Haš.* 1:8; and *b. B. Qam.* 88a. See appendix 2 for the relevant texts, and a discussion of their significance.

35. The law with regard to the oath of testimony is found in Lev 5:1–6.

36. *m. Nid.* 6:4: "whoever is eligible as judge is eligible to testify."

revered and often quoted paradigm in relation to the testing of witnesses. Despite the received law proscribing the testimony of women, in actual practice it eventually became necessary for women to be admitted as competent witnesses at least in matters within their particular knowledge;[37] for example, in the case of customs or events in places frequented only by women;[38] in matters of their own and other women's purity; for purposes of identification, especially of other women; or in matters outside the realm of strict law. In post-talmudic times, the evidence of women was often admitted where there were no other witnesses available, or in matters not considered important enough to bother male witnesses.[39] Tal Ilan contends that while the Rabbis "disqualified women as witnesses . . . the judicial system in Palestine of that period (the Greco-Roman period) did not operate to any extent according to the Pharisees and in fact often needed testimony from women."[40] Richard Bauckham has raised a query about the precise meaning of "often" in this statement of Tal Ilan, and we certainly have to beware of anachronistically reading later practices in the interpretation of law back in time, though it has to be remembered that even medieval and sixteenth-century teachers believed they were passing on authentic oral traditions. Bauckham has also specifically questioned the views of R. G. Maccini and Robert J. Karris for assuming too readily that the Mishnah informs us as to the law in operation in the late Second Temple period.[41]

Even so, there was certainly an ancient *takkanah* relating to the witness of women, which is even today regularly cited as the classic precedent for admitting the evidence of women. This is one of two instances when the school of Hillel reversed its own ruling and adopted the ruling of Shammai[42] concerning the testimony of women in relation to the death of a husband, which provides a legal precedent for the admissibility of women's testimony more generally. There is therefore at least sufficient justification for raising a question about the way in which the ancient law disqualifying women from giving evidence was actually applied in practice in specific situations. The fact that two women are explicitly mentioned in the empty tomb story as those who witnessed the burial, and that they were therefore in the position to have noted its precise location, and that these women believed they were returning to the same

37. Thus, Wegner, *Chattel or Person? The Status of Women in the Mishnah*, observes that "the Mishnah's framers permit a woman's testimony only because they cannot otherwise get at the truth" (122). Maccini likewise insists that the Mishnah allows women's testimony in certain cases (*Her Testimony Is True*, 68).

38. *Rema ḤeMapah* 35:14; *Darkhei Moshe ḤeMapah* 35 n. 3; *Terumat ha-Deshen* Resp. no. 353.

39. A disucssion of detailed references relating to this issue may be found in appendix 2.

40. Ilan, *Jewish Women*, 163–66, and especially 227.

41. Bauckham, *Gospel Women*, 270. See Maccini, *Her Testimony Is True*, 68; and Karris, "Women and Discipleship in Luke," 18–19. Karris follows Wegner's assessment of the status of women in *Chattel or Person*, 120–21. See also Meiselman, *Jewish Women in Jewish Law*, 73–80.

42. *m. 'Ed.* 1:12 and parallel in *m. Yebam.* 15:2, of which *'Eduyyot* appears to be the earlier. See Elon, *Jewish Law, History, Sources, Principles*, 524.

tomb, means, in the absence of men, that they were the *only* ones who could competently give reliable testimony to it. In this circumstance their testimony may well have been heard. Had men been present the women would no doubt have been superseded as witnesses, but without men the situation is clearly different.

On the other hand, there is a cultural possibility that *only* women were permitted to touch a dead body and prepare it for burial; in other words, this is possibly a women's ritual. In this case, *only* the witness of women could be called upon. It is noteworthy that the *Gospel of Peter* says that the women came to the tomb because they "had not done at the Lord's sepulcher the things which the women are wont to do for those that die and are beloved by them."[43] If Mark's reference to the procession of the women with spices (in Mark 16:1) for the purpose of anointing Jesus' body indicates that this cultural rule was operative in the first century, then the application of the rule about the general inadmissibility of women witnesses may not have applied. Without evidence to exclude the operation of the cultural requirement to inhibit men from touching a dead body for reasons of purity in the first century, we cannot simply assume how the law of testimony operated. In this case, the *only* competent witnesses would have been the women who could have provided the required evidence.

Without considering the need of its interpretation in relation to the specific circumstances of its application, the law remains abstract and general. How an abstract general law about the incompetence of women would actually have applied in the particular case of the story of the empty tomb remains indeterminate. Indeed, the Gospel traditions of the empty tomb suggest that the veracity of the story was originally questioned not necessarily because the witnesses were women, but because of the extraordinary nature of their claims. It is perhaps significant that in his reported critique of resurrection belief among Christians, "Celsus himself makes nothing of the fact that Christian claims rest on the evidence of women; instead he points out scornfully that the alleged Son of God 'was not able to open the tomb, but needed someone else to move the stone.'"[44] We cannot therefore be at all sure that Paul abandoned any interest in the empty tomb story, if indeed he knew of it, on the basis of an abstract legal principle without considering the subtleties of its interpretation and application in the context of the particular circumstances to which it may or may not have applied.

Moreover, it is equally possible that, if he knew of it, Paul did not mention it because it was not really all that useful to support his particular understanding of the transformed nature of the resurrection body, and the ultimate heavenly destination of the Raised Jesus, as something more transcendental than the matter-of-fact restoration of a material body to *this* world that the emptiness of the tomb implies. N. T. Wright's proffer of the suggestion that Paul tailored his proclamation of the Easter kerygma by omitting any reference to women so as to make it palatable to a

43. *Gospel of Peter*, Fragment xii, 50, 51.

44. Stanton, "Early Objections to the Resurrection," 81, quoting *Contra Celsus* v.52.

"suspicious and mocking world" is fanciful speculation. Entry into the mind of Paul at this point eludes us.

While, generally speaking, the Deuteronomic requirement of at least two witnesses is known to have applied beyond the narrow confines of a strictly legal environment, whether the incapacity of women to give evidence in a strictly legal and criminal environment also applied outside that environment is a question. The often quoted text from the Babylonian Talmud (*b. B. Qam.* 88a) relating to the incompetence at law of women to give testimony, actually involves a detailed discussion of a variety of types of legal cases, such as establishing the validity of a debt, and the undesirability of convicting fathers on the basis the evidence of their children and vice versa. Moreover, the context of the discussion has to do with the giving of evidence in a courtroom with a view to securing a legal conviction in monetary and capital cases. The overriding concern seems to be to ensure that justice be done by eliminating the testimony of those with some stake in a legal outcome. A child cannot give evidence to convict a father, for example, for this reason. But this relates in the Babylonian Talmud to criminal activity, the convictions of criminals, and even capital punishment. This text is not altogether clear about noncriminal activity and noncapital convictions. Given the kinds of legal cases being discussed, it is not at all clear how this often cited Talmudic reference could really be made relevant to Paul's alleged omission of the empty tomb story in writing to the Corinthians.

The argument that any mention of women was omitted in the resurrection tradition passed on by Paul to the Corinthians for reasons of legal scruple also has to surmount the difficulty that, in writing to the Corinthians, Paul was not actually giving evidence before a Rabbinic court (*Beit Din*), but writing to one of the communities, presumably comprised predominantly of Gentile Christians, which he himself had established. Consistency dictates that we could normally assume that Paul would have approached the Corinthian church as a community in which, by virtue of baptism, "all are one in Christ." It is unlikely that the Corinthian community was intended to be any less inclusive of everyone, than the community of the Galatians, to whom Paul had already articulated his vision of the inclusive eschatological community in Christ (Gal 3:28). This was a community worlds apart from a Jewish court of law. It was a community in which members enjoyed an equality of status by virtue of their baptism into Christ, regardless of the usual humanly devised divisions based upon race, or social class, or gender difference.

Indeed, Paul quotes Gal 3:28 twice in 1 Corinthians. In 1 Cor 12:13 he explicitly addresses the question of the social implications of baptism and reception of the Spirit, and in 1 Cor 7:17–24 appeal is made to the principle of the Galatians text in the context of advice specifically to slaves.[45] It is clear that in the community of Christ, unlike a Jewish court of law, divisions based upon distinctions of race, social status, or gender no longer necessarily held sway. Indeed, given that Paul has a good deal to say in his epistles about the tension between law and grace, and the ensuing freedom won by the gift of the Spirit, account must be taken of the over-riding importance of the operation of grace above and beyond the minimal set of requirements imposed by the law.[46] Despite the specific issues that troubled the Corinthian community, there is no reason to believe that Paul operated on the basis of some kind of inconsistency or double standard at this point between writing to the Galatians and then to the Corinthians.

It also has to be noted that, while Josephus explained that the incapacity of women as witnesses was due to the "levity and temerity of their sex,"[47] by which he apparently meant their alleged lack of gravitas or their lack of standing as "social light-weights,"[48] the Babylonian Talmud, which is so often cited as evidence for Paul's omission of the evidence of the empty tomb because of its reliance on women witnesses, provides an explanation of this in juridical terms. There, it is explicitly said that women are not covered by the law of evidence because they are not circumcised and therefore not "under the law."[49] What Paul would have made of this is anyone's guess, but his clearly expressed negative views about the operation of the law and its requirement of circumcision among those "in Christ" hardly supports the view that his lack of interest in the evidence of the women about the tomb (if indeed he knew of it) was explicitly discounted on the grounds cited by the Babylonian Talmud—i.e. that the law of evidence does not apply to women because they are not circumcised and therefore not under the law.

We therefore have here an additional quite serious difficulty relating to the discussion of the status of women witnesses. We cannot simply elevate a perception of women's lack of reliability articulated by Josephus, and a general legal principle defined in a few Rabbinical texts, or even a general deprecation of the social role of women in the ancient classical world, and import all this into the context of Paul's dealing with a community of baptized Christian believers, to the point where it overrides the fundamental Pauline principle of the free operation of grace among the baptized. This was a community that clearly included both men and women.[50] Some of those women in the communities of Corinth and its vicinity, such as Chloe in Corinth, Phoebe, the

---

45. 1 Cor 7:23: "You were bought with a price, do not become human slaves." Also, 1 Cor 6:20.

46. 2 Cor 3:17: "Where the Spirit of the Lord is, there is freedom."

47. Josephus, *Ant.* 4.219.

48. In a way that is thoroughly offensive to us today.

49. *b. B. Qam.* 88a.

50. See Schüssler Fiorenza, *In Memory of Her*, 219: "we must recognize that the Corinthian community probably consisted of a large number of active Christian women, who had a voice in the community's theology and practice."

deacon of nearby Cenchraea, and Prisca in Rome, exercised roles of leadership, and were women for whom Paul expressed respect as his co-workers (1 Cor 1:11; Rom 16:1, 3). This makes it doubly odd for us to accept the contention that an abstract legal principle operated in such a way as to eliminate all mention of the concrete historical testimony of women in relation to the Resurrection. This is especially so, given that such testimony was crucial to the defense of Easter faith among this community of people at Corinth, including both men and women, who, specifically in relation to resurrection belief, were backsliding. If, in the eschatological community constituted by the Spirit of Christ, social divisions based upon race, social status, and gender difference no longer held sway, it would be odd for Paul to omit crucial evidence relating to the Resurrection, if indeed he knew of it, simply on the ground that women witnesses were its original source.

On the other hand, we know of at least one woman by name, Junia, who is mentioned by Paul himself in Rom 16:7 along with her husband Andronicus. Junia and Andronicus are identified by Paul as his relatives, who were imprisoned with him, and they are also said to have been "in Christ" even before he was. Furthermore, Andronicus and Junia are described as being "highly esteemed among the apostles." Whether they were themselves "esteemed apostles" or whether they were simply esteemed *by* the apostles is not entirely clear, though the weight of scholarship now seems to favor the case for Junia's actually being numbered among the apostles in Paul's understanding of things.[51] Richard Bauckham conjectures that Junia is in fact Joanna, who at a later time is mentioned by Luke on a number of occasions as having been in the company of Jesus (Luke 8:3; 24:10), and whom Luke identifies as one of the women who discovered the tomb (Luke 24:8).[52] This identification of Joanna/Junia may appear to some to be something of a stretch.[53] But the fact remains that, whether Junia was actually an esteemed apostle herself or only a woman esteemed by the apostles, it is hard to imagine that she was not appreciated by Paul as being sufficiently esteemed to be thought capable of bearing witness to the resurrection faith.[54]

51. See the full discussion in Bauckham, *Gospel Women*, 172–80.

52. Bauckham, *Gospel Women*, 165–69.

53. Bauckham argues this on the grounds that, as one who was "in Christ" even before Paul, Junia/Joanna must have originally been a Palestinian and possibly even a Jerusalem Christian before going to Rome, and that it was a common practice particularly for diaspora Jews to adopt Latin names that sounded similar to Semitic names, hence Joanna/Junia. In this case, Joanna/Junia is identified as the wife of Chuza, Herod's household manager, who also features elsewhere in Luke's Gospel as one whom Jesus had healed (Luke 8:3), and who had been in the company of his followers on a number of occasions. This means that Andronicus is either her second husband with whom she is living in Rome, or else he too adopted a Latin name, hence Chuza/Andronicus. All this, while being possible, is surely very speculative.

54. See Bauckham's discussion of Joanna/Junia as apostolic witness in *Gospel Women*, 186–94.

But that is not the end of the matter. In 1 Cor 15:7 when Paul cites the appearance to James he adds "and all the apostles." For Paul, as distinct from Luke, the band of the apostles was much more extensive than just the twelve who had "gone in and out with Jesus" from earliest days.[55] Paul himself understood that he qualified as an apostle because he had "seen the Raised Christ" (1 Cor 9:1), even though he had not earlier been in the company of the disciples of the historical Jesus. Indeed, if Junia is to be identified with Joanna by another name, as Richard Bauckham would have us believe, then she would have qualified for apostolic status on that count also, had election to membership of that group been open to women. In any event, on the basis of Paul's specific understanding of the qualification for apostleship, Junia of Rom 16:7 may well have been regarded by Paul not only as one who was "esteemed" among the apostolic witnesses but she, along with her husband Andronicus, may well have been counted among "all the apostles" to whom the Raised Christ was said to have appeared along with James in 1 Cor 15:7. Certainly, if Paul counted Junia/Joanna among "all the apostles" to whom the Raised Christ had appeared, the idea that the empty tomb story was omitted by Paul from the kerygmatic summary of 1 Cor 15:3–8, specifically because of the fact that women were its witnesses, becomes even more problematic.

We have already noted that there were other influential women in leadership positions in the early Christian communities,[56] and Paul in his letters regularly addressed communities which apparently included both "brothers and sisters" without apparent discriminatory qualms.[57] It is true that in the original Greek texts Paul regularly addresses them simply as "brothers" (*adelphoi*); however, it is unlikely that this was understood in a gender exclusive sense. It was grammatically correct, in Greek as well as Latin, for masculine plural nouns to include a mixed sex grouping, and if males were present, then the masculine form of the noun would be chosen. The New Testament certainly appears to use *adelphoi* elsewhere also in an inclusive sense. For example, the NRSV translation of *adelphous* in Matt 5:47 as "brothers and sisters" in Jesus' exhortation to greet more than just immediate acquaintances; and *adelphos/on* in Matt 18:15, where the reference is to the private handling of unacceptable behavior in the church. The NRSV translates this inclusively as "members of the church" for the apparent reason that, despite the use of "brothers/brethren" in the text, Jesus' teaching

55. For Luke, the requirement of having been in the company of Jesus from the earliest days was stipulated at the time of the election of Matthias to replace Judas Iscariot. See Acts 1:21–22, where they seek to elect "one of the men who have accompanied us throughout the time that the Lord Jesus went in and out among us, beginning from the baptism of John until the day when he was taken up from us—one of these must become a witness with us to his resurrection."

56. In Romans 16, Paul mentions other women by name: Prisca and Phoebe. We also note the role of Chloe (1 Cor 1:11).

57. For example, 1 Thess 1:4; 2:1; 2:9; 1 Cor 1:1; and again in 15:1.

appears not to be directed only to males. Likewise, women seem to have been included in the company of about one hundred and twenty believers prior to Pentecost, whom Luke has Peter address as "*men [and] brethren*" (*Andres/adelphoi*) in Acts 1:16. There is considerable contemporary support for the view that "brothers" (*adelphoi*), as it is regularly used by Paul, implies the inclusion of women in a way that is analogous to the way the word "men" was used inclusively in English-speaking countries until comparatively recent times. That Paul himself apparently uses *adelphoi* inclusively can be observed already in his first letter, First Thessalonians, where many instances are to be found. In 1 Thess 1:4, he writes: "Knowing, beloved *adelphoi*, your election of God." It is hard to believe that women were excluded from membership within "the elect of God." Also, see 1 Thess 2:1: "You yourselves know, *adelphoi*, that our coming to you was not in vain . . ."; or 1 Thess 2:9: "You remember our labor and toil, *adelphoi*; we worked night and day, so that we might not burden any of you while we proclaimed to you the gospel of God." These examples suggest that right from the start of his letter writing, it became a matter of regular practice for Paul to use "*adelphoi*" to refer not to men only, but to include women also. Indeed, for him it seems that the inclusive use of "brothers" to mean both "brothers and sisters" is almost synonymous with addressing "Christians" generally in a particular locality. This seems to be a consistent Pauline usage across the range of his epistles.

Interestingly enough, in his initial greeting to the Corinthians in 1 Cor 1:1, *adelphoi* is apparently also used in this inclusive sense: "I appeal to you brothers (and sisters)."[58] Likewise, later in the epistle, in 1 Cor 15:1 when he addresses the community, again apparently as a whole, explicitly in relation to the resurrection as "brothers," it also seems to be in a sense that is inclusive of "sisters": "I remind you brothers (and sisters) of the good news I proclaimed to you . . ."

In view of this, it is of enormous interest to note that, just a few verses later, in the very Easter tradition that is quoted by Paul (1 Cor 15:3–8), in which he is alleged to have omitted mention of the empty tomb because of the lack of qualification of the women witnesses, Paul passes on the tradition that the Raised Jesus appeared on one single occasion to over five hundred witnesses at the same time (1 Cor 15:6). The members of this large crowd are also identified by Paul as *adelphoi*, but we have to ask whether it is reasonable to assume that this is also intended inclusively so as to indicate the presence of "sisters" as well? Paul goes on to say that while "some have died," most members of this crowd were still alive; the implication being that they could be consulted to test the veracity of their evidence. While we cannot be absolutely sure

---

58. Also, 1 Thess 5:4: "you *adelphoi* are not in darkness"; 1 Thess 5:14: "And we urge you, *adelphoi*, to admonish the idlers, encourage the faint hearted, help the weak, be patient with all of them"; and 1 Thess 5:25: "*adelphoi* pray for us." Likewise, 1 Thess 5:26: "Greet *tous adelphous pantas* with a holy kiss." It seems in all these cases Paul is addressing the whole community. It may be that addressing fellow believers as *adelphoi* derives from the language of guilds and associations (pagan and religious) of the ancient world, but it is hard to deny its distinctive inclusive use in relation to the eschatological community of Christ.

that the reference to "five hundred brothers" in 1 Cor 15:6 is definitely to be interpreted inclusively in this way, it at least seems very likely, given that it would be hard to imagine that such a large crowd of witnesses did *not* include women as well as men. Some contemporary translators therefore take Paul's usage to be inclusive of both as a matter of course, and thus apparently without hesitation translate *adelphoi* in 1 Cor 15:6 as "brothers and sisters."[59]

In this case, we have a further difficulty with the argument that the presence of women witnesses in the empty tomb story was allegedly sufficient reason for Paul not to mention it at all. For by the same token, if the testimony of women was so deficient as to require him to omit such a valuable piece of eyewitness testimony, we would have to explain why he did not also feel obliged to omit or qualify his mention of the appearance to over five hundred "brothers and sisters" at once. This is particularly important given that Paul indicates that this eyewitness testimony could be checked and their evidence scrutinized. Certainly, it would be hard to argue that Paul was comfortable in using this testimony only because of an alleged absence of women from an all-male crowd. In other words, if the testimony of women is to be regarded as being so suspect that it explains why Paul omitted all mention of the empty tomb, how is it that he positively mentions the appearance of Jesus to a crowd which is very likely to have included sisters as well as brothers, and at the same time implies that anyone could check their testimony at any time? It is hard to believe that this crowd quite definitely did *not* include women, or that Paul meant that the testimony only of the males could have been checked!

In any event, if Paul had difficulty in taking the witness of women seriously, why did he not nevertheless at least mention such a crucial piece of evidence as that the tomb was found empty, if he knew of it, and simply pass over the detail that it was first found by women? Also, we might note that a consciousness of the importance of the reliability and trustworthiness of witnesses might be a factor in situations in which he was apologetically urging the acceptance of his case, and that this was the specific situation in Corinth. However, the fact that he does not so much as allude to the empty tomb, even in passing, in the entire corpus of his letters, remains a mystery. This is particularly so where Paul is speaking outside of such apologetic contexts, where therefore the reliability of actual testimony was not at issue, and especially where it

59. NRSV as a matter of course has "brothers and sisters"; also see Bauckham, *Jesus and the Eyewitnesses,* 37 and 307. While accepting that Paul omits mention of the empty tomb because of the presence of women witnesses in the story, Richard Swinburne adopts the translation "brothers and sisters" as witnesses to an appearance all at the same time, noting that the Greek carries no explicit implication "either that women were or were not involved on this occasion" (*The Resurrection of God Incarnate,* 147 n.6). Gerald O'Collins also assumes that the crowd mentioned in 1 Cor 15:6 was comprised of "brothers and sisters," *Believing in the Resurrection,* 61.

might well have been really appropriate to the discussion of the theological point he was pursuing. For example, when Paul is speaking of the nature of the resurrection body (especially in 1 Corinthians 15), or the saving significance of Christ's death, or more generally of his Resurrection from the dead, mention of the empty tomb, had he known of it, might well have been appropriate. If indeed he knew of the empty tomb, and if he thought it important for the understanding of the Resurrection, the absence of reference to the empty tomb is a continuing source of puzzlement.

I think we must conclude that, while the strange absence of named women from the earliest traditions mentioned by Paul in 1 Corinthians 15 *might* be explained by appeal to the inferior status of women and their lack of legal competence as witnesses at Jewish law, this hardly constitutes a sure proof that Paul definitely knew of the empty tomb tradition, and simply chose for this particular reason not to mention it. Unless we assume the absolute inadmissibility of women as witnesses in all cases, including in matters that were not strictly speaking matters of law, and rule out any flexibility about the competence that could arise through specific circumstance, such as when only women were present (as at the burial), it cannot be at all certain that this was the conditioning factor in Paul's omission of mention of the empty tomb. While we are free to regard this as a thinkable possibility, it relies upon an argument from silence, which falls far short of historical proof. At best it is a conjecture not a proof. In the absence of St. Paul himself to tell us how he was thinking, we have simply to admit that we do not really know why he omitted mention of the empty tomb, if indeed he knew of the empty tomb story at all. It may have been, of course, that he simply preferred to proclaim the Easter Gospel on the basis of other evidence, such as the tradition of the appearances as visionary appearances "from heaven," and the subsequent concrete experience of the life-transforming gift of "the Spirit of Christ" among those who were "in Christ." This is, after all, exactly what he does do over and over again throughout his epistles, without any reliance upon the empty tomb tradition.

6

The Empty Tomb
The Gospel Narratives

The comparative lateness of the first mention of the tradition of the empty tomb in the documentary record of the New Testament has naturally invited a good deal of speculation. Given that it first appears in the Gospel of St. Mark (ca. AD 65+) at the beginning of the second generation of Christian faith and practice, it naturally raises the fundamental question of whether it was received by Mark as an oral or even written tradition that pre-dated him,[1] or whether it was in fact Mark's own literary creation.[2] The Gospel narratives of the appearances, by contrast with the empty tomb tradition, are anticipated by much earlier independent "kerygmatic summaries" or lists of appearances now found in the letters of St. Paul and the early sermons reported in *Acts*; however, the narratives of the empty tomb appear "out of nothing" as it were. In the absence of any earlier documentary evidence attesting the empty tomb tradition than Mark's Gospel, it is at least a notional possibility that it could be his own literary creation. Indeed, this thesis has been enthusiastically promoted in recent time by John Dominic Crossan, and Adela Yarbro Collins who goes on to argue that Mark used the story not to signal Jesus' restoration by resurrection from the dead so much as his assumption into heaven.[3] It may even be suggested that the statement of Mark 16:8, that the women fled from the tomb and "did not say anything" to anyone, is a veiled explanation of the fact that the tradition of the empty tomb had been unknown prior to Mark's narrative account of it.

---

1. Bultmann argued for a pre-Marcan tradition. See *The History of the Synoptic Tradition,* 285–86. Also Lüdemann, *The Resurrection of Jesus,* 111–18, and Hengel, "Das Begräbnis Jesu," 127–35.

2. Crossan, "The Empty Tomb and Absent Lord," 152; Collins, *The Beginning of the Gospel,* 119–48 and *Mark: A Commentary,* 781–82.

3. On the basis of the biblical precedent of Moses and Elijah, who in this way apparently avoided death.

In the absence of the possibility of cross-examining Mark himself, we appear to have no easy way of ascertaining an answer to the question of whether the empty tomb tradition enjoyed an oral or textual history prior to his inclusion of it in his Gospel, just as we have no opportunity to ask Paul whether he actually knew of the empty tomb tradition, but decided not to use it in view of the fact that it relied on women witnesses. *Prima facie* we therefore seem to be without a definitive way of determining whether it is a tradition that predates Mark or not.

To argue that the empty tomb was a natural conclusion based upon the original proclamation of the appearances (as outlined by Paul in the kerygmatic summary of 1 Cor 15:3–8),[4] or that the Easter faith of the first Christians could not have survived without there having been an empty tomb,[5] already presupposes what needs to be proved. For this assumes that the specific understanding of resurrection entertained by Paul and the first generation of believers involved the physical restoration of Jesus' body in material form—a restoration of such a kind as would leave a tomb empty. But this is exactly what N. T. Wright hopes to prove by critical historical research on the basis of the evidence of the empty tomb and the subsequent "meetings" with the Raised Jesus. This is why the veracity of the tradition of the empty tomb has to be established beyond reasonable doubt. Otherwise a purely historical quest to prove the occurrence of the Resurrection is put at a serious disadvantage from the start.

This does not mean, of course, that we can confidently say that an original kernel of the developed empty tomb tradition definitely did not have an earlier life either as an oral, or written, or even eyewitness tradition (now lost), before Mark received it and incorporated the first written version of it that we have into his Gospel.[6] It is just that we have no concrete documentary evidence with which to support even this notional possibility.[7] It may seem then that there is no way of proving that the empty tomb story was not, as John Dominic Crossan and Adela Yarbro Collins have contended, actually the literary creation of Mark himself.

By the same token, there seems to be no way of actually proving that it was produced by someone else, prior to Mark himself, which seems to be the conclusion favored by Daniel Smith, who otherwise shares Collins' contention that the story was used by Mark to signal an assumption into heaven rather than a resurrection of a

4. As Gerd Lüdemann argues, *The Resurrection*, 121.

5. As Pannenberg argued in *Jesus—God and Man*.

6. Hengel argues that Paul *must* have known the details of the empty tomb story as part of the "narration" which accompanied the proclamation of the Gospel and the confession of faith from the beginning. He repeatedly speaks of the "Urgemeinde," the earliest core community of believers to locate the origin of the story, which we now have in the Gospels. See "Das Begräbnis Jesu," 127–35. Smith rightly questions whether this can be squared with the "theological reflection and literary development" found in the Gospel accounts of the empty tomb story (*Revisiting the Empty Tomb*, 42).

7. Daniel Smith observes: "The problem is that there is no independent evidence for the existence of the empty tomb tradition outside of the canonical resurrection stories, which themselves are literary products not nearly as old as Paul's letters" (*Revisiting the Empty Tomb*, 42).

physical body.[8] This leaves us with the standing question of the historicity or otherwise of a supposed original kernel of the empty tomb story, probably involving only women witnesses, which Mark could conceivably have received.

In this quest all is not entirely lost. In support of the contention that Mark was not himself the author of the empty tomb story, and that an oral (or written) tradition had been received by him, it is possible to point to apparently Marcan stylistic elements that are found predominantly in the first half of his Gospel, but that are missing from the Passion narrative onwards. This kind of evidence might certainly point to the possibility that this latter material, including the story of the discovery of the empty tomb, was already in set form when Mark received it.[9]

One of the most characteristic and idiosyncratic stylistic features of Mark's Gospel is his use of "*kai euthus*" ("and immediately"), not as an adverb of time, but as a discourse marker at episode boundaries. In order to couple a string of otherwise discrete historical episodes together, Mark simply used this basic connecting device. By contrast with the other Gospels, Mark uses "*kai euthus*" twenty five times, and "*euthus*" forty one times, to connect isolated incidents of Jesus' teaching and activity together. In other Gospels the equivalent is "*kai idou*" ("and lo!") which Mark uses only occasionally.

Now, I think it very interesting that the instances of *euthus/kai euthus* predominate in the first half of his Gospel. That they are less prevalent from the passion narrative onwards may mean it was already a connected literary unit when Mark used it. Though it has to be admitted that there are two instances of *kai euthus* in the concluding episodes of the Gospel, one at Mark 14:43 and one at Mark 15:1, in the empty tomb story of chapter 16 this characteristically Marcan stylistic device is not found at all.[10] This might be regarded as a good indication that he was not the original author of it, but rather that it was something he received.

It has to be acknowledged, however, that this is an argument from silence, and that this omission of *kai euthus* from the passion narrative could also just be fortuitous.[11] After all, at this point Mark is not in the business of connecting together a plethora of otherwise isolated and disconnected incidents in which Jesus is repre-

8. Collins, *Mark*, 422. Certainly, of the two, Smith is the more inclined to concede that Mark reworked a tradition he had received. See Smith, *Revisiting the Empty Tomb*, 76–77.

9. See Schupbach, "'*kai euthus*' as Discourse Marker?"

10. Schupbach, "'*kai euthus*' as Discourse Marker?" 14: "there are large portions of the text in which the word *euthus* does not appear at all, such as the 152 verse stretch from 11.4 to 14.42—over 22% of the text without a single use."

11. Even in the first half of the Gospel, where *kai euthus* is predominately found, there are some chapters where it does not appear (e.g., chapter 3, where *euthus* only appears once, and in this case as a temporal adverb, rather than as discourse marker).

sented as teaching or acting. Chapter 16 consists of only eight verses, which together narrate the single episode of the discovery of the empty tomb. The absence of episode boundaries means that the need of this discourse marker would not have been felt by Mark. I think therefore we probably have to admit that the absence from the Passion narrative onwards of *kai euthus* as a discourse marker that is otherwise characteristic of Mark's own work, may not be ultimately decisive.

On the other hand, while being prepared to countenance the idea that the bare bones of the story may have been received by Mark, Gerd Lüdemann is of the view that, "It is doubtful whether a complete story about the tomb existed before Mark, as the text is overlaid with Marcan redaction."[12] One obvious continuing sign of Mark's own fingerprint is the description of the terror of the women in Mark 16:5–6. The verb "to be terrified" occurs in the New Testament only in Mark—Mark 9:15; 14:33; and twice in 16:5–6 (see also 1:27; 10:24, 32). That Mark left behind signs of his own redactional activity does not, however, mean decisively that the kernel of the story was not originally found in traditional material that he received.

Richard Bauckham has mounted a spirited case for regarding the Gospel material generally as the product of "eyewitness testimony" in a way that minimizes automatic recourse to the fashionable assumption that the traditions about Jesus originally circulated orally among anonymous worshipping communities that allowed the free and unrestrained development of the tradition, as the form critics once had us believe.[13] The fundamental thrust of Bauckham's argument is that there is nothing to require us to think of the reported incidents in which Jesus taught and did certain things as the inventive creations of the post-Easter communities in response to their own needs and concerns, let alone as mythological developments of faith. Moreover, Bauckham is not only convinced, in relation to the material of the New Testament generally, that we are not just dealing with traditions that were adapted by early worshipping communities to meet their own needs at some remove from the original events. In addition, he argues that eyewitnesses could in principle have survived well into the last decades of the first-century, and could have still been alive when the Gospels were being written. In this case, they therefore could have exercised a kind of quality control to restrain the free development of the Jesus traditions, even at the hands of the evangelists. This makes for a basic presumption of reliability concerning the material that is now found in the Gospel narratives. This would have included the empty tomb tradition. It is, after all, in principle as early as other Gospel traditions relating to the historical activity and teaching of Jesus now found for the first time in Mark's Gospel, which appear to have been

12. Lüdemann, *Jesus after 2000 Years*, 114.

13. Bauckham, *The Gospels as Eyewitness Testimony*. Also, this fundamental contention is already implicit in his earlier work, *Gospel Women*.

based on original eyewitness testimony. So why should its historicity be doubted any more than other material which, after a period of oral transmission, also first appears in written form in the Gospel of Mark? Bauckham also argues that there is no actual evidence to suggest that the narrative stories of resurrection appearances grew out of an original kerygmatic summary, such as 1 Cor 15:3–8—rather, the narrative stories and the summaries are judged to be two independent traditions of different genre that appear to have existed in parallel. We need to be aware, of course, that there is no mention of the empty tomb in the kerygmatic summary in 1 Cor 15:3–8 out of which the narrative story *could* grow. It appears from "out of nowhere" as it were. In this way it is entirely in dependent of the Pauline tradition. In any event, Bauckham argues that the form critics' fundamental contention that the narrative traditions of the Gospels were the creative products of anonymous communities in response to their own needs and concerns is to be forthrightly challenged in the interests of restoring, and even privileging, the category of "eyewitness testimony."

However, because we can think of the possibility that eyewitnesses *may* have been around to exercise some constraint on the unrestrained development of the traditions, does not mean that they in fact actually did so. A logical or thinkable possibility does not entail an actual possibility. While, generally speaking, there may be nothing "to require" us to believe in the creative development of the tradition at the hands of primitive communities of faith and worship in response to their own perceived needs and concerns, and that space must therefore be made for the consideration of the function of eyewitness testimony, there may in fact be some very good reasons in particular cases for so thinking. In other words, the texts themselves often indicate a need to consider the possibility that we are dealing with some kind of apologetically motivated in-put into the tradition at the hands of anonymous communities in the process of their transmission of the tradition. This is not to mention what appears to be the obvious redactional activity of known and identifiable evangelists, whose reworking of the received traditions so as to express a particular theological standpoint seems incontrovertible, as the redaction critics of the second half of the twentieth-century were so keen to point out and celebrate.

We are well aware, for example, of Mark's own creative editorial activity. This may be discerned in his characteristic literary method of inserting one incident within another, so as to create a kind of literary sandwich. One example is the inclusion of the story of the woman with an issue of blood within the story of the healing of Jairus' daughter (Mark 5:21–24 [25–34] 35–43); a second is the inclusion of the story of the casting out of the thieves from the Temple within the story of the cursing of the unproductive fig tree (Mark 11:12–14 [15–19] 20–24). A third example of this literary technique is the sandwiching of the story of the Syro-phoenician woman between the two feedings of multitudes (Mark 6:30–44 [7:24–30] 8:1–10), apparently to highlight the significance of the crumbs that "fall from the master's table."

Sometimes the insertion of "a story within a story" is provided with a linking "tag" as we would call it today. For example, the number twelve in "twelve years" of suffering on the part of the woman with the issue of blood (Mark 5:25) and "twelve years of age" in relation to Jairus' daughter (Mark 5:42); or the "tag" of references to "crumbs"—the abundance of the baskets of crumbs in the stories of the feedings either side of the Syro-phoenician woman's statement about foreigners picking up the crumbs from under the table (Mark 7:28). The point is that even eyewitness testimony is clearly subject to the creative editorial activity of Mark, which is not difficult to identify and appreciate, and this is not to mention his overall arrangement of the traditional material, with parables and healing stories being gathered together in the first half of the Gospel, apart from only one or two exceptions in the second half, while in the second half the focus is on his more open or "plain" teaching (Mark 8:32a) on the nature of his messiahship and the kind of discipleship it commands. Certainly, this arrangement of received material appears to have been motivated by theological purpose rather than by a governing desire faithfully to preserve some kind of factual sequence dictated by the informal controlling interest of those who could still draw upon eyewitness testimony.

Clearly, even allowing for the role of eyewitness testimony both at the very beginning of the tradition and as providing a possible continuing authenticating restraint on its development, the texts themselves nevertheless sometimes dictate the need to consider the creative role of the editorial work of the evangelists in arranging and presenting the material that they received. And while the traditions concerning Jesus obviously had a beginning in eyewitness testimony, the possibility of evolutionary developments in the course of its oral transmission cannot be entirely discounted.

While we may not be *required* to think thus and so, lack of a general requirement does not therefore dictate that there cannot sometimes be very good reasons for thinking, at least in specific instances, of the creative role of even anonymous faith communities in the prior development of the tradition and/or of the in-put of the faith of the evangelists themselves. The story of the empty tomb is one such specific instance. Apart from the comparative lateness of its appearance in the written Easter tradition, the evidential usefulness of the empty tomb story from a historiographical point of view also seems problematic to many contemporary scholars because of the range of detailed discrepancies that are found among the various narrative versions of the story, which appear to speak of its development over time. These are found across all four of the Gospel accounts which, when taken together, make it difficult for them to be accommodated along with the material of the Gospels generally in any straightforward way under the category of "eyewitness testimony."

For a start, these discrepancies furnish some legitimate reasons for thinking that, if there was an oral antecedent of the narrative tradition of the empty tomb story now found in the New Testament, it was subject to elaboration in the course of its transmission even long before the writing of the Gospels, perhaps in an apologetic context where resurrection faith had to be defended. On the other hand, if the story originated with Mark, then the same apologetically motivated development of his account is a clear outcome of its treatment by subsequent Gospel writers.

The suggestion is regularly made, for example, that a military guard was introduced into the version of the story of the empty tomb now found in Matthew in response to the felt need to answer the charge that Jesus' body had been stolen.[14] This element is, of course, absent from the original story of the discovery of the empty tomb received from Mark, and so must clearly be accepted as an addition to it, whether by Matthew himself or by some source that was available to him. Though even the appearance of soldiers in the developed tradition is not seen as a difficulty by Richard Bauckham. Bauckham appears to assume the veracity even of this element of the story simply because he believes we are dealing with eyewitness testimony, but this insistently begs the question. We know also that the suggestion that the body had been stolen was not just a theoretical invention of the form critics of the first half of the twentieth century, given that the tradition itself indicates that it was already in the air from an early time; Mary Magdalene is reported naturally to have assumed this explanation of the tomb's emptiness herself (John 20:2, 13). The possibility that the body had in fact been stolen may therefore have been entertained even by those who are reported to have first found the tomb empty, and it may certainly have been aggressively used by the Jewish opponents of faith in polemical argument also from an early time. It is even not beyond conjecture that an original assumption on the part of Mary Magdalene that Jesus' body had been taken away, became in the course of the telling, a story about the placement of the soldiers to prevent this possibility. That the story of the placing of guards at the tomb was added in the version now found in Matthew (27:62–66; 28:11–15) for the explicit purpose of answering this charge does offer at least a credible explanation for this idiosyncratic development in the tradition.

Clearly, if the kernel of the empty tomb story is at least true, it must be traced to original eyewitnesses, but there is no way of proving that the detail concerning the placement of soldiers was itself definitely an authentic piece of that original eyewitness testimony. Even if we were to embrace the theoretical possibility that the empty tomb story originated with eyewitnesses who were around long enough to safeguard its passage through time, the absence of any reference to the placement of the soldiers

14. Matt 27:64–66: "Therefore command the tomb to be made secure until the third day; otherwise his disciples may come and steal him away, and tell the people, 'He has been raised from the dead,' and the last deception would be worse than the first.' Pilate said to them, 'You have a guard of soldiers; go, make it as secure as you can.' So they went with the guard and made the tomb secure by sealing the stone."

to guard the tomb from the more original version of the story as we have it in Mark surely remains troublesome.

Moreover, the argument for the historicity of an original eyewitness testimony of the empty tomb story has to face the added difficulty that the story is not just about the discovery of an empty tomb. What are we to make as twenty-first-century historians of the reported appearances of angels? If we assume that the "young man" mentioned by Mark is meant to be understood as an angel, given his function in delivering a message, then angels are integral to all four accounts of the discovery of the empty tomb. If *angelophanies* are integral to all versions of the story, we have to decide whether these are to be accepted as straightforward historical accounts of what original eyewitnesses actually saw, or whether they are typical first-century heuristic devices added to the original story of the tomb's discovery by the women for the specific purpose of interpreting the meaning of its being found empty. Without them the empty tomb could be explained in a number of diverse ways: the body could have been stolen, as indeed was initially assumed in the tradition itself; or the women may have gone to the wrong tomb, and so on. Clearly, the reader has need of an interpretative message to clarify the meaning of the tomb's emptiness; eventually this problem was solved christologically by the provision of an actual appearance of the Raised Christ, as in Matthew's version of the story where the Raised Jesus meets the women and repeats the angelic message to "go into Galilee" (Matt 28:9–10). But what are we to make today of these angelic elements in determining whether the story originated as eyewitness testimony rather than as a later expression of faith?

In other words, the question is whether these references to angels are the product of faith, or an original element of eyewitness testimony upon which faith was based? James D. G. Dunn contends that the inclusion of encounters with angels "neither adds to nor detracts from the testimony regarding the empty tomb; visions of angels were part of the 'mechanics' of revelatory experiences."[15] However, the issue here is whether these reported experiences were historically accurate at the point of origin of Christian belief or a later attempt to communicate resurrection faith, not just whether they are a normal part of reports of revelatory experiences. If the alleged presence of angels suggests that the empty tomb story reports a "revelatory experience" then an additional question is raised concerning the historicity of exactly what is said to have been experienced. An angelophany does after all involve the perception of a heavenly reality and presupposes the coloring of faith. The introduction of angels into all versions of the story and inconsistencies in relation to the number of angels, plus different ways in which the angels are said to have behaved, cannot but raise a question

15. Dunn, *Jesus Remembered*, 833 n.30.

about the historical reliability even of the original Marcan story of the bare discovery that the tomb was empty.

Luke and John increase the number of angels to two. Some have argued that the presence of one angel in *Mark* and *Matthew*, and two angels in *John* and *Luke*, suggests that there may have originally been two independent versions of the empty tomb story in early circulation during the time of its oral transmission. This is purely hypothetical, but in any event, despite the fact that there may have been two early versions of the story, one with one angel and the other with two, the more important question is: what are we to say of the likelihood of the possible historicity, whether multiple angelic appearances or otherwise, given that what is said to have transpired in the accounts of John and Luke contrasts in some remarkable respects with the stories of Mark and Matthew?

Apart from the problematic issue of the possible apologetic motivation behind the provision of a military guard in Matthew's version of the story, and of the reported role of faith-generated angels in all versions of the story, there are some questions about who the first eyewitnesses actually were or could have been.

For example, the names of the women witnesses are notoriously as various as the detailed accounts of their reported actual experiences. Mark has Mary Magdalene and two other women, Mary "the mother of James" and Salome, going to the tomb; they find the stone rolled away and the tomb already empty, and the "young man," presumed to be an angel, directs them to go and tell Peter and the other disciples to "go into Galilee" where they will see him. Matthew has just two women, Mary Magdalene and "the other Mary"; an angel descends from heaven as a "great earthquake" occurs and actually rolls the stone away in front of them, and then sits on it; the soldiers who have already been introduced into the story to guard the tomb become potential witnesses to the Resurrection, though they are paid to say they went to sleep on the job and so missed the Easter excitement.[16] It is significant, however, that this military presence means that the women cannot just find the stone already rolled away and the body gone as in Mark's version of the story, for the role of the guards is precisely to prevent this from happening. Hence, the earthquake and the more active involvement of the angel in the removal of the stone appears to be a logical consequence of the appointment of the military guard.

In principle, the presence of different women's names in different Gospels might not itself be an insurmountable difficulty for those concerned to probe the question of the historicity of the story. Various women witnesses could have returned to the tomb to check it out, for this would perhaps have been a very natural thing to have occurred,

16. Though, to the delight of a plethora of artists who have attempted to depict this scene, they are represented as having been unperturbed by the reported earthquake and remained asleep.

and this could have given rise to the variation in number of women witnesses. In this case, a principle of selectivity may be behind Mary Magdalene's separation from a broader group, and could also condition the appearance of different names in different Gospels. Likewise, a kind of harmony of the accounts of what happened could conceivably be achieved by appeal to the notion of confusion even in the testimony of eyewitnesses, particularly in relation to the perception of exactly what happened in a momentous event and who was there to witness it. Strict accuracy is often not achieved in group experiences which have to strive for agreement in the detail relating to what actually happened. Indeed, perhaps this is to be expected in a circumstance like the discovery of the empty tomb, which we can assume, was naturally fraught and confused.

That said, it is perhaps significant that Mary Magdalene is the only name consistently found in all four versions of the story. In John's account she is (at least at first) presented as though she were alone, though the use of the first person plural in her words "*We* do not know where they have taken him" (John 20:2) might suggest that others were with her. Whether this is a token acknowledgement of the existence of a tradition that included other women in the story, of which John had at least some knowledge, is therefore a thinkable possibility. Even so, John's focus is exclusively on Mary Magdalene, either as leader of the group, or singled out simply to serve his narrative purposes, given her ensuing reported dialogue with Jesus at the tomb (20:15–17). The kernel of the story as we have received it certainly suggests that Mary Magdalene originally discovered the empty tomb on a single occasion, though perhaps not necessarily with others.[17] The question is, therefore, whether the original core tradition of the empty tomb story involved Mary Magdalene alone as is suggested in John's version of the story?

However, in addition to the question of whether there were other women witnesses or whether Mary Magdalene was alone, there is a significant development in the tradition insofar as men are also introduced into the later versions of the story of John and Luke. Indeed, in these later Gospels men in fact play a part of some significance. Luke has a number of unidentified women who had followed Jesus from Galilee, and two "men in shining raiment," presumably angels, outside of the tomb; the women tell the others (unlike the women in Mark who "do not say anything" to anyone) and then Peter, unequivocally a male human being who is entirely absent from Mark's original and also from Matthew's redaction, is introduced into the story as one who runs to the tomb and finds it empty, save for the remnant linen cloths (Luke 24:12). There is (somewhat curiously) no actual account of an encounter of Peter with the Raised Jesus here; Peter simply observes the place where Jesus' body had been laid and the linen cloths left behind. But this strategy allows Luke, apparently quite deliberately, to detach the appearances tradition from Galilee in the interests of centering the Easter

---

17. A possibility acknowledged by O'Collins, *The Easter Jesus*, 42: "In the original tradition she may have been the sole visitor to the tomb."

Event in Jerusalem. There is no suggestion of a passage of time to allow for Peter's return from Galilee, or of a story of Peter "hurrying back from Galilee" that became an account of his "running" to the tomb. Rather, by awkwardly incorporating this brief account, Peter (allegedly not having gone to Galilee but being still in Jerusalem) is said to have run to the tomb immediately on hearing the reports of the women. In this way, Luke locates Peter in Jerusalem on the first day of the week when the tomb was discovered, for the whole movement of the preaching of repentance and remission of sins among all nations has its "beginning in Jerusalem" (Luke 24:47).

Moreover, the travelers to Emmaus, who encounter Jesus in the breaking of bread, are explicitly said to return to Jerusalem (Luke 24:33) where they find the eleven not scattered but "gathered together" and hear the report that Jesus had appeared to Peter: "Jesus is Risen indeed, and has appeared to Simon/Peter" (24:34). This is even despite the curious fact that Luke has no actual appearance narrative involving Peter. Then the eleven and others are gathered in Jerusalem when the Raised Christ "stands in the midst" and appears to them and says "Peace be unto you" (24:36). They are all then in turn commanded to stay in Jerusalem (24:49), pending the receipt of "power from on high." Clearly, though the tradition of Mark and Matthew suggests that Galilee was the place of the first appearances, the Lucan tradition is conditioned by another agenda.

When we take up John's somewhat more independent version of the Gospel story, we find that, while Mary Magdalene first appears to be alone when she discovers that the stone had been rolled away (and perhaps sees inside, for she assumes that the body had been stolen), she then (as in Luke) runs to tell Peter who in this way is suddenly introduced into the story, though this time by contrast with Luke 24:12, he is in the company of "the disciple whom Jesus loved" (John 20:2–10). John thus abruptly introduces Peter, and in addition "the disciple whom Jesus loved" into the story, which may originally have involved only Mary Magdalene (20:1, 11–18).

There are good reasons for believing that John's references to Peter and the Other Disciple are later insertions into an earlier version of the story involving only Mary Magdalene. Corroboration of the possibility that the original kernel of the story involved only Mary Magdalene is suggested by the fact that at the beginning, and again at the end of his version of the story, she appears to have been alone (John 20:1 and 11–18). The additional episode concerning Peter and the disciple whom Jesus loved (vv. 2–10) is abruptly slotted into this story of Mary Magdalene at the tomb. There is no mention of Peter and the Other Disciple being with her in the introduction to the story (John 20:1). Instead, the men are abruptly introduced without any previous reference to any interaction with Mary, and then they disappear as abruptly as they were introduced, leaving Mary alone once again in the continuation of her story: they "return to their homes." Thus Mary Magdalene is left alone once again at the tomb (vv. 11–18). In other words, no sooner is the account of Peter and the Other Disciple running to the tomb (vv. 2–10) introduced into the story of Mary Magdalene, than they disappear from it again. In this way, John's version of this story may be said to yield telltale signs of the cut-and-paste addition of this tradition involving Peter running to the tomb with the disciple whom Jesus loved, to an apparently independent tradition involving only Mary Magdalene. Rather than appearing to be the composition of a single integrated narrative, this appears to be an editorial conflation of what were originally two traditions each of separate origin.[18] On these grounds, it may therefore be doubted if the presence of Peter and the Other Disciple featured in the original version of the empty tomb story concerning Mary Magdalene.

John then has Mary Magdalene alone once again (20:11), and the two angels also, but here inside the tomb when she looks in (one at the head and one at the feet where Jesus' body had been laid, 20:11), replacing the grave clothes found at separate locations as described in the experience of the Beloved Disciple and Peter (20:5–8). In a way that is too similar to Luke's version of this episode for this to be a mere coincidence, John, also later on "that same day" of the discovery of the tomb by Mary Magdalene, has the disciples assembled in Jerusalem "for fear of the Jews" when Jesus actually "stands in the midst" and says "Peace be unto you" (20:19–23).

It is obviously significant that though Peter does not rank any mention in the earlier versions of Mark and even of Matthew,[19] he figures so prominently in these traditions incorporated by Luke and John. And the question is whether these changes can be accommodated within the general category of "inadvertent variations of detail," and somehow harmonized under the general umbrella of alleged New Testament "eyewitness testimony" into a coherent narrative of a single chain of events, or whether the textual evidence itself actually suggests the work of a much more intentional editorial mind.

It has to be said that the obvious close verbal agreements between Luke and John suggest that it may well have been that John's episode concerning Peter and the Other Disciple (John 20:2–10) may have been an amplification of Luke's brief statement concerning Peter's running to the tomb and finding it empty in Luke 24:12.[20] For example, apart from the obvious similarity of the actual incident, the words "and looking in he sees . . . the linens" in Luke 24:12 are also found in John 20:5, which strongly sug-

18. Among redactional critics, the lack of textual integrity is cited as evidence of cut-and-paste composition. See Fuller, *Formation of the Resurrection Narratives*, 135–36. This explanation of the composition of John 20 is accepted, almost as a matter of course, Smith, *Revisiting the Empty Tomb*, 140–44. See also my own original acceptance of this: Carnley, *Structure of Resurrection Belief*, 19 and 45.

19. Despite the generally speaking "good press" that Matthew accords Peter.

20. The close verbal agreements between Luke and John are the subject of careful study by Neirynck, "Luke 24,12: An Anti-Docetic Interpolation?"; and Neirynck, "Once More Lk 24,12." A useful discussion of the interdependence of Luke 24:12 and John's account of Peter at the tomb in John 20 is to be found in Smith, *Revisiting the Empty Tomb*, 113–18. Neirynck's views are discussed by Smith on 116–17.

gests that John may be dependent upon Luke as a source.[21] The same applies to Jesus' resurrection appearance "standing in the midst" of the disciples in Luke 24:36 as the possible source of the story of the appearance of Jesus, also "standing in the midst" of the assembled disciples in the room behind closed doors of John 20:19–23.[22]

When we turn to Luke's mention of Peter's presence in Jerusalem and his running to the tomb in Luke 24:12, there are some good reasons for regarding this as an interpolation into Mark's story that originally involved only women. Indeed, it is noteworthy that this entire verse, along with some other scattered phrases in Luke 24, do not appear in a number of western manuscript traditions, most notably that of the Greek uncial Codex Bezae Cantabrigiensis (D), by contrast with the codexes Sinaiticus and Alexandrinus.[23] This gave rise to the theory of B. F. Westcott and F. J. A. Hort that the original manuscript, as it left Luke's hands, was without these additional non-Western readings, which came to be added to it later.[24] There is a family of non-Western manuscript instances of this phenomenon. Bart Ehrman argues on the basis of this that the longer readings of the non-Western manuscript tradition were interpolations into the original text of Luke. The entire verse Luke 24:12 therefore becomes a much later insertion into Luke's Gospel, designed to promote the view that resurrection belief involved more than an encounter with a *pneuma* (Luke 24:36), but involved bodily restoration (such as would leave linen clothes lying). Ehrman categorizes this corrective strategy as an attempt to combat Docetism.[25] These purported additions to Luke's text are thus "anti-docetic corruptions" added to the non-Western texts as scribal interpolations.

The more recent consensus, however, is that Luke 24:12 is in fact authentic to Luke.[26] Daniel Smith, for example, is convinced by Frans Neirynck's strong defense of Luke's own authorship of Luke 24:12 on the ground of its typically Lucan language: the pleonastic use of the participle "having got up" (*anastas*), the verb "to wonder" (*thaumazein*), and the participle "that which had happened" (*to gegonos*),[27] and the general consistency of Luke 24:12 with Luke's view that, though the tomb had been found empty, the women also did not see the Raised Christ (see Luke 24:24).[28]

---

21. This is particularly so in view of the grammatical construction with the curious use of the present tense of "he sees" in each case.

22. There may also be a parallel insofar as Jesus' appearance triggers "terror and fear" in Luke 24:37, whereas the disciples are assembled "for fear of the Jews" in John 20.

23. Also the Old Latin MSS and Marcion.

24. Westcott and Hort, *The New Testament in the Original Greek*, 2:295.

25. Ehrman, *Orthodox Corruption of Scripture*, 211.

26. See Metzger, *Textual Commentary*, 184 and 191–93; Metzger, *The Text of the New Testament*, 134.

27. *Revisiting the Empty Tomb*, 215.

28. Smith's discussion of this issue may be found in *Revisiting the Empty Tomb*, 116–17. N. T. Wright is anxious to ensure that Luke 24:12 is understood to be original to Luke's Gospel despite its omission from western manuscripts, citing as a reason the reference back to it in v. 24. See *RSG*, 648.

On the other hand, unfashionable though it might at first seem, it is at least thinkable that these same agreements admit of a possibly that, vice versa, Luke in fact relied upon John.[29] Though Bart Ehrman is more interested in proving the possible interpolation of Luke 24:12 into Luke's original Gospel by a much later third party (using John), it is significant that the phrase "stooping down" or "peering in" (*parakupsas*), and the word used for the linens (*ta othonia*), that Ehrman argues is non-Lukan language, is found at the beginning of the story.[30] While Frans Neirynck has argued that the joining of the words "*thaumazōn to gegonos*" in one expression "creates a valid example of Lucan style" at the conclusion of the story,[31] if Luke was dependent upon John, perhaps this may be explained by the fact that Luke (by contrast with John) has no interest in relaying the "coming to faith" of the Beloved Disciple (or Peter for that matter) on the basis of the sight of the linens (John 20:8). Rather, Luke is content to have Peter come away "wondering at what had happened" (*thaumazōn to gegonos*, Luke 24:12). This part of the tradition, in other words, is necessarily a creation of Luke himself; it is not part John's story. At this point language peculiar to Luke is understandable. It is significant that it is where Luke is in sympathy with John that the linguistic similarities appear.[32]

It is significant that scholarly opinion is divided about the linguistic inter-dependence between John and Luke, and there remains a possibility that the initial verbal agreement with John might be an indication of the fact that Luke himself was directly dependent upon John. If Luke's Gospel is dated very late, perhaps even early in the second century,[33] then it is thinkable that Luke may well have relied upon John. As Daniel Smith observes in passing, these verbal agreements must mean that, if it was not the case that "the author (or redactor) of the Fourth Gospel used Luke," then a later redactor of Luke must have used "the Fourth Gospel as source material."[34] However, perhaps the "redactor" was Luke himself, adding to the original empty tomb

---

He does not explicitly discuss the Ehrman thesis about an "anti-docetic" interpolation, nor Neirynck's rebuttal of Ehrman. Smith's discussion of both was published, of course, long after Wright's work on the Resurrection in 2003.

29. The possibility that Luke 24:14 may be dependent upon John is mentioned in passing by Daniel Smith, *Revisiting the Empty Tomb*, 116, where he observes that it is a possibility that "the author (or redactor) of the Fourth Gospel used Luke" or that an interpolator "added Luke 24.12 'using the Fourth Gospel as source material.'"

30. Ehrman *Orthodox Corruption*, 214.

31. Neirynck, "Luke 24.12: An Anti-Docetic Interpolation?" 148. Also, Neirynck, "Once More Luke 24,12," 324.

32. Wright notes the parallels in John 20:3, 5–6, and 10, and acknowledges the possibility that Luke 24:12 is a compilation of these verses, but prefers to say that "it seems more likely that Luke knew, at this point at least, an abbreviated version of a story like John's" (*RSG*, 613 n.64).

33. It was O'Neill's view that Luke/Acts is to be dated quite late in the first half of the second century. See *The Theology of Acts in Its Historical Setting*. For a serious discussion of the possibility that Luke in fact relied upon John, see Shellard, "The Relationship of Luke and John."

34. The thesis of Ehrman.

story of Mark and using the Fourth Gospel as source material.[35] James D. G. Dunn is of the somewhat speculative view that Luke 24:12 is not the interpolation of a much later redactor into Luke, but relies upon a tradition going back to the Beloved Disciple.[36] Alternatively, of course, Luke and John could both have relied upon a common source.

That said, perhaps a Lucan dependence on John can be established, less on linguistic grounds, but more by attending to Luke's fundamental theological commitments. We have already noted that Luke notoriously disengages the Easter traditions from Galilee so as to center the divine revelatory and redemptive activity in Jerusalem. For this purpose, it is necessary for him to re-caste the angel's message at the tomb, so that it no longer becomes a directive to "Go into Galilee" to rendezvous with the Raised Christ there; instead the angel *reminds* those present *that* Jesus once said (when he was in Galilee) that he would be crucified and would rise from the dead (*Luke* 24:6–7). The discovery of the empty tomb, with Peter now also as a witness, is then followed by the story of the travelers on the road to Emmaus who afterwards return to Jerusalem. Indeed, the disciples are commanded to "stay in Jerusalem" pending the gift of "power from on high." It is curious that while Peter is introduced as a witness to the empty tomb, and the returning Emmaus travelers find upon their return that Jesus "had appeared to Peter," Luke includes no account of an actual appearance to Peter. Daniel Smith concludes that Luke did not have access to an appearance story involving Peter, "otherwise he would have used it."[37] Instead, Luke is said to have been generally aware of the priority of Peter in the Easter traditions, starting with Paul's kerygmatic summary, which cites Peter as the first to whom, with "the twelve," the Raised Christ appeared (1 Cor 15:5). This assumes that John used Luke and not vice versa. On the other hand, if Luke had access to John he conceivably did have access to the account of the appearance to Peter and six other disciple fishermen by the lake in Galilee where they catch a great many fish (*John* 21). If so, why did he not use it? The answer is surely that this story is of little use to him, given his clear determination to disengage the resurrection experience from Galilee and locate it in Jerusalem. This alone may explain his omission of the episode concerning Peter and the other fishermen that is described in John 21. If Luke had access to this story he certainly suppresses it, at least as an account of a resurrection appearance. Instead, however, the essentials of this same story are incorporated by Luke as an incident in Jesus' lifetime, an incident also involving the putting down of a net and a great catch of fish in which

35. Smith, *Revisiting the Empty Tomb*, 116. Frans Neirynck is of the view that John used Luke; "Luke 24.12: An Anti-Docetic Interpretation?" 152–56. Neirynck believes that "the Fourth Gospel betrays Luke's influence."

36. Dunn, *Jesus Remembered*, 833–34.

37. Smith, *Revisiting the Empty Tomb*, 105.

Peter has a prominent role (*Luke* 5:1–11).[38] By this editorial strategy, Luke ensures that Peter's Galilee resurrection experience is successfully omitted while essentially the same story is recycled as an incident in Jesus' historical life. Instead of an experience of the Raised Christ by the Lake in Galilee as in *John 21*, at Luke's hands, Peter thereby becomes one of the witnesses to the Resurrection in Jerusalem.

Given Luke's obvious concern to detach the Easter experiences from Galilee, and to re-locate them in Jerusalem, it is difficult to avoid the conclusion that the reference to Peter's presence in Jerusalem, and his running to the tomb (Luke 24:12) was also a later addition by Luke to an original empty tomb tradition involving only women. In this case, the tradition of the empty tomb being discovered by women without the presence of men continues to make its claim to authenticity. For there are some very good reasons for thinking that an original version of the story involving Mary Magdalene's discovery of the empty tomb (either with or without the company of other women) was later amplified so as to incorporate reference to Peter with the Other Disciple (John), or just Peter (Luke). In this case, the contention that the original kernel of the story involved either a woman witness—Mary Magdalene, alone (John 20:1)—or multiple women witnesses "who had come with Jesus from Galilee" (Luke 23:55) still stands, while references to the inclusion of the men may be accommodated as later additions.

Now, very curiously, N. T. Wright, in defending the historicity of the story of the empty tomb, accepts the historicity of the entire episode including Peter as a participant (and the Other Disciple) as we find it both in John 20 and Luke 24:12. He contends that there are no grounds for the suggestion that Peter and the Other Disciple feature only because of later editorial additions to an original version of the story involving Mary Magdalene alone. In the case of Luke 24:12, he rejects the suggestion that it is an interpolation into the non-Western texts and supports its original place in the composition of Luke.[39] He is unsympathetic to the view that Luke may have used John, and suggests instead that Luke used a source "like John's."[40] He also questions whether the introduction of Peter and the Other Disciple into the empty tomb story by John is a redactional addition to an original tradition involving only Mary Magdalene.[41]

---

38. As in John 21, this story of Luke 5 also begins with Jesus by the lake; it involves Peter and also James and John, and quite explicitly two fishing boats, the experience of catching nothing after fishing all night before the great catch of fish at Jesus's command, and the response of awe and wonder. In Luke's story the nets are, however, said to break because of the number of fish. In John 21, the nets are said not to break despite the size of the catch of 153 fish (the triangular number of 17). However, the parallels in basic elements of the story are obvious.

39. *RSG*, 648.

40. *RSG*, 613 n.64.

41. *RSG*, 664 n.6.

Indeed, he forthrightly declares that "It is quite unwarranted to suggest that the story of Peter and John [i.e. the Beloved Disciple] has been inserted or interpolated, at a late stage in the tradition, into an originally independent story of Mary."[42] In other words, the historicity of the actual involvement of Peter and the Other Disciple in the episode narrated in John 20 is accepted, even in the face of the suggestion that they appear there only as the result of later editorial insertion into the original story which involved Mary Magdalene alone. Unfortunately, this is not argued or in any way defended by Wright. This means he is prepared to side-step the internal textual issues of John 20:1–11 that are raised by the abruptness of the appearance of Peter and the Beloved Disciple in the story (in vv. 2–10) and the immediate lack of any continuing references to Mary Magdalene in these verses, and then her sudden re-appearance alone again in v. 11, as telltale evidence of an insertion of one story into the other.

However, apart from what may well be telltale evidence of the conflation of two independent traditions in the literary formation of the Johannine tradition of the empty tomb, we have to note the fact that in the earlier synoptic versions of the story, there is no mention of Peter and the disciple whom Jesus loved at the site of the tomb at all, while there is a positive tradition that the male witnesses fled to Galilee and were not in Jerusalem at the site of the tomb on the day of its discovery. These factors certainly suggest that it may be a mistake simply to accept John 20 as a straightforward factual account of what actually happened.

N. T. Wright has sufficiently insulated himself from the conclusions of twentieth century redactional criticism so as to by-pass them in favor of a surface reading of the received text, which he harmonizes as best he can with other Gospel narratives of appearances. In this way, Wright simply assumes the historical realism of the received text of John 20 just as it currently stands. This then tends to be integrated into the whole series of "meetings" of the disciples with the Raised Jesus across all four Gospels as one extended composite account of "what happened." Many will find this a very problematic procedure.

However, if Wright aims to hold on to the historicity even of the details of the Johannine version of the story in John 20, then we end with a story that, as it stands, does in fact also include some male witnesses. If Peter was really present at the tomb, as Wright apparently wants us to believe, then Peter (and the Other Disciple) could easily have corroborated the evidence offered by women, or at least by a woman, if it is the case that Mary Magdalene was the sole witness of the emptiness of the tomb. But this means that Wright's own treatment of John 20 drastically undermines his contention that the absence of men from the empty tomb story attests to its authenticity. The same may be said of Luke's reference to Peter running to the tomb in Luke 24:12. On one count, Wright argues that any story generated for apologetic reasons would *not* have drawn only upon women witnesses; the fact that it is a tradition that depends

---

42. *RSG*, 664 n.6. The example given of otherwise unidentified culprits who make this assertion is "Carnley, 1987"; Carnley, *Structure of Resurrection Belief*, 19 and 45.

upon the witness of women who are to be judged legally incompetent to provide such testimony speaks positively of its original historicity. If it were a fabricated story, it would have been furnished with some "fine upstanding men." But he then seems to want us to accept the historicity both of John's version of the story in John 20, and Luke's abbreviated account of the same story in Luke 24:12, which positively includes men as well as a woman/women.

This seems doubly curious, on one hand, because Wright's defense of the historicity of the empty tomb story rests upon the contention that it is furnished with women who lacked legal competence. As he says, if it were a legendary development of a free-flowing religious imagination, or the product of the inventive skill of early believers simply as a way of expressing their Easter faith, then some "fine upstanding male witnesses" might have been called into the empty tomb story to render it reliable. That the story involves only women witnesses is, for Wright, positive evidence that therefore supports its original historicity. It would have been unusual to furnish an invented story with unreliable, and indeed, legally noncompetent women witnesses.

On the other hand, in his treatment of Paul, N. T. Wright's contention is that Paul knew of the empty tomb tradition but was reluctant to utilize it, and therefore did not mention it anywhere in his letters, even in contexts where reference to it might seem eminently appropriate. This is based on the same reasoning as his argument for the historicity of the empty tomb tradition: Paul is said not to have used it precisely because of its reliance on legally noncompetent women witnesses. This part of the tradition is said, for this specific reason, to be of no apologetic value to him.

On one hand, therefore, credibility is said to be loaned to the empty tomb story because of its reliance even on noncompetent women witnesses and, on the other, Paul is said not to rely on it also precisely because of this appeal to women witnesses rather than men.

But given this reasoning, Wright's defense of the historicity of both Luke and John's account of the discovery of the empty tomb, which is said from the beginning to have involved Peter (and in the case of John, 'the Beloved Disciple' as well), furnishes the tradition with two, whom we might justifiably speak of as "fine upstanding men." The fundamental criterion for accepting the historicity of the tradition is thus pulled from under it.

Clearly, Wright's preparedness to accept the historicity of the inclusion of male witnesses in John and Luke's treatment of the story of the discovery of the tomb therefore undermines his own argument that the presence of women alone speaks of the veracity of the empty tomb tradition. I do not think Wright can really have his cake and eat it.

If this were not enough, Wright seems to have overlooked the account which Luke reports in Luke 24:24, where those on the road to Emmaus report that after the women reported the discovery of the empty tomb "some of those who were with us went to the tomb and found it just as the women had said." Even without Peter in

Luke 24:12 (and in John 20:2–10), according to Luke there *were* corroborative male witnesses of the empty tomb after all! This, along with Luke's inclusion of the episode of Peter running to the tomb Luke 24:12, is entirely congruent with Luke's concern to locate the Easter event in Jerusalem, but if Wright is committed to the historical realism and reliability of these narratives, more or less as they stand, then this is a major problem. Insofar as he is anxious to explain Paul's lack of interest in the evidence of the empty tomb because it relied only on women witnesses, and at the same time, insofar as he relies on the presence of only women witnesses in the empty tomb tradition to establish its historicity, his arguments are undermined by his preparedness to accept the historicity of the inclusion of Peter in John 20 and Luke 24:12, and additional men in Luke 24:24, along with the Beloved Disciple also in John 20.

It seems obvious that the veracity of the story of the introduction of Peter and the Other Disciple into the narrative of the empty tomb, and Luke's use of this to effect the relocation of the Easter Event from Galilee to Jerusalem, cannot somehow just be assumed to be accurate reporting of historical fact on the ground of a fundamental presumption that it all falls within the category of eyewitness testimony. It may be more appropriate to think that specific and identifiable reasons, and apparently good theological purposes, motivated the development of these traditions, and even the awkward conflation of alternative traditions, apparently at a time somewhat removed from the incidents that are reported to have originally given rise to them.

What conclusions, then, may we now draw about the historicity of the story of the empty tomb? Clearly, we can speculate or we can choose in a voluntaristic way to assume that the story of the empty tomb *must* have been based upon eyewitness reports and that these eventually got into the hands of Mark. But such an assumption hardly qualifies as a historical proof. I myself incline to the view (even despite the inconclusiveness of the *kai euthus* evidence) that it is unlikely that Mark created the story *ex nihilo*; but I have to admit that I am unable to prove this. In this case, we are back with the Bultmann/Marxsen/Lüdemann view that the empty tomb story may have been an "apologetic legend," the product of faith rather than the evidential grounds of faith, or even, with Adela Yarbro Collins, that it was the creation of Mark himself. Given the lateness of the earliest appearance of the written testimony of the empty tomb in Mark and its complete absence from the letters of Paul, and the obvious indicators of redactional development across the different Gospel versions of the story subsequent to Mark, that were apparently dictated by the differing apologetic concerns of, and the theological motivation behind, the editorial work of the respective Gospel authors, then we have no way of proving that it was *not* the product of legend-making subsequent to the origin of faith. On the other hand, clearly, Wright's imagined incontrovertible argument to the effect that Paul knew of the tradition of the empty tomb but did not mention it, even in his earnest attempt to win back the Corinthian Christians to the fundamentals of Easter faith, must also be judged to be entirely speculative. It may be a thinkable thesis in the sense that it is logically possible, or thinkable without self-contradiction. But, given the lack of compelling evidence, whether it is actually possible or even probable remains an unanswered question.

In addition, the capacity of the empty tomb story to provide sufficient evidence to ground the logical conclusion that Jesus definitely rose from the dead is hindered by the obvious fact that an empty tomb can be explained in a variety of other ways—the traumatized women could have gone to the wrong tomb, or the body could have been stolen. This was not just the initial conclusion of Mary Magdalene when she discovered it empty. According to Luke 24:12 Peter, having looked into the empty tomb, departed "wondering in himself at that which was come to pass." An empty tomb by itself can hardly amount to sufficient proof that a resurrection has occurred.

If resurrection were understood to involve the restoration of a physical body to this world, the emptiness of the tomb would be a *necessary* condition of the truth of that contention. But the emptiness of the tomb is not itself a *sufficient* condition to warrant this assertion, given that its emptiness may be explained in other ways. It is therefore understandable that critics of the Christian movement explained the report of the empty tomb by arguing that Jesus' body could have been stolen. As Origen of Alexandria was to make clear, this later became a favored strategy, most notably of Celsus in the second century.[43] But Matthew's version of the story of the tomb already suggests that this explanation of it may have been in circulation well before the end of the first century (Matt 27:64–66).

The puzzle of the absence of any reference to the empty tomb in the earliest Pauline stratum of the Easter tradition in 1 Cor 15:3–8 therefore remains. Given the lateness of the first written appearance of the empty tomb tradition in *Mark*, a full generation after the reported event is understood to have occurred, along with the developmental elaboration of the story from Gospel to Gospel, the question is whether its historicity as an early oral tradition can be established, and this is a continuing unexplained mystery. New Testament theologians seeking to re-construct an account of what appears to have happened at Easter are entitled to use their historical imaginations and to suggest possibilities and probabilities. No real harm is done. However, the systematic theologian who is interested in the more constructive work of articulating a coherent understanding of faith for today may justifiably be reluctant to overlook the variety of possible explanations of the empty tomb tradition that are still current. There is little for constructive systematic theology to build upon if we start out only with

43. Celsus wrote around AD 178. The response of Origen of Alexandria (c. AD 184–c. 253) is found in his *Contra Celsum*.

possibilities and probabilities. I think we must conclude that the question of whether the story of the empty tomb was certainly part of the initial Easter proclamation, or a later way of expressing faith, remains an open question in current theological debate. If the systematic theologian is looking to New Testament scholars for reasonably agreed grounds on which to build, he or she will be disappointed.

An apologetic and defensive attempt to justify traditional beliefs about what happened by always giving a text "the benefit of the doubt" may likewise be judged not to be all that satisfactory. We must resign ourselves to living with evidential ambiguity. It seems better frankly and honestly to admit that the attempt to prove the account of the discovery of the emptiness of the tomb by women, and the Resurrection of Christ as a historical event on the basis of it, purely as a conclusion of critical historical research, fails. The story of the empty tomb leaves us with an unexplained enigma.[44]

While N. T. Wright sets out to prove the occurrence of the Resurrection on the basis of the evidence of the empty tomb and the appearances, the real challenge is to establish the historical reliability of this purported "evidence." We may have to admit that we may never know the true story of the pre-history of the tradition of the empty tomb and whether, indeed, it was in circulation prior to *Mark*, or whether Mark was the author of it himself.

44. Thus Dunn sums up the current situation in relation to the story of the empty tomb: "It must suffice to say that literary analysis of the gospel traditions has proved decisive neither for nor against its primitiveness." (*Jesus and the Spirit*, 119).

7

The Nature of Faith

N. T. Wright's contention that the first Christians received a "strictly limited" and fixed dictionary definition of the term "resurrection," and that their Easter experience simply conformed to the expectations generated by it, tends to encourage a kind of *a priori* approach to belief. For given the alleged expectation that the term implied that the resurrected body was simply a material body, physically restored to this world, Wright therefore tends to the view that the tomb *must* have been empty. Its emptiness seems already to be implied by the inherited meaning of the term "resurrection" itself and the contention that the first believers could not have thought in any other way. In other words, if they believed in the Resurrection, then they *must* have believed in the empty tomb as a necessary implication of that belief. If this is so, they could have checked out their belief by going to inspect it. The conformity of their thought to an inherited understanding of the meaning of "resurrection" also means that the nature of the appearances or "meetings" with the raised Jesus must also be understood to have conformed to the same expectation as very matter-of-fact physical encounters.

Wright also argues that, given the received "strictly limited" understanding of what "resurrection" allegedly meant, both traditions—that of the empty tomb and that relating to the appearances—must have been in circulation *together*. The first believers, he says, could not have come to believe in Jesus' Resurrection otherwise: "Neither the empty tomb by itself . . . nor the appearances by themselves, could have generated the early Christian belief."[1] Thus, he says, the empty tomb without the appearances would have been "a puzzle and a tragedy."[2] We might also add that without the appearances tradition, the empty tomb could also have been explained in other ways—the body could have been stolen, the women might have gone to the wrong tomb, and so on. However, according to Wright's argument, these explanations are

1. *RSG*, 686.
2. *RSG*, 686.

rendered inadmissible by the tradition of the appearances, which demonstrated the true cause of the tomb's emptiness.

On the other hand, Wright contends that without the story of the empty tomb, the "Sightings of an apparently alive Jesus, by themselves, would have been classified as visions and hallucinations."[3] In other words, the appearances without the tradition of the empty tomb would have led to the conclusion that the appearances were themselves merely illusory. The empty tomb demonstrates that this was not so. Therefore, "an empty tomb and appearances of a living Jesus, taken together, would have presented a powerful reason for the emergence of the belief."

All this depends on a prior acceptance of the "strictly limited" definition of the meaning of "resurrection" in the world of Second Temple Judaism: "The meaning of resurrection within Second Temple Judaism makes it impossible to conceive of this reshaped resurrection belief emerging without it being known that a body had disappeared, and that the person had been discovered to be thoroughly alive again."[4]

How this alleged misinterpretation of the appearances as visions and hallucinations could really have been possible, given the purported experience of "meeting" with the Raised Jesus, talking and eating with him, as Wright envisages these meetings, is a question. But in any event, the empty tomb tradition is said to head off talk of appearances as "visions and hallucinations." Thus, in order to come to belief in the Resurrection, given the definition received from Second Temple Judaism, the tomb *had* to be empty and the appearances *had* to be physical and material in form so as to leave the tomb empty.[5] In other words, once a claim to resurrection faith was made, a specific historical outcome is already dictated by the dictionary definition of the term "resurrection." Given the received conceptual understanding of the first believers, the tomb had to be empty and the appearances had to be congruent with its emptiness, and so Jesus' body had to be physically restored to this world. Otherwise, there would have been no possibility of a child of Second Temple Judaism coming to resurrection belief.

Once again, all this is an implication of the inherited understanding of "resurrection." It meant the physical restoration of a material body to this world of such a kind as would leave a tomb empty. One suspects the blatant *a priori* reasoning here actually dictates what needs to be proved: it is not so much that the incontrovertible evidence of the empty tomb and of the appearances proves that the Resurrection occurred; rather belief in the Resurrection (understood in the "strictly limited" way prescribed by Wright) means that the tomb *must* have been found to be empty and the

---

3. *RSG*, 686.

4. *RSG*, 686.

5. Thus Wright says: "Once we locate the early Christians within the world of Second Temple Judaism, and grasp what they believed about their own future hope and about Jesus' own resurrection, these two phenomena are firmly warranted." (*RSG*, 686).

appearances *must* have occurred in a way that is congruent with its emptiness in order for resurrection belief to emerge.

It is important to Wright's argument that both traditions—the empty tomb and the appearances—of necessity had to be in circulation together from the beginning. However, while these implications follow from an initial acceptance of a particular preunderstanding of the concept of "resurrection from the dead," as it had been inherited from Second Temple Judaism, it is difficult to assert that the two traditions had always been found together in the face of actual evidence. If we go to the evidence of the earliest stratum of the tradition, the Epistles of St. Paul, the contrary appears to be the case. As we have already noted a number of times, Paul provides us with references to the appearances tradition but does not mention the empty tomb in his Epistles. There is thus no concrete early written evidence of the traditions of the appearances and of the empty tomb being in circulation together anywhere in Paul's Epistles. The same may be said of the Gospel tradition. The earliest Gospel, *Mark*, which provides us with the first written report of the story of the empty tomb, is without any narrative tradition of an appearance attached to it. In other words, the earliest stratum of the New Testament evidence, speaks, if anything, to the contrary of what Wright would have us believe about the necessary circulation of these two traditions in tandem.[6]

It is obviously perilous to begin with a "strictly limited" dictionary definition of a term, and then pull the evidence into conformity with it so as to make resurrection belief possible. After all, it would not normally be thought wise to assume that there must have been a bush-fire with a heavy fall-out of black ash, in order to account for the blackness of indigenous Australian swans, simply so as to preserve belief in the conformity of reality to a received concept of the whiteness of swans as they were hitherto conceived to be. It is likewise disastrous to argue, on the basis of a received dictionary definition, that resurrection belief would only have been possible among the first generation of believers if the tomb were in fact found to be empty and if the Raised Jesus appeared in a manner entirely and straightforwardly congruent with its emptiness. To argue that these two traditions are mutually interpretative and that they *must* have been in circulation together, even in the absence of any concrete evidence of this, is to assume what needs to be proved. These are contingent matters that can only be resolved by appeal to actual evidence.

This raises a fundamental question about the actual procedure taken by N. T. Wright in arriving at the conclusion that the Resurrection of Jesus did in fact occur. At this point he produces something of a surprise for his readers. For, after earnestly striving to prove the occurrence of the Resurrection as a historical event by arguing that the evidence in support of its occurrence is both necessary and sufficient to prove

6. Wolfhart Pannenberg is of the view that it is very unlikely that the first witnesses would have gone back to Galilee *after* the discovery of the empty tomb. If, on the other hand, they returned to Jerusalem after experiencing the appearances in Galilee, it follows that "it is very likely that the appearances and the discovery of Jesus' empty tomb happened independently of each other and became connected only in later stages of the tradition" ("Did Jesus Really Rise from the Dead?" 135).

his case, at the end of the day Wright is forced to make a telling admission. In summing up his argument he concedes: "I do not claim that it constitutes a 'proof' of the resurrection in terms of some neutral standpoint."[7]

This comes as a complete surprise, for at the beginning of the whole exercise Wright claimed that the attempt to prove the occurrence of the Resurrection as a historical event was open to anyone of any persuasion using the historical reason.[8] Indeed, at the outset Wright argued for the appropriateness of a historical investigation of the Resurrection precisely because "historical knowledge . . . can be discussed without presupposing Christian faith."[9] He forthrightly rejected a theology with "a closed epistemological circle, a fideism from within which everything can be seen clearly but which remains necessarily opaque to those outside."[10] He therefore set out to prove the occurrence of the Resurrection as a historical event using the techniques of critical historical research in the belief that the historical reason could stand on its own feet without faith-informed presuppositions.

However, after his own exhaustive discussion of the relevant historical evidence, his much more modest concluding claim is that an appeal to the concept of "resurrection" is, in his view, the best explanation of the evidence, and "a historical challenge to other explanations."[11] Apart from this admission that there are in fact "other explanations" of the available evidence, this unfortunately assumes a great deal of what needs to be proved. For we have first to secure the actual evidence: it has to be proved that a tomb was indeed found empty before we begin to argue that the Resurrection of Jesus is the best explanation of it. As we have seen,[12] we cannot actually establish with any certainty that the story of the discovery of the tomb was even an element of the earliest tradition. Given the absence of any reference to it in the writings of St. Paul this remains problematic. Likewise, we have to establish that what Wright describes as "meetings" of the kind portrayed with graphic detail in the later Gospels of Luke and John actually took place more or less as they are described in these respective Gospel

---

7. *RSG*, 717.

8. *RSG*, 21.

9. *RSG*, 22.

10. *RSG*, 21. In fact, some kind of "closed epistemology" is inevitable, since those who do not possess the linguistic tools to make an identification in a claim to knowledge are thereby prevented from doing so. For example, those who do not know what a Quokka is will not be able to claim to know one, even when one is directly encountered. (Quokkas are a kind of "miniature kangaroo" found only on Rottnest Island off the coast of Perth, Western Australia, that were mistaken for large rats by the Dutch explorers of the seventeenth century, hence "Rats' nest Island"). Likewise, the knowing appropriate to faith is closed to those not in possession of the linguistic tools and rules for their use within a community of faith operating as a linguistic community. One cannot claim to know the presence of the "Spirit of Christ" in faith without some understanding of the meaning of this form of words. A quest to transcend this kind of "closed epistemology" may be entirely futile.

11. *RSG*, 717.

12. In chapters 5 and 6 above.

narratives before we can conclude that "resurrection" is the best explanation of them.[13] Indeed, we still have to contend at least with the possibility that the matter-of-fact manner in which those encounters are described in these later Gospels may be the result of the development of the tradition from an earlier less graphic and materializing original kernel over the course of a couple of generations of public transmission. The absence of this graphic detail from the earlier two Gospels of Mark and Matthew only compounds this problem. The possibility that these details were acquired in the course of the transmission of the tradition has yet to be conclusively disproved.

This obliges us to conclude that, insofar as Wright argues that appeal to "resurrection" is the *best* explanation of the available evidence, we also have to face the possibility that there is really no "front runner" among possible explanations, and that the available evidence is actually insufficient to warrant *any* clear historical result with anything like a claim to have been incontrovertibly and securely established. Indeed, as historians we may have to be content to admit defeat in the face of the tantalizingly enigmatic nature of the available evidence.

Curiously, Wright admits that he cannot establish that the historical occurrence of the Resurrection is even the best explanation of the evidence with mathematical certainty or with "the watertight conclusiveness demanded in symbolic logic."[14] By this he apparently means that the occurrence of the Resurrection is not established with the same kind of certainty that pertains in matters of logical necessity, such as in the case of the conclusion that "2 + 2 must equal 4" or (in ordinary language) that "If Tom is a bachelor then he must be unmarried." A statement that Jesus' Resurrection definitely occurred does not follow from the evidence with that kind of logical certainty. But then, on page 687 of *The Resurrection of the Son of God*, Wright admits that his preferred conclusion does not follow from the available evidence with any kind of certainty at all. The admission that his case is not really proven after all follows from the concession that the available evidence constituted by the story of the empty tomb and the reports of post-mortem "meetings" is only sufficient to establish a probability, albeit in his estimate, a high probability, but not a certainty. In summing up his thesis he says: "It is therefore historically highly probable that Jesus' tomb was indeed empty on the third day after his execution, and that the disciples did indeed encounter him giving every appearance of being well and truly alive."[15] Then, tucked away in a footnote on the same page, he explains his use of the term "probable." It is

13. We still have to contend with the possibility that the first appearances were visionary manifestations of an already exalted Christ "from heaven," as was already noted in chapter 4. As we shall see in chapter 9 below, there are still other possible explanations of the evidence, such as the nineteenth century suggestion that they were "subjective hallucinations."

14. *RSG*, 687.

15. *RSG*, 686.

used in what is said to be "the common sense historians' way . . . of indicating that the historical evidence, while comparatively rarely permitting a conclusion of 'certain', can acknowledge a scale from, say, 'extremely unlikely', through 'possible', 'plausible' and 'probable' to 'highly probable.'"[16] In other words, his contention is that the historical factuality of the story of the empty tomb and of the developed narratives of the appearances, while admittedly not having been established with certainty, but only with a high degree of probability, is at least as good as historiography usually gets. The suggestion is that, because "certainty" allegedly always eludes historians, the historian of the Resurrection is in no worse situation than that in which historians generally find themselves.

Wright's entire project to attempt to prove the occurrence of the Resurrection of Christ as a straightforward historical event of the past thus ultimately trickles away into dry sand. Despite his initial confident claim that the Resurrection can be proved to any right thinking person of any persuasion or none, at the end of the day he concedes that the evidence actually allows the drawing of that conclusion only with, in his estimate, a high degree of probability.[17] Having examined the same evidence, many others may think even this a somewhat optimistic view of things. Some might prefer to speak at best in terms only of something perhaps possible or plausible given a prior belief in God, or at best "thinkable," rather even than historically probable or highly probable, and then pursue an approach to an alternative understanding of faith based upon other grounds.

On the other hand, the suggestion that historians generally deal in probabilities and rarely in certainties is cold comfort. Wright is, of course, not alone in believing that historical judgments regularly (if not always) fall short of certainty. Indeed, this was once accepted as *par for the course* for much twentieth-century dogmatic theology, which made a virtue out of the alleged inadequacies of all critical historical research in order to ground faith elsewhere. This was specifically the case in relation to the perceived inadequacies of nineteenth-century liberal attempts to construct historical lives of Jesus. As Albert Schweitzer pointed out over a century ago in *The Quest of the Historical Jesus*,[18] all those lives of Jesus were different, and reflected the various historically and culturally conditioned interests and perspectives of successive authors. As a consequence of the perceived inadequacy of historiography to fur-

---

16. *RSG*, 687 n.3.

17. He in fact contrasts the alleged "historians' way" of employing the concept of "probable" with "the highly problematic philosophers' way" of using the term, mysteriously citing "Lucas, 1970" (*RSG*, 687 n.3). Unfortunately, the name "Lucas" does not appear in the bibliography or in the index of *The Resurrection of the Son of God*. In any event, perhaps Wright has in mind a kind of certainty that follows with logical necessity, as in the case of the analytic truth of the statement that "all bachelors are unmarried" as against contingently possible/probable/certain truths based on evidence. However, why this should be spoken of as a "highly problematic philosophers' way" of using the term "probable" is difficult to fathom.

18. Schweitzer, *The Quest of the Historical Jesus*.

nish believers with a secure basis for the commitment of faith, a whole generation of theologians through the first half of the twentieth century therefore took delight in seeking to focus attention on a variety of other options—on the "Christ of faith" over against the "Jesus of history," or on the revealed biblical and dogmatic tradition, or on the Christ proclaimed in the *kerygma* of the Church,[19] rather than the confusing shifting sands of the welter of historical reconstructions of professional historians. The surpassingly dominant twentieth-century "Word" theologies of Karl Barth and Rudolf Bultmann were the most famous result. As Barth said specifically in relation to the Resurrection of Christ in his *The Epistle to the Romans*: "If the Resurrection be brought within the context of history, it must share in its obscurity and error and essential questionableness."[20] Bultmann even went beyond the contention that historical results have "only relative validity" by declaring that in historiography "the conception of truth is dissolved"![21]

The basis of the Christian commitment of faith had therefore to be found elsewhere; in Barth's case the discernment of the Word of God *in* the words of Scripture, whereas in Bultmann's theology faith became an exercise in existential self-understanding in response to the hearing of a de-objectified exposition of the *kerygma* as a "Word of address." Given the all-pervasive acceptance among twentieth century theologians of the methodological maxim that historiography is incapable of arriving at fixed and certain truth, it is understandable that Paul Tillich rejoiced in the contention that the emancipation of faith from historiography constituted the "greatest contribution of historical research to systematic theology."[22]

This widespread disenchantment with the judgments of historiography in the first decades of the twentieth century was formalized into some apparently trenchant philosophical arguments by Ernest Troeltsch, whose work then fanned the search of much subsequent twentieth-century theology to find a basis for faith of a free-standing kind, independent of any reliance on the alleged insecure findings of critical historical research. Troeltsch argued that the judgments of historians do not just vary from historical perspective to historical perspective, but can never be asserted with certainty because of the ever-present possibility that another document might be found which would cause even the most confident historian to look at her material in a new light, and therefore prompt the revision of an initial view of things.[23] Historiog-

19. See Kähler, *The So-Called Historical Jesus*.

20. Barth, *The Epistle to the Romans*, 204.

21. Bultmann, "The Quest for meaning in History," 329; also, *Faith and Understanding*, 30, and *Essays Theological and Philosophical*, 18.

22. Tillich, "Foreword," in Kähler, *The So-called Historical Jesus*, xii.

23. The broad and persistent sweep of the influence of Troeltsch's argument in this regard, right through the twentieth century and to the present day, is reflected in James Dunn's unquestioning

raphy was therefore thought to be blighted by an incurable tentativeness with respect to its results. In addition, Troeltsch noted that cultural developments in the changing social context within which each successive historian inescapably works might alert him or her to aspects of the past that hitherto had gone unnoticed. Because new perspectives are prone to open up with persistent regularity, the interpretation of the past was therefore said always to be subject to revision and change. As a consequence, twentieth-century theologians were all urged to allow for this by exercising extreme caution. By necessity, only a modest degree of probability could be claimed for historical judgments; they were said never to be capable of being asserted with absolute certainty. As the basis of a commitment of trusting faith with all one's heart, mind, and soul, historical judgments therefore failed to qualify.

Even though N. T. Wright does not himself directly refer to these arguments, and certainly does not unpack or examine Troeltsch's reasoning in relation to this particular issue, he, along with a plethora of theologians over the last century, appears to accept the general conclusion of historical skepticism which may rightly be sheeted back to Troeltsch, by accepting the dictum that historians are always obliged to deal with possibilities, probabilities, and at best high probabilities, but not certainties. Wright therefore admits that even though the occurrence of the Resurrection has not been established with certainty, but only, at least in his own view, with a high degree of probability, this is simply of a piece with the writing of history generally. Given this alleged congenital flaw in all historiography, we are therefore bidden not to fret. We are in effect assured that this is as good as it ever gets for historians, who have to be content to secure their judgments about the past only with degrees of probability.

It is not too difficult to put paid to this Troeltschian principle of the inescapability of historical skepticism. Though it may sound a plausible thesis at first hearing, it is in logical terms flawed. Briefly put, the problem with Troeltsch's contention, that judgments about the past can only be asserted with a degree of probability because of the ever-present possibility that new evidence could be found that would require a revision of opinion, is that logical possibilities of error do not dictate actual possibilities of error. Even though it may be logically possible or, in other words, thinkable without self-contradiction, that there *could* be evidence that would unsettle the veracity of a historical judgment, it is not thereby entailed that the evidence that would do this actually exists, or even that it *should* be thought to exist.

---

acceptance of it in *Jesus Remembered*, 103: "And given that more data may always emerge—in ancient history, a new inscription or, prize of prizes, a new cache of scrolls or documents—any judgment will have to be provisional, always subject to the revision necessitated by new evidence or by new ways of evaluating the old evidence." For Dunn, therefore, "certainty is not attainable for the historian": "In historical scholarship the judgment 'probable' is a very positive verdict." (104).

Furthermore, when sufficient evidence has been accumulated to prove that an event occurred, then the historian can actually in some circumstances dismiss the thinkable or logical possibility that there might yet be evidence such as would cause him or her to revise a particular historical judgment. Claiming to be "certain" means, among other things, being in the position to discount thinkable possibilities of this kind. It is thus quite certain that there was a World War in Europe one hundred years ago between 1914 and 1918. We can dismiss the thinkable possibility that someone will find a document at some future time that will prove this to be entirely mistaken. It is also certain that Winston Churchill was Prime Minister of Great Britain during the Second World War. It is no less certain that Winston Churchill on occasion smoked a cigar. I am also quite certain that my father died in February 1992. These are not mere possibilities or probabilities, or even just high probabilities. We can be certain about such things and can therefore justifiably claim to know them. If we ever were to have doubts about any of them we could consult the relevant evidence and come to a judgment which would allow us to eliminate the possibility that further evidence might be found to refute them. We are thus justifiably able to assert them with certainty.[24] The operative principle here is: logical possibilities of error do not entail actual possibilities of error.

There may be plenty of other historical judgments, of course, for which the evidence is inadequate. For example, there may be a great deal of debate about the actual causes of the First World War; interpretations of what happened on particular occasions in the past may also vary enormously and be the subject of great debate among historians. In this sense the historian is obliged to deal in possibilities and probabilities. But other historical judgments, such as the factual judgment *that* a particular event either happened or did not happen, are regularly established with certainty. The flight from historiography of much twentieth century theology, which Tillich imagined was the "greatest contribution of historical research to systematic theology," was therefore based upon an entirely erroneous premise.

Indeed, to argue that one can never be certain in making a historical evaluation of even the best available evidence is tantamount to saying that historical *knowledge* is impossible, for claims to be "certain" and claims to "know" are, in logical terms, closely linked. It is not possible, for example, to say "I know *that x*, but I am not certain *that x*." Likewise, one cannot say "I am certain *that x*, but I do not know it." In other words, to deny the possibility that one can ever be certain about any historical judgment is to deny the possibility of historical knowledge. Clearly, this is a nonsense. The past is not closed off to us as an area of scientific inquiry that leads to perfectly justifiable knowledge claims. Unfortunately Wright, like James D. G. Dunn, and a

---

24. I argued this case long ago in "The Poverty of Historical Scepticism." This reference does not appear in either Wright's or Dunn's bibliography. However, as far as I am aware, nobody has ever refuted the argument set out in it. For positive assessments of it, see Robinson, *The Human Face of God*, 127; also, Mascall, *Theology and the Gospel of Christ*, 65–67, and 97–101.

legion of other contemporary New Testament scholars too numerous to mention, has uncritically accepted this fundamental logical and methodological error of the theology of the twentieth century.

It is therefore not possible to argue that the evidence for the historicity of the Resurrection of Christ constituted by the reports of the empty tomb and the appearances, though in some degree inadequate, can be accepted with "a high degree of probability" though not with certainty, and then suggest simply that this is as good as historians can ever, or even generally do. The fact is that Wright's attempt to prove the occurrence of the Resurrection purely as a historian using reason alone and the techniques of critical historical research actually fails, not because of an alleged congenital defect of all historiography, but because it falls short of proof through want of adequate evidence.

The seriousness of this willingness on the part of Wright to accept the alleged congenital defectiveness of all historical research, is that it leads to a theological *cul-de-sac* in which Christian faith becomes for him a kind of inadequately evidenced propositional attitude: it means that at the end of the day, the Christian is asked to believe *that* the Resurrection did in fact occur, despite the shortfall in the evidence that renders it at best only "highly probable." At this point rational argument necessarily has to give way to *belief* as an act of will. As Wright himself admits: "Saying that 'Jesus of Nazareth was bodily raised from the dead' is not only a self-*involving* statement; it is a self-*committing* statement . . ."[25] Indeed, after admitting that, given the short-fall in the available evidence, it is "perfectly possible to say that one cannot decide" whether the Resurrection did or did not occur,[26] Wright nevertheless urges his readers "not to live on such a knife-edge" of indecision but to decide in favor of the occurrence of the Resurrection because "what alternative account can be offered which will explain the data just as well?"[27] There is no other explanation "which can provide an alternative *sufficient* explanation for all the evidence and so challenge the right of the bodily resurrection to be regarded as the *necessary* one."[28] I do not understand the logic of the word "necessary" here. If there is no other better explanation it might be more prudent simply to accept the evidential shortfall and admit that the whole episode is, in historical terms, unclear and shot through with inexplicable mystery.

In any event, it is clear from all this that, in Wright's thinking, Christian commitment becomes a propositional attitude of belief even despite the evidential shortfall.[29]

25. *RSG*, 717.

26. *RSG*, 717.

27. *RSG*, 718.

28. *RSG*, 718.

29. A similar position is reached by Dunn, for whom faith in Jesus becomes a trust based at best upon historical probabilities: faith is a kind of epistemic fall-back position. He is driven to this given

It is the belief *that* the Resurrection of Christ did occur in the face of an admitted evidential deficit, which then grounds a commitment to live *as though* it were in fact certain, and to work out the personal implications of this. Given the admission that it is "perfectly possible to say that one cannot decide,"[30] this in the end means that Christian commitment becomes a matter of "regarding"[31] the evidence to be both sufficient and necessary to warrant the commitment of faith anyway. We are urged to make this self-involving and self-committing decision, otherwise the Resurrection is left at the center of "a jigsaw puzzle."[32] Exactly.

This sounds suspiciously like talk of the need of a faith commitment rather than the conclusion of a secular faith-neutral exercise in critical historical research, using reason alone, that is in principle open to anyone. Whether it is rationally justified to assume an attitude of certainty, and to commit one's life "with all one's heart, with all one's mind, and with all one's soul, and all one's strength" to the truth of a proposition when the available evidence only supports it as a possibility or even a probability is a good question. It might be a more prudent course to heed the dictum of David Hume: "A wise man proportions his belief to the evidence,"[33] and then maintain a posture of reticence with regard to the historical evidence relating to the Resurrection.

Also, it is important to note at this point that if Wright's treatment of the Resurrection resolves into a matter of believing *that* something occurred in the past despite an admitted shortfall in the evidence that renders it at best only "highly probable," then faith clearly becomes not just a propositional attitude but also a merely retrospective *fides historica*. Its object is an alleged event of the past. It also means that faith has to do with a knowing only by description: it is the belief *that* x is true, where x is a proposition such as "*that* the tomb was empty" or "*that* Jesus was seen alive after his death," or "*that* Jesus rose from the dead." But surely we can do better than this.

An alternative understanding of the Resurrection of Christ, essentially as a revelatory event, a divine disclosure, rather than simply as an event of the past history of this world that might be handled with the techniques of critical historical research alone, will necessarily call for an altogether different theological approach. For a start, it will be entailed from the outset that the Resurrection of Christ will be appropriated by faith understood as a kind of knowledge (*fides*), which grounds a response of trust

---

the impossibility of reaching certain conclusions on the basis of critical historical research, which he judges (erroneously) always to be defective. See *Jesus Remembered*, 103.

30. *RSG*, 717.

31. This is Wright's own word. It means that faith becomes an "on-look": a decision of the will in the face of the lack of conclusive proof.

32. *RSG*, 718.

33. Hume, *An Inquiry Concerning Human Understanding*, Section 10, in the context of Hume's discussion of miracles.

(*fiducia*). This means that faith will be understood not as a matter of accepting the truth of some inadequately evidenced propositions, but of claiming to perceive the continuing presence of the Spirit of the Raised Christ. It will involve a knowing not by description, but by actual acquaintance with a concretely given experienced reality. As such its object will be not just propositional, but personal and relational.

After all "faith," (*pistis*) as it is used by Paul across all his letters, is primarily a relational matter. Beginning with 1 Thessalonians, through Galatians, Philippians and Romans, and into the deutero-Pauline letters—Ephesians (which admittedly remains very close to Paul), and even the Pastoral Epistles, 1 and 2 Timothy, essentially the same understanding of faith prevails. It has to do with a trust or faithfulness that is grounded in the perception of the changeless and eternal faithfulness of God[34] that was placarded before humanity in historical time in the steadfast obedience and "faithfulness even unto death" of the historical crucified Jesus.[35] This is the historically demonstrated divine faithfulness that was confirmed by the fact that God highly exalted him. This faithfulness unto death in turn drew a response of the same kind of trust or faithfulness from Paul himself and those who heard his message of the good news of the faithfulness of God in Christ.[36] For all who heard the Gospel, not just the Jews, could understand themselves to be chosen people of God (1 Thess 1:4), called to faith as children of Abraham. As God's elect they were therefore called to be "blameless until the coming of the Lord Jesus Christ" (1 Thess 5:23). Timothy is thus "a faithful/*pistis* son in the Lord" (1 Cor 4:17), who is sent by Paul to the Thessalonians "to strengthen and encourage them in their *pistis*/faithfulness" (1 Thess 3:2). The resulting "community of trust" between God, Christ, and the Christian fellowship is thus essentially a matter of inter-personal relationality.[37] Insofar as unwavering, trusting, faithfulness of this kind involves knowledge, it is not propositional knowledge. It is the relational knowledge *of* the trustworthiness of God and of Christ in whom trust is therefore justifiably placed. Moreover, this is not just an individual matter, for the whole "community of faith" is caught up together in it. Paul is very clear about the communitarian dimensions of this experience. Even at the start he acknowledges in Gal 1:13 that originally he had set out to destroy the "assembly of God" but after his own conversion he was found to be a part of that very community, now proclaiming the faith/*pistis* that he once sought to destroy.[38]

---

34. Thus in 1 Thess 5:24 Paul says that God is *pistis*, faithful to his promises.

35. The faithfulness of Jesus that is demonstrated in his obedience towards God is spelled out by Paul in Galatians 1 and 2.

36. Paul lives "in the faithfulness/*pistis* of the Son of God" (Gal 2:20). The Galatians themselves are justified not by keeping the law but because of their pistis/faithfulness (Gal 2:16).

37. There is a development by the time of the Pastorals insofar as faith also includes the trustworthiness of the tradition. E.g., 1 Tim 1:15 and 2 Tim 2:11, which speak of faithful or trustworthy "sayings," but these are not the primary object of trusting faith.

38. Gal 1:23.

In addition, faith is not just a response of assent to the truth of abstract propositions proffered in the preaching of Paul, for it is always accompanied by the experience of the "power of the Holy Spirit." Thus the trustworthiness not just of God and
Christ but of Paul himself is commended in his preaching activity, so that Paul is able
to say: "our gospel did not come to you in word only, but also in power, and in the
Holy Spirit, and in much assurance; as you know what manner of men we were among
you for your sake" (1 Thess 1:5). The effect of Paul's preaching is thus to catch up those
who heard it in "bonds of affection" so that what was imparted was "not the gospel of
God only, but also our own souls, because you were dear to us" (1 Thess 2:8).

Likewise, the Galatians received "the Spirit through faith" (Gal 6:1) and are to
"live by the Spirit" (5:16), having received "the fruit of the Spirit" (5:22), and through
his preaching Paul "ministers the Spirit" among them. Thus the "hearing of faith" is always accompanied by the concretely perceived "power of the Spirit," so that "the Gospel of God," the good news of God's faithfulness, not just towards Jews but Gentiles
as well, is matched by the simultaneous experience of incorporation into the inclusive
"community of faith" by the Spirit of Christ.

Clearly, if we are to be true to the New Testament, faith cannot be reduced to a
kind of notional assent to the truth of abstract propositions, such as "*that* the tomb of
Jesus was found empty," "*that* Jesus appeared to his first disciples," or therefore "*that*
Jesus was raised from the dead." It is true that the continued questioning triggered by
the study of the historical issues raised by the evidence of the empty tomb and the tradition of the appearances, and the unresolved nature of the puzzle left by them, may
prompt a kind of religious interest which has to do with the development of a relationship with God, or with the possibility of a relationship with an imagined Raised Christ
of a more clearly religious and personal kind. But Paul does much better than this. For
Paul, faith is not an inadequately evidenced propositional attitude: it has to do with
an unwavering trusting commitment grounded in a concrete relational knowledge
appropriated through acquaintance with the perceived living Spirit of Christ.

If the inadequately evidenced propositions of a specific piece of historiography cannot
claim the whole of our attention as the end of the matter, this immediately alerts us to
the deficits of a methodological approach to the Resurrection of Christ which focuses
exclusively on the methods and techniques of critical historical research. We must
therefore turn to an alternative possibility. But this leaves us with a good deal of more
work to be done.

If the Resurrection of Christ is released from Wright's materialist reductionism
so as to become the religious object of trusting faith, then the justifying grounds of
such a faith, and the epistemological structure of the kind of religious knowing appropriate to it, as against the purely rationalistic and propositional conclusions of critical

historical research, obviously have to be spelled out. This will require a consideration of the manner of the perception in faith of the living presence of the Raised Christ as an object of contemporary acquaintance, rather than a propositional belief established by the critical historical reason. In this case, we will be involved in a present-centered exercise of systematic theology rather than just the past-centered enterprise of critical historical research appropriate to the exegesis of the New Testament texts.

At the same time, a theology of the Resurrection will also necessarily acknowledge the limitations of human reason when it comes to the handling of a transcendental reality. An acknowledgment of the limitations of human reason in handling matters of faith means that account has to be taken of the impact, specifically in relation to the theology of the Resurrection, of the metaphorical nature of all theological discourse, which by definition always falls short of a clear and distinct description of its Object. This is for the obvious reason that the Infinite must always transcend the capacities of finite minds, which dictates that we have to be cognizant of the limitations of finite discourse to encapsulate and contain it.[39] Just as the Infinite God is always by definition "beyond" our humanly crafted images of God, so likewise the transcending mystery of the Raised Christ will always be beyond finite images of him. Like the historical Jesus in the midst of his hostile critics in the Gospel story of Luke 4, he, "passing through the midst of them," will go his way (Luke 4:30). This means that the theology of the Resurrection, no less than discourse focused upon the being of God, must necessarily retain an *apophatic* face.

At the outset it is necessary to consider whether an orientation of thought towards a transcendent reality outside and beyond history might be quite fundamental if we are to do justice to the New Testament resurrection traditions, even if such an approach possesses a family likeness to what Wright wants to speak of as "platonic." In other words, it is necessary to challenge the apparent assumption that name-calling of this kind will be sufficient to persuade us to dismiss it. Alas, as we shall see, an alignment with the great tradition of Christian theology through the centuries that has treated Plato as a helpful ally, rather than summarily dismissing him as an enemy, could actually turn out to be a theologically profitable strategy.

It is important to note that in seeking to airbrush allegedly "platonic" influences out of the Christian theology of the Resurrection, Wright tends to end up with a sophisticated kind of biblical fundamentalism, focused on a literal articulation and acceptance of the apocalyptic hopes generated by the melodramatic imagination of Second Temple Judaism. He is also in danger of dispossessing historical Christianity of its faith. It is undeniable, for example, that Christian theologians from a very early time exploited the opportunity to mine Plato's philosophy for helpfully supportive

39. Following Barth: "It is not possible to give direct information concerning God and his revelation. The truth of God can never be expressed in a single word, but always only in statement and counter-statement. Every positive proposition has to be complemented and corrected at once by an opposing negative one." On Barth's "dialectical theology," see Zahrnt, *The Question of God*, 29.

ideas. It would be sheer folly to imagine, for example, that one can simply expunge the influence of Plato from the thinking of the Christian tradition of the first millennium of its history, which persisted at least until a renewed interest in Aristotle broke upon the medieval world in the thirteenth century. Without wanting to compile a compendium of those who were open to the helpful assistance of Plato, one only has to think of the theological legacy of Clement of Alexandria, Origen, or of St. Augustine of Hippo, whose thought has been so influential in the West. Certainly, St. Augustine's thought cannot be understood apart from the influence of Plato, whether this was acquired directly from Plato's own texts or mediated to him through the Neo-Platonism of Plotinus.[40] Given Augustine's popularity through the sixteenth century Reformation, it is not a surprise that a valuing of Plato is at some points as true of classical Protestant theology as of the theology of the historical Catholic tradition; witness John Calvin's reflections on the survival of souls when freed from "the prison houses of their bodies."[41] It was precisely Plato's depiction of the immortality of the soul that was one main reason why Plato was "highly esteemed in older Christianity."[42] But even in the twentieth century, no less a Christian thinker than the great Protestant theologian Karl Barth systematically articulated a theology based upon the fundamental categories of revelation and faith, and emphasized the folly of the human religious quest to reach God by utilizing reason alone. Barth's whole enterprise hinged on the drawing of a radical platonic-type distinction between historical time and the eternity of God—the "infinite qualitative difference between time and eternity."[43] It is not insignificant that when Barth, in his speech of acceptance of the Sonning Prize at Copenhagen in April 1963, acknowledged his dependence on theologians who influenced the theology of his early period, he mentioned specifically Søren Kierkegaard and others, but also, though perhaps somewhat surprisingly, he acknowledged his dependence on Plato: "the great Plato—yes, that is what I said, Plato!"[44]

Likewise, one only has to think of the Cambridge Platonists,[45] and of W. R. Inge in the Anglican tradition,[46] to appreciate the wide-ranging importance of Plato across a broad theological spectrum in the long history of Christian theology.[47] Given that we live and work in the wake of a long line of Christian theologians through the centuries who have seen Plato as an ally rather than an enemy, it may be prudent to

40. As Chadwick rightly says, Augustine "lay the foundations for the synthesis between Christianity and classical theism stemming from Plato . . ." (*Augustine*, 3).

41. Calvin, *Institutes* 1.15.2 (Note also the connection of Calvin with Wis 9:15)

42. An observation of Barr, *The Concept of Biblical Theology*, 164.

43. Barth, *The Epistle to the Romans*, 29 (following Kierkegaard).

44. See Zahrnt, *The Question of God*, 27.

45. Cudworth, More, et al., in the sixteenth century.

46. See for example Inge, *The Religious Philosophy of Plotinus* (1914); *The Philosophy of Plotinus*; and *The Platonic Tradition*.

47. I am gratified to note the very positive assessment of the usefulness of Plato's *Phaedrus* in the recent work of Catherine Pickstock, *After Writing*.

pause therefore before corralling everything suggestive of the "Wholly Other" and transcendent or "heavenly" into a pen labeled "platonic" so as then cavalierly to write it off as alien to "authentic" Christian thought.

In fact this long tradition of Christian theology which has received an "Other Worldly" orientation of thought of a generally platonic kind, by appropriating Plato as an ally rather than as an enemy, actually has its roots within the pages of the New Testament itself. The resurgent interest in Plato between 100 BC and AD 200, which produced an amalgam of Stoic and Platonic ideas, with Platonism gradually becoming the dominant partner, and to which we refer today as Middle Platonism, had an impact within ancient Jewish communities as much as any other around the Mediterranean at the time. This is of enormous importance in understanding the intellectual environment in which St. Paul and the first generation of Christian believers necessarily participated. Indeed, it can be argued that justice will not be done, specifically to the primitive understanding of the Resurrection of Christ, by interpreting it exclusively through the eschatological lens of Second Temple Judaism, and thus handling it only as a historical event of the past history of this world, even with an interest in its hopeful implications for the future. For an over-concentration of interest on the implications of the past for the discernment of the shape of the eschatological future leads to an understanding of the nature faith that tends to evacuate the present of theological significance as an arena of concrete religious experience. It tends to overlook the possibility that Christian faith in the Raised Christ may have to do with the discernment and identification of his living presence in the temporal present, and not just in the remembered past and the anticipated future of Christian hope.

N. T. Wright's methodological commitment to the handling of the Resurrection exclusively as a historical event with eschatological implications is therefore unnecessarily self-limiting. On the other hand, the Middle Platonist amalgam of ideas originally of Stoic and Platonic origin provides us with some additional important pointers to the way in which Christ's living presence as a "life giving Spirit" (Paul) or "the abundant Spirit" (John) was understood to be perceived and known in faith among the first generation of Christian believers as the religious Object of their continuing religious experience. As important as the eschatological hope of Second Temple Judaism was to the Jewish mentality of the first century, the first Christians did not just look back in memory to a past historical event and forwards in hopeful expectation of the Day of the Lord. We must also attend to the nature of the continuing experience of the presence of the Raised Christ through the revelatory medium of his Spirit that grounded their continuing faith-claims and justified their hope. Inevitably, we must explore the epistemological and ontological presuppositions of the world that the first generation of Christians inhabited that are implicit in these faith claims.

A concentration of attention on the experience of the presence of the Spirit of Christ as an important constitutive element of resurrection faith, and not just as a kind of reward for faith, or a secondary accompaniment of faith, means that the evidence of the empty tomb and of the appearances tradition does not stand alone. Indeed, as I originally argued in *The Structure of Resurrection Belief*, the Pauline tradition amply demonstrates that early faith and hope were "not exclusively traced back to a visionary experience of the past."[48] And this is not to mention the empty tomb, which Paul does not so much as mention. Rather, Paul's exposition of the nature of faith and hope "is regularly traced back, not to an experience or vision of the bodily Jesus of some kind, but to the continuing presence of the Spirit of Christ."[49] The operative word here is "exclusively," for there are clearly some occasions when Paul does return to the tradition of the original appearances.[50] Nevertheless, the over-whelming thrust of Paul's talk focuses on the importance of the experience of the presence of the Spirit of Christ as the continuing basis of faith and hope: the experience of the Spirit of Christ is the *object* of faith and the *ground* of hope.[51]

Perhaps it is not surprising that N. T. Wright has taken exception to this contention. He alleges for starters in *The Resurrection of the Son of God* that no grounds were offered in *The Structure of Resurrection Belief* in support of the view that early Christian faith and hope were regularly sheeted back to an experience of the Spirit of Christ. Then secondly, he contends that no grounds *could* in fact have been offered in support of this contention, given his own argument (as he presents it in chapters 5, 6, and 7 of *The Resurrection of the Son of God*)[52] that faith and hope must be understood as responses to the occurrence of the Resurrection understood as a historical event of the past that he believes is firmly secured by the evidence of the empty tomb and appearances. While Wright naturally has confidence in his own powers of historical argument as he employs them in the chapters of *The Resurrection of the Son of God* to which he refers,[53] we may nevertheless prefer to rely upon the epistles of St. Paul himself regarding the fundamental importance (or otherwise) of the continuing experience of the Spirit of Christ for an understanding of the actual content of early Christian faith and hope. Not least, we have to take with absolute seriousness St. Paul's declaration that the Spirit that is perceived in faith is the ground of hope, for the concrete experience of the Spirit is to be interpreted in a promissory way as the "down-payment" of a hoped-for yield to come (2 Cor 1:22/Eph 1:13–14) or the "firstfruits" of

---

48. Carnley, *Structure of Resurrection Belief*, 249.

49. Carnley, *Structure of Resurrection Belief*, 249–50.

50. 1 Cor 15:5–8 is the obvious example.

51. For a more detailed treatment of Paul's appeal to the experience of the Spirit of Christ, and of the important place of *pneuma* in the Stoicism of his time, see the companion volume to this, *The Reconstruction of Resurrection Belief*, chapters 3 and 4.

52. *RSG*, 373 n.169.

53. *RSG*, chapters 5, 6, and 7.

the future fulfillment of a great harvest (Rom 8:23), just as the community of the Spirit is the prolepsis of the Kingdom.

Curiously, Wright seems to have forgotten that in these very chapters of *The Resurrection of the Son of God* on the "Resurrection in Paul," he himself makes regular appeal to Paul's references to the Spirit in his own descriptions of Paul's understanding of resurrection faith and hope. Indeed, Wright can hardly avoid mention of Paul's emphasis on the eschatological *role* of the Spirit, originally in the Resurrection of Jesus,[54] and in relation to the future resurrection of all the righteous faithful at the End Time; not to mention the continuing role of the Spirit that, as Wright himself says, was "even now at work to anticipate and guarantee that final event."[55]

Nevertheless, he is apparently reluctant to concede that the experience of the Spirit had an *originative* cognitive role in resurrection faith and hope. Undoubtedly this is because he purports to establish the historicity of the Resurrection exclusively on the basis of the evidence of the appearances and the empty tomb: "When we ask the early Christians themselves what had occasioned this belief," he writes, "their answers home in on two things: stories about Jesus' tomb being empty, and stories about him appearing to people, alive again."[56] Unfortunately, this judgment is entirely fanciful. It clearly cannot apply to St. Paul, who does not so much as mention the empty tomb in his own expressions of faith, let alone "home in on it," nor can we say with confidence that it applies to the communities whose faith Paul describes, for when he writes to them about the nature of their faith, it is also without ever mentioning the empty tomb. By contrast, while the empty tomb ranks no mention at all, Paul's actual references to the appearances tradition are not only few, but tend to be appealed to for the purpose of underlining his own status as an apostle rather than as the basis of faith. For example, in 1 Corinthians 9:1, his own experience, apparently on the Damascus Road, is said to have brought with it the conviction that he enjoyed the status of an apostle equal to other apostolic witnesses, and that he was thereby commissioned to proclaim the Gospel of the Resurrection to the Gentiles. When Paul writes to those to whom he had proclaimed the Resurrection to remind them of their faith in Christ, and its accompanying obligation to live moral lives appropriate to this newfound relationship with Christ, he calls their attention to their experience of the transformative Spirit of Christ (for example, in Gal 3:1–5).

A great deal has already been said concerning Wright's contention about the mutually supportive inter-relation of the evidence of the empty tomb and the tradition of

54. *RSG*, 245: "the resurrection was accomplished by the Holy Spirit."

55. *RSG*, 373. In his subsequent study of the theology of Paul in *Paul and the Faithfulness of God*, where the focus is on the Resurrection, Wright corrects his original tendency to minimize the importance of the experience of the Spirit, though it remains absent from his account of the logical structure of resurrection faith. See, however, *Paul and the Faithfulness of God*, Part III, 940, on the vital final eschatological role, and 1398–402, on the nature of the Resurrection in Paul with reference to the views of Troels Engberg-Pedersen.

56. *RSG*, 686.

the appearances insofar as one is said to interpret the other:—the empty tomb being a pointer to the nature of the resurrected body, and the appearances in turn being represented in such a concrete and physical form as to entail that the tomb *must* have been left entirely empty.[57] This is not to be compared, however, with the importance of Paul's concentration of attention upon the actual experience of the Spirit as the continuing object of the response of faith, over against either the story of the empty tomb or the narrative tradition of the appearances. On the other hand, while Paul's kerygmatic summaries of the appearances are few, and certainly are not cited exclusively or left to stand alone either as the object of early faith or the ground of hope, his allusions to the importance of the experience of the Spirit of the Raised Christ recur over and over again. As Troels Engberg-Pedersen remarks: the Spirit is "a concept that—as soon as one has spotted it—appears to be everywhere in Paul."[58]

The experience of the life-giving Spirit of Christ, received as a gift that was understood to have come "from heaven," implied that the Resurrection *must* have occurred; for Christ must have been exalted for the Spirit to be experienced as it was. In this respect, it is not insignificant that Paul's theology of the Spirit appears to have been inherited by John, who in fact expands upon it and develops it as a fundamental theological theme of his Gospel. The crucial Pauline theme of the gift of the Spirit to the baptized is signaled by John already at John 3:5, where he has Jesus declare that those who enter the Kingdom of God must be "born of water and the Spirit." In a sense, the Gospel of John is the Gospel of "he whom God has sent" who both "utters the words of God" and "gives the Spirit without measure" (John 3:34). For John, by contrast with Luke, the Spirit is bestowed by the Raised Christ upon the assembled disciples in the Upper Room appearance when he breathed on them and said: "Receive the Holy Spirit" (John 20:22). Moreover, it is clear in John's mind that the gift of the Spirit to believers is consistently understood as an objectively given post-Easter reality. In John 7:37–39 when Jesus calls on those who are thirsty to come and drink from the rivers of living water that flow from him, John adds: "This he said about the Spirit, which those who had come to believe in him were to receive; for as yet there was no Spirit, because Jesus had not been glorified." This is to be read in conjunction with Jesus' farewell promise to send "the Paraclete" who will only come once Jesus has left his disciples (John 16:7). In other words, the Spirit which Jesus had received at his baptism (according to John 1:32–34), was received and shared after his death and Resurrection among his believers as "the Paraclete." Moreover, the significance of the Spirit as the objectively given reality that is perceived and known in faith is underlined in 1 John 3:24: "And by this we know that he *abides* in us, by the Spirit which he has given us." This is important enough to be repeated: "By this we know that we abide in him and he in us, because he has given us of his own Spirit" (1 John 4:13).

---

57. Wright emphasizes this interdependence in *RSG*, 686–96.

58. Engberg-Pedersen, *Cosmology and Self*, 14.

While Paul celebrates the fact that Christian faith and forward looking hope have been secured because the concretely experienced reality of God's love "has been poured into our hearts by the Holy Spirit who has been given to us" (Rom 5:5), the First Epistle of John fills out the nature of the quality of the experience of the "divine love" that is mediated through Christ as God's Son, and known by the baptized in faith, when it says:

> In this the love of God was made manifest among us, that God sent his only Son into the world, so that we might live through him. In this is love, not that we have loved God but that he loved us and sent his Son to be the expiation for our sins. Beloved, if God so loved us, we also ought to love one another. No one has ever seen God; if we love one another, God abides in us and his love is perfected in us. (1 John 4:9–12)

The take-away from this for a systematic theology of faith is that it is not that faith is the gift of the Spirit; rather the Spirit itself is the gift of life and love which is received and known in experience through faith. Historically, it has often been imagined that the principal role of the Spirit was to bring believers to faith by giving them the "eyes to see." Calvin, for example, is often cited as one who saw the role of the Spirit in terms of working internally to produce within the hearts of men and women the conviction and persuasion that results in acceptance of scriptural truth. In this way, the Spirit witnesses to the truth of scripture by the removal of blindness and distrust and by facilitating a right apprehension of the mind and confirmation of the heart. In *Institutes* 3.2.1, Calvin thus speaks of the need to be "led by the Spirit" and thus "stimulated to seek Christ," and at *Institutes* 3.2.34, of being drawn by the Spirit and being illuminated by that "internal teacher" so as to receive "a new eye." The work of the Spirit is thus to inspire the human intellect which was previously "stupid and senseless" for, as Calvin says, "we are blind by nature." The danger here is that faith tends to become a gnostic secret knowledge or illumination that is given to some in a privileged kind of way but is in principle inaccessible to others. In both Paul and John, however, it is rather that Christ's Spirit is itself the objectively given reality of life and love in which faith comes to rest. This is the reality that is in principle available to everyone with eyes to see and ears to hear should they attend to it. Just as a moth is drawn to light, the Spirit leads into all truth not as an "internal teacher," but by its own objectively given innate power of attraction. Rather than as an inner whisperer in the ears of potential believers, or as one who removes scales from their eyes so as to enable the gift of faith, the Spirit is itself the objectively given gift of life and love whose presence is both perceived and received through faith. It is in this sense that John speaks of the Spirit as "the *pneuma* of truth." Thus, in John 14:17, "the Spirit of truth whom the world cannot receive, because it does not attend to him, neither knows him" is said to be known by the disciples because "he dwells with you, and shall be in you."[59]

59. See also John 15:26, where the role of "the Spirit of truth which proceeds from the Father" is

Instead of reducing the Resurrection of Christ to the dimensions of a straightforward factual event of past historical time, this opens us in the twenty-first century to the possibility of coming to faith by recognizing and claiming to know the living presence of the same "life-giving" and "abundant Spirit" of which Paul and John spoke, as also a reality of our own present experience. Thus, we are able to interpret Paul's references to "the Spirit of Christ" (Rom 8:9), "the Spirit of God's Son" (Gal 4:6), or the "Spirit of Jesus Christ" (Phil 1:19), on analogy with our own experience of faith. When we read Paul's descriptions of the early Christian experience of faith, it is not as though we are learning of something entirely foreign and alien to our own experience; it is as though we are recognizing something with which we are also acquainted. Like Paul himself, we use this very same language to affirm our own living conviction of enjoying a concrete acquaintance with "Christ himself" (Rom 8:10). Thus, from the perspective of faith, understood as a knowing of the Raised Christ, not just by description in the past, but by acquaintance in the present, we are today able to appreciate what it was that Paul and John were in different ways seeking to express and communicate. It is a mistake to think that Paul was only interested in re-affirming his Damascus Road experience as the exclusive ground of his eschatological hope for the return of Christ as Judge at the End of the Age. His letters make it abundantly clear that an additional component of faith, to which he far more constantly drew the attention of his readers, was their continuing relation to the *Christus praesens*, and to their obligation to behave in a manner compatible with this relationship. Likewise, John's exhortation to be "born again of water and the Spirit," and to "abide in God" just as "God abides in you," and to keep Christ's commandment to love one another, speaks of the eternal reality towards which faith is oriented from within historical time, and its behavioral obligations.

It can therefore be argued that an approach to resurrection faith as a kind of knowing of the living presence of the Raised Christ by acquaintance through the medium of his Spirit, by contrast with the remembering, mostly at second hand, of an essentially past historical happening, may actually be discerned within the pages of the New Testament itself, starting with St. Paul, and with St John following close on his heels. In reminding those in the communities he founded of the importance of their faith in Christ, Paul pointed to the transformative presence of his Spirit that was known not just by abstract verbal description, but in faith by actual concrete acquaintance. By contrast just with a matter-of-fact remembered event of human history that is allegedly like Caesar's crossing of the Rubicon, or Augustus' death, and that could be described in a few well-chosen and literally interpreted words so as then to be handled today exclusively as a historical event employing the historical reason

---

to bear witness to Jesus; and John 16:13 where Jesus promises that the Spirit "will guide [the disciples] into all truth: for he shall not speak of himself" but shall speak what is (divinely) communicated to him, and will show the disciples the "things to come." What is to come at this point is the post-Easter reality of life and love, which is to be received as a consequence of Jesus' death and Resurrection through the gift of the Spirit.

alone, Paul appears to be struggling to come to terms with the reality of an intensely shared and essentially *religious* kind. Even if the verbal expression of it is in some sense "beyond words," as a mystery with a transcendental face must always necessarily be, the continuing object of faith is nevertheless incontrovertibly for Paul a concretely perceived reality of Christ's living presence.

Wright's aversion to the possibility that on-going faith and hope might be grounded in the continuing experience of the Spirit of Christ is understandable, given his own methodological commitments. His own insistence on handling the Resurrection only as an event of the historical past in which the body of Jesus, now said to have been rendered materially and physically incorruptible, is alleged to have been restored to *this* world, almost automatically eliminates any role that the Spirit may have as an epistemic Object in the make-up of faith. Clearly, for Wright, this past event, understood in the precise way in which he understands it, and approached as the subject of historical investigation, assumes an exclusive importance in what is in fact a form of theological foundationalism based upon the exercise of reason. Once understood as a historical event whose occurrence is said to have been proved by the exercise of the historical reason alone, this event then becomes the alleged rational foundation for an understanding of the nature of faith and hope as second order responses that are subsequent to it and dependent upon it. While the Resurrection itself is said to be proved by historical reasoning, faith comes to focus on the role of God as its ultimate cause, and also on the consequential status and identity of Jesus as Messiah and Lord, whose return in glory at the Eschaton is therefore awaited in hope. These propositional judgments of faith and hope are said to issue from the Resurrection understood as an event whose occurrence is allegedly proved by historical research based upon the evidence of the empty tomb and the appearances alone. But this means that the continuing experience of the Spirit in this case becomes a kind of add-on to "anticipate and guarantee" their hope, while the actual basis of their faith is said to be independently secured by the appeal of critical historical research to the evidence of the empty tomb and appearances.

It may be frankly acknowledged that, once an understanding of the Resurrection is released from the constraint of having to be thought of only retrospectively as a historical event, life does not necessarily become less difficult or less challenging for Christian theologians. When the Resurrection is understood as a "going to God," the resurrected, transformed, and exalted Christ, having been located in the first instance "with God in heaven," or "at the right hand of the Father," may be said to have "appeared" to the first witnesses and thus to have been known in a revelatory experience "from heaven." While, in this case, a methodological commitment to handling the Easter Event *only* retrospectively as an historical event, employing the techniques of critical historical research, becomes very problematic (if not entirely impossible), the theological task of accounting for the human perception of a heavenly reality of this kind is not without its own difficulties and theological challenges.

The companion volume to this book, *The Reconstruction of Resurrection Belief*, therefore endeavors systematically to address the epistemological issues that arise from an understanding of faith as a commitment of trust that is grounded in the claim to perceive and know the living presence of the Raised and exalted Christ. We must here be content to consider the actual language to which the first Christians resorted in their attempts to understand and express what had occurred within their own religious experience. For one of the firmly established results of critical historical research on Christian origins is that, whatever happened on the first Easter Day and in the months and years that followed, it issued in an efflorescence of highly distinctive faith claims, which in turn employed a highly distinctive vocabulary. Inherited terms, such as "Lord" and "Christ," came to be used of the exalted Jesus who was now understood to be located "at the right hand of the Father." It is understandable that this language appears often to have originated in the context of community gatherings for worship and prayer to Christ, or to God through Christ. These titles were used along with an equally distinctive application of the titles "Son of Man" and "Son of God." The logical processes by which the first Christians appear to have come to engage in this distinctive form of discourse are instructive with regard to the nature of the experienced Object upon which their faith came to rest and which triggered their eschatological hope. By attending to their christological discourse, we can ourselves also begin to come to terms with the transcendent and heavenly nature of the reality with which they claimed to have to do.

8

The Verbal Expression of Faith

As the first generation of Christian believers processed their Easter experiences, they naturally responded by making faith-claims in which they expressed their understanding of what it was that had occurred. In this sense they were intentionally reporting something; almost certainly they saw themselves in the role of its witnesses. On the other hand, they began to express their faith in worshipful acts of reverence and devotion. At the same time that they expressed their understanding of what had happened to Jesus, they were unwittingly revealing something of the subjective impact on their own lives of what had happened. In this sense they were speaking autobiographically of the affect of Jesus' Resurrection on them and of its continuing significance in their lives.

In the first instance, as they searched for words to explain what had happened with respect to Jesus, and in the making of faith-claims expressing their understanding of where Jesus had gone, and what all this meant in eschatological terms, they naturally drew upon the inherited tradition of their religious language. As Ulrich Wilckens once observed, those who experienced the Easter Event were obliged to make it known "with the resources of the tradition." Clearly, these witnesses had no other means of expressing themselves than those which their tradition placed at their disposal.[1] But, inevitably, as they spoke of their Easter experience, their inherited language was charged with a set of quite new nuances of meaning, sometimes expressed with bold, even audacious, enthusiasm. In this way their actual Easter experience itself cannot but have conditioned what they had to say about it, even though they were naturally employing language and concepts drawn from their religious tradition.[2]

At the outset, in their attempts to explicate the ultimate meaning of the Resurrection in reference to the Raised Jesus and their understanding of his newly vindicated

1. Ulrich Wilckens, "Der Ursprung der Überlieferung der Erscheinungen des Auferstandenen," 56 and 89.

2. As has been argued already in chapter 3.

status, they began to refer to him and even to address him, using a specifically chosen set of inherited titles. At the top of the list of most commonly used titles were "Lord" and "Messiah/Christ," along with "Son of Man"[3] and, very significantly, "Son of God." Though other titles were also used, these four appear in the post-Easter traditions most frequently, and may be regarded as the most theologically telling and significant.[4] Even if some of these titles had surfaced during the life and ministry of the historical Jesus, with one or two of them at least perhaps actually having been used either in direct reference to him or even by Jesus himself, there is general agreement that after his crucifixion an appeal to them in a renewed and invigorated process was certainly initiated by, and dependent upon, the claimed experience of his Resurrection. This, along with the fundamental belief that what had happened had been brought about by the express will and act of God, entailed that the language was inevitably charged with transcendental meaning.

Given the pre-history of these titles in the Jewish religious tradition, they brought with them a set of associated images. The title "Son of Man," for example, came loaded with allusions that may well have been acquired from its use in the book of Daniel. In 1977, C. F. D. Moule made a carefully considered case in support of the belief that Jesus may have used the title "Son of Man" himself,[5] even suggesting that when he referred to himself as "*the* Son of Man,"[6] he had in mind the specific image found in Dan 7:13, where the Son of Man, perhaps originally symbolic of all Israelites who remained resolutely loyal in time of persecution, appears vindicated before the throne of God, the Ancient of Days.[7] If Jesus did use this title and saw his own mission and destiny in relation to it, it would naturally have acquired an additional specific significance in the context of its use in the post-Easter community in the light of the experience of his Crucifixion and Resurrection. However, many New Testament scholars, in the wake of Moule's work, have questioned whether a reference to Dan 7:13 is somehow implicit in Jesus' use of "the Son of Man," and prefer to treat it simply as a generic term of self-reference in which what is said of the Son of Man is true of all human beings.[8] In this case, we cannot anticipate being able to glean a great deal from it that

3. Which strictly speaking may not necessarily be a title, since it could be a generic idiom of self-reference. E.g., "The Son of Man has nowhere to lay his head" may simply mean "A man/someone has nowhere to lay his head" or "I have nowhere to lay my head." Many of the more than eighty occurrences of the phrase "Son of Man" in the New Testament are of this kind.

4. Other titles that were also used are: "Son of David," "God's Servant," "Prophet," "King," "Leader," "Holy One," "Righteous One," "Judge," and "Rabbi/Teacher."

5. See Moule, *The Origin of Christology*, 12–22.

6. Notably in Mark 9:31; 10:33, 45; Matt 24:27, 30; 25:31; and Luke 21:27 and 22:69.

7. John J. Collins, in *Daniel*, also argued for an individualized reading of Daniel's vision, though Wright is more inclined to see it as a "collective symbol." See Wright, *The New Testament and the People of God*, 291–97.

8. Maurice Casey denies any role to Daniel 7 in Paul's thinking. See Casey, *Son of Man*, 151–54. In one interesting discussion of this alternative view of doubting the importance of Daniel, Richard Bauckham specifically engages with Barnabas Lindars' view that an idiomatic use of the generic article

might throw light on its post-Easter significance as an indicator of the Raised Jesus' vindicated status and heavenly destiny.

This contrasts with the post-Easter coloring acquired by the titles "Messiah/ Christ" and "Lord." The title "Messiah," though Jesus may not have used it in reference to himself,[9] appears at least to have been used *of* Jesus by others during his lifetime, as for example in the case of Peter's confession of faith at Caesarea Philippi (Mark 8:27–30; Matt 16:13–20). In this case, Jesus was remembered as one who either himself resolutely endeavored to re-define the precise nature of an acceptable kind of messiahship to be signaled by it, or was perceived by others to have done so indirectly through his teaching and manner of life. In any event, this title became subject to quite radical further revision in the light of faith in his Resurrection from the dead. He was now understood to have been exalted and *designated* to return at a future time to exercise his messiahship as the Christ of God (see Acts 3:20). Certainly, the other two related titles, "Lord" and "Son of God," both of which carry obvious allusions to Jesus' assumption of divine authority and sovereignty, appear to have come into currency with a vengeance as a post-Easter phenomenon.

The combination of titles and the images traditionally associated with them that were used in the formulation of early christological faith-claims, means that those claims are windows into the primitive understanding of what had happened to Jesus as a consequence of his Resurrection from the dead, along with its ultimate transcendental and eschatological implications. Moreover, even if they were not necessarily intended to do so, the use of these titles helpfully points to the quality of the Easter experiences themselves. Not least, the christological language to which the first generation of believers resorted throws light on the nature of the religious Object that was perceived in faith and that was understood to have given rise to it.

The link between the Easter experiences of the first generation of witnesses and their resort to the use of these christological titles is explicitly made by Paul when he says in Rom 1:3–4 that "though Jesus was descended from David according to the flesh," he was "declared to be *Son of God* with power according to the Spirit of holiness, by resurrection from the dead, Jesus *Christ our Lord*." Later in Romans, Paul affirms the same linkage when he says that "*Christ* died and lived again, that he might be *Lord* of both the dead and the living" (Rom 14:9).

---

indicates that the speaker is referring to a class of persons with whom he identifies himself, as in "a man in my position." See Lindars, *Jesus, Son of Man*, 24, and Bauckham's response in "The Son of Man," 250.

9. Though N. T. Wright is of the view that Jesus did use the title in reference to himself, in view of the fact that the idea of the Messiah can hardly be divorced from his self-conscious proclamation of the dawning Kingdom of God in and through his own mission.

Even prior to Paul, however, the same linkage between the Resurrection and the subsequent affirmation both of Jesus' messiahship and of his lordship was already established in the key christological hymn that he quoted in Phil 2:5–11. The anonymous author of this ancient hymn, after first rehearsing a statement of the lowly nature of the servant-humanity remembered to have been lived out by the historical and crucified Jesus, then makes it clear that the Resurrection grounded the conviction that Jesus had received the divine reward of a martyr's faithfulness unto death in the form of his exaltation and glorification, with the promise of ultimate triumph over all his enemies as "Lord" of all things "in heaven, and on earth, and under the earth." Clearly, the Easter experience was of such a kind that it was believed appropriate to claim that, as a consequence of the Resurrection, God had highly exalted the crucified Jesus and given him a name above every name.[10]

The first part of the ancient Christology expressed in this hymn, beginning as it does with a statement of the kenotic "self-emptying" character of the distinctive quality of the lowly servant humanity remembered to have been lived out by Jesus, of which his humiliating death on the Cross was the symbolic exemplification (Phil 2:8),[11] embodies essentially the same theological insights that, as we have already seen,[12] were later developed systematically into the *theologia crucis,* in the decade after Paul, by Mark in his Gospel. In subsequent Christian history, the Resurrection was clearly understood to be the fulcrum of the dramatic transition from Jesus' lowly servant-hood, and apparent humiliating rejection and death on the Cross, to the declaration of his

10. Given the essentially cognitive nature of these claims, it is very difficult to accept the contention of Gerhard Ebeling that "The faith of the days after Easter knows itself to be nothing else but the right understanding of the Jesus of the days before Easter" (Ebeling, *Word and Faith,* 302), or the noncognitive understanding of faith promoted by Marxsen in *The Resurrection of Jesus of Nazareth,* 149–54. For a justification of the perception of "a special transcendent element," in contrast to accounts of the Easter experience in "statements citing just inner-worldly factors," see Baxter, "Historical Judgment, Transcendent Perspective."

11. It has been traditionally fashionable to read notions of pre-existence into this pre-Pauline text and to assume that the reference to condescension related to a divine act of becoming man. In this case, these words quoted by Paul tend to be interpreted along incarnational lines of the pre-existent Word of God in the prologue of St John's Gospel. See for example, Marshall, *The Epistle to the Philippians,* 50; and Witherington, *Jesus the Sage,* 263: "The choice being described in Philippians 2 is the choice to take on human flesh, a choice only a pre-existent one could make." Likewise this is argued in Byrne, "Christ's Pre-Existence." This was simply assumed by an earlier generation of scholars, such as the Anglican Bishop Charles Gore (in his Bampton Lectures of 1891, titled *The Incarnation of the Son of God,* and in *Dissertations* in 1907; Frank Weston (in *The One Christ,* also published in 1907); and P. T. Forsyth (in *The Person and Place of Jesus Christ* in 1909). However, this emphasis on pre-existence may almost certainly be a mistake, for rather than being the divine choice to become human (his humanity thus temporarily obscuring his full divinity), the kenotic choice may be understood as the self-emptying choice of the human Jesus. It is the choice to "empty himself" and take on the lowly role of the servant—the decision to embrace a *distinctive style* of humanity. It is this form of servant-humanity that is *revelatory* of the nature of God for Paul. See Schoonenberg, "He Emptied Himself"; Schoonenberg, "The Kenosis or Self-Emptying of Christ"; Moule, "Further Reflections on Philippians 2:5–11"; and Moule, "The Manhood of Jesus." Also, Macquarrie, "Kenoticism Reconsidered."

12. In chapter 3.

heavenly victory and exaltation to glory. When interpreted from the perspective of the eschatological hopes of Second Temple Judaism, it could be anticipated that he would return in the imminent future in a demonstrative manifestation of this ultimate state of affairs under the sovereign reign of God. In this way, the Resurrection was naturally regarded as the trigger that made the application of christological titles appropriate, if not necessary, in the interpretation and expression of the divine significance of what had happened and of its anticipated eschatological implications.

As a consequence of the Resurrection, it was therefore deemed appropriate to refer to and, indeed, to address the victoriously vindicated Jesus as the "*Messiah/Christ*" of God and also as "*Lord.*" Even in the interim, while the world awaited his return and the messianic showing of his divinely warranted authority in power and glory, he was envisaged already to be exercising a kind of cosmic sovereignty over all things "in heaven, on earth, and under the earth"[13] as *Lord* and *Christ*.

There can be no dispute that, in the first instance these christological titles and the possible descriptive imagery associated with them, were already found in the preceding religious tradition of Second Temple Judaism, even if a new and more immediately poignant content of meaning now came to be injected into them. Indeed, the first Christians are said to have come to the conviction of the appropriateness of the use of the inherited titles in relation to Jesus as they sifted through their scriptural traditions in search of clues to interpret and explain all that had happened to him. By bringing traditional scriptural material into juxtaposition with their newfound Easter experience, they were able to conclude with confidence that Jesus had been vindicated and exalted to heavenly glory. N. T. Wright's very appropriately chosen term for describing this process is that they "ransacked" their religious tradition to this end.

Apart from the fact that the Easter Event is said to have initiated or "triggered" the efflorescence of Christology, the contemporary debate about the nature of the linkages between this inherited linguistic tradition and its application to the Raised Jesus often takes the form of a discussion of a rather abstract and cerebral kind, which is (somewhat surprisingly) often detached from a consideration of the nature of the actual Easter experience that gave rise to it.[14] First, the contemporary christological discussion

13. Phil 2:10. Also, in Acts 2:36, the suggestion is that in the interim until the awaited *parousia* and the full revealing of the Messiah in power and glory, he had already been "*made* Lord and Christ." This is by contrast with his "designation to be" Lord and Christ, whom at some future time "God shall send" (Acts 3:20). See Robinson, "The Most Primitive Christology of All?" for the suggestion that the Christology of Acts 3 may in fact be earlier than that of Acts 2.

14. This is particularly the case with regard to N. T. Wright's treatment of Paul's "messianic theology" which, though triggered by the Damascus Road experience, is explained by reference to its conceptual background. He thus relies heavily on the exploration of the possible *verbal sources* of Paul's "in Christ" language. The result is a text-based account of this language, by contrast with one grounded in and fed by Paul's continuing religious experience.

invariably begins with a debate about exactly which Old Testament scriptural texts were being drawn upon, and then, what precisely the inherited titles actually meant or entailed in the historical context of their original use. In this enterprise the first Christians are said especially to have found help, for example, not only in the "Son of Man" images of the book of Daniel (in chapters 10 and 12 as well as chapter 7), but in an array of Psalms, which were of particular assistance in expounding the theme of exaltation, glorification, and heavenly enthronement. Psalms 8, 16, 68, 80, 102, and especially Psalm 110, were obviously found particularly helpful in clarifying an understanding of the post-Easter status of the Raised Jesus as he was envisioned to be in heaven at the "right hand of the Father," now not just as the martyred but victorious "Son of Man," but as their exalted and sovereign heavenly "Lord."[15] Their reflection on what had transpired in the light of their pre-existing religious tradition is thus said to have confirmed his identity as the long awaited "Christ" or "Messiah" of God, who was believed to be destined to appear from the radical hiddenness of heaven, so as to show his divinely authorized power and strength, on the future eschatological "Day of the Lord." But it also indicated where he was currently understood to be located, and therefore also something of the divine status and power he already now enjoyed, and had at his disposal, as the Christ of God. He was even now vindicated with "his enemies under his feet." Given belief in the Resurrection, these scriptural references thus grounded the conviction that he was now enthroned in heavenly glory, not just as the triumphant and vindicated "Son of Man," but as one who would one day return as the Messiah/Christ to reveal his hidden glory and to administer judgment with divine authority and power.

Indeed, it is impressive that notions of Jesus' exaltation and glorification of the kind expressed in this way are found peppered across a wide spectrum of New Testament writings. Outside their use in the letters usually accepted as certainly coming from Paul's own hand (like Philippians and Romans), the passage from Ps 110:1 is also well represented in the Deutero-Pauline and post-Pauline literature. It is the inspiration, for example, for Eph 1:20–23, which speaks of the God who

> raised [Jesus] from the dead and seated him at his right hand in the heavenly places, far above all rule and authority and power and dominion, and above every name that is named, not only in this age but also in the one to come. And he put all things under his feet and gave him as head over all things to the church, which is his body, the fullness of him who fills all in all.

Similarly, *Col* 3:1 draws on the same image. Here faithful believers are called on to seek "those things which are above, where Christ is, sitting at the right hand of God." In the *Epistle to the Hebrews*, a similar thought process allows a passage from *Psalm*

---

15. See Hay, *Glory at the Right Hand*, 26–27; also Horbury, "The Messianic Associations of 'the Son of Man,'" 125–55.

102, that was originally addressed to God, to be addressed now to the Raised Christ.[16] Once again it is clear that this transference is also achieved with the help of *Ps 110:1*, when *Hebrews* goes on to say: "But of which of the angels has he said at any time, 'Sit on my right hand, till I make your enemies the footstool of your feet'?" (Heb 1:13). In *1 Pet* 3:21–22, it is made clear that "through the resurrection," Jesus Christ had "gone into heaven and is at the right hand of God."

The same allusions occur again in the context of the early sermons attributed by Luke to Peter in Acts. For example, this now familiar passage from Ps 110:1 is found again in Acts 2:34, following upon a quotation from Ps 16:8–10 in Acts 2:25–27. By the time of Luke, because of the apparent delay of the *parousia*, a more expansive sense of time necessarily had subtle implications with respect to the understanding of the exercise of lordship by the Raised One. Acts 3 may possibly preserve the earliest Christology of all,[17] insofar as the first witnesses declared that Jesus had been "designated to be" Lord and Christ at some indeterminate future time; but in Acts 2 the suggestion is that he had already been *made* Lord and Christ (Acts 2:36). In this case, the future revealing of the Eschaton may be understood as the manifestation of an already existing, and even partially and proleptically experienced, state of affairs. It is this apparently early ambivalence between the "now" and the "not yet" of the role of the vindicated Messiah as Lord that is systematically worked out by Luke, as the delayed *parousia* tends to be pushed further into the future in his theology of salvation history. Meanwhile, in the good purposes of God, Luke could envisage the church pursuing its mission in the world under the lordship of Christ.

This widely dispersed christological language appears to have been originally generated within a range of specific contextual circumstances. The first believers not only *referred* to Jesus in the third person now as their "Lord and Christ," but, as a consequence of their resurrection faith, they could with startling boldness actually *address* him using these titles. The early Aramaic prayer *Maranatha*, "O Lord, come!" is an obvious example. In other words, it was language that occupied a place in the context of prayer and worship.[18]

In addition, this distinctive language appears to have been employed in a heuristic or interpretative sense, in the first instance as believers sought to draw out something

16. Heb 1:10–12 quotes Ps 102:25–27: "And, you, Lord, in the beginning laid the foundation of the earth, And the heavens are the works of your hands: They shall perish; but you continue: And they all shall wax old as a garment; And as a mantle you shall roll them up, as a garment, and they shall be changed: But you are the same, And your years shall not fail."

17. See Robinson, "The Most Primitive Christology of All?"

18. Hurtado has championed the fundamental importance of early devotional practices as the context for the efflorescence of Christology, rather than as a secondary evolutionary development subsequent to the verbal formulation of christological insights. See, for example, Hurtado, *How on Earth Did Jesus Become a God?*, 13–30.

of the meaning of what had occurred in their own self-understanding and to explain it to others. But then, almost immediately, it appears also in what we can imagine to be more emotionally charged apologetic contexts. There are indications, for example, that the making of christological claims concerning Jesus' newfound status and power developed as the first believers sought not just to proclaim something of the significance of what had occurred, but to *defend* their understanding of things in the face of doubt from within their own ranks, and hostile and critical questioning from without. This meant that, in making christological claims, they were also proclaiming *arguments* that were designed to convince others. While, on the basis of the Easter experience, it could be concluded by Christian believers in their own self-understanding that Jesus was *their* "Lord" and "Christ," in apologetic argument, the same language was used to contend that the Raised Christ was in process of exercising sovereignty as "Lord," not just over those who responded to his call in faith and obedient discipleship, but over his former enemies as well.[19] The early sermons of Acts are already directed towards those who crucified Jesus. Even if the Raised Christ did not return vindictively and with coercive power to turn the tables on his enemies and to put them down, but rather with the proffer of forgiveness, he was proclaimed as "Lord" even of those who had persecuted and crucified him.[20] Already in the pre-Pauline hymn of Philippians 2, it was concluded that his sovereign rule was of cosmic significance, as the raised "Lord and Christ" was understood to have been transparently shown to be associated with the good purposes of God. It is not too difficult to make the next logical step so as to affirm that, as the Raised Lord, he was intimately related to God as "God's Son."

It has to be admitted that on some occasions Old Testament references, particularly those from the Psalms, are pressed into christological service in this way only somewhat awkwardly. Given that there was no expectation in the literature of late Judaism that the Messiah would die and rise again,[21] it was necessary to find material that could be brought to bear on what had been experienced, even if originally it was unrelated to notions of resurrection. Psalm 16, for example, apparently originated in the context of sickness, and the accompanying experience of anxiety in the face of the threat of death.[22] In this parlous condition, the Psalmist quite naturally expressed the hope that, with God's help, he would be restored to health so that the fate of death, and the subsequent corruption of the body in the grave, would therefore be avoided (even if only for a time).[23] The Psalmist's words are obviously open to be applied to life be-

---

19. See the classic treatment by Lindars in *New Testament Apologetic*.

20. As in Acts 2:36: "This Jesus '*whom you crucified*' has now been made *Lord* and *Christ*."

21. See Mowinckel, *He That Cometh*, 325–33.

22. As is pointed out by Lindars, *New Testament Apologetic*, 40.

23. Psalm 22 expresses a similar sentiment.

yond death once this becomes a clearer option, particularly in the mentality of Second Temple Judaism. Certainly, when taken into the context of faith in the Resurrection of Christ, this cry from the sick-bed is applied to the specific post-mortem reality of the Raised Jesus who was understood, not to have avoided death itself, as the Psalmist might have originally meant, but to have triumphed over it, never to die again.[24] This Psalm indeed, is almost certainly the source of the idea that Jesus' resurrected body was made incorruptible,[25] though it has to be said that the Psalmist's original hope is more likely to have been that he would not suffer the fate of death and subsequent consignment to Sheol or bodily corruption (Ps 16:10), not that the body would be forever made resistant to corruption in an eternal or heavenly eschatological sense.

In any event, given that the first generation of Christian witnesses to the Resurrection trawled through the inherited Jewish tradition for clues with which to interpret the significance of what had happened in their recent experience, we still have some way to go in order to identify something of the actual thought processes by which they felt justified in appropriating these titles, and the images which were associated with them, to the Raised Jesus.

In *The Resurrection of the Son of God*, N. T. Wright seems content to say that once Paul, for example, became convinced *that* Jesus was the Messiah (or Christ) of God, all that was necessary to unpack its further significance and to justify the use of the other titles was a deductive process of reasoning. It is as though the christological developments were just a matter of making explicit what was somehow already implicit in his Damascus Road experience. Subsequently, in *Paul and the Faithfulness of God*, Wright argues that there is "more than a grain of truth" in the view that "Paul's Damascus Road experience provided him, then and there, with the christological categories he proceeded to develop."[26] We are to imagine that one initial messianic insight led to another, as it were, by processes of deductive thought, until it led to a set of formed theological conclusions of a propositional kind, such as, in Wright's own words, *that* God had "exalted" Jesus "to be *the world's true Lord*," or *that* "He is the *kyrios* at whose name every knee shall bow"; or *that* "He is the 'son of man' exalted over the beasts, Israel's king rising to rule the nations"[27] . . . and eventually *that* he was "equal with God," "*that* he was God's Son," and ultimately *that* he shared in the divinity of the one true God. Thus, once a conclusion was drawn about Jesus' messianic status and identity, the other christological titles and images associated with them provided additional

24. This Psalm is quoted in the resurrection sermon reported by Luke in Acts 2:22–36, where it is interpreted as a prophecy that was fulfilled by Jesus' Resurrection, which in turn establishes his Messiahship and Lordship.

25. Luke uses this Psalm again in Acts 13:34–37.

26. Wright, *Paul and the Faithfulness of God*, 649.

27. *RSG*, 395.

clues as to where he was understood now to be located ("at the right hand of God"), what status and power he now enjoyed in this heavenly place to which he had been exalted (with his enemies now under his feet), and what could therefore be expected at his hands in the imminent eschatological future of this world.

Likewise, once a connection is made between the Raised Christ and Daniel's visionary figure of the heavenly "Son of Man," clothed in linen and victoriously re-warded before the heavenly throne of the Ancient of Days, it is understandable that further speculative conclusions could naturally follow deductively from it. If, as C. F. D. Moule doggedly argued, Jesus himself used the image of "*the* Son of Man" and explicitly drew upon the image in Daniel, then perhaps, in the light of the Resur-rection, it was remembered that Jesus had used this language. If so, Jesus' followers could have deductively assumed the more specific identity of Jesus as Daniel's "Son of Man." Indeed, it remains possible that even Jesus himself could have interpreted his role and mission in these terms. Though originally this signaled one with a vocation to be utterly loyal even unto death, and the confident hope of an ultimate heavenly vindication, in the light of Jesus' Resurrection this then grounded some fairly obvious conclusions about his heavenly location and identity.

However, the exact logical track from the Easter experience *itself* to the associa-tion of the Raised Christ, even with the heavenly figure of Daniel, is not always quite so clear. For example, if we start with Wright's contention that Christology, was, for Paul, a kind of deductive flow-on from the Damascus Road experience, we might ask how Wright's description of the Resurrection as the return of Jesus to *this* world with a material body now transformed and made resistant to corruption (perhaps grounded in Ps 16:8–11), links logically and naturally with talk of heavenly exaltation and glo-rification, such as is expressed for example in Daniel's visionary images? Likewise, how does resurrection, understood as a physical restoration of Jesus' material body to *this* world, lead deductively to the contemplation of the *heavenly* Raised Jesus "at the right hand of the Father" envisaged with the help of Psalm 110? Indeed, we have to ask whether this language arises more naturally in relation to the experience of an Object that was empirically perceived *in faith* and, contrary to Wright's depiction of it, with an essentially transcendental and heavenly quality? Furthermore, we might well ask whether these christological claims are rightly understood simply as speculatively deduced logical conclusions anyway, or do they primarily perform another function more attuned to the interpretation and description of the actual resurrection experi-ence itself?

At the outset of this discussion it has to be conceded that, while N. T. Wright is at pains to stress the importance of the primitive Easter experience of historical encounter or "meeting" with the Raised Jesus (and notably Paul's Damascus Road encounter) as the trigger of the alleged deductive processes that led to the making of the various christological claims, he is equally insistent that it was not pursued as an entirely abstract exercise, or *purely* as a matter of logic alone. Quite specifically,

Wright argues that, insofar as Paul played a key role in pursuing this quest to unpack the significance of what had occurred, it is not to be imagined that Paul employed the supposed essentially deductive processes of thought in a logic-chopping or purely abstract, dispassionate and detached kind of way. "We should not suppose," says Wright, "that Saul of Tarsus, having come instantly to believe that Jesus was the Messiah, then worked out, by a process of logic and biblical reflection alone, that the Messiah was after all divine."[28] Rather, Wright qualifies this by hastening to say that, though it was a process of deductive thought that was triggered by the original experience of encounter with the Raised Christ on the Damascus Road (to which Paul is said regularly to have reflectively referred back), the development of christological claims took place within the context of *prayerful reflection* in the fellowship of other believers.[29]

In other words, on the basis of his "memory of the original vision" on the Damascus Road, Paul is, in a context of "prayerful reflection," represented as taking the logical "steps," and making deductive "discoveries," which led him to place the exalted and glorified Raised Christ in juxtaposition with the heavenly throne of God. Clearly, notwithstanding the trigger of the remembered experience of the Resurrection in a context of prayerful reflection, Wright nevertheless presents the entire exercise as though it were a cerebral and abstractly verbal matter of drawing out speculative conclusions of an essentially deductive kind about the ultimate meaning of Jesus' Resurrection. This is understood to have been done, of course, with the help of those texts of the Jewish scriptures that were deemed relevant for the purpose.

Given Wright's initial commitment to the retrospective understanding of the Resurrection as a historical event, it is once again natural, if not unavoidable, that the point of origin of the efflorescence of christological claims comes to focus upon the initial encounters or "meetings." In Paul's case, it is the meeting on the Damascus Road that is said to have triggered christological reflection and discourse. However, this raises a question as to whether these initial experiences of appearances, or "meetings" as Wright understands them, including pre-eminently Paul's own "meeting" with Jesus on the Damascus Road, are in themselves *sufficient* to explain and validate the explicit set of christological claims that are said to have been deduced on the basis of them—especially those relating to Christ's heavenly location and divinely exalted status. Paul's conviction that he had "seen Jesus" is said by Wright to have led him to take "steps" and to make "discoveries" based on scripture as he reflected and prayed.[30] But the question is: does a deductive process of speculative thought, even in the context of prayerful reflection on a remembered "meeting" on the Damascus Road, especially in the very specific "material and physical" way in which Wright encourages us

28. *RSG*, 397.

29. *RSG*, 398. Wright says: In making these "breathtaking explorations" . . . "Every step Paul took he found in scripture; but the reason he took those steps was what he had seen on the road, and what he continued to discover . . . in prayer and the fellowship of other believers . . ."

30. This process is outlined in *RSG*, 396–98.

to envisage this event, sufficiently account for the specific selection of Old Testament titles and associated *heavenly* images that are such a clear feature of the efflorescence of christological language?

The deductive processes of thought by which Paul is said to have come to these conclusions means that the precise nature of the christological language must necessarily be congruent with, and justified by, the *remembered* historical event of the Damascus Road. However, exactly how Paul's Damascus Road experience, even when prayerfully and retrospectively reflected upon, actually leads to the detailed christological images of exaltation, glorification, and heavenly enthronement that were found in an intentional selection of Old Testament scriptural texts, is not made entirely clear by Wright. Indeed, we need to remember that the historicity of the reported transcendental elements of Luke's presentation of Paul's Damascus Road experience in Acts, essentially as a "heavenly vision" accompanied by phenomena of a light and voice, is denied by Wright. In his view, this is only Luke's own literary creation. What Paul actually is said to have experienced is much more "earthed"; it is a "meeting" with a revivified "still physical" Jesus.[31] How this "earthed," robustly physical meeting leads deductively to the images of heavenly exaltation is the question.

It is true that Luke's presentation of Paul's Damascus Road experience in Acts as a "heavenly vision" accompanied by the mysteriously ethereal tokens of a light and a voice, would certainly help establish a logical linkage of the kind we are looking for between this kind of experience and the christological language of heavenly glorification and exaltation. Indeed, apparently sensing the need for this very kind of requirement, Wright even at one point acknowledges that *in Luke's mind* the "context of Saul's coming to believe that Jesus was the Messiah was a *vision*" which "seemed to him at the time much like the biblical theophanies."[32] Clearly, the experience of a "heavenly vision" or Christophany akin to an Old Testament theophany would naturally ground a deductive conclusion that Christ had been raised to a heavenly status. But, curiously, Wright has already discounted the historicity of Luke's account of Paul's *visionary* experience, dismissing it as a Lucan literary invention that was quite foreign to whatever it was that Paul actually experienced.[33] Indeed, Wright's analysis of Luke's presentation of Paul's Damascus Road experience actually destroys the possibility of establishing a logical linkage between Luke's portrayal of Paul's experience as a "heavenly vision" and christological talk of Jesus' heavenly glorification and exaltation.

Instead, Paul is said by Wright to have claimed to have seen the Raised Christ in the context of a much more mundane (in the sense of this worldly) "meeting"

31. *RSG*, 398.

32. *RSG*, 397 (italics original).

33. *RSG*, 388–93.

with him. Though exactly what Paul saw is far from transparently clear in Wright's presentation of this "meeting," his insistence on Jesus' restoration to *this* world as a material and "still physical" body, now made incorruptible, means we are left with the impression that we are to envisage the perception of it in uncomplicated matter-of-fact historical terms. Except for the fact that there is really no interest at all in Jesus' bodily physical features in the resurrection tradition, we might even expect the Raised Jesus to have been recognized by his physical features, for example, just as we might recognize a person who has been absent for a while by noting his/her remembered physical features. However, apart from the crucifixion wounds that establish the continuity of his resurrection body with the one who was crucified, there is a profound lack of interest in physical features of the kind that could be used identifyingly in the Pauline literature. Indeed, there is really no interest at all in Jesus' bodily physical features either in the resurrection tradition or in the Gospel traditions of his historical life. If anything the Easter tradition suggests that physical features initially hindered rather than helped to make such an identification: Mary Magdalene mistook him for a gardener; those travelling on the Road to Emmaus initially also actually failed to recognize him. In any event, while Paul clearly shared in a vivid impression of Jesus' character, particularly as exemplified in his life of "servant-hood" and the self-giving of the Cross, it is unlikely that he could have recognized Jesus by tokens of a physical kind, given that he had not known the historical Jesus "according to the flesh."

Despite these difficulties, Wright nevertheless leaves us with the impression of an apparent "matter-of-factness" that allegedly attached to the Easter "meetings" as he speaks of them, including the meeting with Paul on the Damascus Road, just as they are portrayed in the later Gospels.[34] However, it is this very straightforward, this-worldly "matter-of-factness" that means that the linkage between the resurrection experience and the specific language of glorification and exaltation of the subsequent christological claims becomes elusive: as Wright envisages the Resurrection in terms of a body physically restored to this world and made materially incorruptible, the link with the christological language of heavenly exaltation and glorification can only be very awkwardly, even arbitrarily, drawn. Whether recourse to a purely deductive process as the basis of this understanding of the Easter experiences, even when pursued in the context of "prayerful reflection," sufficiently explains the language used in the making of the christological claims is therefore questionable.

34. As Wright puts it, "Paul says that he saw Jesus, and that remains our primary historical datum" (*RSG*, 393). This "seeing" is not to be accommodated to Luke's visionary presentation of it in Acts, or just in terms only of the seeing of a light and the hearing of a voice. Rather, Wright insists that Paul himself should be privileged as an earlier source, and his own account of his experience is to be associated with "the Easter stories in the canonical gospels (where Luke, famously, depicts a thoroughly embodied risen Jesus)" (*RSG*, 393).

We can readily admit that, even given Wright's specific understanding of the nature of the Resurrection, it is possible that initial inklings into Jesus' messianic identity as the "Messiah/Christ of God" would have been decisively clarified and confirmed. According to the early sermons in Acts, it was so declared with confidence, even to those who had crucified him. But the question is: what is the logical link that may have drawn the explicit imagery of heavenly exaltation and glorification such as we find in the heavenly visions of Daniel, and Psalm 110, into association with this understanding of his messianic identity? For, when the Resurrection is understood in the way Wright urges us to think of it, as the physical restoration of a material body to *this* world, the linkage with the christological language of triumphant exaltation in *another* world, at "God's right hand," begins to become curiously troublesome. Indeed, if anything, Wright's understanding of the Resurrection as the material restoration of Jesus's physical body to *this* world actually countermands any christological interest in his heavenly location and exalted status "at the right hand of the Father." In fact, this is the "platonic" option that Wright consistently avoids and even condemns.

This becomes further complicated by Wright's insistence that "glorification" means not a transformation to a heavenly status or an entry into "the glory of God" (Rom 5:2) for which believers might hope, for this would be to capitulate to a "platonic" schema. Rather, for Wright "glorification" is redefined as the bodily achievement of "physical incorruption" within this material order! In this case, Wright insists that "the risen body will be glorious" in that it will "no longer be subject to decay and death."[35] In other words, the semantic opposite of the achievement of "glory" in this worldly sense is therefore to be understood as the humiliating physical corruptibility of the earthly body. He thus understands the contrast between Paul's references to "the body of humiliation" and "the body of glory" to be parallel with bodily corruption (which is thought of as "dishonorable") and bodily incorruption (which is thought of as "honorable").

Wright justifies this essentially nonheavenly approach to the concept of "glorification" by noting that *kabod* (as used for example in Psalm 73) can be translated "with honour" as well as "to glory."[36] He goes on to contend that in the mind of St. Paul (for example in Philippians 3), a contrast between humiliation and glory refers to an embodied state in which believers will share with "honor and glory" (as we might say today) in a "future rule over the world" with the Messiah.[37] Far from their enjoyment of heavenly glory, it involves their restoration to this world where they are destined to rule and exercise authority on behalf of God. The "hope of glory" then becomes

35. *RSG*, 257–58.
36. *RSG*, 106.
37. *RSG*, 232.

the hope of the return of all the dead to this world with bodies made permanently incorruptible, and their sharing in the kingly reign of the messiah (Rom 5:17). For Wright, "the glory that shall be revealed" therefore has to do not with the eschatological revelation of heavenly reality on earth, so much as with the changed future of this world. In all this the emphasis is on a kind of inner-worldliness at the expense of a (platonic) transcendental "other-worldliness."

In order to arrive at this outcome, Wright is therefore obliged to side-step Paul's characterization of the Raised Christ's sharing in the "glory of God" in heavenly terms. Even the heavenly association of imagery of "shining" in celestial glory is suppressed. Wright says "there is nothing particularly godly, after all, in shining like a star."[38] Unfortunately, while this may be so for Wright in the twenty-first century, it may not have been so for those to whom Paul was communicating, insofar as they shared a Stoic mentality. For them, the analogy of shining like the stars was closely associated with the idea of the divine "intelligible fire." It is from out of this cultural context of Stoicism that it became natural for Paul to speak of the gift of the Spirit in terms of a light that shines out of darkness, and of "the light of the knowledge of God's glory" in the face of Jesus the Messiah (2 Cor 4:6). Clearly, the concept of "glory" can be redefined in terms of sharing in the this worldly exercise of sovereign rule of the Messiah only by arbitrarily dismissing this kind of Stoic imagery as being of no real significance in understanding Paul. But this does not help in explaining the logical linkage between the Easter "meetings" with the Raised Jesus and the efflorescence of christological claims in which a glorified and exalted Jesus is said to reign "at the right hand of God."

The question of the logical linkage between the efflorescence of christological language, with its implicit references to Christ's exalted and glorified divine status, and the nature of the primitive Easter experience thus continues to be troublesome.[39] Wright contends that from out of his alleged "prayerful reflection," Paul "*discovered that he needed the phrase 'son of God' to function in a new sense.*"[40] But exactly why Paul might have felt this alleged need, given the precise way in which Wight portrays the Easter event, remains problematic. Indeed, Wright is prepared to venture that "Paul had an increasingly clear sense that this God was to be known as the one

---

38. *RSG*, 257.

39. Following Bowker, in "'Merkabah' Visions and the Visions of Paul," Wright tentatively suggests that perhaps Paul "was actually meditating on the throne-chariot and *discovered* that the figure seated on the throne was Jesus." Likewise Paul's use of Psalm 110 is said to echo its use in the synoptic tradition: "he *discovered* that David's son was David's lord." This *discovery* is said to be warranted by 1 Cor 15:25–28 "coupled with an understanding of the risen Jesus as 'the son' who will eventually be subject to 'God'." (*RSG*, 397). However, Paul's alleged appeal to Daniel 7 is hardly a matter of scholarly consensus. Maurice Casey denies any role to Daniel 7 in Paul's thinking. See Casey, *Son of Man*, 151–54.

40. *RSG*, 397.

who sent the son and the Spirit of the son" (Gal 4:4–6),[41] The entirely speculative entry into Pauline psychology here should not be allowed to conceal the fact that the logical linkage between this alleged "increasingly clear sense" and the "physically incorruptible material body" of Jesus, which we must assume Paul remembered to have encountered on the Damascus Road, remains opaque. A prayerfully reflective context notwithstanding, how does the one lead to the other? The overall impression left by Wright is that, having come to the conviction that the Resurrection confirmed Jesus' identity as the Christ, Paul was led, in a subsequent context of prayerful reflection, to a set of deductively arrived at, but purely speculative, "bright ideas" or "discoveries" with the help of images somewhat arbitrarily drawn from his inherited religious tradition. But exactly *how* the Easter experience itself warranted and justified the use of the christological titles and their associated images of heavenly exaltation and glorification remains a mystery.

Perhaps sensing something of the gravity of this problem, in *Paul and the Faithfulness of God*, Wright proffered the view that an additional key historical factor, also inherited from the religious culture of Second Temple Judaism, was operative in generating and defining early christological developments: This was the theme, attested in many Second Temple Jewish texts, of the return of YHWH to Zion after apparently having abandoned Jerusalem to her fate, and the consequent future reversal of the fortunes of Israel,[42] with universal and *cosmic* effects.[43] Interpreting Jesus' Resurrection in the light of the theme of the personal return of YHWH to Zion is thus said to provide the initial impetus for the making of christological claims about his divine status and identity. Thus, Paul was not just drawing detached deductive conclusions on the basis of the Damascus Road experience, as was argued in *The Resurrection of the Son of God*; rather, the surfacing of the theme of YHWH's return to Zion was what "pushed the early Christians" to the view that Jesus was somehow included "within the reality of the one God." This thus resulted in the making of "high" christological claims about him.[44] This is clearly a significant departure from the position espoused in *The Resurrection of the Son of God*. Now, it is explicitly said that "Paul's view of Jesus cannot have been simply the result of a private revelation. Even if his Damascus Road experience was indeed the moment when, and perhaps also the means by which, he himself arrived at the view that when one saw the face of Jesus one was looking at the glory of God, Wright contends that this was "simply his own particular unconventional path to the goal which 'those who were "in the Messiah" before him' (as he puts it in Rom

41. *RSG*, 398.

42. For example as found in Mic 1:2–7 and Hos 6:1–3.

43. For example, in Isa 59:15–21; 66:12–16; and Zechariah 14.

44. Wright, *Paul and the Faithfulness of God*, 648.

16:7) had reached by other means."[45] The "other means" referred to here is now the Jewish religious inheritance of pre-Christian ideas about Israel's God and what was hoped for from him; this, in the wake of the triggering of the Resurrection, led the first Christians to use "God-language for Jesus" and "compelled them to use Jesus-language for the One God."[46] If the Damascus Road experience was Paul's individual "unconventional" path to this outcome, for "the entire early church," the inherited hope of YHWH's return to Zion was the "hidden clue to the origin of Christology."[47] As with Paul, they are also said to have "pondered Biblical promises" and "wondered what it would look like" when YHWH appeared, and then "came to see" and, indeed, "deduced" that it had happened in the ministry, life, death and Resurrection of Jesus.[48]

In order for this suggestion to have any traction at all, Wright is obliged to distinguish an alleged inherited hope in YHWH's *personal* return to Zion from a less immediate kind of return effected by surrogate "chief agents"—such as patriarchs, Abraham, Enoch, Moses, a Messiah of some kind, even the archangel Michael.[49] The uniqueness of Jesus means that he was not just a quasi-divine figure to be reverenced in some way like these figures of the tradition, but instead was associated with the more immediate *personal* return of YHWH to Zion.

In response to this thesis of Wright, Larry Hurtado has very convincingly argued: (a) that this contrast between YHWH's *personal* return and his less immediate return mediated through some kind of "chief agent" is entirely unjustified in the Jewish tradition;[50] and (b) that in any event, the New Testament evidence suggests that the theme of the return of YHWH to Zion came to be used in association with belief in the *parousia*, rather than (as Wright contends) with Jesus' earthly ministry, death and Resurrection.[51] This focus on the *parousia* of Christ in association with the return of YHWH to Zion can be seen at 1 Thess 3:13 (apparently adapting a reference to YHWH's eschatological appearance in Zech 14:5) and at 1 Thess 4:13–18; 2 Thess 1:6–8; and 2:8. At that future time, God would come bringing the righteous dead "with him" (1 Thess 4:14) to manifest his sovereign rule in association with the return of Christ.[52] In other words, it seems that the theme of YHWH's return to Zion was brought to the developing christological reflection of the first Christians and functioned as an element within this process, rather than its trigger. Insofar as their hope for the return of the exalted Christ in glory at the *parousia* was itself developed on the basis of Easter

45. Wright, *Paul and the Faithfulness of God*, 648.

46. Wright, *Paul and the Faithfulness of God*, 655.

47. Wright, *Paul and the Faithfulness of God*, 653–54.

48. Wright, *Paul and the Faithfulness of God*, 654.

49. Whom Wright calls "mediator figures" (Wright, *Paul and the Faithfulness of God*, 653).

50. Hurtado, "YHWH's Return to Zion," especially 425–30 on YHWH and Chief Agents.

51. Hurtado, "YHWH's Return to Zion," 430–33 (following Adams, "The 'Coming of God' Tradition and Its Influence").

52. Outside of the writings of Paul, it is also found in Heb 10:37 and 2 Pet 3:10–13, where Isa 26:20; 65:17; and 66:22 appear to have been in mind.

faith, it was the Resurrection itself which triggered this development. Thus, the origin of christological reflection upon the divine status of Jesus as the Messiah/Christ of God, who was now vindicated and exalted in glory, and who would one day return at his *parousia,* was the Resurrection. The same may be said of Phil 2:6–11. Hurtado therefore concludes that the earliest convictions about Jesus' divine status originated from the experience of his Resurrection, and led to the processes of christological reflection within which the theme of the return of YHWH to Zion came to be associated. This theme cannot itself stand as the trigger of this development.[53]

This brings us back to Wright's abiding christological problem, which can be sheeted back to his initial view of the Resurrection as the return of Jesus to *this* world in material and robustly physical bodily form; indeed, in a form "more material than material" (i.e. material now made incorruptible). This view of the Easter Event hardly explains how the early Christians accorded Jesus a divine status, reverence, and worship, or their use of the titles, especially of "Lord" and "Son of God" in relation to him, not to mention the efflorescence of christological images of the going of a pneumatically transformed, exalted, and glorified Christ to share in the immortal glory of God. Larry Hurtado, with an apparent sense of some perplexity puts his finger on the nub of the problem: "It appears that Wright practically limits 'the resurrection itself' to a divine confirmation of a prior belief in Jesus' messianic status." "Wright seems to me," he says, "reluctant to grant that Jesus resurrection accorded him anything significantly new."[54] The simple fact is that there is a glaring disconnect between the Resurrection as Wright conceives of it and the response of faith, worship, and the christological celebration that so clearly ensued from it. Hence the need for Wright, in *Paul and the Faithfulness of God*, to co-opt the help of the theme of the return of YHWH to Zion to bring a divine and heavenly reference into association with Jesus. Ultimately this need arises because of the incongruity of his specific view of the Resurrection and the way the Raised Jesus was alleged to be involved in purely physical and material "meetings" with his disciples. Indeed, in this way a transcendently divine and heavenly view of the Resurrection and the manner in which it was perceived in faith is actually what Wright excludes from his understanding of the Easter Event.

Clearly, in *The Resurrection of the Son of God*, Wright ran into difficulty in establishing the logical connection between the Easter Event, specifically as he described it, and the efflorescence of actual christological claims, couched as they are in the language of exaltation, vindication, glorification, and heavenly enthronement at God's

---

53. As Hurtado says, "the initial conviction that generated subsequent Christological development and devotional practice was that God had raised Jesus from death and exalted him to share in divine glory and the divine name, and now required Jesus to be reverenced accordingly" (as evidenced in Acts 2:34–35, 17:31; 1 Pet 1:21, and 3:22). (Hurtado, "YHWH's Return to Zion," 433).

54. Hurtado, "YHWH's Return to Zion," 422.

right hand. The alleged deductive link between the resurrection event as Wright described it, in terms of the return of a material body restored to *this* world, and (in the light of Psalm 16) its being made "incorruptible," and the early recourse to the post-Easter Christology with its heavy freight of references to exaltation to heavenly glory and other associated transcendental imagery thus remains elusive, if not in a sense inexplicable. Indeed, there is a troublesome sense in which it even appears to be somewhat arbitrary. So we must ask again: how was it that the first Christians were able to draw explicitly on this language and imagery with such confidence in its apparently unquestioned appropriateness?

The fact is that the Easter experience that led to the making of faith claims brought with it a sense of the exaltation and glorification of Jesus such that it could be immediately perceived that, *like God*, he was no longer subject to the constraints of space and time. He was no longer subject to the "constraints of history" to use A. E. Harvey's phrase. Rather, as a consequence of his Resurrection, Jesus, *like God*, was now (as classical Christian theism was to affirm) omnipresent and eternal. Like God, he now "filled all things." If the story of the empty tomb leads some to think, in resuscitationist terms, that Jesus simply walked out of the tomb and was subsequently involved in earthly "meetings" with his former disciples, then this transcendental aspect of the experience of the appearances of Easter Jesus tends naturally to be obscured. It was with this difficulty in mind that Karl Barth spoke of the empty tomb as a kind of "crater" left by an explosion of eschatological light, rather than a mundane emptiness simply left by Jesus' walking out of it into the light of day. Indeed, perhaps it was the need to avoid this kind of suggestion, or not so much as even to countenance this kind of suggestion, that led Paul (if indeed he even knew of the story of the empty tomb) not to draw upon it in the course of writing his entire corpus of letters. If it is used as in the Gospel accounts simply to declare that Jesus was no longer there and to direct the disciples to look elsewhere, it was misused if it was pressed into service to ground specifically resuscitationist accounts of the nature of the return of Jesus' revivified body. For Paul, the Raised Christ was no longer known as he had been known in the days of his historical existence. Rather, Paul's clear conviction was that he had achieved "equality with God," as the highly exalted and glorified one, as a consequence of his Resurrection. In the judgment of faith he is therefore no longer known "according to the flesh." Rather, he is now known in faith in a way that is entirely congruent with the efflorescence of christological language which flowed from it.

Wright's chief christological difficulty may thus be sheeted back to his idiosyncratic portrayal of Christ's Resurrection as a return of the historical Jesus to *this* world of historical space and time. Given Wright's retrospective concentration of interest upon the memory of Paul's Damascus Road experience, and the reported initial "meetings" of the Raised Christ with other early witnesses, he inevitably has to rely upon *purely deductive* processes of speculative thought to explain the efflorescence of christological talk. Even though these deductive processes are said to have been pursued in the context of reflective prayer along with the memory of the initial Easter event, they are understood to have been intended only to interpret and draw out implications of what *had happened* by utilizing a selection of scriptural texts that were deemed appropriate and helpful for the purpose. However, given Wright's understanding of what had happened in the idiosyncratic inner-worldly way to which he is from the start methodologically committed (merely as a historical event that was contained within this world of space and time), it tends to be milked of the transcendental face that is essential to it; this explains why there is unfortunately something arbitrary and disconnected about Wright's portrayal of what happened at the Resurrection, on one hand, and the early choice of christological titles, on the other. There is a missing link of an experiential kind between Christ's Resurrection and the specific transcendental and heavenly references of the scriptural texts that were employed in association with it. Were the first Easter experiences understood as essentially "appearances from heaven" (Christophanies) or "heavenly visions" we would be in a better place, but this is what Wright denies.

The chief difficulty with Wright's heavy retrospective reliance on Paul's original Damascus Road encounter and conversion experience as the sufficient trigger of the making of the christological claims, is that, apart from occurring in a context of prayerful reflection, this deductive process tends to be presented as something that takes place in an experiential vacuum: it fails to take account of the *continuing* nature of the religious experience of faith and the new quality of life enjoyed by the first believers generally, to which the New Testament Easter testimony bears such clear witness. Larry Hurtado also reminds us that it does not take account of the fact that the early resurrection faith implicitly involved the acknowledgement of Jesus' heavenly exaltation as *Kyrios*/Lord, which immediately associated Jesus with the glory of God, and entailed that right from the start intense devotion and worship was accorded Jesus along with the God who had raised him.[55]

In fact, the primitive use of the christological titles does not suggest that these titles bounced into use simply in response to a felt need to "take steps" and "make discoveries" by drawing abstract conclusions of a purely deductive and speculatively propositional kind *only* on the basis of a remembered past event, even with the help of the Second Temple hope of the return of YHWH to Zion. Rather, the evidence provided by Paul itself suggests that this christological language was actually used by

---

55. See for example, Hurtado, *How on Earth Did Jesus Become a God?* 30: "we have to posit powerful revelatory experiences of followers of Jesus early in the days after his crucifixion that conveyed the assurance that God had given Jesus unparalleled heavenly honour and glory."

the first Christians, with an apparent poignant sense of its appropriateness, primarily because it was patently congruent with the way in which they continued to experience *the actual persisting presence of the raised, exalted, and glorified Christ mediated through the gift of his Spirit.* Moreover, there is a sense in which the use of christological titles and the drawing out of their implications is not just the result of an abstractly *deductive* exercise. On the contrary, very often they appear to be used in a *descriptive* way of the continuing religious experience of the first Christians. This means that the use of these titles was arrived at by *inductive* rather than deductive processes. Indeed, the use of the titles and their associated heavenly images really only makes sense insofar as it is appreciated that this language was deemed to be appropriate precisely in an endeavor to describe, and to account for, the transcendental and *heavenly* quality of these *continuing* Easter experiences.

In other words, there is a sense in which the christological claims are not just *speculative* claims or abstract "discoveries" about the supposed heavenly location and divinely exalted status of the one who *had been* raised, but are graphically descriptive claims using language that came into use as the first believers, including Paul, actually wrestled to communicate something of the continuing nature of the experienced reality with which they had to do, and which uniquely drew from them responses of devotion and worship. Apart from its link with the originative Easter Event, which is said to have "triggered" it, the christological language was both appropriate and valid insofar as it went some way towards describing an encounter with the continuing *heavenly* reality of the "life-giving Spirit of Christ." It thus had a role in pointing to, and explaining, the distinctive nature of the continuing reality of the experience of faith and Christian life. This means it was arrived at not just by *deductive* processes of thought (even within a context of prayerful reflectiveness) based upon a retrospectively *remembered* past event, but by *inductive* processes of thought that were pursued as repeated occasional or episodic experiences of the Spirit pointed to the Raised and glorified Christ as their heavenly and divinely exalted originating source.

If, as was argued in the last chapter, we cannot come to grips with the nature of the object of Easter faith unless we take seriously the claim that the Raised Christ had become "a life-giving Spirit" or "Spirit of life" (Paul), or an "abundant Spirit" or "Spirit without measure" (John), then it follows that we must acknowledge the importance of this kind of *continuing experience* as the warrant for the linguistic development of christological claims. These were not just deductively arrived at, at a point temporally subsequent in time to a remembered experience, but inductive conclusions drawn as a direct consequence of the repeated and continuing nature of post-Easter experiences.[56] In other words, apart from drawing abstract deductive and speculative

56. As Hans Frei correctly observed, "The providential action of God over and in his creation is

conclusions by applying Old Testament images and titles to the Raised Jesus on the basis of the memory of a single past event, the christological language used by the first generation of believers had to account for the transcendental coloring of their own continuing experience of Christ as a "life-giving" and "abundant" Spirit, and of his sovereign "lordship" over their lives. Indeed, the christological titles and the images associated with them are themselves eloquent pointers to the truth that this Easter experience is misunderstood if it is not conceived essentially in transcendental and heavenly terms.

In this sense, the Easter experience which grounded the faith and hope of the first believers in Christ is not to be understood just as a visual experience that was entirely of a piece with the visual cognition of material and physical objects of *this* world. Instead, it is to be understood essentially as a *religious* experience, an engagement with other-worldly reality in faith. They could appropriately call the Raised Jesus "Christ" because, as an element of the complex texture of the life-giving experience of his Spirit, they continued to experience him *as* their leader and potential savior. They called him "Lord" because they continued to experience his sovereign presence, and the moral pressure of his will for them in the living of lives of faithful discipleship. In other words, Christ's exalted heavenly location "at God's right hand" could be seen as the elevated vantage point from which his "lordship" was actually mediated to them with the coloring and authority of its clearly perceived heavenly source. This continued to be so experienced, as a constant element of their response to his persisting call to faith and discipleship. Indeed, it was language that continued to account not just for their faith, but also for their *practice* in living lives of moral obedience. As Jürgen Moltmann has helpfully noted, Christology arises not just out of a cerebral faith commitment and deductive processes of theological reasoning, but also out of Christopraxis.[57]

To put this in another way, an understanding of the distinctive quality of the "spiritual gifts" distributed to Christ's faithful righteous ones in their continuing experience pointed the first generation of believers to the heavenly source of those gifts. This is explicitly made clear in *Ephesians* where it is declared that it was from the Raised Christ's exalted vantage point "far above all the heavens, that he might fill all things" (Eph 4:10), that he "gave gifts to his people."[58] Not least among these gifts was the gift of a uniquely distinctive love, which they identified both as "Christ's love" and

---

not that of a mechanical fate to be read off on one occasion." (Frei, *The Identity of Jesus Christ*, 163).

57. Moltmann, *The Way of Jesus Christ*, 41: "christopraxis is the source from which christology springs."

58. Eph 4:8; see also Eph 4:10. At this point, the author of Ephesians quotes Ps 68:19 with some textual modification apparently dictated by the belief that the exaltation of the Messiah (who is said to have "ascended on high") enabled the function of the Messiah as distributor of spiritual gifts. Hence the idea of the receiving of gifts in the original text of Ps 68:19 is understood to be for the purpose of distributing them to others. See the insightful discussion of the early Christian use of Ps 68:19 in Lindars, *New Testament Apologetic*, 51–59.

the "love of God." In other words, what they continued to experience as the gift of the Spirit was a distinctive kind of love, which was connected back to a heavenly source. Indeed, it could be identified as a divine gift precisely because they experienced it as a heavenly sourced reality; a distinctive kind of love was in this way the primary identifying quality of the gift of the Spirit (as in Rom 5:5: "God's love has been poured into our hearts by the Holy Spirit who has been given to us."). There is a sense, in other words, in which the christological language, in order credibly to continue in valid use, had to be congruent with this complex texture of continuing religious experience and life, grounded in the concrete perception of the presence of Christ in faith, precisely as a "life-giving" and "abundant" eschatological Spirit.

This means that, instead of arising within a process of deductive thought, simply on the basis of the remembered Damascus Road experience, in which logical "steps" might have been taken and logical "discoveries" made, Paul's christological language actually arose out of, or "mapped on to," and thus descriptively accounted for, the continuing shared experience of faith and hope that was grounded in the perceived gift of the "life-giving Spirit" of Christ, and the continuing shared commitment to the moral norms of Christian discipleship. Moreover, and very importantly, instead of being based upon the remembered experiences of the *few* who first reported the appearances, the christological claims of the first generation of believers were empirically grounded in the shared experience of the *many*. Its empirical grounding is found in the fundamental Easter experience of all baptized believers.[59]

It was now apparently deemed appropriate for them to address the Raised Christ as "Lord," for example, not only by identifying him as the now vindicated and exalted martyred Son of Man by association with transcendental images from Daniel, whom, they may have believed, would eventually show himself eschatologically in power and glory. Rather, this kind of language was appropriate also insofar as he was actually *experienced* as one who exercised some kind of claim to their continued allegiance, and thus as one who continued to exercise a form of moral sovereignty as *Lord* of their lives.[60] They were not just deductively putting two and two together; they were actually in the business of *describing* aspects of their shared Easter experience which dictated the necessity of acknowledging the "lordship" of the Raised Christ in their lives. These were lives that were conscious of receiving direction from Christ, and which called forth the response of obedient discipleship and allegiance to him.

This is indicated already in the remnant survival of the earliest Aramaic stratum of the post-Easter traditions. On two occasions, once in the New Testament in 1 Cor 16:22, and again in the *Didache* 10:6, the title "Lord" in the Aramaic form of "*mare*"

---

59. Thus Moltmann: Christology "remains related to its practical situation, its *Sitz im Leben* in the community of Christ." (Moltmann, *The Way of Jesus Christ*, 41).

60. See Scott Cowdell, quoting Hans Frei: "For Frei, it is the very experience of Jesus' Lordship itself which provides our evidence that he is risen, obviating any need for further support from historical events which critical history could never verify." (Cowdell, *Is Jesus Unique?* 69–70).

is used in the prayer "Maranatha!"—"O Lord Come!"[61] On a third occasion, in Rev 22:20, the same prayer appears, this time in Greek translation, the original Aramaic "*mare*" now becoming "*kyrios*." In all three instances the really interesting thing is that the context of the use of this prayer is essentially the same: it comes in the context of a rehearsal of the obligations of the divine law. It thus functions as a kind of warning: the prayer is for the Lord to come as Judge of the recalcitrant and as Savior of the repentant. Clearly, the Christian coloring given to the title "Lord" in this early Aramaic use makes it more than just an honorific or deferential title—like the title "Sir" used to address a teacher by a contemporary schoolboy. By contrast with a somewhat domesticated honorific of polite familiarity, it carried overtones of the transcendental authority and sovereignty that the Raised Jesus was understood to be exercising over their human lives in continuing Christian experience. This is what grounded their hope for his imminent future appearing as Lord and Judge. It is out of a fundamental experience of this kind, rather than a this-worldly "meeting" on the Damascus Road, that somehow made it possible to conjure up images, such as (perhaps) Daniel's image of the vindicated and exalted "Son of Man" and (certainly), with the help of Psalm 110, to apply it to the Raised Christ located at "the right hand of the Father."[62]

Furthermore, this means the concrete experience of Christ's lordship is not pushed off only into the future as an object of eschatological hope, but is something that was proleptically realized and perceived in faith. It is significant that this appearance of the early Aramaic form of "*mare*"/Lord in the *Didache* is in the context of the Eucharist, where the repentant are called into the communion of the church. In the next stratum of its use, now in Greek, the title "Lord" (as *kyrios*) appears to have been regularly associated with this experience of the lordship of the Raised One in a Eucharistic context. This is indicated by the appearance of the title "Lord" explicitly in references to "*the Lord's* Supper" (1 Cor 11:20), and to the body and blood of "*the Lord*" (1 Cor 11:27). In 1 Cor 10:21 we also read of "the table of the *Lord*" and "the cup of the *Lord*." Furthermore, the anamnetic liturgy begins "The *Lord* Jesus, on the night before he died . . ." (1 Cor 11:23). Very significantly, there is reference to the death of "the Lord" in this context, whereas the usual expression would have been in relation to "Christ's death."[63] The Eucharistic proclamation of the *Lord's* death is to continue "until he comes" (precisely to exercise judgment as "Lord"). We can therefore detect here something of the tension between a future orientation towards the imminent coming of the Lord as Judge, and the already realized experience of the presence of the Lord in the life of the Eucharistic community. The use of the title "Lord" does not just refer to some kind of abstract and wholly notional view of "sovereign lordship" deductively

---

61. Or perhaps "Surely, the Lord will come!"

62. It should noted, of course, that others deny the influence of Daniel 7 or at best perceive only traces or occasional allusions in Paul. See Casey, *Son of Man*, 151–54; and Evans, "Daniel in the New Testament," 523–26.

63. See the reference to the 'Lord's death' also in v. 26.

arrived at and projected into the future as an item of abstract hope. Rather, it was used in reference to a concrete experience of Christ's Lordship as something already at least partially actualized in an anticipated kind of way in the lives of believers. Christ's Lordship was thus known *in experience* in the Eucharistic presence of their Raised leader as he was corporately perceived and known in the shared day-to-day life of the post-Easter community.

Paul's resort to the use of christological titles, from out of his own continuing experience of faith and life, is illustrated when in Rom 5:1–2, for example, he refers to the "Lord Jesus Christ; through him we have obtained access to *this grace in which we stand.*" The christological affirmation of Christ's lordship over the dead and the living in Rom 14:9 is also not just an abstract logical deduction, which Paul based upon a remembered past event of an episodic kind, even given that this event could well have been reflected upon in the light of Daniel's image of the Son of Man's appearance before the heavenly throne, or the enthronement Psalm 110.[64] Rather, to read Paul's words is to recognize that Paul is speaking out of his continuing experience of Christ's sovereign lordship over his own continuing life. This is why the parenetic moral advice that is found in the countless *prescriptive* passages of Paul's epistles is grounded in *descriptive* passages relating to the nature of the experience of the life of faith. It is here that we see the close relation of Christology to what Moltmann terms *Christopraxis.*

Long ago, C. F. D. Moule, following M. Bouttier,[65] while admitting that Paul refers alternately, sometimes to "Christ" and sometimes to "Lord," and that this may merely be stylistic to relieve the monotony of using only one title, nevertheless noted evidence of variation of context as the possible reason for this. While the Raised Jesus is referred to as "Christ" in the context of verbs in the indicative mood and of statements particularly relating to what God had accomplished in and through Christ, the title "Lord" is characteristically used in the context of exhortations or commands in the subjunctive or imperative, and relate to the importance of living in accordance with the newly established relation to Christ. Moule therefore concluded that there is a Pauline tendency for the title "Christ" to be "associated with the *fait accompli* of God's saving work, and 'the Lord' with its implementation and its working out in human conduct."[66] This is exactly what one would expect, given the experienced need to respond in moral obedience to the exercise of the sovereign will of "the Lord," where the saving work of God "in Christ" is more straightforwardly described in indicative statements. In other words, nuances of expression are dictated by an implicit under-

---

64. By contrast see Wright's speculative hypothetical that Paul somehow "discovered" that "the figure seated on the throne was Jesus" (*RSG*, 397).

65. Bouttier, *En Christ*, 55; Moule, *The Origin of Christology*, 59.

66. Moule, *The Origin of Christology*, 59.

standing of different aspects of the continuing experienced reality of the life of faith and its behavioral demands.

If these insights are correct, this means that the resort to christological language of "lordship" was not just the outcome of reflecting deductively upon a past event to which Paul had access only retrospectively through the mechanism of his own memory and the second-hand descriptions of others. Nor was it grounded only upon the initial conviction *that* Jesus was the Messiah, as if subsequently used christological titles and the images associated with them, or connoted by them, could be deductively "drawn out" by logical processes from this initial insight. Rather, it was a matter of speaking about a continuing perceptual experience of the presence of the Raised Jesus understood as a divinely exalted reality, whom Paul knew by acquaintance in faith *as* his Messiah and, through the experience of the moral pressure of his will, *as* his sovereign "Lord" and Judge who commanded obedience *as* an essentially *heavenly* authority.[67]

Clearly, when he uses this christological language, Paul is not just looking back nostalgically, merely remembering something and drawing deductions from it, even if in a context of prayerful reflection. His language is the language of inductively perceived faith commitments arising out of his contemporary and continuing experience of an objectively given empirical reality which he perceived in trusting faith. This becomes clear when he declares, for example, as an element of his Easter faith, that Christ as the last Adam "has become a *life-giving* Spirit" (1 Cor 15:45) and that God has sent "the Spirit of his Son into our hearts" (Gal 4:6). His continuing experience of obligation to the sovereign life-giving Spirit of Christ also allowed him further to acknowledge Christ's lordship, and thus to declare boldly that the "Lord is the Spirit" or, vice versa, that "the Spirit is the Lord" (2 Cor 3:17). It was the same continuing experience that he describes when he goes on to declare that "where the Spirit of the Lord is, there is liberty" and, in remarkably platonic-sounding phrases, that "we all, with unveiled face beholding as in a mirror the glory of the Lord, are transformed into the same image from glory to glory, even as from the Lord the Spirit."[68]

Thus, when it came to reckoning profits and losses since coming to faith in Philippians 3, Paul does not just access and "count as gain" simply the remembrance of the original event on the Damascus Road; indeed, it is not mentioned at all in this context. Rather, what he counts as gain is "the surpassing value of knowing Jesus Christ." This in turn, and not just the memory of the Damascus Road experience, is what grounds his ultimate hope. As he lives into his continuing Christian experience, he says that he earnestly desires "to know Christ and the power of his resurrection"

67. Philosophically perceptive readers will correctly detect the influence of Ludwig Wittgenstein's notion of "seeing-*as*" here. These Wittgensteinian insights are employed in the process of articulating a systematic understanding of resurrection faith in Carnley, *The Reconstruction of Resurrection Belief*.

68. 2 Cor 3:17–18, apparently as the very same spiritual reality, from which "nothing can separate us."

(v. 10) and, very significantly, to be "found in him." (v. 9). Then, having "the mind that was in Christ Jesus," and "sharing his sufferings by becoming like him in death," he declares his own hope of attaining "the resurrection from the dead" (v. 11). All else is loss. It is this continuing experience of knowing the Raised Christ as his "Lord" in his present experience, and the hope of being found in him at the End Time, that grounds his continuing christological assessment of Christ and his raised and exalted status as his Lord.

A similar inductive dynamic informs the early use of the title "Son of God." In St. Mark's Gospel, the title of "God's Son" operates as bookends at the beginning and the end of the narrative so as to leave the reader in no doubt about the identity of its chief subject: Mark introduces his story by declaring "the beginning of the Gospel of Jesus Christ, the Son of God" (1:1); at the end Mark has the soldier at the foot of the Cross, after witnessing the manner of Jesus' death, declare "Truly this man was the Son of God" (15:39). In between, Jesus' Sonship is established initially in an apparently "adoptionist" manner, marked by the descent of the Spirit upon him at the time of his baptism ("This is my beloved Son, in whom I am well pleased," 1:11), and again in the Transfiguration story ("This is my beloved Son, hear him," 9:7). In 12:6, Mark seems to presuppose the concept of God as Father with Jesus as the Son in the "parable" of the son who is sent to bring to heel the husbandmen in the vineyard, in the belief that "They will reverence my son." It seems clear enough that Jesus' identity as "God's Son" was well set by the time Mark wrote.

Undoubtedly, Jesus' identity as "God's Son" originated with the historical Jesus' own apparent practice of addressing God as "Father,"[69] for the unanimous Gospel testimony is that this was a feature of all Jesus' prayers, with no contrary testimony, save for the cry on the Cross "My God, My God, why have you forsaken me" (Mark 15:34 and Matt 27:46). Here, however, the cry of dereliction and apparent abandonment that is attributed to Jesus is expressed in the words of Ps 22:1. The suggestion that Jesus' use of "Abba, Father" signaled "unusual intimacy" is almost certainly overdrawn by Jeremias,[70] and it is an incontrovertible fact that its use is not exclusive to Jesus.[71] However, it seems clear enough that Jesus' use of *abba* in prayer was a remembered identifying characteristic, even if it was not exclusive to him.

Nevertheless, something of the process by which the conclusion of his Sonship was actually confirmed in the post-Easter community is reflected in Paul, for whom

69. As in Mark 14:36; Matt 6:9; 11:25–27; 26:42; Luke 10:21; 11:2; 23:34 and 46. See Jeremias, *New Testament Theology*, 1:62; and Jeremias, *The Prayers of Jesus*, 54–57.

70. As pointed out in Conzelmann, *An Outline of the Theology of the New Testament*, 104.

71. Vermes, *Jesus the Jew*, 210, insists that it was an ancient Hasidic practice to speak of God as "Father." Even Plato speaks of the Creator also as "Father" in *Timaeus,* a well-known text in the Hellenistic world of Middle Platonism.

Jesus' identity as the Son of God was publicly declared "with power, according to the spirit of holiness, by the resurrection from the dead" (Rom 1:4). In other words, it was not just something deductively arrived at on the basis of Jesus' apparent practice of addressing God as "Father." As in other christological argument, Paul turns to an Old Testament tradition for the interpretation of what happened to Jesus: in this case, the story of Abraham's willingness to sacrifice his own son (in Genesis 22) is brought to the narrative of Jesus' life and death as Paul understood it. God had "sent his own Son" (Rom 8:3; also Gal 4:4), for, like Abraham, "God did not withhold his own Son, but gave him up for all of us" (Rom 8:32; see Gen 22:12, 16). However, even here, it is not just that Paul simply employed abstract deductive processes to draw out parallels from the story of Abraham and his son Isaac.[72] Paul's understanding of the existential experience of baptized believers is also brought to bear inductively upon the significance of Jesus' Sonship, for it is clear from what Paul has to say that the concrete experience of the gift of the Spirit among the baptized brought with it a sense of *their* adoption as sons and daughters of God, "for as many as are led by the Spirit of God, they are the sons of God" (Rom 8:14//Gal 4:5). It is clearly the gift of the Spirit in their concrete experience that confirms their baptismal identity as children of God. This is not a fearful spirit of bondage and repression, but rather "the Spirit of adoption, whereby *we* cry, Abba, Father" (Rom 8:15).[73] In this way, "The Spirit itself bears witness with our spirit, that we are the children of God" (Rom 8:16). And this adoptive sense of being God's sons and daughters brings with it a sense of salvation and ultimate victory as the inheritors of the promises of God, for if they were children, then they were heirs: ". . . heirs of God, and joint-heirs with Christ; if so be that we suffer with [him], that we may be also glorified together with him" (Rom 8:17). In Rom 8:29, Paul thus exhorts his readers "to be conformed to the image of God's Son," that "Christ might be the firstborn of many brothers (and sisters)."[74]

All the while, the concrete experience of the Spirit in the life of the church is understood to have been made possible because Jesus, as a consequence of his Resurrection, is where he now is. He is exalted "at the right hand of *the Father*" in heaven. One of his messianic functions is understood to be the distribution of the gift of the divine Spirit *from heaven*. There is thus an integral connection between his exalted place in heaven and the experience of the Spirit mediated by him to those who are baptized in his name. To use the titles "Lord" and "Son of God" of him was a shorthand way of communicating this interrelated nexus of insights, all expressing not abstractly

72. This tends to be the conclusion to be drawn from the views in Campbell, "The Story of Jesus in Romans and Galatians."

73. See the parallel in Gal 4:6: "And because you are sons, God has sent forth the Spirit of his Son into your hearts, crying, Abba, Father."

74. For a discussion of Jesus' experience of God and of the possibility of his consciousness of his "Sonship," see Dunn, *Jesus and the Spirit*, 21–23 and 318–26.

deduced "bright ideas," but inductively formulated descriptions of something uniquely experienced in Christian faith and life as a consequence of the Resurrection.

Now, if the meaning content of the "Lordship" and "Sonship" of the Raised Christ, insofar as this was expressed in the application of the titles "Lord" and "Son of God" to him, was discerned within the texture of the experience of faith as an implication of the specific way in which life-giving presence of the Spirit of Christ was perceived and known, then the title "Christ" itself also acquired an entirely new freight of meaning in this same process.

As was noted in chapter 3, St. Paul's use of the phrase "in Christ" expressed something of the new continuing relationship that the first believers understood themselves to enjoy with the Raised Jesus, apparently conceived as a transcendent presence whose life they now "participated in," or in some way shared. At the risk of laboring a point that should by now be more than clear, the use of the title "Christ" in this way can hardly result just from deductive processes arising out of prayerful reflection on the Damascus Road experience alone. Rather, the phrase "in Christ" has a role in actually describing an inductively arrived at conviction based upon a continuing experience of faith and community life. Thus, Paul does not just exhort his readers to a mere *imitatio Christi*, so much as to call on them to immerse themselves in his risen life, to be led by the Spirit of Christ, and to be open to its transformative power "in Christ."

At the end of the day, N. T. Wright cannot avoid this aspect of the Pauline tradition. In fact, at the conclusion of his discussion of the way in which Paul "worked out" the fuller implications of the relevant Old Testament texts for an alleged deductive understanding of Jesus' divinely exalted status, Wright acknowledges that the "continuing experience . . . of knowing this in the fellowship of the church," was what Paul was talking about in 2 Cor 4:1–6.[75] In this passage, Paul speaks of the continuing experience of God who "has shone in our hearts to give the light of the knowledge of the glory of God in the face of Jesus Christ." The apparently Stoic allusions here are not acknowledged, or perhaps even recognized by Wright, but he does concede that there is theological continuity between what Paul says there, and what can be said by Luke, "and by us two thousand years later."[76] In other words, it is acknowledged that christological language is not just deductive and abstract and speculative in nature, but essentially descriptive of an empirically experienced reality that is available even to us today.

Despite this, we are positively discouraged by Wright from endowing this statement of 2 Corinthians with any real significance in relation either to the epistemology of Easter faith or to the origin of Christology. Instead, we are bidden to return to "the

75. *RSG*, 398.
76. *RSG*, 398.

initial event on the road to Damascus" as that which triggered Paul's quest to draw out the christological significance of those Old Testament texts that were deemed to be specifically relevant to this purpose. Wright is quick to say therefore that "2 Corinthians 4 is not describing that [Damascus Road] event."[77] All this is in accord with Wright's initial methodological commitment to proving the occurrence of the Resurrection as a historical event of past history, and then building faith and theological and christological reflection exclusively upon it. Thus, it is on the basis of the Damascus Road event that Paul is said to have taken the series of deductive "steps" of a purely logical, abstract, and speculative kind in the context of "prayerful reflection" to arrive at his christological assessments of the significance of what had happened.[78]

In this way, the importance of the continuing participation by faith in the resurrected life "in Christ" through the Spirit that is experienced by Paul and Luke and "by us two thousand years later" is neutralized by Wright and rendered both epistemologically and christologically of diminished significance. Instead, this continuing Christian experience becomes a kind of add-on; of less significance for faith and theology than the originative historical event constituted by the appearance to Paul on the Damascus Road.

Finally, if the Christology of primitive Christianity was essentially the Christology of the *Christus praesens*, this confirms the understanding of the nature of faith outlined at the end of the last chapter. Far from just involving a retrospective belief *that* the Resurrection of Christ happened as an event of the past, faith actually involves an engagement, by acquaintance rather than just by description, with the actual presence of Christ as the "life-giving Spirit" of the Christian *koinonia*, the "Spirit of life" or, as John says, the "Spirit without measure."

By referring to, and addressing, the Raised Christ as "Lord" and "Christ," Paul and the first Christian believers indicated that, in faith, they perceived that they had to do with the Lordship of Christ in their lives—a Lordship that was sovereign over them as they responded to the moral pressure of his will in their own historical existence from day to day. It was not just a matter of sitting quietly in a corner and "working out" by deductive processes *that* Jesus was Lord because he was Christ. Rather, they had a concrete experience of his Lordship by *being led* by the Spirit, by consciously and obediently *doing* his will, and by *living* in the Spirit of Christ. This is what they described as Christ *in* them, and especially what they described when they spoke of being "in Christ." It was not just a matter of reminding themselves that the Resurrection had happened, still less of trying to prove that it happened. After all, one does not have to prove that the Sydney Opera House was built, and opened on 20 October 1973

77. *RSG*, 398.

78. *RSG*, 398: "the reason he took those steps was what he had seen on the road . . ."

if one enjoys a form of life that centers upon and around it in the present. That is one good reason why St. Paul shows no interest anywhere in his letters in the story of the empty tomb, and only occasionally cites the tradition of first appearances, including his own experience on the Damascus Road. His primary interests lie elsewhere than in the past. His overriding concern is in describing the continuing life and experience of faith through baptism and the gift of the Spirit. This is why in a letter such as Galatians, for example, as even Wright himself is obliged to concede,[79] there is no explicit reference to the Resurrection as an event of the past. At best that is something that has to be inferred; if it is there, it is in the background, or "under the surface." What is explicit is Paul's over-riding interest in describing the actual existential and communitarian experience of the Spirit, and not least the role of the Spirit in creating a single inter-personal communion out of previously separated ethnic communities of Jews and Greeks. This is what is appropriated not by fulfilling the requirements of the law of Moses, but by faith like Abraham's, in response to the gift of the Spirit.

If the primitive christological language thus touches down in the continuing concrete experience of life conditioned and interpreted by *faith*, then we automatically move away from handling the Resurrection of Christ with an exclusive methodological concentration on the secular techniques of critical historical research. Rather, we have to make a transition from an interest in historiography so as to a focus on *faith* as a response of trust (*fiducia*) that is grounded in a form of religious empiricism involving the perceptual knowledge (*fides*) of the presence of the Raised Christ apprehended through the medium of his Spirit in the immediate present of our own lives.[80]

79. *RSG*, 224.

80. For an epistemology of faith of this kind, see the companion volume to this: Carnley, *The Reconstruction of Resurrection Belief.*

9

The Subjective Vision Hypothesis

We begin this chapter with a conundrum: the attempt to prove the occurrence of the Resurrection of Jesus as a historical event, by appeal to the evidence of the empty tomb and the tradition of appearances, necessarily has to work with a very concrete and material understanding of the nature of Jesus' resurrected body. If the Resurrection is understood as an event like any other event of human history, this is inevitable. Jesus' raised body has to be the kind of body that could have been visually observed in just the way it could have been observed being laid in the tomb. Had cameras been available, it was a body that could in principle have been photographed. It could also have been described in straightforwardly literal language. This kind of presentation of what happened at Easter, sometimes referred to as a Christepiphany, is a matter-of-fact showing or manifestation of the restored Jesus, alive and walking again, in physical, bodily form.

One difficulty attaching to this kind of understanding of "what happened" at Easter is that it runs into the danger of assimilating the Resurrection to a mere resuscitation; the physical return of Jesus to resume life in this world, similar in significant respects to the kind of thing that we read about in press reports of the resuscitation of a patient in a hospital. Just as a person rescued from the brink of death in this kind of circumstance returns to resume a former life, so Jesus is said to have emerged from the tomb to resume life in the history of this world. This is the way we are encouraged to picture the Resurrection of Jesus by N. T. Wright's account of it as a historical event. It is of a piece with any other event of human history, except for the rider that some kind of bodily transformation ensured that Jesus' raised body had been made materially incorruptible. As a consequence of becoming "more material than material," he would never die again. We need not spend time probing the question of how this quality of "incorruptible materiality" might have been empirically apprehended (let alone verified) by the first Christian witnesses, though admittedly that remains an unresolved issue. It is sufficient to note that, apart from the fact that it was believed therefore that

Jesus would never die again, it is difficult to determine how the empirical experience of his Resurrection, understood in this kind of way, might differ from the experience of a mere resuscitation.[1]

A second difficulty follows from this. The more concretely material and matter-of-fact Jesus' Resurrection becomes when treated as an event like any other event of human history, then the more the actual death of Jesus is called into question. On "meeting" the Raised Jesus (to use Wright's favored term), the natural reaction would have been: "Oh! We thought they had killed you, but clearly we see that you did not die after all!"[2] This is the price that is paid if the experience of encountering Jesus' resurrection body is made to conform to a "meeting" with him in an uncompromisingly "still physical" form that is in principle of a piece with the way he was encountered in the days of his historical existence.[3]

However, we now have frankly to acknowledge that the alternative presentation of the resurrected Jesus in terms of the more heavenly and revelatory appearance of an exalted and much more radically transformed *pneumatic* body, such as might more appropriately be called a Christophany, runs into the opposite difficulty: it could be argued that it might best be understood and explained as nothing more than a psychologically induced vision. In other words, the more ethereal and "heavenly" it is made to be, and the less physical and material, the more it tends to be suggested that it may be explained (if not explained away) as some kind of purely subjective vision or psychogenic hallucination.

If a Christophany is thought of in some way analogous to Old Testament Theophanies, in which something rather elusive and divinely mysterious was revealed "from heaven," one positive implication is that the reality of Jesus' death is certainly retained and not called into question. If anything it is positively affirmed, for it clearly implies that Jesus must have died and gone from this world. At the same time, the glorified heavenly life of the crucified and raised one *with God* is therefore also more clearly affirmed.[4] However, a further more troublesome question must then be faced with candor and honesty: if the appearances of the Raised Christ are presented as though they were "from heaven," and are understood as some kind of nonmaterial vision or apparition, why should we *not* conclude that they were probably purely subjective experiences? For many, the conclusion seems unavoidable that the reported appear-

1. This is the conclusion also of Michael Welker in his excellent and thorough review of *The Resurrection of the Son of God* in the *Scottish Journal of Theology*.

2. A point forcefully made by Cupitt, *Christ and the Hiddenness of God*, 157.

3. Historically, this is the explanation of the Resurrection that was promoted by H. E. G. Paulus, *Das Leben Jesu als Grundlage einer reinen Geschichte des Urchristentums* ("The life of Jesus as the basis of a purely historical account of early Christianity") in 1828. See, Morgan, "Flesh is Precious," 13: "A physical resurrection looks dangerously like resuscitation, and invites the rationalist explanation that Jesus did not really die on the cross. It is better avoided."

4. As in the early New Testament traditions of his placement at "the right hand of the Father" (following Psalm 110).

ances, understood as psychologically induced episodes, had no more objective reality than figments of an over-enthusiastic flight of imagination.

In 1835–6, David Friedrich Strauss proposed what has since become celebrated as the "subjective vision hypothesis" to account for the Easter appearances. In the two volumes of his enormously controversial *Das Leben Jesu, kritisch bearbeitet,* he at least acknowledged that the historical Jesus did actually exist, but according to Strauss's rationalist reading of New Testament texts, the presentation of a purely human Jesus was achieved by emptying the stories of the Gospels of all supernatural overtones: the miracles are to be understood, for example, as mythical re-presentations of ordinary events in Jesus' life. It was perfectly in harmony with the rationalist motivation of this kind of reductionism for Strauss to go on to argue that the reports of Easter appearances were to be understood, not in any sense as miraculous interventions of God, but as psychogenic hallucinations. They were said to have been produced by the mental disturbance of the distraught disciples, who had been so cruelly and abruptly deprived of their leader. Indeed, the mental state of the disciples in the wake of the violence and injustice of the death of Jesus was represented as little short of psychotic.

The initial sensation caused by the publication of *Das Leben Jesu* was only matched by a subsequent furor that was triggered by Strauss's nomination, in 1839, as Professor of Theology at Zurich. On this occasion, in order to side-step the outcry, the university authorities responded to parliamentary pressure by retiring Strauss on a pension before he even took up his new position. It is a measure of the hostility which his portrayal of Jesus unleashed when it appeared in English translation by George Eliot in 1846 as *The Life of Jesus Critically Examined,* that Lord Shaftesbury called it "the most pestilential book ever to be vomited from the jaws of hell." It is understandable that Strauss's name has become synonymous with the "subjective vision hypothesis."[5]

Despite repeated apologetic attempts over the last couple of centuries to quarantine the "subjective vision hypothesis," it continues to re-appear sporadically, often being presented as the most likely and reasonable way of explaining the tradition of the appearances. One recent revival of interest in it was triggered by some tentative suggestions of John Hick, who ventured to explain the appearances as psychogenic projections, similar to visionary episodes that are sometimes reported as part of near-death experiences, and also similar to the experiences of the recently bereaved, who regularly report an awareness of the presence of a deceased loved one.[6] Those surviving near-death episodes often report vivid experiences of "seeing" into another world,

5. In 1865, the English edition of his *Life of Jesus for the German People* was published as *New Life of Jesus* (2 vols.), in which Strauss re-presented his conclusion that Jesus did "nothing superhuman or supernatural" (1:216), and urged that we should "refuse to acknowledge in the resurrection of Jesus any miraculous objective occurrence" (Strauss, *New Life of Jesus*, 1:408). Instead, he said, "The whole thing gives the impression, not of a life objectively restored, connected in itself, but of a subjective conception in the minds of those who think they see him, of separate visions" (Strauss, *New Life of Jesus*, 1:411).

6. Hick, *Metaphor of God Incarnate*, 24–26.

sometimes featuring a heavenly light, and even involving the approach of a figure who is identified as "Jesus." On the other hand, reported experiences in which bereaved people become aware of the presence of a deceased loved one are now well-attested in literature on bereavement as a not unusual part of bereavement sequences.

Gerald O'Collins responded somewhat negatively to Hick's suggestions at an interdisciplinary symposium on the Resurrection held at Dunwoodie, in New York State, from 7–10 April 1996.[7] In a review of the then current state of the questions relating to the Resurrection of Jesus, Fr. O'Collins pointed out that it was hardly legitimate to draw a parallel between the New Testament tradition of appearances and reports of people who have been revived after being pronounced dead or after being "near to death," for that was clearly not part of the experience of Peter, Paul, Mary Magdalene, and other witnesses.[8] To be fair to Hick, this is far from what he actually suggested; it was not the circumstance of the experience but the quality of it that Hick had in mind. Hick's suggestion was that the appearances reported by Peter, Paul, Mary Magdalene, and others, might be understood by us to be *like* the "seeing into another world," reported in our own day by those who have been through near-death experiences, not that Peter, Paul and Mary had been through similar episodes.

In any event, in a "Response" to Gerald O'Collins at the Resurrection Summit of 1996, I myself argued that these suggestions of Hick should be taken more seriously.[9] I alluded to other episodes of the biblical record that do approximate to something more akin to what is reported by those who have been through near-death experiences: Luke, for example, has Paul say in Acts 22:17–18 that as he was praying in the Temple, "I fell into a trance and saw Jesus saying to me . . ." On the other hand, the reported experience of Stephen in the course of his being martyred, as this is found in Acts 7:55, speaks of Stephen "gazing into heaven" and seeing "the glory of God and Jesus standing at God's right hand." This might justifiably be understood at least as a kind of "near-death" experience. Paul also speaks in 2 Corinthians 12 of "visions and revelations" of the Lord and of a man (whom some commentators speculate was Paul himself) who, fourteen years prior to writing (ca. AD 40), claimed to have "seen into the third heaven." Though it is usual for New Testament scholars to try to distinguish these apparently more subjective "visions and revelations of the Lord" from Paul's primary experience of the Easter Jesus on the Damascus Road (which is held to be a more "objective" kind of vision), this distinction may be hard to sustain. Wolfhart Pannenberg, at the end of the day, admits that he cannot find criteria to distinguish "subjective" from "objective" visions.[10]

7. The proceedings of this "Resurrection Summit" were edited by Stephen Davis et al., and published as *The Resurrection* in 1997.

8. See O'Collins, "The Resurrection," 11–12.

9. See Carnley, "Response," 30–31.

10. Pannenberg, *Jesus—God and Man*, 93–94. See my discussion of Pannenberg, and of the views of H. Grass on "objective visions" (*Ostergeschehen und Osterberichte*, 1962) in Carnley, *Structure of*

On the other hand, Hick's second suggestion that the Easter appearances might be understood by comparison with reports of visionary experiences of a vivid but fleeting glimpse of a deceased loved one, comes much closer to what Strauss had in mind in articulating the "subjective vision hypothesis." In these cases, there is no suggestion of the subject's being in a trance or altered mental state, or anything approaching the state of unconsciousness that is a feature of near-death experiences. Often, those who report such experiences were at the time simply going about their daily business. Hick's contention was that the experiences of the disciples after Calvary might well be understood as experiences of a similar kind.

Gerald O'Collins's point in reply to this particular suggestion was that, as a unique event, the Resurrection of Jesus should not be generalized by being drawn into comparison with a range of human experiences that are said to be very common among bereaved people. This, however, is to beg the question of the uniqueness of Jesus' Resurrection. We cannot rule out the possibility of a suggestion on the ground that it generalizes what *a priori* has been deemed to be unique and therefore inappropriately compared with anything else. The uniqueness of Jesus' Resurrection is what needs to be proved, both in relation to the "subjective vision hypothesis," and in relation to the possible analogy provided by the reported experiences of bereavement sequences.[11]

A rather more intensively and aggressively argued version of the "subjective vision hypothesis" was pursued by Gerd Lüdemann in *The Resurrection of Jesus*,[12] in the year following Hick's suggestions. Lüdemann sought to add credence to the psychogenic explanation of the visions as bereavement episodes by pointing to the antecedent operation of guilt in the mind of Paul, the persecutor, and of deep remorse in the case of Peter, the betrayer. Given the obvious impossibility of cross-examining the first-century witnesses to the appearances, it is difficult to see how a valid judgment about these suggestions could possibly be made. Even a reasonably conservative New Testament scholar such as James D. G. Dunn acknowledges that the "subjective vision hypothesis" could be one explanation of the origin of the Easter appearances tradition, "given the nature of the evidence we have."[13] Robert Morgan is more forthright: "The appearances in 1 Corinthians 15.3–8 are easily construed as visions, and if the distinction between visions and hallucinations reflects faith's judgment about the trans-subjective reference of the event rather than an observable difference, that is appropriate too. Paul did not doubt the divine reality of the event, but seems not to have conceived the appearances as realistically as the evangelists."[14]

Resurrection Belief, 68–72; and, 244–45.

11. A more full discussion of O'Collins' views may be found in my "Response."

12. Lüdemann, *The Resurrection of Jesus*, especially 49–84 (in relation to Paul) and 96–109 (in relation to Peter).

13. Dunn, *Jesus and the Spirit*, 133.

14. Morgan, "Flesh Is Precious," 11.

In the face of the obvious difficulty of distancing the Easter appearances from subjective visions, Dunn resorts to the tradition of the empty tomb so as to tip the balance in favor of the "objectivity" of the visions as against their "subjectivity." N. T. Wright follows the same course. The tradition of the appearances, without the support of the story of the empty tomb, is admitted to be enigmatic and inconclusive: "Sightings of an apparently alive Jesus, by themselves," he says, "would have been classified as visions or hallucinations, which were well enough known in the ancient world."[15] But equally, Wright's view is that without the appearances tradition, the story of the empty tomb itself would be "a puzzle and a tragedy." Both traditions are mutually interpretative and supportive.[16]

Unfortunately, this thesis depends on the view that the empty tomb tradition and the stories of appearances circulated together from the beginning. Otherwise, the suggestion might be that one was a later development on the basis of the other. However, as we observed in chapter 5, the absence of the story of the empty tomb from the writing of Paul, and his exclusive reliance on the kerygmatic summary of the appearances to bolster resurrection belief among those to whom he wrote in Corinth, suggests that this was not necessarily so. Likewise, Mark, who supplies us with the earliest version of the empty tomb story that we have, does not append an appearance narrative to it. The notion that both traditions were found together from the start is without evidential support. At this point, talk of what "must have been," or conclusions that are said to be "good enough" in the face of an evidential short-fall, are themselves simply not good enough. It is a perilous course to assume what needs to be proved.

Meanwhile, the suggestions of Gerd Lüdemann tend to be summarily dismissed by N. T. Wright. In *The Resurrection of the Son of God*, Wright says: "I find the lengthy traditio-historical analysis of Lüdemann 1994, 33–109 almost entirely worthless."[17] In a way this is understandable, for all the while Wright works with the alleged "strictly limited" definition of resurrection said to have been inherited from Second Temple Judaism, which necessarily requires both an empty tomb and concrete appearances to make for the straightforward restoration of a transformed but "still physical" body to *this* world. No alternative can really be countenanced.

It seems fairly clear that we can choose to ignore the possibility that the origin of the appearances tradition might be found in psychologically induced visions of some kind,[18] but in the absence of more concrete evidence of the exact nature of the original appearances, and in the face of our obvious contemporary inability to cross examine

15. *RSG*, 686.

16. As was noted in chapter 7 above in the context of Wright's discussion of the evidential deficits in securing the historicity of the Resurrection as a historical event.

17. *RSG*, 319 n.17.

18. Wright, for example, refers to this possibility only in passing without seriously considering it. The name of D. F. Strauss does not so much as appear in the bibliography or index of Wright, *The Resurrection of the Son of God*. Likewise, the suggestions of Gerd Lüdemann tend to be dismissed without serious discussion.

the original witnesses, it is difficult to lay the "subjective vision hypothesis" to rest. In the course of a valiant and sustained attempt to handle the Resurrection as a historical event, Wolfhart Pannenberg was himself prepared to speak of the appearances in terms of the category of "visions," on the ground that they were phenomena that were not open to public scrutiny: "Any event of this sort," he says, "must be designated as a vision. If someone sees something that others present are not able to see, then it involves a vision."[19]

What then are we to make of the "subjective vision hypothesis," and how may we appropriately respond to it? Nervous attempts of an apologetic kind to try to disprove it on the basis of the disciples' subsequent courageous missionary behavior, and their determination in the face of persecution, are not convincing. To argue that one does not commit oneself in faith, and then determine to go out on mission to all parts of the known world, and even face death by martyrdom, on the basis of a mere hallucination, does not adequately face the possibility that the first believers, though absolutely secure in their convictions, may nevertheless have actually been mistaken about the exact nature of the content of their experiences. The fact that they believed that their experiences were tokens of something real, so real that they were prepared to embrace death in the face of them, does not itself disprove that they may nevertheless have misinterpreted an illusory phenomenon for something objectively real. Clearly, they were convinced that they were not mistaken. However, their firmness of subsequent belief, to the point of dictating the outline shape of their ensuing behavior, does not validate the content of the belief itself.

That mistaken perceptions are not rendered valid by the human actions that are subsequently based upon them may be illustrated in a number of ways. Humans assumed that the earth was flat and conducted their lives on the basis of this belief for centuries: they are said to have been naturally reluctant to sail too far to the west for fear of falling over the edge. Prior to 1492, many no doubt very firmly resisted alternative cosmologies, but that does not prove that the earth is in fact flat. Likewise, it was once very firmly believed that the Sun moved across the heavens and that the earth was the center of the universe. Even the most committed and firm attachment to a belief does not validate a mistaken belief.

19 Pannenberg, *Jesus—God and Man*, 93. See also Grass, *Ostergeschehen und Osterberichte*, 229. It should be noted, however, that the perceptual blindness, experienced by some and not others, is not in fact confined to visions as assumed by Pannenberg. The contemporary philosophy and psychology of perception speaks of "inattentional blindness" in relation to instances where a perceiver is apparently blind to something simply because attention is directed to something else within a field of vision. Thus, this statement of Pannenberg is mistaken. However, we take his point that the appearances *could* be understood as visions.

Likewise, the so called "beaten men" argument, and the appeal to the reality of the Easter experiences as the *only* explanation of the dramatic turn-around of a dispirited and dejected group of mourners into an enthusiastic and energy-filled company of joyful missionaries, does not deal with the possibility that they may have been confused and perceptually mistaken. Indeed, the T-shirt mantra of the 1960's—"*Che lives!*"—is suggestive of the fact that the opposite is the case: the dispirited and confused are among the most likely to deal with their trauma by the assertion of defiant victory.[20] This means that we still have to come to terms with the possibility raised by Strauss: that the appearances were in fact what we would call today "subjective visions," or psychologically induced hallucinations, even if those experiencing them believed otherwise.

At the outset of the discussion of this possibility, some care is called for in using the term "hallucination" itself, for its meaning is somewhat promiscuous and difficult to pin down. Professor Oliver Sachs has done us a service in clarifying, in a frank and positive way, the nature of what it is that we are talking about by speaking of "hallucinations." Sachs is not coy in openly using the term in relation to a range of phenomena, for example, which he shows are regularly shared by people who are far from psychotic. In addition, his extensive study has clearly demonstrated that hallucinations are neither imaginary nor simply to be dismissed as fantasy. For instance, he says that hallucinations are reported by people suffering from acute migraine, whose coming attacks are apparently preceded by warning experiences of seeing zigzag lines before their eyes. These are not purely subjective in the sense of being the self-contained experiences of isolated individuals, for they are in fact regularly shared by migraine sufferers who are able to discuss and cross-check their experiences. They are certainly not to be regarded as somehow imaginary, unreal, or illusory. Nor are they the product of disturbed minds, for those suffering from migraine are clearly perfectly normal in other ways.[21] Sachs therefore was perfectly comfortable with the use of the word "hallucinations" of such experiences, while in no way suggesting that they are in any sense unreal.

Another example, among the very extensive range of phenomena documented by Sachs, comes originally from John Hughlings Jackson (the father of English Neurology) and his partner William Gowers. Gowers was particularly fascinated by the visual symptoms of a coming epileptic seizure: in relation to one patient he reported that "the warning was always a blue star, which appeared to be opposite the left eye, and to come nearer until consciousness was lost." "Another patient," he says, "always

20. A point made in Cupitt, *Christ and the Hiddenness of God*, 141. Likewise, Cupitt observes that the *Times* on 18 August 1969 reported that, in Ireland, "James II is not dead."

21. Sachs, *Hallucinations*, chapter 7, "Patterns: Visual Migraines."

saw an object, not described as light, before the left eye, whirling round and round. It seemed to come nearer and nearer, describing larger circles as it approached, until consciousness was lost." Once again, this kind of phenomena falls under the category of "hallucinations" for Sachs, without suggesting its unreality.[22]

Despite the extensive range of experiences scientifically studied by Sachs under the heading of "hallucinations," Sachs unfortunately did not (at least in the study he published under the title *Hallucinations*) deal with examples of those who report experiences of the presence or nearness of deceased loved ones in the emotionally numbing wake of the death of a close friend or near relative. This deficit has, however, been amply filled by the sustained researches of Dr. Dewi Rees of Wales. In an initial study, published in the *British Medical Journal*[23] of the experiences of 227 widows and 66 widowers, Rees reported that nearly half this number had experienced encounters of some kind with what they understood to be the presence of a departed loved one. In some cases, those interviewed claimed to have felt the presence of the deceased, or to have seen them, listened to them, spoken with them, and even (occasionally) touched them. Some had multiple and varied experiences, and a large proportion (36.1 percent) had experiences of this kind which lasted over some years.[24]

These reported experiences appear to have involved something more than a general sense of the continuing presence of a departed loved one. When Alfred Tennyson heard that the grieving Queen Victoria wanted a private audience with him in April 1862, just four months after Albert's death, he consulted the Duke of Argyll about how he should behave, and what he should best say. The Duke warned Tennyson not to refer to the Prince Consort as "late," but to remember the "strong reality" of the Queen's "belief in the *Life Presence* of the Dead."[25] A little earlier, in January of the same year, just a month after Albert had died, Victoria had herself publicly expressed this very belief. When, at that time, over two hundred men and boys perished in a mine disaster at New Hartley, Victoria immediately wrote to her "kind sister widows," and told them of the comfort she had received since her loss of Albert from "the constant sense of his unseen presence," and her belief of eventually being united with him.[26] Those with a background in the pastoral care of the bereaved know that a strong Christian belief in the afterlife is often accompanied by a general sense of the continuing nearness of a departed loved one of this kind. However, the reported experiences of those studied by Dewi Rees involved, not so much a general sense of the nearness of a departed loved one or the awareness of an "unseen presence," so much as an actual encounter of an arresting kind in which sight and hearing, perhaps even touch, is also claimed to

22. Sachs, *Hallucinations*, 136.

23. Rees, "The Hallucinations of Widowhood," 37–41.

24. Dewi Rees followed up his 1971 article with a review of similar studies in *Death and Bereavement*. See also, Klaus and Walter, "Processes of Grieving."

25. Baird, *Victoria*, 322.

26. Baird, *Victoria*, 321–22 and 336–7.

have been involved. Those who report such experiences speak of "seeing" something and of listening to, and even speaking with, the deceased. Clearly, there seems to be a prima facie analogy between the reports of these experiences and the New Testament Easter traditions.

The first thing to be noted in response to the reflections of Dewi Rees on this material is that, like Oliver Sachs, he initially used the term "hallucinations" of these experiences.[27] In response to this, Gerald O'Collins expressed the view that this was "a loaded term," and contended that what Rees reported was not anything like what "would normally be called 'hallucination.'"[28] Subsequently, Rees himself showed some reluctance to use the term "hallucination" to designate the kind of experiences he described.[29] Though he noted that "medics use the term in a specialized sense," as indeed is the case with Oliver Sachs's use of it, Rees appreciated that its more popular sense was to refer to "something that is not there."[30] N. T. Wright assumes a popular negative sense of this kind when he nonchalantly and dismissively couples "hallucinations" and "fantasy."[31] Larry W. Hurtado is likewise wary of the use of the term "hallucinations" in reference to the appearances or visions of the Raised Christ, because to "refer to these experiences of early Christians as 'hallucinations' would indicate a negative philosophical/theological judgment about them . . ."[32]

For this same kind of reason, Rees came to prefer not to use the term "hallucinations" if it failed to convey a sense of the normality of the experiences, or misled people into thinking that those who report them are in some way mentally deranged. Clearly, if in popular understanding the term "hallucinations" unfortunately suggested an entirely subjective experience, disconnected from anything real, he believed it was best avoided. What he described of the experience of widows and widowers, he said, had nothing to do with the unreality of "wishful thinking," or something caused by psychotic illness, or induced by psychedelic drugs, acute toxic states, or

27. Dr. Rees's MD thesis of 1971 was titled "Hallucinatory Reactions of Bereavement." The publication of his findings in the *British Medical Journal* in the same year was titled "The Hallucinations of Widowhood."

28. O'Collins, "The Debate Continued," 596 n.8. In *Easter Faith*, 109, O'Collins noted the observation of Wiebe, *Visions of Jesus*, 195, that the term "hallucinations" is "a theory laden expression. It might appear to be straightforwardly descriptive, but . . . it conceals many assumptions about what is real and what humans are capable of knowing." In O'Collins, *Believing in the Resurrection*, O'Collins confirmed that he regarded the term "hallucinations" to be loaded because it judges the experiences of the bereaved as "merely imaginary and not real" (72).

29. Rees, *Pointers to Eternity*, 187–88.

30. Rees, *Pointers to Eternity*, 187–88.

31. *RSG*, 7. See also 686, on visions and hallucincations.

32. Hurtado, *Lord Jesus Christ*, 71.

the withdrawal of drugs or even alcoholism.[33] Rees was very anxious to say that the experiences of bereaved widows and widowers are not hallucinations in this sense, for these experiences were accepted as tokens or pointers to something objectively real. For this reason, Rees therefore saw the difficulty of using the term "hallucinations" in reference to experiences which he was at pains to show to be "common, normal and helpful."

While Sachs likewise believed that hallucinations are also common and normal, and certainly not the product of psychotic states, he nevertheless spoke of them as experiences that are self-contained within the experiencing subject. There is no sense in which they are cognitive experiences of objects external to the subject. This is the case even when different subjects are able to share and talk about their experiences, and so discover that their experiences are essentially the same as the experiences of others. A shared experience of the kind studied by Sachs does not necessarily mean therefore that it is an experience of something external to the person experiencing it.

Rees, unlike Sachs, however, came to prefer not to use of the word "hallucinations," precisely because they are interpreted by those experiencing them not as self-contained subjective experiences, but as pointers to a state of affairs that is objectively real. Indeed, given that the experiences of widows and widowers are not the "seeings" of mentally disturbed people, nor the experience of visions under the influence of some kind of drug, nor the imaginary seeing of something which is entirely without reality, Rees therefore believed he was justified in arguing that there is an analogy between these experiences of widows and widowers and the reported experiences of the first Christians who interpreted their experiences as real encounters with the Raised Jesus, and not just as fanciful episodes of imagination.

Gerald O'Collins has taken exception to the drawing of this analogy on the ground that a detailed comparison of the two sets of experiences shows up serious differences. For example, O'Collins points out that Jesus' first disciples "remembered him as having made extraordinary claims to personal authority and then having died an utterly shameful death in a place of public execution. Rees reports no cases of anything like that among his 293 widows and widowers."[34] Furthermore, the cases examined by Rees were said not to parallel the New Testament reports of the experiences of the disciples in other respects: the bereaved widows and widowers of Rees' study were all *individuals*, whereas Jesus regularly appeared to people in groups. Nor did the appearances to the disciples last for years. More significantly, perhaps, the disciples immediately passed on the good news to others, but it was a feature of those interviewed by Dewi Rees that 72.3 percent of them kept their experiences to themselves.

---

33. Rees, *Pointers to Eternity,* 188. Rees concedes that a "new, generally acceptable, terminology is needed" for the purpose of distinguishing those whose bereavement experiences he reports from psychiatric patients. Klaus and Walter also saw the need for a new term: Klaus and Walter, "Processes of Grieving," 436; as did Olson and others in "Hallucinations of Widowhood," 543–47.

34. O'Collins, "The Debate Continued," 597.

Indeed, in the case of the disciples, their lives changed dramatically, "and they became missionary witnesses to the crucified and risen Jesus."[35] For all these reasons, O'Collins was of the view that Rees's suggested analogy "is not close or illuminating."[36] Likewise, Hick's conjecture about an analogy between the Easter experiences and bereavement experiences, along with my own 1996 plea for this to be taken seriously, was said by O'Collins to be not "particularly appropriate or illuminating."[37] Furthermore, unlike Rees's scientific study of the experiences of the bereaved, the view expressed by Hick and myself is said to be only a suggestion: "it is not an argument based on scientific studies of some group of bereaved disciples whose beloved master had died in a horrible way in a place of public execution and after making extraordinary claims to personal authority."[38] Thus, O'Collins concludes that "We misrepresent the two cases if we allege a close analogy,"[39] for "the experiences of bereaved persons do not closely and directly parallel the Easter appearances reported by the New Testament."[40]

The chief terminological difficulty between Rees and O'Collins is therefore really not so much about the use or the appropriateness of the term "hallucination" so much as about their respective understandings of the concept of an "analogy." When Rees responded to O'Collins in *Pointers to Eternity* in 2010, he provided a much more full account of his interviews with the bereaved than he had done earlier[41] and, while acknowledging obvious differences between the New Testament accounts of the appearances and the experiences of bereaved people generally, nevertheless defended the drawing of an analogy between them.[42] While acknowledging differences, Rees insisted that "the divide is not absolute."[43] Nevertheless, whereas Rees was anxious to establish some kind of analogy between the experiences of widows and widowers concerning their reported perceptions of the presence of their departed spouses and the New Testament appearances, O'Collins, while insisting on dissimilarities that entail that there is no "close and illuminating analogy,"[44] does implicitly acknowledge *some* kind of analogy. Under pressure of Dr. Rees's insistent defense of the drawing of an analogy, O'Collins concedes that an analogy may be drawn even though it is not "close and illuminating."

---

35. O'Collins, "The Debate Continued," 597.

36. O'Collins, *Easter Faith*, 13.

37. O'Collins, "The Debate Continued," 597.

38. O'Collins, "The Debate Continued," 597.

39. O'Collins, "The Debate Continued," 597.

40. O'Collins, *Easter Faith*, 14.

41. He also discussed a range of other phenomena relating to the perception of the presence of Jesus among retired Anglican bishops, and also deathbed experiences that do not impinge so much on this discussion.

42. See Rees, *Pointers to Eternity*, chapter 11, "Are the Experiences Comparable?"

43. Rees, *Pointers to Eternity*, 192.

44. O'Collins, *Easter Faith*, 13.

In his initial responses to Rees, O'Collins listed five identifiable points of difference between the experiences of bereaved widows and those of the bereaved disciples. In his subsequent, more sustained treatment of these issues (in his rejoinder to Rees in *Believing in the Resurrection* in 2012),[45] the original five points of difference were expanded to eight points of difference. In this rejoinder, O'Collins also modified his stance on the possible usefulness of comparing bereavement experiences and Easter appearances, though he tended to restrict this to the *confirmation* of resurrection belief, and its pastoral usefulness in the context of ministry to the bereaved, rather than its usefulness in illuminating the nature of the New Testament appearances tradition itself. O'Collins thus concluded more positively that those who read the research findings of Rees and others in the same field "may well find that this somehow contributes to or confirms their Easter faith and hope."[46]

At the end of the day, there may not therefore be a great deal at issue between Dewi Rees' affirmation of an analogy between the experiences of bereaved widows and the Easter experiences of the first believers and Gerald O'Collins' insistence that valid dissimilarities may be drawn between the two.

In addressing the question of the appropriateness of the use of the term "analogy" in relation to the contemporary experiences of bereaved widows and widowers and those of the bereaved disciples of some two thousand years ago, it is as well to note that by definition the term "analogy" already affirms both a similarity and, at the same time, a difference.[47] In other words, the analogical use of a word is neither univocal nor equivocal; it does not just posit an exact sameness or identity between two terms, but nor does it posit a thoroughgoing difference between them either. There are no similarities at all, for example, when the same word "pen" is used (equivocally) of an instrument to write with and of an enclosure for chickens. Clearly, it is not the case, however, that Rees wants to say (univocally) that the Easter appearances and the experiences of the widows and widowers are entirely the same. Indeed, Rees frankly admits that "major differences exist," particularly in the significance accorded the events and the spiritual stature of those involved. When Rees says that an analogy may be drawn between the experiences of widows and widowers following the deaths of their beloved spouses, and the experiences of the first disciples following the traumatic death of their beloved leader, what is being said is that the respective experiences are in some respects different and in other respects similar. An analogy posits a kind of proportionality between the two—a sameness and a dissimilarity at the same time. He therefore insists that, despite obvious differences, a comparison by way of an

---

45. Following upon the publication by Rees of *Pointers to Eternity* in 2010.

46. O'Collins, *Believing in the Resurrection*, 191.

47. A point made by Rees himself in *Pointers to Eternity*, 193.

"analogy" may appropriately be drawn because of *some* clearly identifiable similarities which he believes are of importance. It follows that Gerald O'Collins's list of a number of dissimilarities does not therefore nullify Rees's contention that an analogy may appropriately be drawn between the two sets of reported experiences. Indeed, I think this discussion between O'Collins and Rees may amount to little more than a verbal quibble with little of real substance dividing them.

In fact, Rees spells out the exact points of similarity: the belief that the deceased loved one in question is somehow alive, secure in heaven with God, but in another sense "near at hand," and somehow wanting to communicate an assurance that this is so. All this is common ground with the Easter experience of the first Christians. The drawing of these essentially similar conclusions from the experience points towards an alleged similarity relating to the quality of the foundational experience itself. In using the term "analogy," Dewi Rees is therefore simply saying that the experiences of widows and widowers, insofar as they regularly report events in which they claim to perceive the presence of their beloved deceased spouses, helps us to understand the resurrection experiences of the first Christians, given that some significant similarities may be drawn between the two.

On the other hand, most of the eight "points of difference" listed by Gerald O'Collins have to do either with the antecedent historical circumstances of the two sets of experiences being compared, or differences in status among those involved, or else with the *interpretation* that was subsequently given to the respective experiences, rather than differences that might be drawn between the quality of the experiences themselves. In large part, these interpretations arise because of circumstantial factors relating to differences of context and culture in which the respective analogically understood experiences occurred, rather than to an alleged lack of similarity in relation to the actual experiences being described. For example, O'Collins points out that none of the widows spoke of their sense of the awareness of the presence of their deceased spouses as a "resurrection"; also, none were motivated to go out on mission. Indeed, he points out that in many of the cases examined by Rees, the widows actually kept their experiences to themselves. None spoke of their deceased husbands as the "Messiah of God" (or "Lord and Christ" for that matter). Indeed, Rees's study, while finding that those he interviewed found the experiences beneficial rather than disturbing (at least in all but a few cases), led him to the observation that the people involved did not go on to make additional interpretative claims at all. None of the widows who were the subject of Rees' study thought of them, for example, as a sign of anything beyond the fact that their deceased husbands were indeed alive and in some sense "close" to them, let alone anything even approximating the conclusion that they experienced something that promised the salvation of humanity at "end of the world." Clearly, the significance of the two sets of experiences is interpreted entirely differently. What Rees is attempting to draw to our attention with respect to the experiences of the bereaved following the deaths of their beloved spouses is probably better described as something more akin to the "communion of saints," by contrast with the idea of "resurrection from the dead." These experiences make it possible for them to affirm that their recently deceased spouses thus enjoy some victory over death, which is no longer thought of as exercising an ultimate finality.

That does not necessarily mean, however, that the actual experiences themselves were so entirely different and that no analogy may be drawn between them. Indeed, as I myself pointed out at the beginning of this protracted discussion (in 1996), it could be argued that many of the "points of dissimilarity" described by O'Collins, including the trauma of losing a beloved master, the intensity of their devotion to him, the special standing in which they held him, and the "horrendous end" of dying a horrible death in a place of execution, might actually have heightened the likelihood of the kind of bereavement experience described by Rees, rather than distancing the experience of the disciples from it. In other words, these are not dissimilarities of detrimental effect with regard to the drawing of the analogy. If anything, these particular circumstantial factors may support the validity of the analogy.

In any event, I think everyone will agree that the interpretation given to their Easter experiences by the first-century believers was an entirely different kind of assessment from that to which the widows and widowers of Rees's study had recourse as they processed and interpreted their grief. This, however, may be attributed more to the Hellenistic Second Temple "conceptual grid" through which the Easter experience passed in the mentality of the first-century believers, rather than to some kind of radical difference relating to their experience itself compared with the experiences of widows and widowers following the deaths of their spouses. A discussion of the different ways in which respective experiences were interpreted and processed is one thing, but given possible similarities that may be discerned between them, it is hard to quibble with the contention that an analogy may legitimately be drawn between the actual experiences of the first Christian believers and those of widows and widowers who, as a result of their experiences following the deaths of their spouses, also at least come to the conviction that their spouses are safely alive with God in the life hereafter.

We are all enormously indebted to Dewi Rees for his terrier-like pursuit of the discussion of the analogical similarities between the Easter appearances and contemporary bereavement experiences; this is a discussion that has now been sustained over four decades. Likewise, Gerald O'Collins is to be thanked for an equally sustained attempt to distance the New Testament Easter appearances from the more contemporary awareness of the bereavement phenomena researched by Rees, and in doing so for taking the proposals of Rees seriously into account. At the very least, by taking Rees' analogy seriously we are able to say that the Easter experiences of the first Christians appear to have been, *in some respects*, like the reported experiences of the bereaved.

At least insofar as, in consequence of them, the bereaved became convinced of the well-being of their spouses in an afterlife, and that they were safely "living" in the nearer presence of God, these convictions resonate with the first Christians' Easter experiences as we read of them in the New Testament.

The positive usefulness of the drawing of this analogy is that it opens an avenue for an assessment of the Easter experiences other than by simply speaking in matter-of-fact terms of resurrection as literally the "standing up of a corpse" and its "still physical" return to the materiality of *this* world. The analogy drawn by Rees allows at least the possibility of viewing the Easter experiences as essentially the same as the experience of widows and widowers insofar as there can be no suggestion on the part of the reported experiences of widows and widowers that their spouses did not die. The drawing of the analogy between these purported visual seeings and the Easter appearances may therefore also help to curb the quick conclusion that Jesus did not die. The widows and widowers' experiences may also be distinguished from ordinary events of human history as well, including the near-death resuscitations of hospital patients. At the same time, a clear difference may be signaled from the merely "imagined hallucinations" of mentally disturbed people, or those in altered mental states under the influence of drugs, or whatever.

Now, though the drawing of an analogy of this kind is acknowledged by both Rees and O'Collins to be of usefulness as a support to the commitment of faith, as well as in pastoral ministry as a support to those processing a bereavement, the analogy is, however, also of some methodological significance in the theological enterprise of handling the Resurrection of Jesus, particularly insofar as attempts are made to approach it as a historical event of the past. Somehow, this aspect of things has tended to be lost in the course of the Rees/O'Collins discussion.

Ernst Troeltsch famously drew attention to what he termed the "principle of analogy" in his discussion of the methods employed by historians in understanding their material. He cited this as a basic historiographical principle that he believed important, not just for interpreting and understanding the past in an heuristic sense, but also in making judgments about the veracity, or otherwise, of reported happenings of the past. In other words, he believed that historians were justified in drawing analogies between their contemporary understanding and knowledge, and what is described by witnesses in the past, in the course of their historical-critical assessment of it. In this way, the "principle of analogy" is held to be operative in the making of historiographical judgments not just in relation to questions of meaning, but also in relation to questions of truth.

Let us take an example to illustrate this. The brass rubbing of Sir John de Wautone (who died in 1347),[48] which hangs upon my wall, yields no indication of whether he died peacefully in domestic circumstances or on a battlefield. That part of the original brass on his tomb, which by convention would show him either with his feet resting on a dog (in the case of a domestic death), or on a lion (in the case of a battlefield calamity), is missing. But suppose we come across an ancient chronicle that gives an account of his death, in which he is said to have been riding on the road from Cambridge to Wimbish with a retinue of retainers, when suddenly an "evil angel" drew near from behind and plunged a sword deep into his back between his shoulder blades. He is reported to have screamed out in pain, which he apparently felt right through to his chest, for when the retainers who were ahead of him turned around, they said that they saw him clutching his garments at his chest. The "evil angel" is said to have disappeared as Sir John slumped forward, then fell from his horse to the ground, where he lay prostrate, staring with fixed gaze to the skies. He was pronounced dead within just a few minutes. Then, when his body was examined it was found that, by a miracle, the wound inflicted by the angel of death had entirely disappeared.

Now Troeltsch's contention was that, when a contemporary historian comes across an account of a purported historical event of this kind, and is confronted with assessing what actually happened, he or she interprets it, and judges the veracity or otherwise of the story, by appeal to the "principle of analogy." A judgment is made about what happened in the past by drawing a comparison with present-day knowledge of how and why things of this kind happen, which may in fact be at variance with the actual account provided by the original witnesses. In this circumstance, by appeal to the "principle of analogy," Troeltsch effectively contended that the historian would be justified in concluding that Sir John de Wautone probably died suddenly of a heart attack. This entails that the historian who judges the past on analogy with a contemporary understanding of the "way things go," is actually in a position to claim to know more about what happened than the original witnesses.

A second example: suppose, sometime prior to his death in 1958, Pope Pius XII reported that he was walking in the cool of the evening in the Vatican Gardens, when suddenly he noticed the setting Sun dip quickly down to the horizon, as if to kiss it in a kind of salute, and then return to its normal place in the sky. A contemporary historian, believing that the Sun does not normally move at all,[49] let alone in such an unpredictable kind of way, also knows that for such an occurrence to have happened, the rotating Earth would actually have had to stop its normal rotation and "fast-forward," and then put itself into reverse, before then proceeding as usual on its regular daily course. The perfectly understandable absence of any reports of such an unpredictable occurrence because it is in fact judged to be scientifically impossible, allows the historian justifiably to make a judgment that the Pope must have been somehow mistaken

48. The brass may be found in All Saints' Church, Wimbish, England.

49. Admittedly, except in a galactic orbit.

in his interpretation of what happened. Perhaps a cloud formation, or the effect of heat haze, made the Sun and the horizon look as though they suddenly touched and then parted again, or perhaps the Pope was having some kind of vision or, indeed, "hallucination." Once again, in coming to this kind of conclusion, the historian draws upon the "principle of analogy" by assessing reports of past occurrences in the light of his or her contemporary knowledge.

On any reckoning, a resurrection portrayed as an extended historical event that commenced three days after Jesus' death, involving his bodily emergence from the tomb, and then a series of rendezvous "meetings" at various Palestinian locations, must be judged to be a very extraordinary series of episodes. When judged "on analogy" with our regular understanding, this is not what normally happens after the death of a human person. A secular historian, utilizing the historical reason alone and the techniques of *critical* historical research might therefore normally make a judgment about the veracity or otherwise of such reports *on analogy* with his or her contemporary knowledge of the way the biology of human life and death in the natural universe operates. Working purely as secular historians, in a way that is independent of faith commitments, the inevitable conclusion would naturally be that this kind of thing "does not happen." For this reason, it might well be argued that Jesus' Resurrection must therefore be approached as an article of faith which, for a start, presupposes belief in a God of Almighty power, with a plan for the salvation and renewal of humanity, rather than just as a historical event like any other event of human history. This is the course of argument taken by Richard Swinburne in *The Resurrection of God Incarnate*. Swinburne frankly states that the attempt to inquire into the subject matter of the New Testament concerning the Resurrection "without introducing any theological claims" is a "sign of deep irrationality."[50]

The publication of *The Resurrection of the Son of God* by N. T. Wright coincided in the same year with Richard Swinburne's *The Resurrection of God Incarnate*. There was no opportunity for Wright to respond to the challenge of Swinburne's contention about the irrationality of a methodological approach to the handling of the Resurrection purely as an event of the past employing the secular tools of critical historical research. It is understandable, however, that, given his commitment to handling the Resurrection purely as a historical event that may be pursued by anyone using reason alone, regardless of faith commitments or none, Wright does take issue with the Troeltschian "principle of analogy."[51] Indeed, even working as a historian whose public secular methodology he allegedly employs, utilizing the historical reason and the techniques

---

50. Swinburne, *The Resurrection of God Incarnate*, 3.

51. *RSG*, 16–18. See Troeltsch, *Gesammelte Schriften*, II:732; III:190, and the discussion of this in Coakley, "Is the Resurrection a 'Historical" Event'?," 88–94.

of critical historiography, he declares quite positively that credence is not to be given to the histiographical "principle of analogy." For Wright, it has no validity at all.

This is argued on the basis of the uniqueness of Jesus' Resurrection. Wright contends that the historian is not dealing with something that has happened either before or since. It therefore is not to be compared with anything else: "The fact that Jesus' resurrection was, and remains, without analogy, is not an objection to the early Christian claim. It is part of the claim itself."[52] However, this, he says, also applies, not just to the Resurrection of Jesus, but also to any newly emerging event of historical time that happens for the first time. Thus Wright declares: "We did not have to wait for the second space flight before being able to talk, as historians, about the first one."[53] In effect, Wright interprets Troeltsch's principle to mean that a historical occurrence can only be judged by analogy with a subsequent occurrence or set of circumstances of a similar kind, which somehow permits the admissible possibility of its occurrence.

Likewise, Wright argues that the historical phenomenon of the rise of the Christian church as a whole was itself a phenomenon without precedent, which means, he says, that on Troeltsch's principle we would therefore "be able to say nothing about the rise of the early church." "The rise of the early church," he claims, "thus constitutes in itself a counter-example of Troeltsch's general point."[54] In other words, Wright's understanding of the Troeltschian "principle of analogy" is that nothing can happen for the first time for the historian, for nothing can be described or critically examined that is without precedent.

Unfortunately, this is a misreading of Troeltsch's methodological principle. It is not the case that Troeltsch believed that nothing can happen for the first time for the historian, or that the historian cannot handle an event until a second event has occurred which is analogous to it. It is not that the historian cannot deal with it unless there is a precedent with which to compare it; rather, Troeltsch argued that when a historian reads a report of an occurrence, which may even be a happening "for the first time," its veracity or otherwise is nevertheless assessed on analogy with a current knowledge of what is naturally or humanly possible. For Troeltsch, historiography is always confronted by a kind of tension between the factual record of the past and the historian's contemporary worldview. What is understood to be "humanly possible," or "possible" in terms of a contemporary scientific understanding of the cosmos, here means not just what is logically possible, or thinkable without self-contradiction, but what, contingently speaking, is judged to be actually possible, based on the evidence of our existing knowledge and experience of the universe and how it operates. While resurrections may not have happened either before or since the reported Resurrection of Jesus, the fact is that people have died and have been buried, virtually in infinite numbers, before and since the death of Jesus. On analogy with what usually happens

52. *RSG*, 712.

53. *RSG*, 17.

54. *RSG*, 18.

in such cases, it is known that dead people do not normally stand up again alive after having been dead for three days. If that is said to have happened in a particular case, then the historian, working purely as historian, will naturally seek to explain it in relation to what he or she knows is actually possible. In the face of a report of such a happening, the historian may justifiably suggest therefore that perhaps the purported coming back to life of a person after being dead for three days can be accounted for because he or she was mistakenly pronounced dead, or for some reason was only thought to be dead. Alternatively, if this judgment is based upon a report of an empty tomb, the emptiness of the tomb might be historically explained in other ways. In other words, a historian *qua* historian, using the historical reason alone, is very likely to judge that, after a human death, "that sort of thing does not happen." In order to begin to think otherwise, one has to begin to talk theologically and to make judgments of faith about the being and activity of God, the eschatological plan of God for the redemption of humanity, and so on. Very quickly one will move away from discourse that falls within the category of secular historiography based on reason alone, and into the arena of faith and theology.

The "principle of analogy" may in fact be brought to Wright's own example of space flight. A future historian might well come across a report dating from 1969, relating to an alleged occasion when a human person named Neil Armstrong actually walked on the Moon. This is said to have occurred for the first time on 20 July 1969. After a brief series of similar reported occurrences, alleged instances of walking on the Moon cease; it is something that no longer happens as a regular occurrence of human experience. Now, a historian working, say in 2069 and confronted with deciding whether this extraordinary event actually happened or not in 1969 will, of course, make a judgment by first assessing press reports and video clips of the time. It will be assumed (on analogy with a knowledge of the purpose of news reports in the media) that newspapers and other media outlets back in 1969 were committed to the reporting of events and not to the promotion of fanciful tales. If there is no reason to doubt a news report, a historian will be justified in assuming that the purported report of what actually happened on the Moon on 20 July 1969 did in fact occur. Furthermore, even though this event is said to have happened for the first time in history on that day, and may not any longer happen, assent to the possibility of such a thing once happening would be achieved on the basis of the current understanding of "rocket science" in 2069, and of the ability of space-rocket technology and engineering to defy the laws of gravity to the point of being able to up-lift a freight load such as to propel human beings far into space and to the Moon. If there were in 2069 very good reasons to doubt the very possibility of that technological and engineering capability, then he or she might be obliged to judge the report of a man being on the Moon in 1969 to be of very doubtful authenticity. In other words, this judgment would be made on the basis of an analogy with an understanding of the actual technological and engineering possibilities current in 2069.

It has to be said that Troeltsch's "principle of analogy" does not necessarily entail the positivist principle that nothing can happen contrary to the laws of nature, or even that "miracles cannot happen." Sometimes extraordinary things do happen which appear to be contrary to an accepted law of nature. In this case, as David Hume argued, if the evidence for the occurrence of such an event were found to be overwhelming, then there would be good reason to revise the supposed law. Hume believed therefore that there could be no such thing as a miracle, for if there were very good reasons for accepting the occurrence of an extraordinary happening involving an alleged breach of a law of nature, this would instead require the revision of the law. It follows that there would be no longer a miracle where a miracle is defined as a breach of a law of nature. However, Richard Swinburne has argued, against Hume, that it is thinkable that there might be sufficient evidence to support belief in the occurrence of an extraordinary and surprising event, which therefore could be interpreted in faith as a miracle of God, but without dictating the need to revise an existing law. In this case, a miracle would be understood as a "non-repeatable exception" to a law.[55] In this case an alternative worldview to Hume's, in which miracles are a possibility, would be brought to the assessment of the historical evidence, but it would be a worldview in which the miraculous power of God is an element. In this case, however, the presupposed worldview would accommodate belief in the existence and power of God.

All the while, however, historical judgments of this kind are made on analogy with *some kind* of contemporary understanding of the general laws of nature and how they operate. Whether a Humean or Swinburnian understanding of things is accepted, some such contemporary understanding will come into operation as a historian works to interpret the past. These are the historian's canons of judgment in evaluating evidence on analogy with the norms of a contemporary worldview; without some such canon no critical judgment is possible.

In the case of the Resurrection of Jesus, its unpredictable and extraordinary nature as an apparent violation of a law of nature (the law that normally dead people do not spring back to life after three days) means that it can only be evaluated as a nonrepeatable exception to this general law; i.e. as a miracle of God. In this case it does not call for a revision of the law so much as for faith in the capacity of God to act contrary to accepted laws of nature from time to time.[56] Whether it occurred or not is not ruled out of court on some *a priori* conviction that unusual or unpredictable events cannot happen or that nothing can happen for the first time. Rather, any judgment must be based on an assessment of the available evidence. Furthermore, that evidence will

---

55. Swinburne, *The Concept of Miracle*, 27.

56. I do not wish to pre-empt the possibility of other definitions of a miracle by contrast with talk of "a violation of a law of nature." For example, a miracle may be defined as any extraordinary or unusual event that brings observers to a sense of the presence and activity of God. This tends to be the contemporary popular use of the term, as in media references to a prematurely born baby, who survises against all odds, as "a miracle baby."

inform an understanding of the nature of what is alleged to have happened (the question of meaning), as well as whether it did or did not occur (the question of truth).

Apart from the problematic methodological decision to try to prove the occurrence of the Resurrection purely by employing the secular methods of critical historical research independently of considerations of faith, N. T. Wright's mistake resides in his muddling of the concepts of "analogy" and "precedent." Clearly, Troeltsch's "principle of analogy" does not mean that nothing can have happened for the first time for the historian, or, in other words, that nothing can be handled historiographically unless there is a precedent for it. It is rather that reports of things that are said to have happened in the past, even for the first time, nevertheless have critically to be assessed on the basis of a current knowledge of the regular workings of the natural order, and of human nature and human behavioral capacities, and of "the way things usually go." A judgment about the past is made on the basis of a contemporary worldview. Naturally, there will be similarities and dissimilarities between the occurrences of the past and those of subsequent experience and knowledge with which they may be compared. If the events of the past are entirely incongruent with what is judged to be actually possible, the historian may be inclined to shake his or her baffled head, and admit defeat in the face of a surpassing puzzle. In this case, it may be necessary for the historian *qua* historian to preserve a prudent reticence, or to admit that no purely historical judgment may be made.[57] On the other hand, a contemporary knowledge of the "way things go" may allow the contemporary historian to explain an occurrence of the past, on the basis of the evidence relating to it, in a way that was not available to the actual historical persons involved at the time.

Now, given the operation of Troeltsch's "principle of analogy" the historical assessment of the tradition of Jesus' appearances cannot fail but be compared on analogy with the visions and, dare we say, "hallucinations," that are well-known and regularly reported in the modern world, particularly among those whose lives have been disturbed by the sudden death of much loved and respected persons. In other words,

57. In criticism of Engberg-Pedersen's methodological tendency to judge whether ancient ideas (such as Second Temple apocalyptic hopes, or Paul's talk of "participation" in Christ) are "real options" for us today, Wright also insists on a less critical historical method (Wright, *Paul and the Faithfulness of God*, 1390). Concerning Engberg-Pedersen, Wright says: "But it is strange to find someone whose basic discipline is ancient philosophy complaining that if certain ancient ideas are not 'real options' for us we should be anxious as to whether we can even describe them properly." Wright is anxious about the method known as *Sachkritik*, "by which the expositor claims to be able to 'correct' certain strands in someone's thought in line with 'more central' elements." Engberg-Pedersen's point is that we may need to be cautious in claiming to know exactly what an ancient understanding amounted to when it fails to "match up" in our own experience, while in other cases our own experience dictates clearly that an ancient viewpoint is not a "real option" for us. The difficulty Wright has with this echoes the difficulty he has with Troeltsch's "principle of analogy" as an operative principle of *critical* historical research. For Engberg-Pedersen on this, see *Paul and the Stoics*, 27–28.

from a faith-neutral historiographical point of view, it is perfectly justifiable that the appearances tradition might be understood on analogy with what we know from reports of what appear to be similar phenomena today, such as that documented by Dewi Rees. Indeed, even people of faith may find this explanation of the appearances attractive.

In the case of the drawing of an analogy between the reports of the experiences of widows and widowers following the death of a loved one studied by Dr. Rees, and the reported experiences of the disciples following the death of Jesus, the historian may actually work with a kind of statistically established law.[58] The relevant law would be, for example, "Whenever bereaved widows and widowers are involved in bereavement sequences following the death of a loved-one there is a (statistically established) possibility that in x percent of cases they will have experiences of encounter with what they interpret as the presence of their deceased loved-one."[59] This principle of our contemporary worldview may in turn be brought by historians, and applied by analogy, to the reported experiences of the disciples of Jesus in their assessment of the relevant New Testament evidence.

Those working as historians, using the faith-neutral tools of critical historiography, would certainly be justified in drawing such an analogy between the New Testament reports of appearances of Jesus following upon his death and our contemporary knowledge of the reported experiences of bereaved people following the deaths of their loved ones. On the other hand, it seems to follow that, in order to insist that the veracity of the reports of appearances may be accepted as objective accounts of actual historical "meetings" with the restored Jesus, anybody working as a historian, such as N. T. Wright in his attempt historically to prove the occurrence of the Resurrection, would be obliged to demonstrate that the appearances could *not* have been analogous to the regularly reported experiences of widows and widowers in the modern world. Alternatively, the historian would be obliged to prove that the post-mortem appearances of Jesus reported in New Testament were not *merely* "hallucinatory" in an entirely subjective sense. Whilst ever the possibility of the subjectivity of these experiences remains on the table, however, it has to be accepted that we really cannot, purely as historians, pronounce with any definiteness on the exact nature of the reported appearances of Jesus, let alone make a confident judgment about their veracity.[60]

This also means, that working purely as a secular historian, without introducing considerations of faith relating to the existence of God and the power and plan of God, a critical historical assessment of the appearance traditions of the New Testament will

58. By "law" here, I mean a statement of universal conditional form, such as "if x, then y" or "whenever x, then y."

59. Some such statistically grounded regularity now seems a scientifically established possibility. Apart from the research of Dewi Rees, see also Parkes, *Bereavement Studies*; and Lüdemann *The Resurrection of Jesus*, 99 and 225.

60. This is the prudent conclusion of Dunn, *Jesus and the Spirit*, 107: "it is impossible to demonstrate either answer."

find it difficult to avoid the consideration of what normally happens after the death of a human person—namely, the accepted regularity, or law, that dead people do not normally come back to life after three days. From the perspective of faith this ambiguity might be viewed in another light in relation to the evidence pertinent to Jesus' Resurrection. However, both with regard to the nature of the appearances and the specific sense in which they are said to have been experienced, a historian working from a faith-neutral perspective will struggle for clarity for want of an analogy with which to interpret the relevant evidence. What is known to happen in bereavement sequences may afford the best option.

The question therefore comes down to this: even if the secular historian, employing the techniques of critical historical research and utilizing Troeltsch's "principle of analogy," might come to the conclusion that the appearances were probably apparitions or hallucinatory subjective visions, why should Christian believers continue to think nevertheless that the first experiences of appearances were in fact tokens of something real? For what reason might the Christian believer conclude that they were not just subjective psychogenic experiences, or "hallucinations" in the sense of illusions or fantasies, but pointers to eternal reality?

Perhaps the answer to this question is already at hand, implicit in the reports of post-mortem experiences of those processing the traumatic loss of a loved one. Dr. Dewi Rees argues that the experiences of the widows and widowers he studied were helpful to them as "pointers" to eternity. They were regularly understood to point to a continuing eternal life of a loved one beyond death, and therefore to their well-being and their nearness. But perhaps the argument should run in the opposite direction. It seems that the widows and widowers of Rees' studies came to these experiences with a pre-existing belief in life beyond death, perhaps based upon an even more fundamental background belief in the existence of a God of love and care who promises the well-being of his children "come what may," death itself included. That, after all, is the substance of God's covenant promise for Christian believers. Given this pre-existing belief in the afterlife, widows and widowers were therefore able to interpret their post-mortem experiences as tokens of the continuing life of their deceased spouses, and therefore as confirmatory evidence supportive of their (pre-existing) belief in life beyond death itself.

Likewise, the reported experiences of appearances of the first generation Christians were interpreted on the basis of a pre-existing set of beliefs, even if their experiences were surprisingly unexpected in matters of detail that therefore called for the modification of those inherited beliefs in some respects.[61] Moreover, as I have argued

---

61. These relate to its timing and the involvement of Jesus as an individual before the anticipated resurrection of all the righteous departed.

in this book, the reported appearances and the story of the empty tomb were not themselves the sole basis of their newfound faith, given their claims to the continuing perceived encounter with the presence of Christ as a "life-giving" or "abundant" Spirit. Indeed, given their continuing conviction of assent to what appears to have been for them the palpable and sustained experience of the Spirit of Christ within their shared community life, the members of the early Pauline communities would naturally have been pre-disposed to assent to the reports of the original visionary experiences. These were remembered tokens of the living reality of the one whom they themselves in faith continued to claim to encounter, if in another way through the medium of his Spirit.

Once we abandon the quest to try to prove the occurrence of the Resurrection of Jesus as a historical event of the past by utilizing the historical reason and the faith-neutral techniques of critical historical research, but come to an understanding of Easter faith as a commitment of trust based upon a contemporary knowing of the presence of the Spirit of the Raised Christ by acquaintance, then present-day Christians are in a similar position to their first-century counter-parts. The first point to be made in relation to the discussion of the possible explanation of the appearances as subjective hallucinatory visions, or whether they might be compared with the experiences of the bereaved in relation to their awareness of the apparent presence of their deceased loved ones, is therefore that we have already established an understanding of faith that is independent of the outcome of this discussion. A faith based upon the recognition of the presence of Christ *as* the animating Spirit of the Christian community that is known by acquaintance in present experience, means that we are no longer in the business of having to try to "prove" the occurrence of the first Easter appearances one way or the other. This means that the question of whether the appearances were hallucinations, subjective visions, or something "more real" than that, is not nearly as crucial an issue as it might otherwise be. Clearly, contemporary faith does not depend upon the resolution of this issue.

The ability to claim in faith to know the presence of the one who promised to be with his disciples always "to the End of the Ages," by interpreting present religious experience as a knowing by acquaintance of "the Spirit of Jesus Christ," means that the appearances tradition of the New Testament assumes a different status. For starters, from the perspective of an already established resurrection faith, the reports of appearances, along with the story of the empty tomb, are no longer themselves the ground of faith. After all, this would amount only to a knowing at second hand by description. Faith is not just an assent to the truth of reports of the empty tomb and appearances. Rather, if faith, by contrast, involves a knowing by acquaintance of the presence of Christ within the inner texture of the life of the Christian community as its "life-giving Spirit," the basis of faith is thus a reality encountered in the present and known by acquaintance, not simply "believed in" in the past, even in the face of an evidential shortfall. However, those stories of past experiences of the empty tomb, and appearances of the Raised Christ, nevertheless become at least understandable for present-day believers as tokens of, or pointers to, the living reality of the heavenly, exalted, and glorified Raised Christ. As such, they become amplifications of faith or supports to faith, rather than constituting faith's evidential basis.

Obviously, something happened to trigger the explosion of Christian life and witness, but the historiographical discussion of whether the Easter experiences of the first believers involved appearances of the Raised Christ understood either as apparitions, objective visions, hallucinations, or "seeings" that were analogous to the experiences of contemporary bereaved widows and widowers following the death of their spouses, can be left unresolved without causing too much angst. As we noted in the previous chapter, if I am acquainted with the present reality of the Sydney Opera House and the form of life that goes on in it, I also know that there must have been a time in the history of Australia when it was built and opened. I do not have to prove that this originating event happened in order to enjoy the marvel of the Opera House and the form of life that occurs within it in the present. Likewise, if I come to trusting faith in the Raised Christ, whom I claim to know by acquaintance as the life-giving presence of his Spirit of self-giving, in the distinctive form of life that is characteristic of the Christian community and, indeed, acknowledge that Spirit to be constitutive of its inter-personal communion, then I know that he must have been raised from the dead. Clearly, in this case my experience of faith does not depend on my ability, working as a historian, to prove the occurrence of that originating event. Indeed, given that questions of meaning are logically prior to questions of truth, it is first necessary to determine the nature of what it is that needs to be proved, and the elusive and fragmentary nature of the historical evidence persistently tantalizes us even at the level of its meaning.

This means that the resolution of the issue of whether apparitions or visions of the Raised Christ, or Christophanies, are to be understood to involve something analogous to the reported experiences of bereaved widows following the deaths of their husbands is therefore not a crucial issue *for faith* either. Indeed, at two thousand years remove, and with only meager fragments of evidential reports to work with, which themselves often appear to have been distorted and modified in the course of their transmission and colored by theologically pregnant motifs, we are almost certainly asking too much of ourselves if we hope to be able to resolve this issue using the tools of critical historical research.

On the other hand, it will be perfectly natural for Christian believers, already believing in the Resurrection of Jesus on other grounds, to incline to the view that the original appearances involved something more than the "subjective vision hypothesis" of D. F. Strauss. Hans Grass has forcefully argued, for example, that the very ambiguity of the historical evidence, which allows the possibility of interpreting the reported appearances as "subjective visions" in the manner of D. F. Strauss, also allows the possibility of interpreting them in faith as "objective visions."[62] This contention of Grass has admittedly not been well understood.[63] For example, even though Willi Marxsen would probably agree that the first witnesses could barely have contemplated that the visions could have been the purely subjective result of their own faith, he is clearly perplexed by Grass' contention that the disciples understood their Easter experiences in faith as "objective visions," and thus as the result of God's action in their lives.[64] Grass admits that the visionary experiences were ambiguous and contends that "faith alone prevails over ambiguity."[65] However, while this may certainly have been the case with regard to the first disciples, Marxsen doubts whether a believer *in the present day* can "see God's action in the visions of the disciples" in this way. In other words, Marxsen doubts whether present-day faith can "overcome the visionary experiences *of those days*" so as also to make the judgment that they were objective events. Marxsen's difficulty resides in the inclination of Grass to speak of the visions as "events," which suggested to him that faith meant that they became historiographically accessible in a way that they were not accessible by appeal to reason alone. Just how the events of the visionary appearances can be accessible to faith in such a way as to be judged to be objective events of history is his primary concern: "How can *we* believe that 'in the case of the visions there was no self-deception on the part of the disciples to be explained by presuppositions of their own, but that God acted here and did not leave Christ to die, but restored him to life'?"[66]

Marxsen correctly sees that "In the case of the subjective-vision hypothesis it is the disciples who, so to speak, create the visions by their faith, and that, on the other hand, in the case of the objective-vision hypothesis of Grass it is the faith of *today* which relies on objective visions."[67] While this is undoubtedly correct, it is not that the experiences of the disciples by being viewed in faith as objective-visions are "quietly turned into history," as Marxsen says. Nor is our faith itself a matter simply of viewing the visions *as* historically factual and objective visions *despite* their ambiguity. It is, rather, that our faith today is based upon other grounds altogether, and then from this perspective of faith the appearances may be viewed rather differently than they would be purely from the perspective of the historical reason.

62. Grass, *Ostergeschehen und Osterberichte*, 233.

63. Lüdemann, "Earliest Christian Belief in the Resurrection," in *The Historical Jesus in Recent Research,* ed. Dunn and McKnight, 418: "The thesis of an 'objective vision' has rightly found no echo in more recent scholarship." Lüdemann's own commitment is, of course, to a form of the subjective vision hypothesis; see his earlier work, *The Resurrection of Jesus.*

64. Marxsen, "The Resurrection of Jesus," 29.

65. Grass, *Ostergeschehen und Osterberichte*, 244.

66. Marxsen, "The Resurrection of Jesus," 30. Marxsen is quoting Grass, *Ostergeschehen und Osterberichte,* 249.

67. Marxsen, "The Resurrection of Jesus," 30.

Unfortunately, Marxsen's discussion of the nature of faith is noncognitive. For him, faith is the "right understanding" of the historical Jesus before his crucifixion. His approach is entirely divorced from the realism of an understanding of faith today as the perception of the presence of the life-giving Spirit of Christ. If this is the continuing experiential ground *today* of the conviction that God acted in the raising of Jesus from the dead, the point is that in the light of this conviction of faith, a believer in *these days* finds it not impossible also to believe that God acted in the lives of the first witnesses insofar as he not only raised Jesus from the dead, but revealed the truth of Christ's Resurrection to them in a visionary way. This does not over-ride the ambiguity of the evidence in such a way as to turn it into historical fact that would satisfy any historical inquiry. It is simply a way of interpreting the ambiguous reports of the visions that is congruent with, or analogous with, a present day commitment of faith. Despite N. T. Wright's claim that he can prove the occurrence of the resurrection using the historical reason (without faith) and the secular techniques of critical historical research, at the level of dispassionate historical inquiry, the evidence of the visions remains ambiguous. Furthermore, faith does not depend on proving the historicity of the appearances. Though Grass says "it is faith alone that prevails over ambiguity," it would be better to say that the very ambiguity of the evidence makes room for faith. The judgment is not from faith to history so much as from *our faith* to the *faith of the first disciples* as something possessing diachronic congruence and continuity. Thus, the contention that the visions were "the result of God's action" rather than subjectively induced, is in this way understandable from the point of view of an existing faith. Even if it cannot be proved to be the case from an historiographical point of view, it is possible in faith to contemplate the likelihood that the visions were divinely appointed pointers to something real, just as the living experience of the Spirit that is known today in faith as the energizing Spirit that is constitutive of the Christian community is interpreted in faith as a pointer to the heavenly existence of Christ himself as something real.[68]

The inclination to think of the objective reality of the visionary appearances of the Raised Christ, no less than the inclination to the view that the experiences of bereaved widows and widowers were also tokens of something real, is grounded in a pre-existing faith in God as the God of steadfast love, and of care for his children, who is known also as "the God who raised Jesus Christ from the dead." If what ultimately grounds the conviction that God raised Jesus Christ from the dead is a contemporary acquaintance with Christ's living Spirit, then from this perspective of faith, the tradition of the reported original appearances of the raised Christ "from heaven" takes on a more acceptable hue as at least a thinkable possibility. This means that, even if the original reported experiences of appearances were analogous to the experiences of

68. An epistemology of faith understood in this way is to be found in the companion volume to this: Carnley, *The Reconstruction of Resurrection Belief,* especially chapter 7, "Faith, Freedom, Ambiguity, and Doubt."

widows and widowers studied by Dewi Rees, from the perspective of faith they may nevertheless be accepted as tokens of something real.

Finally, Troeltsch's "principle of analogy" comes into play as a positively helpful tool at this point. Given that Christian believers today claim a knowledge of the presence of the Raised Christ, based upon the continuing experience of the living Spirit of Christ within the texture of life and worship in the inter-personal communion of the church, they naturally read the words, for example, of St. Paul relating to his faith experience, and understand them *on analogy* with their own present experience of faith. When contemporary believers read the scriptural texts, their experience is not so much a matter of *learning* something as of *recognizing* something that they themselves already know. When the texts are read and interpreted within the life of the Christian community, a meaning is discerned in them that may not be discerned by those who read the same texts from an entirely different perspective. For those with eyes to see, what is claimed to have been known in faith, and described in the ancient scriptural texts, is recognized as the very same reality that is known by acquaintance today within the texture of life and worship of the Christian community. When Paul says, for example, that "God's love has been poured out into our hearts by the Holy Spirit who has been given to us" (Rom 5:5), the contemporary Christian believer understands and knows exactly what it is that Paul is talking about *by analogy* with his or her own contemporary acquaintance with what is discerned to be the very same reality. Likewise, when Ephesians has Paul pray "that you may be strengthened in your inner being with power through the Spirit, and that Christ may dwell in your hearts through faith," and that "you may have the power to comprehend, with all the saints, what is the breadth and length and height and depth, and to know the love of Christ that surpasses knowledge, so that you may be filled with all the fullness of God" (Eph 3:16–19), this is not entirely opaque language. This is because understanding is not just at an entirely abstract, theoretical, or *conative* level, because Paul's words continue to *denote* a concrete reality of contemporary experience. This is the experience of faith in the form of the discernment of the gift of a distinctive kind of love *as* the self-giving of Jesus who, as a result of his Resurrection, has become "the Spirit of life in Christ Jesus."[69]

For this reason, the object of faith is therefore actually known and appropriately described as something graciously received; it is experienced as a gift to the community rather than something striven for by human effort. It is something achieved, in

69. As Don Cupitt once said in correspondence with C. F. D. Moule: "The evidence for the aliveness of Jesus is obtained by putting together the life of Jesus, the whole picture of the nature of God which the Bible gives us, and the testimony of our own hearts and our own life-situation. When all these things "click" together into a significant pattern, the Easter faith is born" (Cupitt, "The Resurrection: A Disagreement," 510).

other words, not so much by trying as by faith—by trusting. It is received in trusting faith because it is concretely experienced as something that wells up in the Christian fellowship graciously and spontaneously as a "spring of living water." Hence, when it is read about in the texts from the hand of Paul as something appropriated "by faith" rather than "works," or when it is described particularly by Paul and John, it is not just received as an abstract description of something alien to contemporary experience, but is recognized *on analogy* with something concretely known within the life, worship, and mission of the contemporary Christian community.

It is because Christian believers recognize themselves and their own experience of faith, particularly in what Paul and John have to say about the nature and inner dynamic of the life of the Christian community in Christ, that the textual traditions of the empty tomb and appearances of Jesus can therefore also be received as pointers to something real—the heavenly existence of Jesus "at the right hand of God" who not only promises to give the gift of the Spirit to his people, but who is concretely and empirically known in his own self-gift.

$\sim$

IO

Incorruptibility or Immortality?

The understanding of faith outlined in the preceding chapters of this book depends upon a view of the Resurrection of Christ essentially in terms of his going beyond death to an exalted place "at the right hand of God," from whence he may be understood to have appeared to the first witnesses. This contrasts with N. T. Wright's sustained defense of the view that in the ancient world there was only one understanding of what the word "resurrection" meant, and that this would have involved the thought, not of a going of Jesus to the eternity and immortality of God, so much as his return to *this* world in material and physical bodily form.

Wright's contention that the first Christians cannot have thought of the Resurrection other than in terms of this "strictly limited" understanding that they are alleged to have received from Second Temple Judaism has already been challenged. In chapter 2, the possibility was raised that it is at least thinkable that, in the ancient Jewish religio-linguistic culture of the Greek Diaspora in first-century Palestine, different, and often logically competing viewpoints, about the afterlife were all in circulation at the same time. It is therefore reasonable to hold that the first Christians may thus have had access to ideas of the afterlife other than in terms of the "strictly limited" definition of resurrection specified by N. T. Wright as the only viable possibility.

Apart from the fact that there seems to have been a variety of views of the afterlife in the world of the first century, Wright does not take account of the possibility that the first Christians modified their received view of resurrection in the light of what they actually experienced.[1] In addition to their acquaintance with the tradition of first appearances, and possibly the story of the empty tomb, their continuing experience of the presence of Christ through the medium of his "life-giving" and "abundant" Spirit convinced the first generation of Christians that Christ had been exalted to an

---

1. As was argued in chapter 3; with the exception, of course, that what was understood to have happened in the case of Jesus' Resurrection involved an individual *before* the collective resurrection of all the dead at the Eschaton.

immortal life in heaven, from whence he distributed gifts to his faithful disciples, most notably the gift of himself through the medium of his Spirit. From his eternal and immortal location "at the right hand of the Father," he may be understood to have appeared mysteriously from heaven in revelatory Christophanies that were witnessed in faith by the first believers. Likewise, it was from this same heavenly and exalted location as Lord that he was understood to have distributed his "life-giving Spirit" among the baptized. This is the same Raised Christ whom his faithful ones still claim to know in faith as the animating Spirit of the Christian community today and "until the close of the age."

Wright's fundamental objection to this view is expressed in his contention that this accommodates resurrection belief to a form of "platonism." It is to be rejected as fundamentally a pagan "Christianized Platonism," that is to be sharply contrasted with the more clearly Jewish eschatological view that Jesus was restored to this world with a body that was not made heavenly and immortal, but rather transformed materially and made physically incorruptible.

The primary thesis of this book is that, unfortunately, this is entirely to discount the incontrovertible fact that in the world of the first century, in the amalgam of Stoic and Platonic ideas that comprised what is now known as "Middle Platonism," the thought of Plato was in fact on the rise in terms of its popularity. Instead, it is to assume that a self-contained set of more clearly Jewish eschatological views was streamed to the first Christians from Second Temple Judaism on a narrow frequency band that, at the same time, automatically put a block on all other cultural influences. In fact, the intellectual world of which Hellenistic Judaism was part was rather more complex.

It is now possible to take this discussion a step further by forging a direct link between this Hellenistic cultural environment and St. Paul himself in a way that increases an appreciation of the influence of both Stoicism and Platonism in his actual thought. For we do know on the evidence of Paul's own words, and with a high degree of probability, that Paul was actually acquainted, if not directly with the Wisdom of Solomon,[2] then with a Hellenistic understanding of the very kind which we find already expressed in Wisdom. In other words, at the very least we can say that Paul accepted views remarkably similar to those found in Wisdom and appears to have used them as his theological guide.

Paul's observation, for example, that "the wages of sin is death; but the free gift of God is eternal life in Christ Jesus our Lord" (Rom 6:23), can be sheeted back to an acquaintance with a tradition of thought also found in Wisdom. James Barr has pointed

---

2. Which we may date from late second and early first-century BC Alexandrian Judaism (following Schütz, *Les idées eschatologiques du livre de la Sagesse*; and many others through to Reese, *Hellenistic Influence on the Book of Wisdom*. Zimmerman, "The Book of Wisdom" provides an alternative view).

out[3] that it is Wisdom's gloss on Genesis, rather than the book of Genesis itself, that Paul relies upon when he says that "the wages of sin is death," for it is in Wisdom that we find the suggestion that death is the punishment received by Adam and Eve after their misadventures in Eden. Wisdom's assumption seems to be that Adam and Eve were originally created immortal in the Garden of Eden and that death, and hence the condition of mortality, was the punishment for their disobedience. By contrast, in Genesis itself, there is no suggestion that Adam and Eve already enjoyed immortality in Eden and would not die. Rather, for them, as for human beings generally, mortality and death is a normal part of life. Like the rest of us, they are represented as mortals who would one-day face death. In Genesis itself, therefore, the punishment for their disobedience is not death, but expulsion from Eden. Though they did not already enjoy immortality, they thereby forfeited the opportunity of reaching immortality, for the Tree of Life in the center of the Garden, with its promise of immortality, was thereby removed from their reach. By contrast, in Wisdom, it is death and mortality, rather than expulsion from Eden, which becomes the punishment, and Paul takes up this same idea when he declares that "the wages of sin is death." Paul's dependence therefore either on Wisdom, or on a tradition similar to that found in Wisdom, seems clear.

James Barr also points out an additional thematic similarity between Paul's theology and that of the Wisdom of Solomon. In Romans, as in Wisdom, immorality is linked with idolatry. As Barr says: "among all biblical or near-biblical books, it [Wisdom] devotes especial attention to the theme of idolatry, and traces a clear linkage between idolatry and all later immorality, in a style which is very closely followed by Paul in the letter to the Romans."[4] Once again, Paul's reliance on the tradition of theological reflection represented in the Wisdom of Solomon seems clear.

If Paul was acquainted with this Hellenistic strain of thought about death, it means that it was very likely that he was also acquainted with Wisdom's emphasis on the reward of immortality with God, not to mention a corresponding lack of emphasis on the resurrection of the material body understood as a return to this world. As we shall see, Wisdom's (suspiciously Platonic sounding) reference to the body as an "earthly tent" (Wis 9:14)[5] also finds an echo in Paul in 2 Cor 5:1 where he declares that ". . . we know that if the earthly tent we live in is destroyed, we have a building from God, a house not made with hands, eternal in the heavens." In addition, mention should be made of his references to *eternal life* as the gift of God, for example, in Rom 6:23 and to the "*mortal putting on immortality*" in 1 Cor 15:53–4. All these echoes of the language of Wisdom seem to suggest, therefore, that Paul definitely knew, if not

3. Barr, *The Garden of Eden*, 16–17.

4. Barr, *The Garden of Eden*, 17.

5. Compare parallel texts: Rom 1:18–32 with Wis 13:1–19 and 14:8–31; Rom 2:4 with Wis 12:10; Rom 9:14–23 with Wis 12:12–22; Rom 9:20–21 with Wis 15:7; Rom 13:1–7 with Wis 6:3.

the book of Wisdom itself, then the same Hellenistic tradition of thought of which Wisdom is representative.

This means we are no longer just talking about the possibility of a diversity of belief about the afterlife in the Hellenistic culture of first-century Palestine in very general and abstract terms, without any direct linkages with the first Christian believers. Paul himself appears actually to have had access to the Wisdom tradition, and was well acquainted with its Hellenizing approach to talking about life after death for the righteous. This means that when Christians of the first generation were faced with the challenge of handling their new-found Easter experience conceptually, it is certainly possible that they approached the task with more than just a single "strictly limited" understanding of what might be entailed by notions of life beyond death, and of what was meant by the term "resurrection."

The crucial issue therefore for the current theology of the Resurrection is whether the concept of "resurrection" must be understood in terms of categories of thought that are exclusively in line with the apocalyptic imagery of Second Temple Judaism's eschatology, as the return of the Raised Jesus after having been dead for three days to *this* world, and thus as a historical event, as N. T. Wright vehemently contends. Or, alternately, whether commerce with the Greek idea of "immortality with God" in a timeless eternity beyond this world was brought to bear on the understanding of Christ's Resurrection, so as to modify it by removing it from the arena of historical time to the arena of God's immortality. In this case, it becomes the subject matter of theology, with only a secondary toehold in history in the form of the religious faith claims and the reported experiences of the first generation of Christian believers. The question of interest thus becomes whether the originally Greek idea of the "immortality of the soul," and the originally Hebrew idea of "the resurrection of the dead," so rubbed shoulders in that ancient world as to produce a kind of amalgam of these two streams of thought.

The appearance even of the word "immortality" in the New Testament clearly poses something of an embarrassment to N. T. Wright. While conceding that the originally Platonic idea of the "immortality of the soul" was present among the Greek modes of thought that were in the intellectual atmosphere of first-century Palestine, and that Christians, such as St. Paul, even actually used the term "immortality,"[6] Wright's readers are shepherded towards the view that what Paul *meant* by it was nevertheless something entirely distinct from anything Platonic or characteristically Greek. In other words, the possibility that specific meanings connoted by, or associated with, the term "immortality" in its original Greek context might have penetrated

6. In 1 Cor 15:53–4: "For this perishable body must put on the imperishable, and this mortal body must put on immortality. When the perishable puts on the imperishable, and the mortal puts on immortality, then shall come to pass the saying that is written . . ."

Hebrew/Christian thinking in a synthetic way, so as to color the original Jewish understanding of resurrection or to modify it, is studiously resisted.

The earlier generation of New Testament scholars of the Biblical Theology Movement also found Paul's use of the term "immortality" very confronting. Krister Stendahl, who was among the most notable proponents of that style of New Testament scholarship (specifically in relation to the Resurrection), endeavored to get over the embarrassment posed by Paul's use of the term "immortality" in 1 Cor 15:53, by trying to argue that it was simply a rogue term with only a very marginal toehold in the New Testament. The noun *athanasia* (immortality), it was said, only occurs twice. Apart from its use by Paul in 1 Cor 15:53, it appears only once more, in relation to God's immortality (1 Tim 6:16). Stendahl explained the unwelcome appearance of this "alien" Greek term in the New Testament by putting it down to the fact that Paul was quoting somebody else. It was not therefore to be taken seriously. The biblical world, said Stendahl, is just not interested in the immortality of the soul.[7] Unfortunately, as we shall see, the special pleading of Stendahl's argument here leaves a great deal to be desired.

To his credit, N. T. Wright is sufficiently aware that a clear dichotomy between the Greek belief in the immortality of the soul, and the Jewish belief in resurrection, is now somewhat passé in New Testament studies as to distance himself from it; yet he is reluctant to let it go entirely. He speaks of it as at least a "half-truth" that "got hold of something which is in itself quite remarkable."[8] Despite the fact that it is admitted that between 200 BC and AD 200 there were "dozens of options" on offer with regard to belief in the afterlife, including belief in the "immortality of the soul," by the time of Jesus "most Jews," he says, had accepted a form of resurrection belief, and even if they spoke of it as a form of "immortality" it was a belief that is to be contrasted with the fully-fledged Platonic belief in the immortality of the soul as a "permanently disembodied future state."[9]

The residual influence of the Biblical Theology Movement becomes very apparent in relation to Wright's strategies of argument for handling Paul's use of the term "immortality." His purpose is achieved by pulling Paul's use of "immortality" into line with the concept of material "incorruptibility." This is pursued by arguing that the Greek words *aphtharsia* and *athanasia*, which translate into English as "incorruptibility" and "immortality" respectively, "were near-synonyms in Paul's world."[10] For Wright, the transformation of the resurrected body is to be understood strictly in terms of its becoming physically "incorruptible" and certainly not "immortal." Thus the noun *aphtharsia* (incorruptibility) is said to be privileged above notions of immortality right through the New Testament, particularly in relation to what is said

7. Stendahl, "Immortality Is Too Much and Too Late," 196.

8. *RSG*, 129.

9. *RSG*, 130.

10. *RSG*, 358.

to have occurred by way of transformation of Jesus' body. In this way, Paul's use of "immortality" is brought into line with it.

To Wright's mind, the inviolability of the concept of "incorruption" must be defended at all costs. Even in 1 Cor 15:53–4, where Paul employs the term "immortality" (*athanasian*), Wright confidently insists that Paul "is not 'combining' two disparate beliefs."[11] The "two disparate beliefs" here are the Hebrew/Christian view of the resurrection of the body and the Greek view of the "immortality of the soul." Clearly, to think of the resurrected body as "immortal" and heavenly rather than "still physical" and materially "incorruptible" would be to effect the dreaded "combining" of two beliefs.

Wright therefore cannot allow that the meaning of *aphtharsia* (incorruptibility) might actually be being modified in 1 Corinthians 15 by its close association with the concept of "immortality," for this might suggest a Platonic going of Jesus to the "immortality of God," perhaps even to the timeless eternity of God, as to a heavenly life apart from temporal and corporeal life in this world. Rather, *aphtharsia* and *aphthartos* are not to be pulled into association with ideas of eternal immortality, but are to be translated strictly as "incorruptibility" and "incorruptible" or "imperishable." Paul's belief in the resurrection of the body is to be kept distinct from anything even approximating the "immortality of the soul." The idea of going to share in the eternity and immortality of God is therefore dismissed by Wright as a "Platonizing" interpretation of Paul that is alien to a more truly "Biblical" view of things. It is "an unwarranted platonizing of Christian hope."[12]

In arguing that the transformed and resurrected body of Jesus became "incorruptible" rather than "immortal," N. T. Wright follows the same basic strategy that we have already seen him pursue in relation to the alleged monochrome Second Temple idea of "resurrection"; it is a matter of working with a single dictionary definition and insisting that the transformative impact of God in the afterlife can mean only one thing. It is assumed that the noun *aphtharsia* (incorruptibility) and the adjective *aphthartos* (incorruptible) must always apply to corporeal, fleshly bodies belonging to this world, rather than to immaterial heavenly realities. The transformation of the body through death and resurrection is therefore to be thought of in a way that is appropriate to a restoration to this world of material things, rather than a "going to God."

Because Jesus' body is understood to have been restored to life in *this* world, it is therefore understood to have been endowed with a kind of transformed materiality, such that the possibility of ever dying again is eliminated. As a consequence, what is to be understood to have been "put on" by Christ at his Resurrection, or exchanged for the natural or mortal physical body, was not "immortality" but physical "incorruptibility." The first Christians are in this way said to have introduced a "mutation" into the inherited resurrection belief of Second Temple Judaism, while retaining an

11. *RSG*, 164.
12. *RSG*, 367.

alleged unwavering commitment to the understanding of it essentially as a restoration to this world of space and time. It follows from the eschatological significance of Jesus' Resurrection that his restored body, now made physically "incorruptible," could be understood to provide the pattern of what will transpire for all the righteous at the Eschaton: the bodies of all the righteous dead will be made equally incorruptible for they will be furnished with bodies like Jesus' raised and transformed body as they too are restored to *this* world.

To encapsulate something of the nature of the outcome of this transformative process in a single word, Wright coins the term "transphysicality."[13] This is intended to suggest that the resurrection body becomes not less material, in the sense of spiritual and heavenly (as the term "immortality" might suggest, especially when associated with talk of conformity to Christ as "the man from heaven"), but more concretely or permanently material and hence "incorruptible" or "imperishable." Indeed, Wright confidently affirms that, as a consequence of the Resurrection, Jesus' body became "more material than material." Presumably, this means that it became a body not only that would never again die, but also that would never be subject to the ravages of disease or even the debilitating impact of normal processes of ageing. Unlike human bodies that are normally subject to the gradual degeneration of bodily function and progressively diminished physical capacity in this life, and eventually subject to decay and corruption in the grave, some kind of element "additional" to materiality, capable of arresting or reversing this process, is achieved through resurrection from the dead. The result is that the raised body is made even more physically robust than it originally was, and entirely resistant to both death and decay. Jesus' resurrection body was thus saved from the fate of corruption in the grave, not by being made "heavenly" and "immortal," but simply by being made resistant to physical corruption.

Clearly, an enormous weight of speculative thought hangs upon Wright's insistence that *aphtharsia* and *aphthartos* are to be translated as "incorruptibility" and "incorruptible," and must always be related to the qualitative transformation of this corporeal or fleshly body rather than to a radically different *pneumatic* transformation into an imagined immaterial and heavenly immortal reality. This is the price that has to be paid so as to keep resurrection belief at arm's length from any suggestion that the resurrection body may be assimilated to ideas of alleged Greek/Platonic origin concerning immortality. At the same time, it is a conclusion that becomes logically unavoidable given Wright's original methodological commitment to handling the Resurrection of Christ purely as a historical event; an occurrence within the time and space of *this* world, as distinct from a going to a heavenly destiny.

13. *RSG*, 477, 543, 606, 609, 612, 646, 654, 661, and 771.

Unfortunately, in order to secure the force of the preferred concept of "incorruptibility" over against "immortality" Wright, once again, effectively follows a lead set by theologians of the Biblical Theology Movement of a former generation insofar as a contrast is drawn between originally Greek and originally Hebrew ways of thinking. However, this argument for an understanding of the transformation of Christ's resurrection body exclusively in terms of physical "incorruptibility" cannot be sustained for the following reasons.

In endeavoring to argue that "immortality" is not in fact a biblical concept at all,[14] and that "The whole world that comes to us through the Bible, OT and NT, is not interested in immortality,"[15] Krister Stendahl placed a heavy reliance on the fact that *athanasia* (immortality) occurs in the New Testament only twice. By contrast, *aphtharsia* (incorruption) appears much more often.

Though truth is not established by democratic procedures, and not a great deal hangs on a New Testament word count alone, it has to be noted that James Barr once pointed out that, over and above Stendahl's count of only two instances of *athanasia* (immortality) in the New Testament, in the apocryphal books Wisdom of Solomon, and 3 and 4 Maccabees, *athanasia* appears much more often (five times in Wisdom and twice in 4 Maccabees). Also, the adjective *athanatos* (non-death) appears once in Wisdom and three times in 4 Maccabees.[16] Similarly, *aphtharsia* (incorruptibility) appears three times in Wisdom and twice in 4 Maccabees, while *aphthartos* (incorruptible) is found twice in Wisdom. Moreover, and much more importantly, there are a number of instances where the appropriateness of translating *aphtharsia* always as "incorruptibility" is not readily justified. In other words, noting Wright's observation that these two terms were often used interchangeably in the ancient world, this does not mean that *athanasia* (immortality) must therefore always be brought into line and translated as "incorruptibility." If anything, it is the other way around. Indeed, there are in fact a number of clear instances where *aphtharsia* (incorruptibility) is used, but *not* in relation to corporeal or fleshly realities. Instead, *aphtharsia* is actually used in relation to nonmaterial realities, where its meaning in those contexts is most naturally secured precisely by assimilating it to ideas of heavenly immortality.

For example, Paul, in Rom 1:23, speaks of "the glory of the immortal/incorruptible God" (*tēn doxan tou aphthartou theou*), contrasted with the idolatrous images fashioned after "corruptible man" (*phthartou anthrōpou*) along with "birds, four-footed animals and creeping things." While some New Testament translations opt for "incorruptible God" here, this clearly cannot be understood in terms of material or corporeal incorruptibility. It is perhaps thinkable that God could be understood as being "incorruptible" in the sense of "not morally corruptible," or not changeable in the

---

14. Stendahl, "Immortality Is Too Much and Too Late," 196.

15. Stendahl, "Immortality Is Too Much and Too Late," 196.

16. See James Barr's response to the initial proposals of Krister Stendahl, in Barr, *The Garden of Eden*, 111–12.

way that the physical and material order is subject to change and decay. However, it can hardly be said that God is not corruptible in a physical or material sense since God has no "body, parts, or passions." A reading of *aphthartou* assimilated to immortality is clearly far more natural and obvious in relation to God, and is in line with *athanasian* (immortality) in relation to the nature of God in 1 Tim 6:16. This is particularly the case given that Paul is drawing a contrast between the "immortal God" and the corruptible or perishable nature of merely material images of created by humans—in other words, idols.

Similarly, in Wis 12:1 *aphtharton* qualifies *pneuma* when, in address to God, it is said: "your *aphtharton pneuma* pervades all things." Once again, when a nonmaterial reality is being qualified by *aphtharton*, it must certainly be translated "immortal" rather than "incorruptible," hence "immortal spirit." The same may be said of Eph 6:24 where "incorruptible" is hardly appropriate as a qualifier of love: "Grace be with all who have a love for our Lord Jesus Christ that is immortal (*en aphtharsia*)." Despite the use of *aphtharsia*, love cannot be understood as being "incorruptible" in a material or physical sense. Likewise, in 2 Tim 1:10, Christ is said to have "abolished death and brought life and immortality (*aphtharsian*) to light."

It is fairly clear from these instances of the use of *aphtharsia*, that the status of the qualified noun dictates the meaning to be assigned to it as the qualifying adjective. As in the case of "a good meal" and "a good man," the precise meaning to be given to the adjective "good" is determined by the noun which it qualifies. The meaning of the quality of "goodness" will differ from the connotation of size and flavor (in the case of the meal) to a set of moral qualities (in the case of the man). Likewise, in the case of an "*aphthartos x*," the meaning of *aphthartos* will vary according to whether "*x*" is a material or a nonmaterial object. In the first case, it will naturally be translated "incorruptible"; in the second, "immortal." The precise meaning of *aphtharsia* in specific cases then becomes clear. None of the realities—God, Spirit, love—can be thought of as corporeal or fleshly realities to which earthly or material incorruptibility *must* be assigned simply by the use of *aphtharsia* in relation to them. Similarly, it is impossible to move from the mere use of the adjective as a qualifier with respect to Jesus' resurrected body so as to conclude that it *must* be understood as a material and "still physical" and hence "incorruptible" body, rather than a "heavenly," "spiritual" and "immortal" body. That would be to assume what needs to be proved. The mere use of an adjective does not dictate the nature of the noun that it qualifies, unless its meaning is first established and obviously clear. Conversely, some understanding of the nature of the resurrection body will in turn dictate whether the appropriate meaning to be assigned to the adjective is "incorruptible" or "immortal." Given that in many instances of its use, it is more valid to assimilate it (almost as a synonym) to immortality, than to think in terms of physical incorruptibility, it cannot be insisted that it *must* necessarily be translated "incorruptible" in reference to the resurrected body of Jesus.

We have to conclude that any doctrinaire insistence that *aphtharsia* must always be translated "incorruptible," and understood in a physical or material sense, thus distancing it from ideas of heavenly immortality, is entirely unfounded. If anything, I think it is the other way around: it can be argued that Paul's words in 1 Cor 15:53 about the "corruptible putting on incorruption" and the "mortal putting on immortality" is a close, almost poetic parallelism, and is to be understood in a way that is determinative of a primary thrust of meaning in favor of heavenly immortality. Given that *athanasia* and *aphtharsia* were near-synonyms, and the possibility of accommodating one to the other, the weighting is tipped in favor of "immortality" in this usage of Paul because of his reliance on the Wisdom tradition, which is so clearly focused on the reward of the righteous in terms of the achievement of immortality with God.

Wright's own strategies of argument at this point are very instructive. While conceding that the word "immortality" may have found its way into Jewish discussions of the afterlife by the first century, the idea that its meaning content could have been somehow amalgamated with the inherited Jewish belief in the resurrection is strictly vetoed as an impossibility. Paul, he insists, only used the term in a form of words to *refer* to resurrection, but not to import any specific *meaning content* that might impact upon the alleged accepted Hebrew understanding of it. The term "resurrection" was thus said to retain the specific "strictly limited" sense in which it is alleged to have been used in Second Temple Judaism—as a physical return of a dead person to life in *this* world. The term "immortality" was thus used (according to Wright's reading of things) without incorporating any alternative connotations of meaning of an "other worldly" kind that might be said to have been derived from its original Greek source.

Thus, lest contemporary New Testament scholars fall into the misconception that Paul might have been thinking of resurrection in the light of Greek views of immortality, Wright insists that "there was no 'combining' two disparate beliefs."[17] He clearly believes that the idea of "resurrection" was so immune from modification, even under the pressure of alternative Greek modes of thought, that it was somehow steadfastly resistant to contamination by influences of this kind. And this is not to mention the possibility that the early Christian use of the term was conditioned by the actual primitive Easter experience itself.

Wright achieves this conclusion by conceding that the word "immortality" could mean a number of things. Among these, he contends that "resurrection" is itself a "*form* or type of 'immortality,'" though, of course, entirely different from the meaning of the same term as it is used by Plato and those subsequently influenced by him! It is thus contended that it is *thinkable* that when Paul used the term "immortality," he did not mean to suggest anything even remotely platonic or "other-worldly" in relation

17. *RSG*, 164.

to it. But then, this logical possibility (it being *thinkable* without self-contradiction) becomes for Wright an *actual* possibility. What Wright says is "thinkable" to his mind, becomes what Paul was actually thinking!

At the end of the day, this means that, at Wright's hands, Paul's use of this characteristically Greek concept of "immortality" was entirely equivocal: Paul did not actually mean what he appears to have said. When Paul used the term "immortality," he is said to have meant nothing more than "resurrection," and by "resurrection" he is said to have meant nothing more than Jesus' physical restoration to *this* world, quite divorced from any suggestion of a "platonic" going from this world to an exalted, heavenly and immortal divine life. This means that, if Jews, at least from 2 Maccabees onwards to the Pharisees of Jesus' day, used the term "immortality" they in no way compromised their alleged view of the resurrection as the return of a dead body to this world. Wright avers that he does not draw a sharp opposition between the Platonic view of the immortality of the soul and the Second Temple view of resurrection of the body, but even despite these protestations of innocence, it is clear that any possible commonality comes down to a form of words. Even if resurrection was spoken of as a kind of "immortality," it does not import any quasi-platonic ideas suggestive of a going from this world to share in the life of the "immortal God." Nor does it suggest an imagined re-clothing with a kind of nonmaterial, "*pneumatic*," or "spiritual" body appropriate to a heavenly world; rather, it involves simply the return of a reconstituted earthly or material body to *this* physical world in a form that rendered it incorruptible. Unfortunately, all these assertions do not amount to an argument. A close eye needs to be applied to the testing of them.

Wright's strategy of allowing the Jewish use of a term ("immortality") that is comfortably at home in Hellenistic culture, but at the same time denying any possibility that it signaled the sharing of a common conceptual meaning-content, was developed by the Biblical Theology Movement into an art form. Famously, the biblical understanding of "time" in qualitative terms as "the right time" or "the appropriate time," "a time of opportunity" or "the time of the visitation of God," was said to be entirely at variance with an alleged Greek view that thought exclusively only of measured time.[18] It is, once again, James Barr who is to be credited with demonstrating the implausibility of these contentions by identifying countless examples of the commonality of meaning in relation to the understanding of time across the Greek/Jewish divide. Effectively, it was his work in relation to this that brought the ascendant popularity of the Biblical Theology Movement to a somewhat abrupt end.[19]

18. Most notably following Aristotle.

19. Barr, *The Semantics of Biblical Language*; and Barr, *Biblical Words for Time*.

Of more importance for our present concern, another fundamental commitment of the Biblical Theology Movement was that, while the Greeks characteristically thought anthropologically of the human person in a dualistic way, as being made up of an outward physical body and an inner soul, Hebrew thinkers were said by contrast to think synthetically in a "totalist" way of a body/soul unity. The alleged anthropological dualism of Greek thought played out specifically in relation to the characteristically Socratic/Platonic belief in the immortality of the soul, for example in talk of the "escape" of the soul *from* the body at death. By contrast, an alleged "totalist" Hebrew anthropology was said to have led to the thought of the resurrection of the total person, body-and-soul together.

Nevertheless, despite these "totalist" contentions, there could be no denying that the Jews also spoke of the "soul" (*nephesh* in Hebrew), and did so precisely in ways that distinguished it from the body. The classic example is the statement of Gen 2:7 that God breathed into Adam and "he became a living soul." This awkward difficulty for the "totalist" viewpoint tended to be explained away during the period of the ascendancy of the Biblical Theology Movement by saying that when Hebrew thinkers used the word "soul," they actually meant the "total person," a body-soul unity, not a kind of quasi-platonic inner self which could be conceived in separation from the outward body. So when God breathed into Adam we were encouraged to understand that "he became a living total person."

Once again, James Barr pointed out that talk of an alleged Jewish "totalist" anthropology does not really sound very convincing, for even in Gen 2:7 there is an implicit dualism insofar as a distinction is made between the dust from which Adam's body is fashioned and the spirit which is in-breathed into him and which animates him. Certainly, "totalist" thinking does not wash in many other instances of the biblical use of the term "soul." For example, we can say with the Psalmist: "Why are you so full of heaviness, O my soul?" (Ps 42:5). In other words, it is possible to address words to our inner selves, as an inner part of our total selves. But somehow it does not seem to make sense to say "Why are you so full of heaviness, O my total person?" This is especially so when we note that the verse goes on to say "and why are you so disquieted *within* me?" Even if it could be thought possible for a "total person" to address a "total person," it makes no sense at all to speak of a "total person" *within* a "total person." Moreover, there is the embarrassing fact in the Gospel of Matthew that even Jesus himself is clearly reported as distinguishing two identifiable aspects of our human make-up, body and soul: "Do not fear those who kill the body but cannot kill the soul; rather fear him who can destroy both soul and body in hell" (Matt 10:28).

In any event, James Barr convincingly demonstrated that to admit the use of the term "soul" but to try to suggest that it was always used in a distinctively "Hebrew" sense to connote a "total person," rather than in a more dualistic Greek sense to refer to an "inner self" distinct from the body, was also one of the fundamental mistakes of the Biblical Theology Movement. The similarity of this strategy of argument to

Wright's contention that Paul's use of the word "immortality" means nothing more than the inherited Jewish view of "physical resurrection" does not escape us.

N. T. Wright is sufficiently attuned to the contemporary appreciation of the Hellenization of Palestinian culture in the first century to try to distance himself from the Biblical Theology Movement, and to avoid speaking in terms of a rigid polarity between "biblical" and "Greek" categories of thought. Even so, for him there can be no abandonment of the alleged inherited Second Temple belief in the resurrection of the body understood as its return to this world as opposed to something else, originally of Greek origin, of a more transcendental and heavenly kind. This means there is no possibility of thinking of accommodating views of immortality to resurrection belief by a blending of the two. If there ever was a Jewish tendency to accept belief in the immortality of the soul, as, for example, seems to be the case in the book of Wisdom, then Wright insists that this can only have referred to an interim state of the soul's "sleep" prior to the final visitation of God when resurrection, understood in strictly Jewish terms, would occur. Thus, we are to think of a more mechanical end-on sequence of essentially discrete ideas: a temporary intermediate state of persisting souls after death is said to have come first, while they await the resurrection of their bodies. In this way, "resurrection" is thus said to refer to the restoration of physical bodies to new life in *this* world *after* this initial form of "life after death," as it were, of "sleeping souls." By this strategy of argument, the idea of "resurrection" itself in Second Temple Judaism is said to remain uncontaminated by Greek or "platonic" modes of thought.

The attempt of those who, during the ascendancy of the Biblical Theology Movement, sought to eliminate notions of "immortality" from the Jewish mentality of first-century Palestine must certainly be judged to have failed. Indeed, James Barr concluded that the weight of the biblical evidence actually dictates the *restoration* of the concept of "immortality" even to a biblical way of looking at things. He ended his discussion of Stendahl's attempt to remove the concept of "immortality" from the mentality of the New Testament authors by saying,

> The Bible, then, has much interest in immortality . . . Immortality of *the soul* is not the only kind that matters. Immortality of the person, bypassing death, is an important part of the heritage. It is not surprising, therefore, that translations like KJV and RSV use 'immortality' as the rendering at a place like II Timothy 1.10: Christ 'abolished death and brought life and immortality to light.'[20]

In view of all this, it is therefore perfectly legitimate to suggest that the occurrence of *athanasia* (immortality) along with *aphtharsia* (incorruptibility) in 1 Cor 15:53 in

20. Barr, *The Garden of Eden*, 112.

a kind of parallelism, involves one amplifying the other. But it is not necessary, as Wright would have us believe, to draw up an opposition between resurrection and immortality,[21] or to argue that notions of immortality, if used at all, are to be confined to a period of disembodied existence between death and the Eschaton, when the dead are alleged to be "alive somewhere, somehow in an interim state" while awaiting a resurrection with a materially incorruptible physical body.[22] Rather, the Psalmist's words about "not suffering your holy one to see corruption" in the grave,[23] when applied to the fate of Christ, might naturally be understood to refer to an avoidance of bodily corruption that was causally achieved, not by its being made "more material than material," but as a consequence of the gift of immortality by resurrection from the dead and heavenly exaltation and glorification with God. As we shall see in the next chapter, in 2 Corinthians Paul's language actually resonates with the characteristically Greek idea of immortality of the kind that the Biblical Theology Movement mistakenly had us believe was entirely at odds with a biblical understanding of things.

We have to conclude that N. T. Wright's contention that we must always translate *aphthartos* as "materially incorruptible," and thus rule out the alternative "heavenly and immortal" option, is clearly not made. Furthermore, if the contention that the transformation of Jesus' resurrected body *must* be understood in terms of physical "incorruptibility" as the *only* legitimate reading of Paul, rather than as a going to immortality, fails, then Wright's coining of the term "transphysicality" to signal the transformation of the body of the resurrection from an earthly physical body so that it is said to become "more material than material" may also be judged to be lacking in adequate textual warrant.

This clears the way for us to understand early belief in Christ's avoidance of corruption in the grave to be the beneficial outcome of his vindication and exaltation through his going to share in the immortal, heavenly life of God. From his eternal and immortal location "at the right hand of the Father," he may be understood to have appeared mysteriously from heaven in revelatory Christophanies that were witnessed in faith by the first believers. Likewise, it was from this same exalted location as the heavenly glorified Lord that he was understood to have distributed his "life-giving Spirit" to the baptized. This is the same Raised Christ whom his faithful disciples also still claim to know in faith as the animating Spirit of the Christian community "until

21. This opposition also follows in the wake of Stendahl, who insisted that "The NT in a very interesting way speaks constantly about resurrection as against immortality" (Stendahl, *Immortality ahd Resurrection*, 197).

22. The question of the "intermediate state" in which the righteous dead are said to be asleep while awaiting their physical resurrection will be further discussed in chapter 11 below.

23. In Psalm 16, which may originally have simply been intended as a prayer for recovery from illness and the avoidance of death itself. It is quoted by Peter in Acts 2:27.

the close of the age." Certainly, Wright's bid to privilege the idea of "physical incorruptibility" over the notion of "heavenly immortality," as the only acceptable way to characterize the nature of the resurrection body of Jesus, must be said to fall under the judgment of "not proven." It is a contention chosen somewhat arbitrarily so as to ensure that Jesus' resurrection body conformed to the *a priori* requirement that the Resurrection be handled purely as an event of this world, essentially like any other historical event, employing the historical reason and the techniques of critical historical research rather than faith.

~

II

Heaven

The bereaved widows and widowers interviewed by Dewi Rees, who reported experiences that convinced them that their loved ones were safely in the everlasting care of God, appear to have presupposed the traditional Christian belief that the righteous dead "go to heaven" immediately following their individual deaths. Though this belief in heaven as the eternal destiny of the righteous dead "with God" is firmly rooted in the received Christian theology of the afterlife so as now to be widely domiciled as an article of popular belief, in the view of N. T. Wright this is entirely mistaken.

This is an inescapable outcome of Wright's revamped Second Temple apocalyptic schema in which "heaven has not happened yet." It is the logically necessary conclusion to be drawn from the contention that the resurrection of the dead must be understood in accordance with the assumed speculative thought of Second Temple Judaism, as a corporate event that will occur only on the ultimate eschatological day of reckoning. In its Christian format Wright envisages that, on that future day, the righteous dead will be raised together, with restored physical bodies, all made incorruptible after the manner of Jesus' own alleged materially incorruptible body at his Resurrection. Presumably, this is imagined to render them no longer subject to the ravages of disease or the degenerative processes of ageing. With the arrival of the Kingdom of Heaven, the righteous dead will then "run the world on behalf of God." Clearly, because this eschatological outcome is yet to eventuate, it can only be a yet-to-be-realized object of future hope. Heaven has not happened yet. For Wright, it is therefore entirely mistaken to think of heaven as the immortal destination to which the righteous dead individually go to be "with God" immediately upon their deaths.

It is equally mistaken to think, however, that what Wright represents as the traditional Christian view of heaven, as a place of eternal immortality "in the nearer presence of God," has been entertained in a uniformly monochrome way over the centuries. It has in fact undergone a number of subtle, though significant, permutations. Indeed, the variety among historical viewpoints about a heavenly afterlife has in recent time even been spoken of provocatively in terms of the possibility of the writing of a "history of heaven." What is meant is that a "history of ideas" can be written about the nature of heaven.[1]

Broadly speaking, these views of heaven have ranged from *theocentric* notions of life everlasting to *anthropocentric* views; the former having to do with a focus upon the vision of God in heaven, and the latter having primarily to do with restored human relationships and the reunion of families and friends beyond the grave.

The classical Christian theology of the afterlife represented, for example, by Augustine or Thomas Aquinas, has tended to focus on *theocentric* notions—the desired ultimate hope being, respectively, the *visio Dei* or the *Beatific Vision*. Most modern thinking about heaven has by contrast become very much more *anthropocentric*. Though there were some nuanced anticipations of this more anthropocentric view in such works as Cyprian's treatise *On Mortality* in the third century, and even earlier in the thought of Origen (which was subsequently crystalized in the creedal affirmation of belief in the "Communion of Saints"), this view really became popular in a somewhat more sentimentalized form from the seventeenth century onwards because of the writing of the Swedish theologian Emanuel Swedenborg (1688–1772), who was in turn influential on John Wesley, among others.[2]

In any event, N. T. Wright's understanding of heaven is to be placed in diametric opposition to *both* traditional *theocentric*, and to modern, post-Swedenborgian *anthropocentric*, viewpoints. His position entails that both of these fail to measure up to the kind of resurrection belief implicit in Second Temple Jewish apocalyptic, which found its way into the mind-set of first-century Christians and thus into the New Testament.

Wright's view of heaven is really in effect a radically reductionist *anthropocentric* view, which bypasses any *theocentric* interest in heavenly union with God, and assimilates heaven to the history of this world. The notion of "heaven" signals a final or ultimately fulfilled phase of world history in which the hoped-for "Kingdom of Heaven" will be manifestly realized. In this process, it is understood, of course, that the sovereignty of God will be victoriously revealed, but Wright's primary emphasis is on the return of the righteous departed with resurrected bodies-made-incorruptible to *this* world, which God will on that day bring to fruition.

Wright's attempt to historicize heaven in this way, so that it constitutes the climactic end-phase of historical time, apparently then entails that the world itself will become the everlasting venue in which the good purposes of God will be played out.

1. See, for example, McDannell and Lang, *Heaven*; and Lang, *Meeting in Heaven*.

2. Notably Robert Hindmarsh and Robert Hartley, Swedenborg's first English translator. Just a few weeks after the death of her father, Princess Louise, the daughter of Queen Victoria, who was a gifted artist, expressed this view of heaven when, on 10 February 1862, she drew an image of her mother in her bedroom, asleep and dreaming of being reunited with Albert. The dream couple are shown above the bed of the sleeping Queen in glorious light surrounded by the clouds of heaven. They are embracing. The representation of Princess Louise's painting may be found in Baird, *Victoria: the Queen*.

At the Eschaton, all the righteous departed will be restored, with bodies now made incorruptible, to *this* world. Even if the world itself is in some way also renewed, I think we have to envision a world with a spatial capacity ample enough to accommodate all the restored bodies of all the righteous departed who have ever lived.

Whether such a view of "heaven" will be found either pastorally or theologically satisfactory to twenty-first-century people is, of course, an open question. After waiting for the delayed *parousia* for two millennia, the church's patience is naturally wearing a bit thin. Sunday by Sunday worshippers express the Creedal hope that Christ will one day return as "judge of the quick and the dead," but hardly, these days, is this affirmed with a sense of the impending cataclysmic anxiety characteristic of the melodramatic imagination of Second Temple Judaism. A joyful expectancy of the Day of the Lord of the imminent kind that possessed the first generation of Christians has also long-since been dissipated by the passing of time. On the other hand, this long-delayed hope may struggle to achieve the capacity to command any real drawing power pastorally, especially among those bereft of their loved ones, and all who mourn, who are naturally anxious to know that their loved ones are safely "with God" *now*.

Meanwhile, the contemporary secularized equivalent of the early Christianized version of this Second Temple apocalyptic belief, in the form of the scientifically based prediction of the end of global history, is hardly a comforting alternative. Undoubtedly life on planet Earth will come to a finite end long before the point when, in however many billion years' time, as scientific forecasts have it, the Sun will eventually burn itself out.[3] However, this ultimate global catastrophe is so existentially remote as not to be likely to cause immediate concern or generate any demonstrable passion.

There is, admittedly, a transparently clear and growing concern in the modern world to forestall an inadvertent and premature end to the life of this planet, by curbing the human contribution to global warming that, since the industrial revolution, has begun to reach such alarming proportions. The internationally shared anxiety which gives rise to the contemporary sense of the need to exercise responsible stewardship in the present world, for fear of the dire consequences that global warming may have for our own children and our children's children, is in its way a secularized echo of the anxiety of ancient Jewish apocalyptic. Nevertheless, the prospect of the final end of the world, as a consequence simply of its inescapable finitude, may not commend itself as a sufficiently "live issue" to ignite the passions of many contemporary humans who are more pre-occupied with their own earthly survival. Even in the context of this kind of secularized apocalyptic narrative of the End of the world, such a far-off and speculative event, as the ultimate conclusion of the history of the world, may not gain much traction among twenty-first-century people.

---

3. A young boy earnestly explained to me one day on a seminary pathway that the Sun will become a lump of compressed carbon: literally "like a diamond in the sky."

In any event, for Wright, it is the theological counterpart of contemporary scientific pessimism about the ultimate end of this corner of the universe that is of more interest. This involves belief in the future intervention of God, at an exact time obviously known to no human, to bring about an end to things as they currently are, and to establish God's sovereign reign of justice and peace. In N. T. Wright's theology of the Resurrection, this conclusion, based upon a more or less literal reading of the New Testament's narratives of apocalyptic speculation that were ultimately derived from Second Temple Judaism, is, then, what Christian talk of "heaven" should really be about. We do not as individuals "go to God in heaven" at death; that may be written off as "Christianized Platonism."[4] Rather, God will, in God's good time, eventually come to exercise a heavenly reign in *this* world. The righteous dead will then be restored to it with bodies made incorruptible. When this happens, the hope of heaven will at last have been actualized.

Theologically speaking, Wright's contention that "heaven has not happened yet," raises some obvious questions: *where* are the departed *now* located while they await the ultimate denouement of the End-time, and *how* are we to imagine their condition? Wright's answer is that early Christianity, once again following the Hellenized lead of Second Temple Judaism, invites us to think in terms of a kind of interim state, though now obviously very extended through time, which is believed to be populated by the righteous dead, while they await the future resurrection of their bodies. In this "intermediate state" between death and the future eschatological resurrection of all the departed, the dead are said to be "asleep." They are somehow alive in a kind of preliminary "life after death" and are safely "in the hands of God."[5] They are "at peace," but they are not to be thought to have gone to a glorious heavenly fulfillment beyond this world, nor do they share immortality in the sense of participating in the eternal life of the immortal God.

In this way Wright finds it convenient, perhaps even necessary, to make use of the concept of the "soul" as a bridging concept while the righteous departed await the restoration of their refurbished earthly bodies, and their future return to life in this world. To this extent, he embraces an attenuated kind of quasi-platonic belief in the "immortality of the soul," for at death the soul assumes a disembodied form, but, unlike the original, Platonic view of immortality, this is only of temporary duration. Though Wright resorts to this kind of "soul-talk," he thus actually jettisons the concept of "immortality" as a timelessly eternal condition. Despite its Platonic pedigree, the

---

4. *RSG*, 50.

5. Following Wis 3:1–4, though this metaphor is not associated by the author of Wisdom with an intermediate state so much as with the enjoyment of the condition of "immortality."

soul's continuing disembodied quasi-afterlife in the "intermediate state" has nothing to do with the traditional hope of sharing eternally in the immortality of God.[6]

Also, in Wright's understanding of things, in the *Jewish* mind of the Hellenistic period, the "soul" was not thought to be naturally or innately immortal (as in Plato),[7] but is "kept alive"[8] in a state of suspended animation while awaiting the day of the visitation of God at the End-Time.[9] This "intermediate state" in which departed "souls" are "asleep" is indicated, if obliquely, he believes, when Paul describes the Raised Christ as "the first fruits of them that have fallen sleep" (1 Cor 15:20), or declares that he would not have his addressees ignorant about those who are "asleep" (1 Thess 4:13).

Because Wright understands the future resurrection body in uncompromisingly physical terms, notions of the soul's "immortality" are in this way very carefully circumscribed. Indeed, "immortality" is allowed into the picture only with reference to the alleged disembodied existence enjoyed by the dead who are said to hold on to "some kind of personal identity"[10] even after bodily death, while they patiently await their re-clothing with reconstituted corruption-resistant bodies at the general resurrection at the Eschaton. If we are to believe, as he confidently proposes, in an *intermediate* disembodied state between death and a re-clothing with the resurrected body at the Eschaton, then this is to be understood only as a "temporary immortality of the soul," after which the dead may hope for "resurrection" as a re-embodied existence of an unambiguously physical and material kind in this world. The use of "immortality" to refer to this temporary disembodied state is said to be "not inappropriate."[11]

Certainly, when Wright speaks of an "intermediate state," this is not to be understood as a place of purgation of the kind imagined by Dante in the *Purgatorio*, or by Catherine of Genoa, who pictured a post-mortem process of purgation in terms of the imagery of sinful accretions being scraped off the souls of the departed after the manner of barnacles being removed from the hulls of ships, which she had regularly observed in the dry-docks of Genoa.[12] The intermediate state of which Wright speaks is not the kind of place where souls might be helped on their way to an eternal heavenly destination, certainly not through the earthly buying and selling of indulgences. So, when he speaks of an "intermediate state," he does not wish to suggest anything like what the Thirty-Nine Articles appended to the Anglican *Book of Common Prayer*

---

6. *RSG*, 175. Wright says that Hellenistic language about the soul was already at hand for the first Christians; however, "It was capable of being imported without necessarily bringing all its latent Platonic baggage with it."

7. *RSG*, 168.

8. *RSG*, 174.

9. *RSG*, 216, where the body is said to be asleep, but the sleeping dead are 'not necessarily unconscious'. They are just inactive.

10. *RSG*, 164.

11. *RSG*, 164.

12. Catherine of Genoa, *Treatise on Purgatory*, chapters 1 and 2.

call "the Romish Doctrine concerning Purgatory."[13] Rather, it is an intermediate state that is simply presented as a place in which the dead are somehow in a kind of restful repose. As the condition of the "sleeping dead," it is a *kind* of afterlife, but not afterlife proper, as it were, for that must wait until the eschatological day of bodily resurrection. Though Wright is reluctant to assign a name to this intermediate state, his language about it tends to conjure up the image of some kind of post-mortem, subterranean dormitory in which the righteous dead persist in a condition of inactivity, but apparently in a state of semi-consciousness, while they await the end of world history as we know it. Hence, in the interim between death and resurrection, it is contended that the righteous dead are thus rightly said to be "asleep."

Despite these clearly articulated and very firmly asserted views, there is, even so, a little ambivalence in N. T. Wright's writing concerning the use of the terminology of "heaven." He is absolutely certain that he knows what heaven is *not*, for it is certainly not, as in traditional Christian belief, the final destination where the righteous dead might be thought individually to go immediately after their death.[14] This is perfectly clear. But when it comes to thinking about how the term "heaven" might be more positively conceived, there appear to be two possibilities that he admits could be entertained. At a squeeze, the word "heaven" could conceivably be used to refer to the state of suspended animation (or "sleep") in the "intermediate state" itself into which Wright believes the dead do slip after death. However, this is a possibility that Wright admits only begrudgingly: this state in which the dead await the resurrection of their bodies between their individual deaths and the Eschaton "might be called heaven," he says, but only "If you must." If we were so disposed, this intermediate state might possibly be referred to as "heaven," because those who are said to be "asleep" are "safe in the mind, plan, and intention of the creator God."[15] This is a concession, perhaps designed to allay the concerns of the bereaved concerning the fate of their loved ones. However, for Wright, if the word "heaven" is used at all, it is better used to refer to "*the place where the divinely intended future for the world is kept safely in store.*"[16] With reference to the condition of the departed while they await bodily resurrection, Wright clearly prefers to speak simply of an "intermediate state" without recourse to the term "heaven" at all.[17]

13. *Article* XXII.

14. *RSG*, 367–68.

15. *RSG*, 373.

16. *RSG*, 368.

17. See Wright, *For all the Saints?*, for Wright's critique of the church's distinction between "all souls" and "all saints," and the separate liturgical observance of the feasts relevant to this distinction on November 1 and 2. His insistence is that all the baptized are the holy people or saints of God, not a spiritual elite who are thought to have qualified for heaven, while "all souls" are somehow in a less

His real preference, insofar as the object to be denoted by the word "heaven" is concerned, is therefore to opt for the final state of all the bodily resurrected at the end of the world history as we know it. This will be the finally consummated "Kingdom of Heaven," when the dead will be raised and the sovereign reign of God will become clearly manifest. At that time all righteous people, both living and departed, will be clothed with their restored resurrection bodies, just as Wright believes Christ's raised body (as the promise or anticipation of this universal happening) was, at his Resurrection from the dead, restored to this world with a body made incorruptible. Having insisted that the Resurrection of Christ was a historical event in the sense that it involved his bodily return to life in *this* world, then the fulfillment at the Eschatological End, of which it was the promise and anticipation, must also be a historical event of essentially the same kind, involving the restoration of all the dead to everlasting life in *this* world. Thus, heaven has not happened yet, but when it does finally materialize (and "materialize" seems to be the appropriate word here), it will be a kind of "Heaven on Earth." The Kingdom of Heaven will at that time have ultimately arrived.

It certainly follows from these views of Wright that New Testament references to those who "sleep" are not to be interpreted as euphemisms for death itself, but as apparently literal references connoting a temporally extended existence beyond death of those who await their resurrection on "the day of the Lord's revealing." New Testament references to "those who sleep" do not mean to speak metaphorically therefore simply of "those who have died."

When we look carefully for concrete New Testament evidence to support belief in this alleged "intermediate state," it is surprising to find that Wright frankly admits that Paul does not spend a great deal of time speculating about the "intermediate state." In fact, he admits that Paul only ever comes anywhere near an account of an "intermediate state" on two occasions. First, in Phil 1:23 Paul declares his earnest desire "to depart and to be with Christ" for this is "far better" than remaining in the flesh. Second, in 2 Corinthians 5 he speaks similarly of being at home in the body in this world but being "away from the Lord" (5:6), though, clearly, it is more desirable to be "away from the body and at home with the Lord" (5:8). Just how these statements indicate Paul's commitment to belief in an "intermediate state" is not made at all clear. Nevertheless, Wright is prepared to say in relation to these two texts that "this is as close as Paul ever comes to an account of an intermediate state between death and resurrection."[18]

It is perfectly clear that, despite these somewhat enigmatic Pauline texts, Wright's primary impetus for thinking in this kind of way is a purely logical one. It is an entailment of thinking of Christ's resurrection as a *prolepsis* or anticipation of the general

privileged position. All are purported to be together "asleep" in the alleged "intermediate state."

18. *RSG*, 369.

resurrection of all the dead at the Eschaton when all the righteous dead may anticipate "a resurrection like his." When this is coupled with the denial of any (Platonic) belief in individual entry at death into the immediate presence of the immortal God, some kind of intermediate state becomes a logical necessity. As Wright himself acknowledges, belief in an intermediate state becomes "a necessary corollary" if resurrection is understood, not as a "going to the eternity of God," but as a future occurrence "of all the true people of the true God."[19] Thus, once the resurrection is understood as being confined to the dimensions of a corporate event of the future Eschaton, and individual entry to the presence of God in heaven after death is denied, some kind of intermediate state in the interim between the deaths of individuals and the future day of resurrection becomes logically unavoidable.

It is also clear enough that an appeal to the notion of an "intermediate state" of this kind could be one way of resolving the tension in the world of Hellenistic Judaism between the essentially Greek belief in the "immortality of the soul" and Hebrew belief in the "resurrection of the body."[20] In Wright's understanding of things, these alternative options were coupled together sequentially, with no modifying impact on Jewish notions of resurrection, even though the original Platonic concept of immortality *is* said to have been necessarily modified by its being turned into a temporary rather than an eternal condition. Obviously, as Wright makes clear, this outcome can only be achieved by ruling out what he speaks of as the "unwarranted platonizing of Christian hope"[21] that suggests that life after death might be experienced by individuals as a going "to heaven when you die"—a going to share in the timeless eternity of the immortality of God in heaven immediately after death.

Now, the question facing us is whether it is really necessary for Christians today to embrace this suite of views, which really owes its outline shape to the speculations of Second Temple Jewish apocalyptic, or is it possible to suggest a viable alternative? To put the question bluntly, must contemporary Christian resurrection belief continue to conform in the manner of a kind of neo-fundamentalist literalism to this specific understanding of Second Temple Jewish belief at this point? Indeed, is there really any clear evidence that the first generation of Christians actually thought in this way themselves?

The first thing to be said in relation to this is that it needs to be noted that we are exhorted to think in terms of an intermediate state by N. T. Wright on the ground of the "strictly limited" way Second Temple Judaism allegedly thought of the "resurrection of the dead," and the way therefore in which he believes the first Christians also

---

19. *RSG*, 372.

20. Cavallin, *Life after Death*, 128. In discussing Wisdom's reference to the "souls of the just" being in "the hands of God" (Wis 3:1–4) while they await the "visitation" (*episcope*) of the End Time, Cavallin observes that one "logical conclusion would be a theory about an intermediate state." However, as we shall see, Cavallin denies that it would in fact be correct to postulate the idea of an intermediate state in Wisdom.

21. *RSG*, 367.

must have thought, and we are obliged to follow suit. Indeed, it has to be said that belief in an intermediate state *only* becomes logically necessary if there was indeed only one "strictly limited" way of thinking of the resurrection in Second Temple Judaism. As was noted in chapter 2, it seems very unlikely that there was at the time only one "strictly limited" understanding of things and, in any event (as noted in chapter 3), even if there was, any inherited belief would have been subject to modification in the light of the experience of what actually happened in the case of Jesus' Resurrection and how it was understood.

On the other hand, if we go to the Wisdom of Solomon, as the one Hellenistic tract representative of a theology which we can fairly confidently say was directly influential on Paul, we certainly find an emphasis on immortality without mention either of resurrection or of an "intermediate state." H. C. C. Cavallin concludes that, while it is clear that the author of Wisdom promoted belief in immortality as God's gift to the faithful as a reward of a righteous life, and promises both their further glorification and the future public *visitation* of God to demonstrate the vindication of their cause over the seeming temporal success of the wicked, Wisdom nevertheless "speaks about the future life of the righteous without mentioning the resurrection."[22] At best, the author may have "accepted the possibility of miraculous resurrections like those connected with Elijah and Elishah," but it cannot be proved that "the Sage believed in the future eschatological resurrection of all the dead . . ."[23] In the Wisdom of Solomon, "the silence of the resurrection remains a fact."[24]

Instead, Wisdom appears to promote belief in an immediate post-mortem condition of being "in God's hand" and "at peace" which is enjoyed by the righteous immediately after death. As Cavallin says, for Wisdom, "righteousness" equals "immortality," for as Wisdom says at 15:3, "To know you is perfect righteousness, and to acknowledge your power is the root of immortality." Cavallin goes on: "Immortality probably means life after death, as in the rest of the book. Its nature is defined as righteousness and as knowledge of God and communion with God."[25]

There is no doubt also that it is envisaged by Wisdom that this is to be followed by the future *visitation* of God to render eschatological judgment in the form of punishment to the wicked and salvation and manifest glory to the righteous. But there is no clear anticipation of a general resurrection to accompany this visitation of God. Rather, as Cavallin rightly says, these "two types of eschatology are apparently only juxtaposed without very much reflection on the tension between them. Therefore it would not be correct to postulate the idea of an intermediate state here. We have no indications that such an idea was at all in the mind of the author."[26]

22. Cavallin, *Life after Death*, 126.

23. Cavallin, *Life after Death*, 132.

24. Cavallin, *Life after Death*, 127.

25. Cavallin, *Life after Death*, 132.

26. Cavallin, *Life after Death*, 128.

If there was in fact much more variety of viewpoint about the nature of the afterlife in the world of Hellenistic Judaism than Wright would have us believe, and especially if the Platonic idea of "immortality with God" was brought into closer association with resurrection belief, particularly in the light of what the first Christian actually experienced, then the idea of an "intermediate state" becomes logically superfluous. If Jesus' appearances, for example, are understood to have been more visionary than visual,[27] and to have originated "from heaven," then a resurrection like his would be a resurrection to an exalted heavenly destiny with him "at the right hand of the Father." This heavenly destiny "with him" no longer requires talk of an "intermediate state."

In other words, talk of an "intermediate state" is dependent upon a specific view of what is to be understood to be entailed by the concept of "resurrection." At the same time, however, it must be said that the hope of an immediate entry into heaven after death does not preclude the idea of a future eschatological showing of the sovereignty of God at a time of ultimate earthly *visitation* marked by the final redress of the injustices perpetrated at the hands of the wicked in the world. In this case, Paul may be understood, once again, to share this belief with the tradition of Wisdom.

This means that it might well also be argued that Paul's references to those "who are asleep" could be understood as metaphorical references simply to those who have endured death itself, as "the longest sleep of all," and who are now safely in the hand of God and, in fact, "at peace in heaven." In this case, references to "those who sleep" may be understood more as euphemistic talk relating to those who have died, rather than as a literal description of the actual condition of the departed in an alleged intermediate state.[28]

The logical coherence of Wright's speculative talk about an intermediate state is also itself problematic. As we have already noted, in arguing for belief in an "intermediate state," Wright relies heavily on Paul's reflection in Phil 1:21–24 about it being better to endure death so as to "be with Christ" than to remain in the flesh; and in 2 Cor 5:6–8 about it being better to be "present with the Lord" than "at home in the body" but "absent from the Lord."

These texts, which are fondly cited by Wright as "the closest Paul comes" to talking about the "intermediate state" certainly seem to presuppose that Paul anticipated going at death to "be with the Raised Christ," perhaps even while those who remained behind in this world awaited his Eschatological return. If these texts imply that Paul

27. As was argued in chapter 4, above.

28. Christopher Evans notes, "In the New Testament also 'to fall asleep' is a conventional expression for 'to die' (Matt 27.52; Acts 7.60, 13.36; 1 Cor 7.39, 11.30, 15.6), and 'those who have fallen asleep' for 'the dead' (I Thess 4.13,15): . . . the expression is so conventional that it can hardly be pressed to convey real information about the condition of the dead" (Evans, *Resurrection and the New Testament*, 23–24).

hoped to be "with Christ" after death, then these references cannot be interpreted as expressions of the hope of being "with Christ" that would only be fulfilled at the eschatological End of the world.[29] Indeed, in 2 Cor 5:1 the sense of Paul's grammatical construction, employing the conditional form of *protasis/apodosis*, is that *when* death happens *then* something much more acceptable immediately follows.[30] In other words, Paul intended to communicate the view that physical death awaits everyone, but for the believer at death the inhabitant of the body vacates one dwelling to take up residence in another, and will thus be "with" the Raised Christ. This passage provides no support for the idea of an intermediate state. Paul's sense is that the transition from earthly tent to heavenly abode is immediate.

However, even though the sleeping departed of the alleged intermediate state are said by Wight to be "in the care/hands of God," they are explicitly said *not* to be with God sharing in the immortality of heaven. Curiously, while pursuing the *Philippians* passage as "the closest answer we ever get from Paul" about an intermediate state, Wright actually notes that Paul "does not speak of going to heaven, *though he would presumably have given that as the present location of the Messiah.*"[31] This is indeed a reasonable presumption. If not, what has become of the primitive Christian conviction that is represented in so many New Testament texts, that the raised and exalted Christ is in heaven itself, "at the right hand of the Father"? But if Paul's destiny beyond death is to sleep with the righteous departed in an "intermediate state," this would suggest that Paul's expressed hope of being "with Christ" immediately after death entails that the Raised Christ, whom Paul anticipates being "with," is himself now to be understood also to be located there in the "immediate state." However, if Paul envisages being with the Messiah after death, and he located the Messiah with God "in heaven," how can he envisage not being in heaven himself with Christ after death, but somehow in the temporary "holding pattern" of an intermediate state "away from God" in heaven? Either way, whether we locate the Raised Christ, whom Paul hopes to "be with" beyond death, in an intermediate state or "with God in heaven," how does this square with Wright's understanding of resurrection belief in terms of the "strictly limited" Second Temple form of a transformed, incorruptibly material, resurrected body in which Christ is said to have been restored to *this* world? Paul's hope beyond death is necessarily somewhat speculative apart from his firm conviction of being "with Christ," but in insisting on the necessary existence of an "intermediate state," Wright seems to end with a speculative muddle.

Clearly, we may legitimately ask whether Paul in these texts (Phil 1:21–23 and 2 Cor 5:6–8) so much as even implied an "intermediate state" in which the righteous

29. Wright, *RSG*, 226, in fact agrees that in this Philippians passage Paul is facing the prospect of his own death and what might lie beyond it.

30. See Aune, "Anthropological Duality," especially his very detailed discussion of Paul's grammatical construction, 223). Also, Windisch, *Der Zweite Korintherbrief*, 159.

31. *RSG*, 227 (italics added).

departed are all actually understood to be in a kind of semi-conscious sleep. Though this is said by Wright to be "about as explicit as he gets on the question of the 'inter-mediate state,'"[32] we can be forgiven for thinking that Paul is not explicit at all. In fact, it is doubtful that he so much as imagined an "intermediate state." Rather, his personal eschatological hope was to be "with Christ," in the eternity of heaven immediately after his death (should that occur before the Eschaton), even while at the same time he anticipated a final "visitation of God" to declare God's triumphant good purposes among the living and the dead at the ultimate End of world history. As Cavallin observed in relation to Wisdom, these two eschatologies, one relating to the immortal destiny of the individual beyond death, and the other a public and cosmic showing of the ultimate good purposes of God, are held side by side without too much concern as to their integration.[33] This appears to be Paul's position as well.

As it turns out, Wright himself concedes, in a way somewhat damaging to his own cause,[34] that this actually seems to be the view of the author of Colossians, where the eschatological hope is not only focused on the future, but also on its inauguration for individuals already in the present (Col 3:3–4). In Colossians, burial with Christ in baptism, and being raised with him through faith in the resurrection, is said to be already effective through faith in the power of God who raised Jesus from the dead (Col 2:12). The consequence of baptism into Christ's death and resurrection is a new life "hid with Christ in God," which will eventually be fully revealed. This is the kind of scenario that appears to be expressed in Col 3:1–4:

> If you then be risen with Christ, seek those things which are above, where Christ sits on the right hand of God. Set your affection on things above, not on things on the earth. For you are dead, and your life is hid with Christ in God. When Christ, who is our life, shall appear, then you shall also appear with him in glory.

It seems that we may think not just of a self-contained eschatological event *of* future historical time, but of the manifestation *in* historical time of the reality of an invisible heavenly state of affairs; an ultimate showing of a reality now hidden in the timeless eternity of God. This echoes a similar sentiment of Paul himself in 1 Thess 4:14 where at the Eschaton, rather than coming to fetch the dead out of the sleep of an "intermediate state," or even from their graves (as might be implied in other passages), Paul explicitly says that "through Jesus God will bring with him those who have died" (apparently from heaven). In the end, at the time of God's eschatological visitation, both the dead who have been raised, followed then by the living, will be "caught up in the clouds with them to meet the Lord in the air" (1 Thess 4:17). It is not easy to square these images with the idea of the inauguration of a new phase of world history

---

32. *RSG*, 367.

33. Cavallin, *Life after Death,* 128.

34. *RSG*, 368, where Wright seems content to identify Paul as the author of Colossians.

in which the righteous, now with incorruptible material bodies, will be "running the world on behalf of God."

To be fair to Wright's position, we need to note that in 2 Corinthians 5, Paul also expresses some anxiety about the possibility of being found naked, by being divested of the body at death. The use of this Platonic image of the soul's nakedness[35] could perhaps be understood to imply the possibility of a period of time when the soul is divested of the body, and therefore left "naked" in an "intermediate state." Thus, perhaps Paul's reference to being found naked could be said to imply an intermediate state between the "exchanging" of his earthly body for the heavenly. Whether we can import time into this scenario, so as to speak of '*a period* of waiting for the eventual resurrection"[36] in an intermediate state, is itself problematic, as we shall see. Nevertheless, while Wright admits that the language of "changing" one body for another of 1 Cor 15:51–52 and Phil 3:21 may also be reflected in 2 Cor 5:4, he believes it is here a way of indicating that Paul hoped to avoid the nakedness of the "intermediate state." The suggestion is that the return of Christ, and the arrival of the Eschaton before he died, is Paul's preferred option, for he thus speaks of "being clothed upon" (while he was still living) rather than being stripped of his body by death and then reclothed. Understandably, this is to be preferred over dying and waiting in nakedness as a disembodied soul after death in an implied temporally extended "intermediate state."

Alternatively, however, if Paul did not envisage the possibility of an extended "period" of nakedness in an intermediate state at all, in speaking of his fear of being found naked, he may just have been expressing the hope of avoiding the trauma of death and the divesting of the body of the flesh that it involved. In other words, he was expressing his hope of the more immediate arrival of the Eschaton during his lifetime, and little more than that. This does not deflect him from affirming that even the trauma of death may have to be endured, but that, even in the face of death, he knows it will lead to a re-clothing with a heavenly, pneumatically transformed body appropriate to a heavenly existence "with the Lord." Significantly, he actually says that he hopes not just to sleep, or even to be at peace, in an extended period in a disembodied condition in an intermediate state, but simply to be *with* the raised and exalted Christ.

Also in 2 Corinthians 5, as we have already seen, in expressing his longing "to be absent from the body and present with the Lord," Paul contrasted "this earthly tent" with "a house, not made with hands, *eternal in the heavens.*"[37] At the same time, his hope for a clothing with the resurrection body is with a body that is to be received

35. See the judgment of naked souls in the Platonic dialogues *Gorgias* (524d) and *Cratylus* (403b), where the soul is said to go to God "without the covering of the body."

36. *RSG*, 367 (italics added).

37. See Wis 9:15, where Platonic ideas about the immortality of the soul are evident: "A perishable body weighs down the soul and the earthly tabernacle burdens the mind so full of thoughts."

"from heaven" (2 Cor 5:2). In this entire passage, Paul contrasts the *temporality* of being in the flesh with the *eternality* of the heavenly life with Christ for which he hopes. It is difficult to see that what he had in mind as the object of his hope was simply a future, infinitely extended phase of world history.

A little earlier in 2 Corinthians, in a reference to the infirmity of life prior to death, and his suffering because of a "slight momentary affliction," Paul goes on to speak not of going to a "period of waiting" in an intermediate state, but to a contrasting timeless or everlasting "eternal glory." In 2 Cor 4:16–18, Paul says:

> Though our outer nature is wasting away, our inner nature is being renewed day by day. For this slight momentary affliction is preparing us for an eternal weight of glory beyond all measure. Because we look not at what can be seen, but at what cannot be seen, for what can be seen is temporary, but what cannot be seen is eternal.

The apparent influence of a platonic "other worldly" idiom in much of this Pauline material, suggests that instead of thinking of a purely horizontal eschatology in the manner of much Second Temple Jewish speculative thought, in which the End is envisaged as a final phase of the history of *this* world, it may be more true to the primitive Christian insight to think of a final eschatological *showing* in this world of a heavenly and timelessly eternal state of affairs in which the sovereign reign of God is made more gloriously and uncompromisingly manifest in justice and peace. After all, the primary sense of the word "apocalypse" is "revealing." In this case, this position would, once again, have resonated with the idea of the *visitation* of God spoken about in the Wisdom of Solomon. In Wis 4:15, this is described as a time of *charis* ("grace") and *eleos* ("mercy," "compassion," perhaps "pity"). This visitation of God may therefore be understood as a further revealing of glory in which, in the ultimate good purpose of God, the righteous (both living and departed) may be thought to be "caught up to be with Christ" in glory (1 Thess 4:17). In this case, the ultimate hope of the Eschaton expressed in the traditional images of the return of Christ, the Last Judgment, and the Messianic banquet at the end of history, are not to be dispensed with as images of the ultimate fulfillment of the good purposes of God. But neither must they necessarily be substituted for ideas of the heavenly destination of the individual dead in the presence of the timelessness of eternity of God in the meantime.

In 1 Pet 1:3–9, the suggestion seems to be that those who were still living, for whom death was necessarily an occurrence of the future, have a "living hope through the resurrection of Jesus Christ from the dead" that is grounded in the promise of an inheritance that is in turn described as "imperishable, undefiled, and unfading." And, very significantly, this is also said to be "kept in heaven" for them. Meanwhile, those who remain in this world, even though they do not "see Christ," are encouraged by the author of 1 Peter to "trust in him and rejoice with an indescribable and glorious joy," based upon a promissory receiving in the present of salvation by anticipation, a proleptic "salvation of our souls" as the already experienced benefit of faith.

While the faithful await the revelation of the ultimate object of Christian hope in this world, their present consolation is thus in the "protection of the power of God," through "faith for a salvation" that is said to be "ready to be revealed in the last time." In other words, a state of affairs is in some sense already said to be a reality which is held in store, though it is "ready to be revealed." It is not so much that "heaven has not happened yet," but rather that what is yet to happen is that the timelessly eternal or eternally present reality of heaven is to be revealed in this world of time on the Day of the Lord. Despite trials by fire in this world which are said to test "the genuineness of faith," the final consummation of all things is thus "to result in praise and glory and honor when Jesus Christ is *revealed*."

This suggestion, of the revelation of something hidden that is kept in heaven, invites the thought that the righteous dead can legitimately also be thought now to be with Christ "at the right hand of God" in the radical hiddenness of the same heaven. This also explains why, in the eschatological text of 1 Thess 4:14, it is said that on that day the departed "who sleep in Jesus will God bring *with* him."

It has to be said that the highly speculative nature of these images of the ultimate fulfillment of Christian hope are, by nature, not easily systematized into a single coherent narrative of the End-time. However, instead of thinking of the End as the inauguration of a new period of world history in which, following the general resurrection, the righteous will take a share in the running of the world on behalf of God, it is at least possible to think eschatologically simply of the revealing of the justice and peace of God at the End of historical time. In this case, apart from the general resurrection of the living and departed together, the eschatological End may be envisioned as the manifestation of a transcendent, heavenly, and eternal state of affairs, in which the sovereign reign of God will be made fully and openly manifest. The apparent earthly success of the wicked will be redressed, and the righteous vindicated. In this case, we should not hope for the inauguration of a new phase of the history of *this* world, but for the ultimate making manifest both "in Heaven and on Earth" of a timelessly eternal state of affairs in which God will be "all in all."

Certainly, once the idea of an "intermediate state" of temporal duration prior to the Eschaton is no longer entertained, some New Testament texts become more open to this kind of understanding of things as a legitimate theological possibility. Such an account of things would certainly explain Paul's failure to express any interest in explicit talk of an "intermediate state." The conclusion seems to be that he did not express the idea of an intermediate state because he did not seriously entertain the idea of an intermediate state. In response to questions about the existence or otherwise of an "intermediate state," we may therefore choose to reply with words borrowed from the interchange of Laplace with Napoleon: we have "no need of that hypothesis."[38]

Finally, something must be said about "timelessness." Among the ideas pertaining to the afterlife that inhabited the minds of people in the first-century world of Middle Platonism was the notion of the timelessness of eternity. The view that the world was not self-generated or self-substantial, but that it was created, as having being produced by a source outside of itself, led naturally to the contemplation of an eternal timelessness "prior" to Creation. This belief, which is implicit in the Jewish religious tradition from Genesis 1, was, in the world of Middle Platonism, bolstered by appeal to Plato's account of creation in *Timaeus*.[39] However, while *Timaeus* might be understood to suggest that creation simply involved the ordering of a pre-existing chaos, the Middle Platonists clearly preferred to avoid any monistic suggestion of the co-eternality of the divine creator and the cosmos, by insisting on the externality of God to the creation. In this way, they parted company with the monism of Stoicism. Already in the century before Paul, Eudorus of Alexandria noted that the creation of the world must have occurred extra-temporally, for time is understood to be a product of the creation of the world itself.[40] If the created order is dependent upon an external cause, i.e. God, then it is implied that God's act of creation was not "in time" but outside of time. One is tempted to say "before all time," except for the fact that until time is created there is no "before" and "after."

However difficult it may be to think of timelessness, it has to be said that a certain sense of the timelessness of God, as God is in God's self, could certainly be understood to be implicit in the Genesis creation story insofar as time itself appears to be part of the created order. Time comes to be in the process of creation itself when God creates the heavens and the earth and separates the light from the darkness, when "God called the light Day, and the darkness he called Night. *And there was evening and there was morning, the first day . . .*" (Gen 1:5), and so on. Particularly when read through the Platonic lens of belief in the perfection of changelessness by contrast with the change and decay of the passing world of time, the assumption of Genesis appears to be that "before all worlds," there was no chronological time at all.

We know that, closer to Paul's own time, Philo of Alexandria shared the conclusions of Eudorus. In *On the Creation of the World*, it is accepted that time only comes

---

38. For a defense of the traditional Roman Catholic approach to the intermediate state, as distinct from more recent a-temporalist proposals, see Yates, *Between Death and Resurrection*. Yates opts for the traditional view because of the need to retain a cosmic and temporal dimension to Christian eschatological hope, and not just an individualized a-temporal one. However, the suggestion of a revealing in time of a timelessly eternal state of affairs has the capacity to address this concern.

39. For example, Plato, *Timaeus* 37.

40. See Dillon, *The Middle Platonists*, 132.

into being with the creation of the world.[41] Philo elsewhere states that "in Eternity there is nothing past and nothing future, but only present."[42] However, in *On the Creation of the World* the emphasis is on time as a component of the created order. Philo emphasizes the powers of God as "Maker and Father" (once again following Plato in *Timaeus*),[43] but crediting Moses with "attaining the summit of philosophy." Philo asserted that Moses "could not fail to recognize that, in the realm of existence (*ta onta*), there are two elements: an active causal principle and a passive element"—the passive element being the created world. This is not to be understood in a monistic Stoic sense,[44] because the active cause is "the perfectly pure and unsullied Mind of the universe, transcending virtue, transcending knowledge, *transcending the Good Itself and the Beautiful Itself.*" The created world, by contrast, is the Creator and Father's "perfect masterpiece."[45] In the century after Philo, Calvenus Taurus (ca. AD 100–165) echoed Philo's generally Platonic views,[46] and Albinus, Taurus's contemporary, likewise affirmed the creative sovereignty of the Supreme God, and at the same time provided a formal definition of Time as "part of the created order"; Time is "the extension (*diastêma*) of the motion of the cosmos."[47]

For all the importance of Second Temple Jewish apocalyptic talk of the hoped-for action of God in the historical future to redress the obvious imbalances of the world's injustice (of the kind that appears to have been spawned in times of political crisis and social trauma in the context of the persecution of the Jews), we also have to take account of other more philosophical elements of the Hellenistic intellectual atmosphere. Given that we have evidence of a persisting belief in a transcendent God's creation of time only along with the creation of the universe, that we may date at least from the time of Eudorus, not long before Paul, through Philo, Paul's contemporary, and into the following century after Paul, we also have to take seriously the logically associated belief in the timelessness of eternity itself during this same period. As a view that was in circulation within Alexandrian Judaism (the unchallenged dominant intellectual powerhouse of the south eastern Mediterranean of that age), it is hard to argue that Paul's own references to eternity could have somehow remained immune from all notions of "timelessness." This becomes a particularly insistent possibility when we note that he contrasts the temporality of life in this world compared with the eternity of his hope. In the absence of some clear indications in his writing of an alternative idea of eternity as a kind of extended temporal period of everlasting historical duration

---

41. Philo, *Opif.* 26–27.

42. Philo, *Deus* 6:32.1.

43. Plato, *Timaeus* 28c.

44. *Stoicorum Veterum Fragmenta* 1:85.

45. As Philip Melanchthon was to see clearly: "God is present to his creation, not as the God of the Stoics, but as a free agent sustaining his creature" (*Loci theologici*, 639).

46. See Dillon, *The Middle Platonists*, 242–43.

47. *Didaskalikos* 14:170.21. See Dillon, *The Middle Platonists*, 287.

simply of this of world, we are justified in entertaining the possible availability to him of this more clearly Middle Platonic option.

The Middle Platonic marriage of biblical insights based on the ontological independence of God as Creator and the temporality of "the days of creation" of Genesis 1, with an essentially Platonic idea of the "timelessly eternal" by contrast with the passing and ephemeral world of material things, entailed that the "timelessness of God" certainly became an object of theological reflection from Albinus onwards in subsequent Christian orthodoxy. Thus, Augustine sought accurately to interpret Genesis from this perspective: "You have made all times, and before all times only you are, nor does time antecede itself." For Augustine, eternity itself thus becomes a single moment for it is "always present."[48] Thus, in the *City of God* he is able to say:

> If eternity and time are rightly distinguished by this, that time does not exist without some movement and transition, while in eternity there is no change, who does not see that there could have been no time had not some creature been made, which by some motion could give birth to change,—the various parts of which motion and change, as they cannot be simultaneous, succeed one another,—and thus in these shorter or longer intervals of duration, time would begin? Since then, God, in whose eternity there is no change at all, is the Creator and Ordainer of time.[49]

In the developed classical theism of Anselm and Aquinas, one of the implications of God's absolute ontological independence of anything outside of God's self is likewise God's a-temporality. Thus, Anselm: ". . . you were not yesterday, and you will not be tomorrow, but yesterday, today, and tomorrow you are. Indeed, it is not even that you are yesterday, today, and tomorrow, rather, you simply are, outside of all time."[50] Similarly, for Aquinas God is "pure actuality" (*actus purus*),[51] with no potentiality, for God is outside all time. Thus, the timelessness of God was understood as a kind of *nunc stans*, or "stationary now." This means that in God all things are already known as actual, including things that for those in created time are yet to be. As Aquinas says: "the present glance of God extends over all time,"[52] for "eternity lacks succes-

48. Augustine of Hippo, *Confessions* xi:14.17.

49. Augustine of Hippo, *City of God* xi.6.

50. Anselm of Canterbury, *Proslogion*, chapter 19. See also chapter 8, on the passionlessness (impassibility) of God, who, by a paradox, is "compassionate in terms of our experience" rather than in terms of God's own being, for God must be said to be "not compassionate" simply in the way humans are compassionate.

51. Aquinas, *Summa Theologiae*, Q: xi: "God is immutable, or as final actuality (*actus purus*) with no admixture of potentiality he cannot change, nor can he be moved. Since his infinitude comprehends the fullness of all perfection, there is nothing he can acquire and no whither for him to extend."

52. Aquinas, *Summa Theologiae*, Q: xiv.

sion, being simultaneously whole."[53] On the basis of these insights, belief in God's absolute ontological independence (God's *aseity*)[54] entails the string of negative statements of classical theism's *apophatic* or "negative way": God is *in*finite, *un*changeable, *im*passible, *un*affected, *im*material, *a*-temporal, *in*effable, and so on. Indeed, one of Augustine's contributions to the development of classical theism was the conclusion that when we say that God is eternal, immortal, incorruptible, or immutable, we are actually saying the *same thing.*[55]

In the outworking of these insights of classical theism in the theology of the twentieth century, Karl Barth's programmatic conviction of the "infinite qualitative distinction" between time and eternity meant that God's revelation (of God's self, and of God's will), as God calls people to obedient discipleship, necessarily breaks into time from outside of time. The revelation of God can never therefore be conformed or accommodated to the passing values of human history. For Barth, only a pathetic liberalism could think of domesticating God by the assimilation the eternal Word of God to the passing values of this historical world.

It is only by standing apart from this tradition of classical Christian theism, and by narrowly focusing on the graphic images of Second Temple Jewish apocalyptic, that N. T. Wright is able to identify "heaven" as the final concluding phase of world history itself. Meanwhile, the possibility of any talk of the timelessness of God's eternity in which God simply is, and where the righteous dead might be imagined to continue to be "hid with Christ in God" (Col 3:1–3), is eliminated by his idea of awaiting resurrection *for a period* in an alleged "intermediate state" of temporal duration. Indeed, Wright clearly does not find the idea of a "timeless eternity" at all amenable. As we have already seen, for him the very idea of timelessness is an essentially alien, Platonic, and indeed pagan notion,[56] that is to be contrasted with historical time itself, as the (alleged) more authentically "Jewish" way of thinking.

I do not wish to suggest that the idea of timelessness, whether in relation to the Being of God, or the nature of the heaven enjoyed by the righteous departed with Christ in God, is an easy topic with which Christian believers might try to come to terms. It is, after all, one of the transcendent mysteries of God that we can in humility admit

53. Aquinas, *Summa Theologiae*, Q: x.

54. *Aseity*: from *a se esse* = "being from one's self"; this entails God's absolute ontological independence and self-sufficiency.

55. See Augustine of Hippo, *De Trinitate* xv:5.7: "That is also true eternity by which God is unchangeable, without beginning, without end; consequently also incorruptible. It is one and the same thing therefore, to call God eternal, or immortal, or incorruptible, or unchangeable." As Nelson Pike points out in *God and Timelessness*, 39, "to change is to be different from one time to an earlier time . . . in order to change, an object must exist at two moments in time." It follows that not to change is not to be in time.

56. Perhaps, as in its original meaning "from the country."

"passes all understanding." Just to begin to entertain it is to become conscious of the challenges of struggling to come to terms with something that is beyond the limits of human reason alone and even of religious knowledge. And if we ask "What was God doing before creation?" we can sympathize with the Reformers' answer: "He was making switches with which to beat those who ask such foolish questions." We can thus only guess at what the "timelessness of God" might be like, perhaps resorting to analogical experiences, as for example when we ourselves are so fully absorbed that we lose consciousness of the passing of time. These are times when time itself seems to "stand still," as it were. Another inkling into the nature of timelessness might be grasped when the experience of time is psychologized as in the thought of Augustine, for whom the past is memory and the future is expectation, but "the present" is the knife edge between the two—a "present" that has no temporal extension, for the present has already become past in the instant that we begin to focus upon it. This is the so call "specious present" of much-twentieth century philosophical puzzlement.[57] Apart from such experiences, we have to admit that the timeless eternity of God is a mystery that is known to God alone.

Contrary to the urgings of N. T. Wright, there are some very good theological reasons for thinking that Christians might in fact do well to separate talk of the more proximate hope of "heaven" as a form of individual life with God immediately after death, from the ultimate public object of Christian hope in the form of the final cataclysmic revelation at the End of historical time, as two quite separate items of Christian contemplation and reflection. It is a mistake to think of one as "platonic" and of the other as "Hebrew/Christian" in the manner of the Biblical Theological Movement. Certainly, one is unnecessarily jettisoned in favor of the other.

Despite the admitted initial concentration of interest on the return of Christ and the eschatological End that is reflected so often in the documents of the New Testament, and which the first generation of Christians imagined was imminent, this does not, even in the New Testament itself, entirely displace the thought that Christ in the meantime "is above" and that believers should therefore "set their minds on things that are above" and not on "things of the earth." This was for the perfectly good reason that this is "where Christ is, seated at the right hand of God" (Col 3:1). This reflection of the importance of Psalm 110 in the early church's post-Easter apologetic, as the favored way of explaining where the Raised Jesus had gone, locates him now at the "right hand of the Father" where he already "reigns in glory," and "where he ever lives

57. I understand that physics has for a while spoken of "imaginary" or "mathematical" time as the synchronic block time of the entire spatio-temporal continuum, from beginning to end at once—of which our diachronic perspective of the "flow" of time is an "illusion"! Whatever we make of this, it is clear that we live daily with illusions: given that the Sun does not move in relation to the Earth, but vice versa, it is also illusory to say: "The Sun will rise at 6 a.m. tomorrow."

to intercede for us" (Heb 7:25). It is natural for the Christian's individual destination beyond death to be thought of in terms of being in heaven "with Christ."

Given this imagery in relation to Christ, it is obviously difficult not to speak of heaven in terms of a place—the place where we locate the righteous dead with God, along with the Christ whom we imaginatively and metaphorically place at "God's right hand in glory." We dare not modernize Paul by seeking to demythologize the vertically stratified cosmology of the first century. There are occasions when it is clear that Paul, as a man of his time, apparently thought of heaven as a place, as his references to being caught up in the third tier of heaven make clear. If not a place, it is perhaps only natural that people tend to think of heaven at least as a condition or a state—such as a state of happiness or bliss. It is understandable that heaven is popularly conceived as a kind of Christian equivalent of the Buddhist Nirvana—a state of perfect quietude, freedom, highest happiness, and liberation from the repeating cycle of birth, life and death.

However, there are some good theological reasons why Christians might more appropriately think of heaven, neither as a place, nor as a state, but rather, essentially as the fulfillment of a relationship. Despite Paul's tendency from time to time to think in terms that suggest an ultimate going to a place, it seems clear enough that for him spatial location is often incidental to what happens in it, and he thought of what happens in it in essentially relational terms. There is no doubting, for example, that Paul understood the purposeful striving and reaching forward to embrace the new life in Christ as being directed to an ultimate end—or *telos*. In his ethical teaching, one of the perspectives he shared in common with the contemporary Stoic philosophy, apart from the language he used, was the view that ethical behavior was purposefully directed towards a specific outcome—a *telos* or end.[58] However, instead of working out, by the exercise of reason, a desirable set of ethical norms for a manner of living that would be in accord with what nature intended (like the Stoics), Paul exhorted those for whom he continued to exercise a kind of pastoral oversight to behave in a manner appropriate to their *relation to Christ* until the day of his return. He thus married this individual teleological behavioral orientation with his inherited Jewish apocalyptic beliefs concerning the return of Christ to effect a cataclysmic denouement and the inauguration of God's Kingdom. Even so, for Paul, the *telos* or end was not just the ultimate return of Christ for the purpose of the final judgment on good and evil in this world, or even for the *pneumatic* transformation of the baptized into resurrected bodies appropriate to a heavenly existence. It was also the consummation of a relationship with Christ, of which, in a partial and incomplete way, he already in faith enjoyed the foretaste.

Thus, apart from the hope of the imminently dawning Kingdom of God in the future of the world, Paul also had in mind the fulfillment of a relationship; a meeting with Christ "in person" or "face to face." In 1 Thess 4:17, it is clear that the *telos* of the

58. As has been so clearly expounded by Troels Engberg-Pedersen, for example in *Paul and the Stoics*.

public eschatological gathering of those still living, to be with those raised from the dead, is thought of in relational terms and with an eternal dimension: "so shall we ever be with the Lord."

In texts subsequent to the Thessalonian correspondence,[59] it is fairly clear that Paul had come to the conclusion that, should the returning Christ not appear in his own lifetime (in which case this "being with the Lord" was not going to be experienced before his own death), then failing that, what he hoped to experience beyond death was the consummation of his relationship with Christ. At this point, his thought is not primarily about going to a place, or even entering into some kind of state (whether intermediate or otherwise), but is conceived in terms of inter-personal relational fulfillment.

This focus upon inter-personal relationality is thus the crux of what is expressed by Paul in the face of the possibility of death, and the destruction of the earthly body, in 2 Cor 5:1. When he contemplates the destruction of his own body at death, he yearns not to be in a place, or to enjoy some kind of condition or state, but to be "with the Lord." As we have already noted, he even expresses the yearning desire to be away from the body and "at home *with the Lord*." Elsewhere, he speaks of his ultimate personal hope in terms of knowing no longer partially in faith (i.e. incompletely or "dimly," as a reflection in a mirror), but "face to face"—in other words, he looks forward to knowing Christ by meeting him "in person"—thus to know fully "even as [Paul himself] is fully known" (1 Cor 13:12). We should therefore not underestimate the importance of his various expressions of the individualized hope of being "with Christ." It is clear that this in a sense compensates for the experienced deficits and hardships of life in this world. In other words, when Paul expresses his hope of his final destination beyond death, he speaks less in terms of just going to a place, or even in terms of achieving some kind of state of happiness and bliss akin to a kind of Nirvana. Rather, Paul speaks in inter-personal relational terms of being "with Christ," given that "in the body" in this world he is in a sense "away" from Christ.

Even so, this emphasis on thinking of the human *telos* (or end) in terms of inter-personal relationality does not take the form of the kind of thinking of heaven purely in terms of a post-seventeenth-century Swedenborgian anthropocentric approach. The "take-away" from Paul's expression of hope is much less sentimental than the post-Swedenborgian view of "heaven" as essentially involving the restoration of relationships just with family and friends. For Paul, and for much of the New Testament's christological reflection, the ultimate *telos* of human beings in Christ has to do with the new relation to the Father, won through the redeeming work of Christ. It has a theocentric and not just an anthropocentric orientation. Thus in 2 Cor 5:18–20, the whole purpose of the cosmic mission of Christ is couched in relational terms: "God was reconciling the world to himself in Christ, not counting people's sins against them." This in turn gives his disciples the outline shape of their mission in the world,

59. Most notably 2 Corinthians 4–5.

for as Paul goes on to say: "He has committed to us the message of reconciliation. We are therefore Christ's ambassadors, as though God were making his appeal through us. We implore you on Christ's behalf: Be reconciled to God." Ultimately, the hope of those "in Christ," far from having a this-worldly orientation, or even the heavenly orientation of being re-united with family and friends, is to stand with him "at the right hand of the Father," for it is "through him we have access by the one Spirit to the Father" (Eph 2:18). As Ephesians says, our human destiny together with Christ "is to be raised up with him" and to "sit with him in the heavenly places" (2:6). This is the *telos* of the relationship of the believer with God in Christ that begins with repentance and faith and the gift of the Spirit at baptism.

We cannot fail to notice the echoes here of Wisdom's conviction that the immortal life of the righteous has already begun in the course of their life of being righteous (Wis 5:15). In Wisdom, the nature of the immortal life is close communion with God, for the divine glorification of the blessed righteous "brings a man nearer to God." This is a sentiment analogous to that expressed in Ps 73:23–26:

> Nevertheless, I am continually with you:
>> You hold my right hand.
> You guide me with your counsel,
>> And afterward you will receive me to glory.
> Whom have I in heaven but you?
>> And there is nothing on earth that I desire besides you.
> My flesh and my heart may fail,
>> but God is the strength of my heart and my portion forever.

This invites the theological possibility that "heaven" for the Christian should therefore be conceived, not as a place, nor as a state, but essentially as a relationship *with God in Christ*. This relationship with God *in* Christ, and *through* Christ, that is implicit in the notion of the reconciliation won *by* Christ, begins at baptism and the promissory gift of the Spirit. This means it is also a relationship of a corporate nature that comes to be and is nurtured in the communion (*koinonia*) of the church; a relationship with one another "in Christ," understood as the Eucharistic community *instituted* by Christ and *constituted* by his living Spirit. The *koinonia* of the Spirit is the inner texture of the shared life of the community of faith that is inclusive of all, both Jews and Gentiles, for reconciliation in the Spirit with God brings with it human inter-personal reconciliation across boundaries of race, social status, and gender identity.[60] This communitarian outcome of the reconciling work of Christ through the gift of his Spirit is also expressed in Ephesians 2:

---

60. As in Paul's insights into the nature of the eschatological community in Gal 3:28. Also Eph 2:13–18.

> But now in Christ Jesus you who sometimes were far off are brought close by the blood of Christ . . . that he might reconcile both unto God in one body by the cross. (Eph 2:13-16)

The good news of the Christian Gospel thus has to do with the possibility of the reconciliation with God won by Christ, albeit not merely in this world, for it has a set of eternal implications. For the communion of the Holy Spirit that encompasses both Jews and Gentiles is interpreted as a promise of what is to come; the communion of the church that is created by the gift of the Spirit being itself the *prolepsis* of the Kingdom. In other words, the relationality of inter-personal sharing in the communion of the church, which is effected through participation in the life of the Spirit, finds its fulfillment in the "pouring out of the Spirit" on all humanity at the eschatological End of the world.

In this case, "heaven" is essentially the continuation beyond physical death of a relationship with Christ, but also a relationship with God through Christ. It is a relationship that is established by baptism into Christ, on the basis of the response of repentance and faith and the gift of the Spirit. By virtue of this relationship, the sovereign reign of God is already dawning in the lives of those who align themselves in faith and hope with the Raised Christ and the values of his Kingdom. This provides the impetus and the content of the Christian mission to the world, pending its ultimate revealing at the time of God's visitation. Clearly, it is not that "heaven has not happened yet"; rather, even at baptism the life of heaven has already begun, for in baptism we have already "died with Christ" and have been "raised with him." With regard to the imminence of the future eschatological dawning Kingdom of God in the world, Paul was clearly mistaken. But the relational character of his hope, and the fulfillment of his yearning to be "with Christ," nevertheless still stands as a legitimate Christian hope beyond death until Christ's ultimate appearing. The baptized life in which believers have already died with Christ, and been raised with him, is in turn the promise of eternal life with him beyond death, in the form of its corporately relational fulfillment.

The nature of this relationship which Paul described as "communion," the communion of the Holy Spirit inclusive of all the baptized in any particular location, and which Christians enter into at baptism, and share together most intentionally as the worshipping Eucharistic community, provided the experiential context for the development of the doctrine of the Trinity by the Cappadocian Fathers in the fourth century. Basil of Caesarea, for example, appealed to the concept of inter-personal relationality when he spoke of the unity of the Persons of the Trinity, as "Three Persons and one Communion."[61] The baptized do indeed share together the Holy Communion

---

61. In his *Treatise on the Holy Spirit*, AD 371. Though the formula "Three Persons and One Substance" was already in the air (at least since Nicaea), Basil in this work shows a regular preference for

of God, by their incorporation into the life of God the Trinity of Persons, Father, Son, and Holy Spirit. This is the experience of heaven on earth, and the promise of the messianic banquet of the world beyond death. Relationality, then, rather than spatial location in a place, or some kind of qualitative state or condition, whether of sleep or of blissful happiness, is the key to the Christian understanding of the nature of "heaven."

It may be helpful at this point to observe that the language of Christian hope must necessarily resort to images and metaphors. This is particularly so when we seek to focus on an ultimate hope—something that is beyond all imagining. Conceptually speaking, more proximate hopes are more easily managed than longer-term or ultimate hopes. For example, I might hope that my grandchildren will all arrive home from school safely today. That kind of hope can be formulated and expressed in fairly simple literal language. When I seek to envisage their longer-term success in negotiating what might lie ahead of them in the ups and downs of the future, and express the hope that they will live full, happy, and enriching lives, I cannot know or articulate in any specific detail what actual form those hopes might take. I have necessarily to be less explicit, and to speak more generally of an indeterminate "happiness, contentment, and human fulfillment" for them. Likewise, when Christians come to express their ultimate hope in terms of God's "visitation" of the End Time, imaginary picture language is all we have—verbal images of the return of Christ in the clouds of glory, the last trumpet, and the consummation of all things in terms of a "heavenly banquet." Given that the imminent End envisaged by Paul using these kinds of images did not eventuate, as we today naturally set our minds on the things that are above, "where Christ is, seated at the right hand of God" (Col 3:1), it seems reasonable enough imaginatively to place the righteous departed "in heaven" with him. Then, as we express the hope that, despite the vicissitudes of history, ultimately the good purposes of God will prevail and all be revealed, we dare to express the hope that this will be the time of Christ's final appearing using those same Pauline images of the day of the revelation of the Lord. But we really have no detailed notion of what precise concrete form that future fulfillment might take.

Though N. T. Wright is not amenable to the idea that the righteous dead might already be "with God in heaven," dismissing this as a form of "Christianized paganism" spawned by an unwelcome intrusion of "Platonism" into the Christian tradition, we have to own that Paul himself was in fact a creature of the world of Middle Platonism, and that post-Pauline Christianity cannot really shake itself free of this origin. This means that cognizance must be taken of the very mixed nature of an intellectual environment in which Plato could regularly be regarded as an ally rather than an antagonist. The apocalyptic inheritance of Second Temple Judaism did not stand

---

the more dynamic and relational alternative "Three Persons and One Communion."

alone as a solitary influence in Paul's thought. The Stoic and Platonic amalgam of epistemological, ontological, and cosmological ideas of the world of Middle Platonism also played a part in primitive Christian origins. It is wholly congruent with this originating state of affairs that the ultimate eschatological hope of Christianity has come to be expressed both in public and historical terms reminiscent of the apocalyptic hope of Second Temple Judaism and, at the same time, in terms of the more individualized Platonic hope of personal immortality beyond death; the two being linked by the idea of the ultimate visitation of God manifestly to exercise judgment and to disclose the sovereignty of divine rule at the End of historical time. It is in relation to the expression of that ultimate hope that those texts which speak of the coming of Christ "in the clouds of heaven," with a cry of command and the archangel's call, and the sound of God's trumpet, continue in useful currency. As Christians, we dare to express the hope that on that day God will bring the righteous departed "with him" (1 Thess 4:14), and that "when Christ who is our life appears," we also, and all the righteous departed, will "be revealed with him in glory" (Col 3:4).

Appendix 1
2 Baruch 49–51

The Apocalypse of Baruch Son of Neriah (known as *2 Baruch*), from *The Old Testament Pseudepigrapha*, 1, edited by James H. Charlesworth. Garden City, NY: Doubleday, 1980. This originally Greek document was translated into Syriac early in the second century AD.

49 But further, I ask you, O Mighty One; and I shall ask grace from him who created all things. *In which shape will the living live in your day? Or how will remain their splendor which will be after that? *Will they, perhaps, take again this present form, and will they put on the chained members which are in evil and by which evils are accomplished? Or will you perhaps change these things which have been in the world, as also the world itself?

50 And he answered and said to me: Listen, Baruch, to this word and write down in the memory of your heart all that you shall learn. *For the earth will surely give back the dead at that time; it receives them now in order to keep them, not changing anything in their form. But as it has received them so it will give them back. And as I have delivered them to it so it will raise them. *For then it will be necessary to show those who live that the dead are living again, and that those who went away have come back. And it will be that when they have recognized each other, *those who know each other at this moment, then my judgment will be strong, and those things which have been spoken of before will come.

51 And it will happen after this day which he appointed is over both the shape of those who are found to be guilty as also the glory of those who have proved to be righteous will be changed. For the shape of those who now act wickedly will be made more evil than it is (now) so that they shall suffer torment. Also, as for the glory of those who proved to be righteous on account of my law, those who possessed intelligence in their life, and those who planted the root of wisdom in their heart—their splendor will then be glorified by transformations, and the shape of their face will be changed into the light of their beauty so that they may acquire and receive the undying world which is promised to them. Therefore, especially they who will then come will be sad, because they despised my Law, and stopped their ears lest they hear wisdom and receive intelligence. When they, therefore, will see that those over whom they are exalted now will then be more exalted and glorified than they, then both these and those will be changed, these into the splendor of angels and those into startling visions and horrible shapes, and they will waste away even more. *For they will first see and then they will go away to be tormented.

Miracles, however, will appear at their own time to those who are saved because of their works and for whom the Law is now a hope, and intelligence, expectation, and wisdom a trust. *For they shall see that world that is now invisible to them, and they shall see a time that is now hidden to them. *And time will no longer make them older. For they will live in the heights of that world and they will be like the angels and be equal to the stars. And they will be changed into any shape which they wished, from beauty to loveliness, and from light to the splendor of glory. *For the extents of Paradise will be spread out over them, and to them will be shown the beauty of the majesty of the living beings under the throne, as well as all the hosts of the angels, those who are held by my word now lest they show themselves, and those who are withheld by my command so that they may stand at their places until their coming has arrived. *And the excellence of the righteous will then be greater than that of the angels. *For the first will receive the last, those whom they expected; and the last, those of whom they had heard that they had gone away. *For they have been saved from this world of affliction and have put down the burden of anguishes. *Because of which men lost their life and for what have those who were on the earth exchanged their soul? * For once they chose for themselves that time which cannot pass away without afflictions. And they chose for themselves that time of which the end is full of lamentations and evils. And they have denied the world that does not make them that come to it older. And they have rejected the time which causes glory so that they are not coming to the glory of which I spoke to you before.

Appendix 2

Jewish Sources on the Legal Status of Women

Three sources are regularly cited by Christian theologians in support of the contention that St. Paul systematically avoided references to the evidence of the Empty
Tomb because at Jewish law women were not thought to be competent witnesses.
These are from the Mishnah and Babylonian Talmud: *m. Šebu.* 4:1; *m. Roš Haš.* 1:8;
and *b. B. Qam.* 88a.

1. The relevant text from *m. Šeb.* 4:1 is found in the context of a discussion about
the making of oaths of different kinds, some of which apply to women as well as to
men. For example, oaths relating to uncleanliness are not gender specific (*m. Šeb.*
3:10–11). By contrast with other oaths, the "oath of testimony" does not apply to
women, or to specific categories of men who are likewise legally disqualified from
giving evidence. The text of *m. Šebu.* 4:1 is as follows:

> The law about "an oath of testimony"[1] applies to men but not to women, to
> them that are not kinsfolk but not to them that are kinsfolk, to them that are
> qualified [to bear witness] but not to them that are not qualified, and it ap-
> plies only to them that are fit to bear witness;[2] and [it applies whether uttered]
> before a court or not before a court;[3] but it must by uttered out of a man's own
> mouth.[4] If [he was abjured] at the mouth of others, he is not liable until he has
> denied his knowledge before a court. So R. Meir. But the Sages say: Whether
> [he swore] out of his own mouth or [was abjured] at the mouth of others, a
> man is not liable until he has denied his knowledge before a court.

This provision concerning the "oath of testimony" applies to those who are ko-
sher [i.e. halakhically fit to give testimony] but not to *pasul* [i.e., those who are unfit].
Along with women generally, those who are classed as unfit to provide testimony are
specified: a dice player, a usurer, pigeon-flyers, or traffickers in Seventh Year produce.
However, perhaps somewhat surprisingly, according to *m. Sanh.* 2:2. a king, is also

---

1. And as a consequence, the ramifications of transgressing it.

2. Those disqualified are explicitly listed in *m. Sanh.* 3:3–5.

3. A Rabbinic court, a Beit Din, or not before a Beit Din.

4. This excludes hearsay evidence.

exempted from the oath of testimony, as are (less surprisingly) the kinsmen of a suitor, including a suitor's father, brother, father's brother, mother's brother, etc. and even a friend or an enemy. Clearly, these provisions are intended to safeguard and maintain the values of fairness and justice in legal suits.

Even so, in some circumstances the testimony of a woman is permitted in the cause of maintaining the same principle of justice. For example, in relation to the acceptability of evidence relating to the identification of a corpse so as to allow a woman to marry again, *m. Yebam.* 16:5 explicitly says "Even if a man (only) heard women saying, 'Such a one is dead', that suffices." Similarly, a mother's testimony along with that of a father is positively required in the case of condemning "a stubborn and rebellious son" (*m. Sanh.* 8:1–4). Just how these legal principles governing the "oath of testimony" might be brought to bear on matters of testimony where there are no plaintiffs or defendants, but which simply involve the transmission of information (such as, for example, the report of an empty tomb) is not at all clear.

2. The text from the *m. Roš Haš.* 1:8 simply rehearses the general principle which includes women in the list of those considered legally ineligible to testify. The text is as follows:

> These are they that are ineligible:[5] a dice player, a usurer, pigeon-flyers, traffickers in Seventh Year produce, and slaves. This is the general rule: any evidence that a woman is not eligible to bring, these are not eligible to bring.[6]

3. In the following section from Babylonian Talmud, *B. Qam.* 88a, the disqualification of a woman from giving evidence is said also to apply to a slave. It is pointed out that a woman is disqualified because she is not under all the commandments and is not circumcised. Also a child cannot give evidence to convict a father. However, this clearly relates in the Babylonian Talmud to criminal activity, convictions in criminal matters, and even capital punishment.

The full text may conveniently be found at: http://www.come-and hear.com/babakamma/babakamma_88.html. The relevant passage is as follows:

> But again would you now also say that according to the Rabbis, a slave would be eligible to give evidence, since it says, And behold, if the witness be a false witness and hath testified falsely against his brother? 'Ulla replied: Regarding evidence you can surely not argue thus. For that he is disqualified from giving evidence can be learnt by means of an a fortiori from the law in the case of Woman: for if a Woman who is eligible to enter [by marriage] into the congregation [of Israel] is yet ineligible to give evidence, how much more must a slave who is not eligible to enter [by marriage] into the congregation [of Israel] be ineligible to give evidence? But why is Woman disqualified if not perhaps because she is not subject to the law of circumcision? How then can you assert the same in the case

5. I.e., considered unfit to be witnesses.

6. These texts may be found in *The Mishnah*, edited by Herbert Danby.

of a slave who is subject to circumcision? The case of a [male] minor will meet this objection, for in spite of his being subject to circumcision he is disqualified from giving evidence. But why is a minor disqualified if not perhaps because he is not subject to commandments? How then can you assert the same in the case of a slave who is subject to commandments? The case of Woman will meet this objection, for though she is subject to commandments she is disqualified from giving evidence. The argument is thus endlessly reversible. There are features in the one instance which are not found in the other, and vice versa. The features common to both are that they are not subject to all the commandments and that they are disqualified from giving evidence. I will therefore include with them a slave who also is not subject to all the commandments and should therefore also be disqualified from giving evidence. But why [I may ask] is the feature common to them that they are disqualified from giving evidence if not perhaps because neither of them is a man? How then can you assert the same in the case of a slave who is a man? You must therefore deduce the disqualification of a slave from the law applicable in the case of a robber. But why is there this disqualification in the case of a robber if not because his own deeds caused it? How then can you assert the same in the case of a slave whose own deeds could surely not cause it? You must therefore deduce the disqualification of a slave from both the law applicable to a robber and the law applicable to either of these [referred to above]. Mar, the son of Rabina, however, said: Scripture says: 'The fathers shall not be put to death through the children', from this it could be inferred that no sentence of capital punishment should be passed on [the evidence of] the mouth of [persons who if they were to be] fathers would have no legal paternity over their children.

While *Baba Qamma* explicitly addresses criminal convictions and even capital punishment, it is not altogether clear about non-criminal activity and non-capital convictions. Exactly how it is to be brought to bear on the straight forward transmission of information, outside a legal environment in which the interests of plaintiffs and defendants are to be defended, is, once again, a matter of some debate. For example, even in *Baba Qamma* itself the testimony of a woman (and, indeed, even of a minor) is countenanced in relation to an issue about the ownership of swarming bees:

In response "Rabbi Johanan B. Beroka said [that] even a woman or a minor is trusted. Rabbi Judah said in the name of Samuel: We are dealing here with a case where, e.g., the proprietors were chasing the bees and a woman or a minor speaking in all innocence said that this swarm started from here." (*b. B. Qam.* 114b)

It is also noteworthy that a principle of common sense appears to be operating in the teaching of medieval and revered sixteenth century Rabbis in relation to the admission of women witnesses. For example, Rabbi Moses Isseries (known as Rema, 1530–1572) held that the testimony of women was acceptable in relation to matters that were within their own particular knowledge (ḤaMapah 35:14; Darkhei Moshe: ḤaMapah 35, n. 3). This echoes a teaching of Rabbi Israel Isserlein (1390–1460) in the *Sefer Terumat ha-Deshen* (Responsa no. 353) which accepted the testimony of women in the case of customs or events in places frequented by women. Both Rabbi Meir ben Baruch (known as Maharam of Rothenburg, c. 1220–1293) and Rabbi Joseph Colon be Solomon Trabotto (known as Maharik, c. 1420–1480) accepted the evidence of women when there were no other witnesses available (See Responsa Maharam of Rothenburg, ed. Prague, no. 920; Responsa. Maharik, no. 179). Maharik also accepted the evidence of women in matters not considered important enough to bother male witnesses (Responsa Maharik no. 190). This is a position also found in Sefer Kol Bo no. 116. Finally, it is noteworthy that the important Halakhic code known as Tur, composed by Jacob ben Asher (1270–c. 1340), omits women from the list of non-competent witnesses (ḤaMapah 35).

While these legal opinions clearly appeal to a principle of common sense in the interpretation of inherited law, these revered teachers undoubtedly believed that they were passing on authentic teachings of ancient oral origin. In this respect it is significant that the Mishnah itself already addressed the issue of women witnesses in the crucial case of providing testimony relating to the death of a husband. In times when civic authorities were yet to regulate the registration of births, deaths, and marriages, the testimony of a woman became crucial if she was to be permitted to marry again. In this circumstance even the evidence of one woman and not two was said to suffice, particularly in giving evidence relating to the identification of a corpse (see *m. Yebam.* 16:5). On the other hand, *m. Ketub.* 2:6 explicitly allows the evidence of women in matters relating to purity. Similarly, as was noted above, the Mishnah also already provided that a mother's testimony along with that of a father is positively required in the case of condemning "a stubborn and rebellious son" (*m. Sanh.* 8:1–4).

While it is not at all clear just how the legal principles governing the "oath of testimony" might be brought to bear on mattes that did not involve plaintiffs or defendants, what is clear is that a bare statement of legal principles and the question of exactly how those principles were actually applied in practice are two different things. It is certainly entirely inadmissible to jump from the regular provisions of Jewish law relating to the legal inadmissibility of women to give legal evidence, to the conclusion that this explains the reason why Paul omitted any reference to the empty tomb in his writings. A conclusion about Paul's alleged scrupulous adherence to these legal provisions, based upon the three references that are so regularly cited by contemporary New Testament scholars, when we do not actually know how the law was actually applied.in practice is clearly problematic. To conclude that Paul allegedly had knowledge of the empty tomb tradition but did not mention it, simply because of its reliance on women witnesses, is clearly uncomfortably speculative.

∽

Bibliography

PRIMARY SOURCES

Albinus (alias Alcinous). *Didaskalikos.* https://www.esonet.org/the-didaskalikos-of-albinus-145-ad/. A bibliography of studies may be found in John Dillon, *The Middle Platonists, 80 B.C. to A.D. 220,* 419. Ithaca, NY: Cornell University Press, 1977.

Anselm of Canterbury. *Proslogion, with the Replies of Gaunilo and Anselm.* Translated with Introduction and Notes by Thomas Williams. Indianapolis: Hackett, 2001.

Antiochus of Ascalon. *Collection of Fragments.* Edited by Georg Luck in *Der Akademiker Antiochos.* Bern: n.p. 1953. For studies see John Dillon, *The Middle Platonists, 80 B.C. to A.D. 220.* Ithaca, NY: Cornell University Press, 1977, 417.

Apollodorus. *Apollodorus: The Library.* Edited by James G. Frazer. LCL. London: Heinemann, 1921. http://www.theoi.com/Text/Apollodorus1.html/.

Aquinas, Thomas. *Summa Theologiae,* Vol. 55, *The Resurrection of the Lord.* Edited by C. Thomas Moore, O.P. London: Eyre & Spottiswoode, 1976.

The Assumption of Moses. Translation adapted from R. H. Charles, *The Apocrypha and Pseudepigrapha of the Old Testament,* 2: 407–24. Oxford: Oxford University Press, 1913. http://wesley.nnu.edu/index.php?id=2124.

Augustine of Hippo, *The City of God,* in *The Works of Aurelius Augustine.* Edited by Marcus Dods, Vol. 1. Edinburgh: T. & T. Clark, 1871/ Overland Park KS: Digireads, 2017.

———. *Confessions.* Translated with an introduction and notes by Henry Chadwick. Oxford: Oxford University Press, 1991.

———. *De Trinitate,* A republication of *A Select Library of the Nicene and Post-Nicene Fathers of the Christian Church,* Vol. 3. Edited by Philip Schaff. Buffalo: Christian Literature Co., 1886. Translated by Arthur West Haddan, revised by William Shedd: Veritatis Splendor, 2012.

The Babylonian Talmud. Text and translation in Soncino Hebrew/English Babylonian Talmud, edited by I. Epstein. London: Soncino, 1990. http://www.come-and-hear.com/sanhedrin/sanhedrin_0.html

Catherine of Genoa. *Treatise on Purgatory: The Dialogue.* Translated by Charlotte Balfour and Helen Douglas Irvine. London: Sheed & Ward, 1946.

The Holy Bible, with the Books called Apocrypha: Revised Version with Revised Marginal References. Oxford: Oxford University Press, n.d. [1898].

The Holy Bible, Containing the Old and New Testaments with the Apocryphal/Deuterocanonical Books: New Revised Standard Version. Oxford: Oxford University Press, 1991.

Josephus. *Jewish Antiquities*. Translated and edited by H. St. J. Thackeray et al. LCL. Cambridge, Mass: Harvard University Press/London: William Heinemann, 1926–65.

———. *The Jewish War*. Translated and edited by H. St.J. Thackeray et al. LCL. Cambridge: Harvard University Press, 1926–65.

Melanchthon, Philip. *The Chief Theological Topics: Logi Praecipui Theologici* (1559). Translated and edited by J. A. O. Preus. St. Louis: Concordia, 2017.

The Mishnah, Translated from the Hebrew with Introduction and Brief Explanatory Notes. Edited and translated by Herbert Danby. Oxford: Oxford University Press, 1933.

The Old Testament Pseudepigrapha. Edited by James H. Charlesworth. 2 vols. Garden City, NY: Doubleday, 1983–85.

Origen of Alexandria. *Contra Celsum*. Edited by Henry Chadwick. Cambridge: Cambridge University Press, 1953.

Philo. *Works*. 12 vols. Edited by F. H. Colson, et al. LCL. Cambridge: Harvard University Press, 1968–81.

———. *Philo of Alexandria: An Annotated Bibliography, 1937–86, 1987–96, and 1997–2006*. Edited by Roberto Radice and David T. Runia. Supplements to Vigiliae Christianae 8, 57 and 109. Leiden: Brill, 1992, 2000, 2012.

The Psalms of Solomon. Translated by S. P. Brock. In *The Apocryphal Old Testament*. Edited by H. F. D. Sparks. Oxford: Clarendon, 1984. https://carm.org/psalms-of-solomon.

Pseudo-Philo. *Biblical Antiquities*. In H. Jacobson, *A Commentary of Pseudo-Philo's Liber Antiquitatum Biblicarum*. Leiden: Brill, 1996.

Plato. *Complete Works*. Edited with introduction and notes by John M. Cooper. Indianapolis: Hackett, 1997.

Stoicorum Veterum Fragmenta. Edited by. H. von Arnim. Stuttgart: Teubner, 1903–24.

The Testament of Job: An Essene Midrash on the Book of Job. Re-edited and translated by Kaufmann Kohler, in *Semitic Studies in Memory of Alexander Kohut*. Edited by G. A. Kohut. Berlin, 1897, 264–338; English translation by M. R. James, revised by Jeremy Kapp: https://www.scribd.com/document/1251114/Testament-of-Job-Revised-English.

Vermes, Geza, trans. *The Complete Dead Sea Scrolls in English*. 4th ed. New York: Penguin, 1997.

SECONDARY SOURCES

Adams, Edward. "The 'Coming of God' Tradition and Its Influence on New Testament Parousia Texts." In *Biblical Traditions in Transmission: Essays in Honour of Michael A. Knibb*, edited by Charlotte Hempel and Judith M. Lieu, 1–19. Supplements to the Journal for the Study of Judaism 111. Leiden: Brill, 2006.

Aune, David. E. "The Problem of the Genre of the Gospels: A Critique of C. H. Talbert's *What Is a Gospel?*" In *Gospel Perspectives II: Studies of History and Tradition in the Four Gospels*, edited by R. T. France and David Wenham. Sheffield: JSOT Press, 1981.

———. "Anthropological Duality in the Eschatology of 2 Cor 4.16—5.10." In *Paul beyond the Judaism/Hellenism Divide*, edited by Troels Engberg-Pedersen, 215–39. Louisville: Westminster John Knox, 2001.

Baird, Julia. *Victoria: The Queen*. Sydney: HarperCollins, 2017 (first published New York: HarperCollins/Random House, 2016).

Barr, James. *Biblical Words for Time*. London: SCM, 1969.

———. *The Concept of Biblical Theology: An Old Testament Perspective*. Minneapolis: Fortress, 1999.

———. *The Garden of Eden and the Hope of Immortality*. 1993. Reprint, Eugene, OR: Wipf & Stock, 2003.

———. *The Semantics of Biblical Language*. Oxford: Oxford University Press, 1961.

Barth, K. *The Epistle to the Romans* (1922). 2nd ed. translated by Edwyn C. Hoskyns. Oxford: Oxford University Press, 1933.

Bauckham, Richard. *Gospel Women: Studies of the Named Women in the Gospels*. Grand Rapids: Eerdmans, 2002.

———. *The Gospels as Eyewitness Testimony*. Grand Rapids, Eerdmans, 2006.

———. "The Son of Man: 'A Man in My Position' or 'Someone'?" In *The Historical Jesus: A Sheffield Reader*, edited by Craig A. Evans and Stanley E. Porter, 244–55. Biblical Seminar 33. Sheffield: Sheffield Academic, 1995.

Baxter, Anthony. "Historical Judgment, Transcendent Perspective and 'Resurrection Appearances.'" *Heythrop Journal* 40 (1999) 19–40.

Becker, Eve-Marie. "Wright's Paul and the Paul of Acts: A Critique of Pauline Exegesis—Inspired by Lukan Studies." In *God and the Faithfulness of Paul*, edited by Christoph Heilig et al., 151–63. WUNT 2/413. Tübingen: Mohr/Siebeck, 2016.

Bockmuehl, Markus. "The Compleat History of the Resurrection: A Dialogue with N. T. Wright." *Journal for the Study of the New Testament*, 26 (2004) 489–504.

———. "Resurrection." In *The Cambridge Companion to Jesus*. Edited by Markus Bockmuehl. Cambridge: Cambridge University Press, 2001.

Bode, E. L. *The First Easter Morning: The Gospel Accounts of the Women's Visit to the Tomb of Jesus*, Analecta Biblica 45. Rome: Biblical Institute, 1970.

Bonazzi, Mauro. "Eudorus of Alexandria and Early Imperial Platonism." In *Bulletin of the Institute of Classical Studies Supplement*, 94.ii, Greek and Roman Philosophy, 100BC–200AD, (2007) 365–77.

Bouttier, M. *En Christ*. Paris: Presses Universitaires de France, 1962.

Bowker, John. "'Merkabah' Visions and the Visions of Paul." *Journal of Semitic Studies* 16 (1971) 157–73.

Bultmann, Rudolf. *Essays Theological and Philosophical*. Translated by J. C. G. Greig. London: SCM, 1955.

———. *Faith and Understanding*. Translated by L. P. Smith, edited by R. W. Funk. London: SCM, 1969.

———. *The History of the Synoptic Tradition*. Translated by John Marsh. Oxford: Blackwell, 1963/1968.

———. "The Quest for Meaning in History." *Listener* (1 September 1955) 329–30.

Burridge, Richard. *Four Gospels, One Jesus*. 1994. Reprinted, London: SPCK, 2013.

———. *What Are the Gospels?* 1992. Reprint, Grand Rapids: Eerdmans, 2004.

Buttrick, George Arthur, ed. *The Interpreter's Dictionary of the Bible*. 4 vols. Nashville: Abingdon, 1962.

Byrne, Brendan. "Christ's Pre-Existence in Pauline Soteriology." *Theological Studies* 58 (1997) 314–20.

Calvin, John. *Institutes of the Christian Religion*. 2 vols. Translated by Henry Beveridge. Grand Rapids: Eerdmans, 1975.

Bibliography

Campbell, Douglas A. "The Story of Jesus in Romans and Galatians." In *Narrative Dynamics in Paul*, edited by Bruce W. Longenecker, 97–124. Louisville: Westminster John Knox, 2002.

Carnley, Peter. "The Poverty of Historical Scepticism." In *Christ, Faith and History*, edited by Stephen Sykes and J. P. Clayton, 165–89. Cambridge: Cambridge University Press, 1972.

———. *The Reconstruction of Resurrection Belief*. Eugene, OR: Cascade Books, 2019.

———. "Response" to G. O'Collins SJ, "Resurrection: the State of the Questions." In *The Resurrection: An Interdisciplinary Symposium on the Resurrection of Jesus*, edited by Stephen T. Davis et al., 29–40. Oxford: Oxford University Press, 1997.

———. *The Structure of Resurrection Belief*. Oxford: Clarendon, 1987.

Casey, Maurice. *Son of Man: The Interpretation and Influence of Daniel 7*. London: SPCK, 1979.

Cavallin, H. C. C. *Life after Death: Paul's Argument for the Resurrection of the Dead in I Cor 15, Part I: An Enquiry into the Jewish Background*. Coniectanea Biblica, New Testament Series 7:1. Lund: Gleerup, 1974.

Chadwick, Henry. *Augustine*. Oxford: Oxford University Press, 1986.

———. "Philo and the Beginnings of Christian Thought." In *Cambridge History of Later Greek and Early Mediaeval Philosophy*, edited by A. H. Armstrong. Cambridge: Cambridge University Press, 1967.

Chester, Andrew, "Messianism, Mediators and Pauline Christology." In *Messiah and Exaltation: Jewish Messianic and Visionary Traditions and New Testament Christology'*, WUNT 2/207. Tübingen: Mohr/Siebeck, 2007.

Coakley, Sarah. "Is the Resurrection a 'Historical' Event? Some Muddles and Mysteries." In *The Resurrection of Jesus Christ*, edited by Paul Avis, 85–115. London: Darton, Longman & Todd, 1993.

Collins, Adela Yarbro. *The Beginning of the Gospel: Probings of Mark in Context*. Minneapolis: Fortress, 1992.

———. "The Empty Tomb in the Gospel according to Mark." In *Hermes and Athena*, edited by E. Stump and T. P. Flint, 107–40. Notre Dame: Notre Dame University Press, 1993.

———. *Mark: A Commentary on the Gospel of Mark*. Hermeneia. Minneapolis: Fortress, 2007.

Collins, John J. *Daniel: A Commentary on the Book of the Prophet Daniel*. Hermeneia. Philadelphia: Fortress, 1993.

———. "The Son of Man and the Saints of the Most High in the Book of Daniel." *Journal of Biblical Literature* 93 (1974) 50–66.

Collins, Raymond F. *First Corinthians*. Sacra Pagina 7. Collegeville, MN: Liturgical, 1999.

Conzelmann, Hans. *An Outline of the Theology of the New Testament*. Translated by John Bowden. London: SCM, 1969.

Cowdell, Scott. *Is Jesus Unique? A Study of Recent Christology* New York: Paulist, 1996.

Craffert, Pieter F. *The Life of a Galilean Shaman: Jesus of Nazareth in Anthropological-Historical Perspective*. Matrix 3. Eugene, OR: Cascade Books, 2008.

Cranfield, C. E. B. "The Resurrection of Jesus Christ." In *The Historical Jesus in Recent Research*, edited by James D. G. Dunn and Scot McKnight, 382–91. Winona Lake, IN: Eisenbraun, 2005, 382–91. Reprinted from *Expository Times* 101 (1989–90) 167–72.

Crossan, John Dominic. "The Empty Tomb and Absent Lord (Mark 16.1–8)." In *The Passion in Mark: Studies on Mark 14–16*, edited by Werner H. Kelber, 135–52. Philadelphia: Fortress, 1976.

Cullmann, Oscar. *Immortality of the Soul or Resurrection of the Dead?* London: Epworth, 1958.

Cupitt, Don. *Christ and the Hiddenness of God.* London: Lutterworth, 1971.

Dahl, Nils A. "Die Messianität Jesu bei Paulus." In *Studia Paulina in honorem Johannis de Zwaan septuagenarii,* edited by J. N. Sevenster and W. C. van Unnik, 83–95. Haarlem: Bohn, 1953.

———. "Promise and Fulfillment." In *Studies in Paul: Theology for the Early Christian Mission,* 121–36. 1977. Reprint, Eugene, OR: Wipf & Stock, 2002.

Davies, W. D. *Paul and Rabbinic Judaism.* London: SPCK, 1948.

Davis, Stephen T. "'Seeing' the Risen Jesus." In *The Resurrection: An Interdisciplinary Symposium on the Resurrection of Jesus,* edited by Stephen T. Davis et al., 126–47. Oxford: Oxford University Press, 1997.

Deissmann, G. A. *Paul.* Translated by W. E. Wilson. New York: Harper, 1957.

Dibelius, Martin. *From Tradition to Gospel.* Translated by B. L. Woolf. 1934. Reprint, Cambridge, UK: James Clarke, 1971/1982.

Dillon, John. *The Middle Platonists, 80 B.C. to A.D. 220.* Ithaca, NY: Cornell University Press, 1977.

Dillon, Richard J. *From Eye-Witnesses to Ministers of the Word.* Analecta biblica 82. Rome: Biblical Institute Press, 1978.

Dodd, C. H. *According to the Scriptures: The Sub-structure of New Testament Theology.* London: Nisbet, 1952.

———. "The Appearances of the Risen Christ: An Essay in Form-Criticism of the Gospels." In *Studies in the Gospels: Essays in Memory of R. H. Lightfoot,* edited by D. E. Nineham, 9–35. Oxford: Blackwell, 1955.

Donfried, Karl. *The Romans Debate: Expanded and Revised Edition.* Peabody, MA: Hendrickson, 1991.

Dunn, J. D. G. *Jesus and the Spirit.* London: SCM, 1975.

———. *Jesus Remembered.* Grand Rapids: Eerdmans, 2003.

Ebeling, Gerhard. *Word and Faith.* Translated by James W. Leitch. London: SCM, 1963.

Ehrman, Bart D. *The Orthodox Corruption of Scripture: The Effect of Early Christological Controversies on the Text of the New Testament.* Oxford: Oxford University Press, 1993.

Elon, Menachem. *Jewish Law: History, Sources, Principles.* Translated by Bernard Auerbach and Melvin J. Sykes. Philadelphia: Jewish Publication Society, 1994.

Elledge, C. D. *Life after Death in Early Judaism: The Evidence of Josephus,* WUNT 2/208. Tübingen: Mohr/Siebeck, 2006.

———. "Future Resurrection of the Dead in Early Judaism: Social Dynamics, Contested Evidence." *Currents in Biblical Research* 9 (2011) 394–421.

Engberg-Pedersen, Troels. *Cosmology and Self in the Apostle Paul.* Oxford: Oxford University Press, 2010.

———, ed. *From Stoicism to Platonism: The Development of Philosophy, 100 BCE–100 CE.* Cambridge: Cambridge University Press, 2017.

———, ed. *Paul and the Stoics.* Edinburgh: T. & T. Clark, 2000.

———, ed. *Paul beyond the Judaism-Hellenism Divide.* Louisville: Westminster John Knox, 2001.

———, ed. *Paul in His Hellenistic Context.* Edinburgh: T. & T. Clark, 1994.

———. "Setting the Scene: Stoicism and Platonism in the Transitional Period in Ancient Philosophy." In *Stoicism in Early Christianity*, edited by Tuomas Rasimus et al. Grand Rapids: Baker Academic, 2010.

Evans, Christopher. *Resurrection and the New Testament*. London: SCM, 1970.

Evans, Craig A. "Daniel in the New Testament Visions of God's Kingdom." In *The Book of Daniel: Composition and Reception*, edited by John J. Collins and Peter W. Flint, 2:490–527. 2 vols. Supplements to Vetus Testamentum 83. Leiden: Brill, 2001.

Farrow, Douglas. *Ascension and Ecclesia: On the Significance of the Doctrine of the Ascension for Ecclesiology and Cosmology*. Grand Rapids: Eerdmans, 1999.

Feldman, Louis H. *Josephus's Interpretation of the Bible*. Hellenistic Culture and Society 27. Berkeley: University of California Press, 1998.

Fitzmyer, Joseph A. *First Corinthians*. Yale Anchor Bible 32. New Haven: Yale University Press, 2008.

Frei, Hans W. *The Identity of Jesus Christ: The Hermeneutical Bases of Dogmatic Theology*. 1975. Reprint, Eugene, OR: Wipf & Stock, 1997.

———. *The Identity of Jesus Christ: The Hermeneutical Bases of Dogmatic Theology*. Expanded ed. Edited by Mark Alan Bowald. Eugene, OR: Cascade Books, 2013.

Fuller, Reginald H. *The Formation of the Resurrection Narratives*. London: SPCK, 1972.

Gaventa, Beverly Roberts, and Richard B. Hayes, eds. *Seeking the Identity of Jesus*. Grand Rapids: Eerdmans, 2008.

Gerhardsson, Birger. "Mark and the Female Witnesses." In *Dumu-E,-Dub-Ba-A* (A. W. Sjöberg Festschrift), edited by H. Behrens, et al. Occasional Papers of the Samuel Noah Kramer Fund 11. Philadelphia: University Museum, 1989.

Glasson, T. F. *Greek Influence in Jewish Eschatology: with Special Reference to the Apocalypses and Pseudepigraphs*. London: SPCK, 1961.

Grass, Hans. *Ostergeschehen und Osterberichte*. 2nd ed. Göttingen: Vandenhoeck & Ruprecht, 1962.

Haight, Roger. *Jesus, Symbol of God*. Maryknoll, NY: Orbis, 1999.

Hanson, K. C. "How Honorable! How Shameful: A Cultural Analysis of Matthew's Makarisms and Reproaches." Semeia 61 (1994[96]) 81–111.

Harvey, A. E. *Jesus and the Constraints of History*. London: Duckworth, 1982.

Hay, David M. *Glory at the Right Hand: Psalm 110 in Early Christianity*. SBL Monograph Series 18. Nashville: Abingdon, 1973.

Hebblethwaite, Brian. "The Resurrection and the Incarnation." In *The Resurrection of Jesus Christ*, edited by Paul Avis, 155–70. London: Darton, Longman & Todd, 1993.

Heger, Paul. *Cult as the Catalyst for Division: Cult Disputes as the Motive for Schism in the Pre-70 Pluralistic Environment*. Studies on the Texts of the Desert of Judah 65. Leiden: Brill, 2007.

Hellholm, David. "Enthymemic Argumentation in Paul: The Case of Romans 6." In *Paul in His Hellenistic Context*, edited by Troels Engberg-Pedersen, 119–79. Edinburgh: T. & T. Clark, 1995.

Hengel, Martin. "'Χριστός' in Paul." In *Between Jesus and Paul: Studies in the Earliest History of Christianity*. Translated by John Bowden. Philadelphia: Fortress, 1983.

———. 'Das Begräbnis Jesu bei Paulus und die leibliche Auferstehung aus dem Grab.' In *Auferstehung—Resurrection: The Fourth Durham-Tübingen Research Symposium*, edited by Friedrich Avemarie and Hermann Lichtenberger, 119–83. WUNT 1/135. Tübingen: Mohr/Siebeck, 1999.

———. *The Four Gospels and the One Gospel of Jesus Christ*. Translated by John Bowden. Harrisburg: Trinity, 2000.

———. *The 'Hellenization' of Judaea in the First Century after Christ*. Translated by John Bowden. London: SCM, 1989.

———. *Judaism and Hellenism*. Translated by John Bowden. London: SCM, 1974.

———. "Psalm 110 und die Erhöhung des Auferstandenen zur Rechten Gottes." In *Anfänge der Christologie* (Festschrift for Ferdinand Hahn), edited by Villiers Breytenbach and Henning Paulsen, 43–73. Göttingen : Vandenhoeck & Ruprecht, 1991.

Hewitt, J. Thomas, and Matthew V. Novenson. "Participationism and Messiah Christology in Paul." In *God and the Faithfulness of Paul*, edited by Christoph Heilig, et al., 393–415. WUNT 2/413. Tübingen: Mohr/Siebeck, 2016.

Hick, John. *Faith and Knowledge*. London: Macmillan, 1957.

———. *The Metaphor of God Incarnate*. London: SCM, 1993.

Holloway, David. *Where Did Jesus Go?* Basingstoke, UK: Marshall Morgan & Scott, 1983.

Horbury, William, "The Messianic Associations of 'the Son of Man.'" In *Messianism among Jews and Christians: Twelve Biblical and Historical Studies*, 125–55. London: T. & T. Clark, 2003.

Houlden, Leslie. *Connections*. London: SCM, 1986.

Hume, David. *An Enquiry Concerning Human Understanding* (1777 ed.). Edited by L. A. Selby-Bigge. Oxford: Clarendon, 1902.

Hurtado, Larry W. *How on Earth Did Jesus Become a God?* Grand Rapids: Eerdmans, 2005.

———. *Lord Jesus Christ: Devotion to Jesus in Earliest Christianity*. Grand Rapids: Eerdmans, 2003.

———. *One God, One Lord: Early Christian Devotion and Ancient Jewish Monotheism*. Minneapolis: Fortress, 1988.

———. "YHWH's Return to Zion." In *God and the Faithfulness of Paul*, edited by Christoph Heilig et al., 417–38. WUNT 2/413. Tübingen: Mohr/Siebeck, 2016.

Ilan, Tal. *Jewish Women in Greco-Roman Palestine*. Peabody, MA: Hendrickson, 1996.

Inge, W. R. *The Philosophy of Plotinus*. Gifford Lectures at St Andrews, 1917–18. 2 vols. London: Longmans, Green, 1918.

———. *The Platonic Tradition in English Religious Thought*. Hulsean Lectures. Cambridge, 1925–1926. New York: Longmans, Green, 1926.

———. *The Religious Philosophy of Plotinus and Some Modern Philosophies of Religion*. London: Lindsey, 1914.

Jeremias, Joachim. "Artikelloses Χριστός: Zur Ursprache von 1 Cor 15.3b-5." *Zeitschrift für die Neutestamentliche Wissenschaft* 57 (1966) 211–15.

———. *The Eucharistic Words of Jesus*. Translated by Norman Perrin. New York: Scribner, 1966.

———. *New Testament Theology*. London: SCM, 1971.

———. *The Prayers of Jesus*. London: SCM, 1967.

Johnson, Aubrey R. "Hebrew Conceptions of Kingship." In *Myth, Ritual and Kingship: Essays on the Theory and Practice of Kingship in the Ancient Near East and in Israel*, edited by S. H. Hooke, 204–35. Oxford: Clarendon, 1958.

———. *Sacral Kingship in Ancient Israel*. Cardiff: University of Wales Press, 1967.

Kähler, Martin. *The So-Called Historical Jesus and the Biblical Historic Christ* (1892). Translated by Carl E. Braaten. Philadelphia: Fortress, 1964.

Karris, Robert J. "Women and Discipleship in Luke." *Catholic Biblical Quarterly* 56 (1994) 1–20.

Kittel, Gerhard. *Die Probleme des palästinensischen Spätjudentums und das Urchristentum*, Beiträge zur Wissenschaft von Alten und Neuen Testament 3/1, Stuttgart: Kohlhammer, 1926.

Kittel, Gerhard, and Gerhard Friedrich, eds. *Theological Dictionary of the New Testament*. 10 vols. Translated by Geoffrey W. Bromiley. Grand Rapids: Eerdmans, 1964–1976.

Klaus, D., and T. Walter. "Processes of Grieving: How Bonds are Continued." In *Handbook of Bereavement Research: Consequences, Coping and Care*, edited by M. S. Stroebe et al. Washington, DC: American Psychological Association, 2001, 431–38.

Klawans, Jonathan. *Josephus and the Theologies of Ancient Judaism*. Oxford: Oxford University Press, 2012.

Kramer, Werner. *Christ, Lord, Son of God*. Translated by B. Hardy. London: SCM, 1966.

Lang, Bernhard. *Meeting in Heaven: Modernising the Christian Afterlife, 1600–2000*. Frankfurt: Lang, 2011.

Lee, Aquila H. J. 'Messianism and Messiah in Paul: Christ as Jesus?' In *God and the Faithfulness of Paul*, edited by Christoph Heilig et al., 375–392. WUNT 2/413. Tübingen: Mohr/Siebeck, 2016.

Lindars, Barnabas. *Jesus, Son of Man*. Grand Rapids: Eerdmans, 1983.

———. *New Testament Apologetic*. London: SCM, 1961.

Lindblom, J. *Gesichte und Offenbarungen: Vorstellungen von göttlichen Weisungen und übernatürlichen Erscheinungen im ältesten Christentum*. Acta Regiae Societatis Humaniorum Litterarum Lundensis 65. Lund: Gleerup, 1968.

Lohmeyer, Ernst. *Das Evangelium des Markus*. Kritisch-exegetischer Kommentar über das Neue Testament 2. Göttingen: Vandenhoeck & Ruprecht, 1951.

Lüdemann, Gerd. "The History and Nature of the Earliest Christian Belief in the Resurrection." In *The Historical Jesus in Recent Research*, edited by James D. G. Dunn and Scot McKnight, 413–19. Winona Lake, IN: Eisenbrauns, 2005.

———. *Jesus after 2000 Years*. Translated by John Bowden. London: SCM, 2000.

———. *The Resurrection of Jesus: History, Experience, Theology*. Translated by J. Bowden. London: SCM, 1994.

Maccini, R. G. *Her Testimony is True: Women as Witnesses according to John*. Journal for the Study of the New Testament Supplements 125. Sheffield: Sheffield Academic, 1996.

MacCullouch, Diarmaid. *Christianity: The First Three Thousand Years* (first published as *A History of Christianity*, 2009). New York: Penguin/Viking, 2011.

Mack, Burton L. *A Myth of Innocence: Mark and Christian Origins*. Philadelphia: Fortress, 1988.

Macquarrie, John. "Kenoticism Reconsidered." *Theology* 77 (1974) 115–24.

Manson, T. W. "The Bible and Personal Immortality." *Congregational Quarterly* 32 (1954) 7–16.

Marcus, Ralph. "Divine Names and Attributes in Hellenistic Jewish Literature." *Proceedings of the American Academy for Jewish Research* (1931–32) 43–120.

Marshall, I. Howard. *The Epistle to the Philippians*. London: Epworth, 1991.

——— et al., eds. *New Bible Dictionary*. 3rd ed. Downers Grove, IL: Inter-Varsity, 2002.

Marxsen, Willi. *Jesus and Easter. Did God Raise the Historical Jesus from the Dead?* trans., Victor Paul Furnish. Nashville: Abingdon, 1990.

———. *Mark the Evangelist: Studies in the Redaction History of the Gospel.* Translated by James Boyce et al. Nashville: Abingdon, 1969.

———. "The Resurrection of Jesus as a Historical and Theological Problem." In *The Significance of the Message of the Resurrection for Faith in Jesus Christ,* edited by C. F. D. Moule, 15–50. Studies in Biblical Theology 1/8. London: SCM, 1968.

———. *The Resurrection of Jesus of Nazareth.* Translated by Margaret Kohl. London: SCM, 1970.

Mascall, E. L. *Theology and the Gospel of Christ: An Essay in Reorientation.* London: SPCK, 1977.

Mason, Steve. *Flavius Josephus on the Pharisees.* Studia Post-Biblica 39. Leiden: Brill, 1991.

———. *Josephus, Judea, and Christian Origins: Methods and Categories.* Peabody, MA: Hendrickson, 2009.

———. *Life of Josephus, Translation and Commentary.* Brill Josephus Project 9. Leiden: Brill, 2001.

McCullogh, W. Stewart. *The History and Literature of the Palestinian Jews from Cyrus to Herod, 550 B.C. to 4 B.C.* Toronto: University of Toronto Press, 1975.

McDannell, Colleen, and Bernhard Lang. *Heaven: A History.* New Haven: Yale University Press, 1988.

McDonald, James I. *Kerygma and Didache: The Articulation and Structure of the Earliest Christian Message.* SNTSMS 37. Cambridge: Cambridge University Press, 1980.

Meier, John P. *A Marginal Jew: Rethinking the Historical Jesus.* New Haven: Yale University Press, 2009.

Meiselman, Moshe. *Jewish Women in Jewish Law,* Library of Jewish Law and Ethics 6. New York: Ktav, 1978, 73–80.

Metzger, Bruce. *A Textual Commentary on the Greek New Testament.* London/New York: United Bible Societies, 1971.

———. *The Text of the New Testament: Its Transmission, Corruption and Restoration.* Oxford: Oxford University Press, 1992.

Moltmann, Jürgen. *The Way of Jesus Christ: Christology in Messianic Dimensions.* Translated by Margaret Kohl. Minneapolis: Fortress, 1993.

Morgan, Robert. "Flesh Is Precious: The Significance of Luke 24.36–43." In *Resurrection: Essays in Honour of Leslie Houlden,* edited by Stephen Barton and Graham Stanton, 8–20. London: SPCK, 1994.

Morris, L. L. "Resurrection." In *New Bible Dictionary,* edited by I. Howard Marshall et al., 1010–12. 3rd ed. Downers Grove, IL: Inter-Varsity, 2002.

Moule, C. F. D. "Further Reflections on Philippians 2:5–11." In *Apostolic History and the Gospel,* edited by W. Ward Gasque and Ralph P. Martin, 264–76. Exeter: Paternoster, 1970.

———. "The Manhood of Jesus in the New Testament." In *Christ, Faith and History,* edited by S. W. Sykes and J. P. Clayton, 95–110. Cambridge: Cambridge University Press, 1972.

———. *The Origin of Christology.* Cambridge: Cambridge University Press, 1977.

———. *The Phenomenon of the New Testament.* Studies in Biblical Theology 2/1. London: SCM, 1967.

———. "St Paul and Dualism: The Pauline Conception of the Resurrection." *New Testament Studies* xii (1965–66) 106–23.

Moule, C. F. D., and Don Cupitt. "The Resurrection: A Disagreement." *Theology* 75 (1972) 507–19.

Mowinckel, Sigmund. *He that Cometh*. Translated by G. W. Anderson. 1956. Reprint, with a new Foreword by John J. Collins. Grand Rapids: Eerdmans, 2005.

Murphy-O'Connor, Jerome. "Christological Anthropology in Phil., II, 6–11." *Review Biblique* 83 (1976) 22–50.

Nauck, W. "Die Bedeutung des leeren Grabes für den Glauben an den Auferstandenen." *Zeitschrift für die Neutestamentliche Wissenschaft* 47 (1956) 243–67.

Neirynck, Frans. "Luke 24,12: An Anti-Docetic Interpolation?" In *New Testament Textual Criticism and Exegesis: Festschrift J. Delobel*. Bibliotheca Ephemeridum Theologicarum Lovaniensium 161. edited by A. Denaux. Leuven: Peeters, 2002, 145–58.

————. "Once More Lk 24,12." *Ephemerides Theologicae Lovanienses* 70 (1994) 319–40.

Nickelsburg, George. W. E. *Resurrection, Immortality and Eternal Life in Intertestamental Judaism and Early Christianity*. Expanded ed. Harvard Theological Studies 56. Cambridge: Harvard University Press, 2006.

Novenson, Matthew V. *Christ Among the Messiahs: Christ Language in Paul and Messiah Language in Ancient Judaism*. Oxford: Oxford University Press, 2012.

O'Collins, Gerald, SJ. "The Appearances of the Risen Christ: A Lexical-exegetical Examination of St. Paul and Other Witnesses." *Irish Theological Quarterly* 79 (2014) 128–43.

————. *Believing in the Resurrection*. New York: Paulist, 2012.

————. *Christology: A Biblical, Historical, and Systematic Study of Jesus*. Oxford: Oxford University Press, 1995.

————. *Easter Faith*. Mahwah, NJ: Paulist, 2002.

————. *The Easter Jesus*. London: Darton, Longman & Todd, 1973.

————. "The Resurrection of Jesus: the Debate Continued." *Gregorianum* 81/3 (2000) 589–98.

————. "The Resurrection: The State of the Questions." In *The Resurrection: An Interdisciplinary Symposium on the Resurrection of Jesus*, edited by Stephen T. Davis et al., 5–28. Oxford: Oxford University Press, 1997.

————. "Thomas Aquinas and Christ's Resurrection." *Theological Studies* 31 (1970) 512–22.

Olson, P. R., et al. "Hallucinations of Widowhood." *Proceedings of The American Geriatric Society* 33 (1985) 543–47.

O'Neill, J. C. *The Theology of Acts in Its Historical Setting*. London: SPCK, 1961/1970.

Pannenberg, Wofhart. "Did Jesus Really Rise from the Dead?" *Dialog* 4 (1965) 128–35.

————. *Jesus—God and Man*. London: SCM, 1968.

Parkes, Colin Murray. *Bereavement Studies of Grief in Adult Life*. 3rd ed. London: Routledge, 1996.

Paulus, H. E. G. *Das Leben Jesu als Grundlage einer reinen Geschichte des Urchristentums*. 2 vols. Heidelberg: Winter, 1828.

Perkins, Pheme. *Resurrection: New Testament Witness and Contemporary Reflection*. Garden City, NY: Doubleday, 1984.

————. "Review of *The Resurrection of the Son of God*." *Theology Today* 61 (2004) 412–16.

Perrin, Norman. *The Resurrection Narratives: A New Approach*. London: SCM, 1977.

Pickstock, Catherine. *After Writing: On the Liturgical Consummation of Philosophy*. Oxford: Blackwell, 1998.

Pike, Nelson. *God and Timelessness*. London: Routledge & Kegan Paul, 1970.

Pope, M. "Studies in Pauline Vocabulary; of Boldness of Speech." *Expository Times* 21 (1909–10) 236–38.

Bibliography

Radice, Roberto, and David T. Runia. *Philo of Alexandria: An Annotated Bibliography, 1937–86, 1987–96, and 1997–2006.* Supplements to Vigiliae Christianae 8, 57, and 109. Leiden: Brill, 1992, 2000, 2012.

Rajak, Tessa. "The Location of Cultures in Second Temple Palestine: The Evidence of Josephus." In *The Book of Acts and Its First Century Setting 4: The Book of Acts in Its Palestinian Setting,* edited by Richard Bauckham, 1–14. Grand Rapids: Eerdmans, 1995.

Renan, Ernest. *The Life of Jesus.* Translated by Charles Edwin Wilbour. London: Trübner, 1864.

Rees, Dewi. *Death and Bereavement: The Psychological, Religious and Cultural Interface.* London: Whurr, 1997/2001.

———. "The Hallucinations of Widowhood." *British Medical Journal* 4 (2 October 1971) 37–41. (Rees's MD thesis of 1971 was entitled "Hallucinatory Reactions of Bereavement." University of London Library, The Senate House, Russell Square, London).

———. *Pointers to Eternity.* Talybont, Ceredigion: Y Lolfa Cyf, 2010.

Reese, J. M. *Hellenistic Influence on the Book of Wisdom.* Analecta Biblica 41. Rome: Pontifical Biblical Institute Press, 1970.

Richardson, Alan. *A Theological Word Book of the Bible.* London: SCM, 1957.

Riley, Gregory J. *Resurrection Reconsidered: Thomas and John in Controversy.* Minneapolis: Fortress, 1995.

Robinson, H. Wheeler. "The Hebrew Conception of Corporate Personality." In *Werden und Wesen des Alten Testaments; Vorträge gehalten auf der Internationalen Tagung Alttestamentlicher Forscher zu Göttingen vom 4—10 September 1935,* edited by Johannes Hempel et al., 49–62. Biehefte zur Zeitschrift für die alttestamentliche Wissenschaft, 66. Berlin: Töpelmann, 1936.

Robinson, J. A. T. *The Body.* Studies in Biblical Theology 1/5. London: SCM, 1952.

———. *The Human Face of God.* London: SCM, 1973.

———. "The Most Primitive Christology of All?" *Journal of Theological Studies* 7 (1956) 177–89.

Rogerson, John W. "The Hebrew Conception of Corporate Personality: A Re-examination." *Journal of Theological Studies* 21 (1970) 1–16.

Rose, Herbert Jennings. "Herakles and the Gospels." *Harvard Theological Review* 31 (1938) 113–42.

Sachs, Oliver. *Hallucinations.* New York: Knopf, 2012.

Schiffman, Lawrence H. *Qumran and Jerusalem: Studies in the Dead Sea Scrolls and the History of Judaism.* Grand Rapids: Eerdmans, 2010.

Schille, Gottfried. "Das Leiden des Herrn; Die evangelische Passionstradition und irh 'Sitz im Leben'." *Zeitschrift für Theologie und Kirche* 52 (1955) 161–205.

Schmid, Wilhelm von. *Christs Geschichte der Griechischen Literatur.* Sechste Auflage unter Mitwirkung von O. Stählin. Handbuch der Alterumswissenschaft VII/2. Munich: Beck, 1920.

Scholla, Robert W., SJ. *Recent Anglican Contributions on the Resurrection of Jesus (1945–1987).* Rome: Gregoriana, 1992.

Schoonenberg, P. "He Emptied Himself." *Concilium* 2 (1965) 47–66.

———. "The Kenosis or Self-Emptying of Christ." *Concilium* 3 (1966) 27–36.

Schrage, Wolfgang. *Der erste Brief an die Korinther.* Evangelisch-Katholischer zum Neuen Testament. 4 vols. Neukirchen-Vluyn: Neukirchener, 1991–2001.

Schubert, K. "Die Entwicklung der Auferstehungslehre von der nachexilischen bis zur frührabbinischen Zeit." *Biblische Zeitschrift* 6 (1962) 177–214.

———. "Das Problem der Auferstehungshoffnung in den Qumrantexten und in der frührabbinischen Literatur." *Wiener Zeitschrift für die Kunde des Morgenlandes* 56 (1960) 154–67.

Schupbach, S. Scott. "'*kai euthus*' as Discourse Marker in the Gospel of Mark?" https://www.academia.edu/6590469/kai_euthus_as_discourse_marker_in_gospel_of_Mark (2013).

Schüssler Fiorenza, Elisabeth. *In Memory of Her: A Feminist Theological Reconstruction of Christian Origins*. New York: Crossroad, 1983.

Schütz, Rudolphe. *Les idées eschatologiques du livre de la Sagesse*. Strasburg, 1935.

Schweitzer, Albert. *The Mysticism of Paul the Apostle*. Translated by William Montgomery. London: A. & C. Black, 1953.

———. *The Quest of the Historical Jesus: A Critical Study of Its Progress From Reimarus To Wrede*. Edited and translated by William Montgomery. London: A. & C. Black, 1910.

Schweizer, Eduard. "Resurrection—Fact or Illusion?" *Horizons in Biblical Theology* 1 (1979) 137–59.

Sedley, David. *Greek and Roman Philosophy*. Cambridge: Cambridge University Press, 2003.

Segal, Alan. *Life After Death: A History of the Afterlife in Western Religion*. New York: Doubleday, 2004.

———. "Life after Death: The Social Sources." In *The Resurrection: An Interdisciplinary Symposium on the Resurrection of Jesus*, edited by Stephen T. Davis et al., 90–125. Oxford: Oxford University Press, 1997.

Setzer, Claudia. "Excellent Women: Female Witness to the Resurrection." *Journal of Biblical Literature* 116 (1997) 259–72.

Shellard, Barbara. "The Relationship of Luke and John: A Fresh Look at an Old Problem." *Journal of Theological Studies* 46 (1995) 71–98.

Shutt, R. J. H. "The Concept of God in the Works of Flavius Josephus." *Journal of Jewish Studies* 31 (1980) 171–87.

Smith, Daniel. *Revisiting the Empty Tomb*. Minneapolis: Fortress, 2010.

Stanton, Graham. "Early Objections to the Resurrection of Jesus." In *Resurrection: Essays in Honour of Leslie Houlden*, edited by Stephen Barton and Graham Stanton, 79–94. London: SPCK.

Stendahl, Krister. "Biblical Theology." In *The Interpreter's Dictionary of the Bible*, edited by George Arthur Buttrick, 1:418–32.. Nashville: Abingdon, 1962.

———. *Immortality and Resurrection*. New York: Macmillan, 1958.

———. "Immortality Is Too Much and Too Late." In *Meanings: The Bible as Document and as Guide*. Philadelphia: Fortress, 1984.

Steenburg, David. "The Case against the Synonymity of *Morphe* and *Eikon*." *Journal for the Study of the New Testament* 34 (1988) 77–86.

Sterling, Gregory E. "Hellenistic Philosophy and the New Testament." *Handbook to Exegesis of the New Testament*, edited by Stanley E. Porter, 313–58. New Testament Tools and Studies 25. Leiden: Brill, 1997.

———. "Wisdom or Foolishness? The Role of Philosophy in the Thought of Paul." In *God and the Faithfulness of Paul*, edited by Christopher Heilig, et al., 235–53. WUNT 2/413. Tübingen: Mohr/Siebeck, 2016.

Strack, H. L., and P. Billerbeck, eds. *Kommentar zum Neuen Testament aus Tulmud und Midrasch*. Vols. III and IV. Munich: Beck, 1926–61.

Bibliography

Strack, H. L., and G. Stemberger, *Introduction to the Talmud and Midrash*. Translated by Markus Bockmuehl. Edinburgh: T. & T. Clark, 1982/1991.

Strauss, David Friedrich. *The Life of Jesus Critically Examined* (1835–36). Translated by George Eliot, 1846. Cambridge: Cambridge University Press, 2010.

———. *A New Life of Jesus*, 2 vols., London: Williams and Norgate,1865.

Swinburne, Richard. *The Concept of Miracle*, London: Macmillan, 1970.

———. *The Resurrection of God Incarnate*. Oxford: Clarendon, 2003.

Talbert, Charles H. *What Is a Gospel?* London: SPCK, 1978.

Taussig, Hal. "Review of *The Resurrection of the Son of God*" in *Union Seminary Quarterly Review* 58/3–4 (2004) 244–45.

Thackeray, H. St. John, *Josephus: The Man and the Historian*. New York: Jewish Institute of Religion, 1929.

Thackeray, H. St. John, et al., eds., *Josephus,* Loeb Classical Library, 9 vols. Cambridge, Mass: Harvard University Press, 1926–65.

Thiselton, Anthony C. *The First Epistle to the Corinthians*. Grand Rapids: Eerdmans, 2006.

Trites, Allison A. *The New Testament Concept of Witness*. Society for the Study of the New Testament Monograph Series 31. Cambridge: Cambridge University Press, 1977.

Troeltsch, Ernst. *Gesammelte Schriften*. Tübingen: Mohr Siebeck, 1912–25.

Vermes, Geza. *Jesus the Jew: A Historian's Reading of the Gospels*. London: Collins, 1973.

Wegner, Judith Romney. *Chattel or Person? The Status of Women in the Mishnah*. Oxford: Oxford University Press, 1988.

Wedderburn, A. J. M. *Beyond Resurrection*. London: SCM, 1999.

———. "Some Observations on Paul's Use of the Phrase 'In Christ' and 'With Christ.'" *Journal for the Study of the New Testament* 25 (1985) 83–97.

Welker, Michael. "Wright on the Resurrection." Review of *The Resurrection of the Son of God. Scottish Journal of Theology* 60 (2007) 458–75.

Westcott, B. F., *The Gospel of the Resurrection: Thoughts on its Relation to Reason and History*. London and Cambridge: Macmillan, 1866.

Westcott, B. F., and F. J. A. Hort. *The New Testament in the Original Greek*. 2 vols. New York: Harper & Brothers, 1882.

Wiebe, P. H. *Visions of Jesus*. Oxford: Oxford University Press, 1997.

Wilckens, Ulrich. "The Tradition-History of the Resurrection of Jesus." In *The Significance of the Message of the Resurrection for Faith in Jesus Christ,* edited by C. F. D. Moule, 51–76. London: SCM, 1968.

———. "Der Ursprung der Überlieferung der Erscheinungen des Auferstandenen." In *Dogma und Denkstrukturen*, edited by W. Joest and Wolfhart Pannenberg, 458–75. Göttingen: Vandenhoeck & Ruprecht, 1963. **[KC: series]**

Williams, Rowan. "Between the Cherubim: The Empty Tomb and the Empty Throne." In *Resurrection Reconsidered*, edited by Gavin D'Costa, 87–101. Oxford: Oneworld, 1996.

———. "A History of Faith in Jesus." In *The Cambridge Companion to Jesus,* edited by Markus Bockmuehl, 220–36. Cambridge: Cambridge University Press, 2001.

Williams, T. "The Trouble with the Resurrection." In *Understanding, Studying and Reading: New Testament Essays in Honour of John Ashton*, edited by C. Rowland and C. H. T. Fletcher-Louis, 219–35. Journal for the Study of the New Testament Supplements 153. Sheffield: Sheffield Academic, 1998.

Windisch, Hans. *Der Zweite Korintherbrief.* Göttingen: Vandenhoeck & Ruprecht, 1924.

Bibliography

Witherington, Ben, III. *Conflict and Community in Corinth: A Socio-Rhetorical Commentary on 1 and 2 Corinthians.* Grand Rapids: Eerdmans, 1995.

———. *Jesus the Sage.* Minneapolis: Fortress, 2000.

Witt, R. E. *Albinus and the History of Middle Platonism.* Cambridge: Cambridge University Press, 1937/2013.

Wright, Ernest G. *God Who Acts: Biblical Theology as Recital.* Studies in Biblical Theology 1/8. London: SCM, 1962.

Wright, N. T. "Christians Wrong about Heaven." Interview with David Van Biema, *Time Magazine*, Thursday, 7 February 2008. http://content.time.com/time/world/article/0,8599,1710844,00.html

———. *The Climax of the Covenant: Christ and the Law in Pauline Theology.* Edinburgh: T. & T. Clark, 1991.

———. *For All the Saints? Remembering the Christian Departed.* London: SPCK, 2003.

———. "The Messiah and the People of God: A Study in Pauline Theology with Particular Reference to the Argument of the Epistle to the Romans," D.Phil. diss., Oxford University.

———. *The New Testament and the People of God.* London: SPCK, 1992.

———. *Paul and the Faithfulness of God.* London: SPCK, 2013.

———. *Paul in Fresh Perspective.* London: SPCK, 2005.

———. *The Resurrection of the Son of God*, London: SPCK, 2003.

Yates. Stephen. *Between Death and Resurrection: A Critical Response to Recent Catholic Debate Concerning the Intermediate State.* London: Bloomsbury Academic, 2017.

Zahrnt, Heinz, *The Question of God.* London: Collins, 1969.

Zetterholm, Magnus. "Paul and the Missing Messiah." In *The Messiah: In Early Judaism and Christianity.* Minneapolis: Augsburg/Fortress, 2007, 33–55.

Zimmerman, F. "The Book of Wisdom, Its Language and Character." *Jewish Quarterly Review* 57 (1966–67) 1–27 and 101–38.

Author Index

Index of Subjects

Abraham, 54n101
  promises made to, 76–78
  never in Sheol, 90n1
  faith of, 169, 211
  willingness to sacrifice Isaac, 208
Achilles, 118
Adelphoi, (inclusive of women in Paul), 133–35
Albert, Consort of Victoria, 220, 258n2
Albinus (alias Alcinous), 273–74
  Didaskalikos, 273n47
Alexander the Great, 11
Alexandria, 11, 12, 13
Ambiguity, perceptual and faith 21, 94, 110–14
  of evidence relating to empty tomb, 157
  (see also Freedom in perception)
Analogy, of Easter appearances with bereave-
    ment sequences, 222–24, 233–34
  principle of in historiography (Troeltsch),
    227–29
  Wright's attempted critique of, 229–33
  analogy of faith, 237–41
Angels, at the tomb, 144–45
Andronicus, 83, 132–33
Anselm of Canterbury, 274–75
  Proslogion 274n50
Antioch, 13
Antiochus of Ascalon. 12
Antiochus IV Epiphanes, 25
Appearances, kerygmatic summary of, 85–90
  ambiguity of, 90–95
  nature of appearances as revelatory, 87–92,
    116
  materializing tendency of John and Luke,
    92–99, 110
  in view of Stephen Davis (and Wright),
    99–107, 112–13
  view of Form Critics, 107
  Wright's treatment of as "meetings," 7, 21,
    26, 94, 102, 107, 138, 192–93
  as hallucinations, 159 (see also under Sub-
    jective vision hypothesis)
Apocalyptic, in Second Temple Judaism, 172

as "revealing" of eternal state of affairs, 53,
  55, 270–72
Apollodorus, 118–19
  The Library, 118
Apophatic discourse, 104, 171, 275
  (see also, Metaphor in theology)
Aquinas, Thomas. 258, 274–75
  Summa Theologiae, 274n51, n52, 275n53
Argyll, Duke of, 220
Aristobulus, 15
Aristotle, 11, 12, 14, 17n44
Ascension, in Luke, 91, 96, 98
Aseity, 275
Assumption (of Jesus), 118–19, 137, 138–39
Assumption of Moses, 90n13, 118
Athens, fall of, 11, 12
Augustine of Hippo, 258, 274–75
  and Platonism 172
  City of God, 274
  Confessions, 274n48
  De Trinitate, 275n55
Augustus, Emperor, 2

Babylonian Talmud, 122, 126–27, 130–31,
  286–88
Bannus, 38
Baptism, into community of baptized 82–83,
  130–32
  into Christ's death and resurrection, 268
  baptism and the gift of the Spirit, 176–79,
    202–3, 211, 255–56, 279–81
Bartimaeus, 72n20, 73
Baruch, Apocalypse of (*2 Baruch*), 29–36,
  54n101, 283–84
Basil of Caesarea, 280
"Beaten men" argument, 219
Ben Sira (Ecclesiasticus), 13n35
Biblical Theology Movement, 9–11, 17–20, 38,
  40n54, 50, 60
  and Wright, 38, 50, 246–47
  and "time," 252
  and "totalist" anthropology, 253, 276